Translated Texts for Historians

300–800 AD is the time of late antiquity and the early middle ages: the transformation of the classical world, the beginnings of Europe and of Islam, and the evolution of Byzantium. TTH makes available sources translated from Greek, Latin, Syriac, Coptic, Arabic, Georgian, Gothic and Armenian. Each volume provides an expert scholarly translation, with an introduction setting texts and authors in context, and with notes on content, interpretation and debates.

Editorial Committee
Phil Booth, Trinity College, Oxford
Sebastian Brock, Oriental Institute, University of Oxford
Averil Cameron, Keble College, Oxford
Marios Costambeys, University of Liverpool
Carlotta Dionisotti, King's College, London
Jill Harries, St Andrews
Peter Heather, King's College, London
Robert Hoyland, Oriental Institute, University of Oxford
William E. Klingshirn, The Catholic University of America
Michael Lapidge, Clare College, Cambridge
John Matthews, Yale University
Neil McLynn, Corpus Christi College, Oxford
Richard Price, Heythrop College, University of London
Claudia Rapp, Institut für Byzantinistik und Neogräzistik, Universität Wien
Judith Ryder, University of Oxford
Raymond Van Dam, University of Michigan
Michael Whitby, University of Birmingham
Ian Wood, University of Leeds

General Editors
Gillian Clark, University of Bristol
Mark Humphries, Swansea University
Mary Whitby, University of Oxford

A full list of published titles in the **Translated Texts for Historians** series is available on request. The most recently published are shown below.

Three Political Voices from the Age of Justinian: Agapetus – Advice to the Emperor, Dialogue on Political Science, Paul the Silentiary – Description of Hagia Sophia
Translated with notes and an introduction by PETER N. BELL
Volume 52: 249pp, ISBN 978-1-84631-209-0

History and Hagiography from the Late Antique Sinai
DANIEL F. CANER, with contributions by SEBASTIAN BROCK, RICHARD M. PRICE and KEVIN VAN BLADEL
Volume 53: 346pp, ISBN 978-1-84631-216-8

Orosius: Seven Books of History against the Pagans
Translated with introduction and notes by A. T. FEAR
Volume 54: 456pp., 2010; ISBN 978-1-84631-473-5 cased, 978-1-84631-239-7 limp

The Chronicle of Pseudo-Zachariah Rhetor: Church and War in Late Antiquity
Translated by GEOFFREY GREATREX, with ROBERT PHENIX and CORNELIA HORN; introductory material by SEBASTIAN BROCK and WITOLD WITAKOWSKI
Volume 55: 2010; ISBN 978-1-84631-493-3 cased, 978-1-84631-494-0 limp

Bede: On the Nature of Things and On Times
Translated with introduction and notes by CALVIN B. KENDALL and FAITH WALLIS
Volume 56: 371pp., 2010, ISBN 978-1-84631-495-7

Theophilus of Edessa's Chronicle
Translated with introduction and notes by ROBERT G. HOYLAND
Volume 57: 368pp., 2011, ISBN 978-1-84631-697-5 cased, 978-1-84631-698-2 limp

Bede: Commentary on Revelation
Translated with introduction and notes by FAITH WALLIS
Volume 58: 343pp., 2013, ISBN 978-1-84631-844-3 cased, 978-1-84631-845-0 limp

Two Early Lives of Severos, Patriarch of Antioch
Translated with an introduction and notes by SEBASTIAN BROCK and BRIAN FITZGERALD
Volume 59, 175pp., 2013, ISBN 978-1-84631-882-5 cased, 978-1-84631-883-2 limp

The Funerary Speech for John Chrysostom
Translated with an introduction and notes by TIMOTHY D. BARNES and GEORGE BEVAN
Volume 60, 193pp., ISBN 978-1-84631-887-0 cased, 978-1-84631-888-7 limp

The Acts of the Lateran Synod of 649
Translated with notes by RICHARD PRICE, with contributions by PHIL BOOTH and CATHERINE CUBITT
Volume 61, 476pp., ISBN 978-1-78138-039-0 cased

For full details of **Translated Texts for Historians**, including prices and ordering information, please write to the following: **All countries, except the USA and Canada:** Liverpool University Press, 4 Cambridge Street, Liverpool, L69 7ZU, UK (*Tel* +44-[0]151-794 2233, *Fax* +44-[0]151-794 2235, Email janmar@liv.ac.uk, http://www.liverpool universitypress.co.uk). **USA and Canada:** University of Chicago Press, 1427 E. 60th Street, Chicago, IL, 60637, US (*Tel* 773-702-7700, *Fax* 773-702-9756, www.press.uchicago.edu)

Translated Texts for Historians
Volume 62

Macarius, *Apocriticus*

Translated with introduction and commentary

by
JEREMY M. SCHOTT
&
MARK J. EDWARDS

Liverpool
University
Press

First published 2015
Liverpool University Press
4 Cambridge Street
Liverpool, L69 7ZU

Copyright © 2015 Jeremy M. Schott and Mark J. Edwards

The right of Jeremy M. Schott and Mark J. Edwards to be identified as
the authors of this book has been asserted by them in accordance with the
Copyright, Designs and Patents Act 1988.

All rights reserved. No part of this book may be reproduced stored in a retrieval
system, or transmitted, in any form or by any means, electronic, mechanical,
photocopying, recording, or otherwise, without the prior written permission of
the publisher.

British Library Cataloguing-in-Publication Data
A British Library CIP Record is available.

ISBN 978 1 78138 129 8 cased
ISBN 978 1 78138 130 4 limp

Typeset by Carnegie Book Production, Lancaster
Printed by BooksFactory.co.uk

CONTENTS

Preface	vii
Introductory Essays	
I. General remarks and outline of the *Apocriticus*	1
II. Macarius and the Christian Tradition (Mark J. Edwards)	5
III. The Hellene (Jeremy M. Schott)	21
A. Macarius's Use of a Source or Sources	21
B. Identifying the Hellene?	28
i. Celsus	29
ii. Sossianus Hierocles	30
iii. Julian	32
iv. Porphyry	35
C. Conclusions	39
IV. Macarius and the *Apocriticus* (Jeremy M. Schott)	41
A. The Text	41
B. Title, Author, Provenance, and Date	44
C. A Literary Assessment	54
Abbreviations and Sigla	60
Macarius, *Apocriticus, or Monogenēs*	
1. Book 1	61
2. Book 2	64
3. Book 3	103
4. Book 4	203
5. Fragments	274
Bibliography	279
Index of Biblical Passages	295
Index of Proper Names	299
Subject Index	302
Index of Theological, Philosophical, and Rhetorical Terminology	304

PREFACE

This collaborative volume on Macarius emerged out of our ongoing teaching and research on the intertwined histories of early Christianity and later Platonism. Scholarship on both traditions has largely ignored the *Apocriticus* as a text in its own right. Adolf von Harnack's inclusion of large sections of the text in his edition of Porphyry of Tyre's *Against the Christians* has, however, meant that the work has figured importantly, if often silently, in scholarship on "pagan-Christian conflict" in late antiquity. In offering this translation, the first rendering of the complete text in English, our first goal was to make this work widely available to Anglophone scholars and students. The notes and introductory essays that accompany the translation locate the work in its historical and intellectual contexts.

Macarius's prolix Greek does not yield easily to fluid and idiomatic English. We have aimed for a fairly literal translation that achieves readability without obscuring the original.

The translation is a thoroughgoing collaboration, as we both had an equal hand throughout. The annotation and the introductory essays reflect a division of labour to a certain extent, with Dr Edwards focusing somewhat more on theology and Macarius's place in the Christian tradition and Dr Schott concentrating on the philosophical and rhetorical aspects of the text.

We are grateful to those who have read and offered helpful comments on portions of the translation, especially Mark DelCogliano, David Maldonado Rivera, Derek Krueger, Jason Mokhtarian, Eva Mrozcek, John Reeves, Tina Shepardson, and the participants in Indiana University's Late Antiquity Reading Group. Sean Tandy provided particularly helpful editorial comments on the final draft. We would especially like to thank the TTH Editorial Committee and Mary Whitby for shepherding this project to completion. A particular debt of gratitude is due Gillian Clark for her extensive and invaluable editorial advice on rendering Macarius's difficult Greek into comprehensible English.

INTRODUCTION

I. GENERAL REMARKS AND OUTLINE OF THE *APOCRITICUS*

The text presented in this volume—the *Apocriticus* of Macarius—is among the consistently neglected works of late antiquity. As discussed in detail below, the text has a curious transmission history, and was only rediscovered in the 1870s. An apologetic work of the later fourth century, it stands chronologically between the great apologies of the early fourth century (e.g. Eusebius's *Gospel Preparation*, Lactantius's *Divine Institutes*) and those of the early fifth (e.g. Cyril of Alexandria's *Against Julian*, Theodoret's *Cure for Greek Maladies*). In form it claims to be the record of a public disputation between a Christian (Macarius) and an unnamed Hellene,[1] and thus bears comparison with other, better-known dialogues and dispute texts, such as Justin's *Dialogue with Trypho*, Jerome's *Dialogue against the Luciferians*, and Augustine's *Debate with Fortunatus*.

Since the nineteenth century, the *Apocriticus* has received attention primarily as a possible repository of disappeared anti-Christian polemics. Macarius has constructed the "Hellene" in whole or in part from a source—probably a work of anti-Christian polemic written by a Platonist. The list of usual suspects includes the second-century writer Celsus, whose pamphlet *The True Logos* was refuted at length by Origen of Alexandria; Sossianus Hierocles, governor of the Roman province of Bithynia, who penned *The*

---

1 In the Athens manuscript, the interlocutors are designated "Christian" and "Hellene" by glosses marking the beginning of major discourses. The tables of contents preserved in the Vatican manuscript, meanwhile, use the phrase "to the Hellenes" to describe the work. In one of the narrative transitions between discourses, Macarius calls his opponent a "master of Hellenic cleverness" (3.7.3). In late antiquity, "Hellene" could refer generally to non-Christian "pagans"; however, the term was also a self-designation employed by philosophical traditionalists to mark their commitment to Greek cultural values. The "pagan" character in the *Apocriticus* is meant to epitomize this sort of self-conscious intellectual and cultural Hellenism. On "Hellenism" in late antiquity see Bowersock (1990) and, more recently, Johnson (2012).

Lover of Truth, a polemic associated with the Diocletianic persecutions of 303–313 CE; and the emperor Julian, whose *Against the Galilaeans* (written 362–363 CE) drew a lengthy response from Cyril of Alexandria. But the anti-Christian Platonist most often connected with Macarius's Hellene is Porphyry of Tyre (232/3–c.305 CE), who, by any estimation, was the most sophisticated and feared anti-Christian polemicist of late antiquity. In several works, Porphyry levelled historical and philological critiques of the Hebrew Bible, Gospels, and Pauline literature, attacked Christian claims to universalism, and impugned what he argued were the ethical hazards of Christian doctrine. If Porphyry is the source of Macarius's Hellene, then the *Apocriticus* would be among the most important witnesses to Porphyry's lost works.

But the work as a whole is significant in its own right. The *Apocriticus* is neither a paragon of rhetorical prowess nor an epitome of theological or exegetical originality. Macarius is neither obviously pro-Nicene, Homoian, nor Heterousian. He deploys common apologetic tropes, but invents others all his own.[2] To say it is the work of an average talent may seem disparaging or dismissive, but Macarius is significant precisely because he is middling. Like the giants of his age, the Cappadocians and John Chrysostom, Macarius had been trained in the rhetorical schools, and the text is a case study in the ways a rhetor could create a discourse by assembling various stock figures of speech. Macarius also appears to have some philosophical training; as discussed in greater detail below, he engages philosophical and theological questions surrounding the relationship between names and the nature or essence of beings based on knowledge of Aristotle's *Categories*. Thus the *Apocriticus* provides important evidence for the ways in which fourth-century Christians wrestled with erudite exegetical and philosophical criticisms.

Outline of the *Apocriticus*

The *Apocriticus* consisted of five books. Books 1 and 5 have been lost, except for brief quotations. The majority of Book 2, the entirety of Book 3, and almost the entirety of Book 4 survive. Each book portrays a day of public debate between the Hellene and the Christian, and each day, in

---

2 "Nicene," "Homoian," and "Heterousian" designate differing theological trajectories within the ongoing theological controversies between the Council of Nicaea (325 CE) and Constantinople (381). On these terms and on Macarius's place in the Christian apologetic tradition see Mark J. Edwards's essay in this Introduction.

INTRODUCTION 3

turn, is divided into three sets of questions and responses. As discussed in more detail below, the *Apocriticus* thus belongs both among the fictional dialogues of late antiquity and to the popular genre of "question and answer" (ζητήματα καί λύσεις) literature. The rounds of questions and answers are punctuated by narrative interludes in which Macarius describes the ferocity of the Hellene's polemical questions and steels himself for his replies. Occasionally, he calls upon divine aid.

The sets of questions and answers are structured by the sequence of the Hellene's critique, which begins with polemics against the Gospels, proceeds to an attack on the apostles (particularly Peter and Paul), and then to criticisms of Christian ethics, cosmology, and theology. Macarius's speeches are much lengthier than the Hellene's, as the author uses the latter as launching points for excurses on a variety of topics. As elaborated below in Mark J. Edwards's introductory essay on "Macarius and the Christian Tradition," Macarius deploys a variety of exegetical, apologetic, and theological strategies throughout his responses.

Book 1
Lost except for a brief quotation preserved by Photius.

- The extant *pinax*[3] (table of contents) to Book 1 indicates that the Hellene's critiques focused on passages from the Gospels, and emphasized the incredibility of Christ as presented in the Gospels.

Book 2
First pair of discourses [lost]

- The extant *pinax* to Book 2 suggests that the first exchange of speeches focused on miracle stories in the Gospels.

Second pair of discourses
Hellene's critiques [lost] / 2.18.1–2.22.9: Macarius's responses

- Enigmatic statements of Jesus in the Gospels

Third pair of discourses
2.23.1–2.27.7: Hellene's critiques / 2.28.1–2.32.11: Macarius's responses

---

3 A *pinax* (pl. *pinakes*) was a tablet for writing, often made of wood; it came, by extension, to refer to tabular lists (which were often composed on such tablets). Late ancient books often included *pinakes* listing the sections of a work sequentially, and functioned roughly like modern "tables of contents."

- Inconsistency and implausibility of the Passion and Resurrection narratives in the Gospels

- Critiques of Jesus's statements concerning the "Ruler of this world" and the "Accuser"

Book 3
First pair of discourses
3.1.1–3.7.3: Hellene / 3.8.1–3.14.21: Macarius

- Critique of the Crucifixion

- Critiques of the inconsistency, implausibility, and ethical hazard of a variety of sayings of Jesus and miracle stories in the Gospels

Second pair of discourses
3.15.1–3.22.5: Hellene / 3.23.1–3.29.13: Macarius

- Attack on Christian faith and soteriology, based on criticisms of sayings of Jesus concerning the eucharist, faith, and apparent contradictions in Jesus's attitude towards Peter; concludes with attack on Peter's moral character and his "execution" of Ananias and Sapphira

Third pair of discourses
3.30.1–3.36.3: Hellene / 3.37.1–3.43.29: Macarius

- Attack on Paul, based on passages from Acts and the Pauline corpus

Book 4
First pair of discourses
4.1.2–4.10.3: Hellene / 4.11.4–4.18.19: Macarius

- Attack on Paul continues, based on passages from the Pauline corpus

- Attack on Christian eschatology, based on *Apocalypse of Peter*

Second pair of discourses
4.19.1–4.24.8: Hellene / 4.25.1–4.30.37: Macarius

- Attack on Christian theology, angelology/demonology, eschatology

Book 5
Both text and *pinax* are lost. A brief quotation survives in the works of the sixteenth-century Jesuit Francisco Torres (Turrianus).

II. MACARIUS AND THE CHRISTIAN TRADITION

Mark J. Edwards

It was the business of an apologist to present the most catholic view of Christianity, saying nothing of controversies in which one good Churchman differed from another. Even the first apologists, however, had found it necessary to draw a line excluding those whose doctrines seemed to them to fall outside any tolerable latitude of opinion. Justin Martyr had warned the Romans not to take Simon Magus for a Christian;[4] Origen complained that Celsus had quoted a Gnostic fantasy to support a caricature of the new religion.[5] Where the heresy was subtler, so was the polemic. Athanasius, in explaining the incarnation to the Platonists, made no allusion to Arius, yet belief in the full divinity of Christ—the tenet upheld against Arius by the Nicene Council of 325—is treated throughout the work as an axiom that no Christian would presume to doubt. In the generation after this Council synod followed synod, each bringing forth two new divisions for every one that it healed. Some upheld the Nicene proclamation that the Son was *homoousios*, "consubstantial" or "of one being" with the Father; others, to make it clear that Father and Son were not identical, preferred the expression *homoios kat' ousian*, "like in respect of being," while others again maintained that it was heresy to apply the term *ousia* to the Godhead.[6] Many adhered to the formula that the Son is "like the Father in all respects" or the "perfect image of the Father," which had satisfied bishops of impeccable orthodoxy before the Nicene condemnation of Arius.[7] Nevertheless, there were those for whom the term "image," when used of the superhuman element in Christ, seemed to imply that he was a creature rather than the second *hypostasis*

---

4 Justin, *1 Apology* 26.1–4, trans. Minns and Parvis (2009), 147–148.
5 Origen, *Against Celsus* 26.1–4, where an "Orphic diagram" depicts the soul's escape from the material realm to its lost abode by way of the planetary spheres.
6 See further Ayres (2004), 133–166; Edwards (2009), 103–136.
7 See Edwards (2012), 1–21.

of the Godhead;[8] others wished to proscribe the noun *hypostasis* itself, on the grounds that three *hypostases* could only mean three gods.[9] Macarius does not align himself expressly with any of these parties, though he says nothing to contradict the Nicene Creed, which in the years between 360 and 381 came to be acknowledged as an oecumenical standard of orthodoxy. At 4.25.22 he assumes that the Christian faith proclaims three *hypostases* in one *ousia*, but does not appear to think this a contentious position.[10] His catalogue of heretics at *Apocriticus* 4.15 is made up largely, perhaps entirely, of men whose adherents would not have been permitted to attend a synod under imperial sanction. The first is Manes[11] or Mani, invidiously but not altogether unfairly described as a Persian who had claimed to be a second Christ (4.15.3); since Christ had never asserted that the world is a tragic product of the immersion of divine light in the primal darkness, there was evidently no place in the Church for this latter-day apostle. The next name is that of Montanus, the second-century enthusiast, who was generally regarded as an impostor outside Africa and his native Phrygia (4.15.4). He is followed by a posse of infamous dualists—Cerinthus the bugbear of John the Evangelist, Simon Magus the sorcerer, Marcion the despiser of the Old Testament, and Bardaisan the eclectic Syrian—and by two less familiar malcontents, Droserius and Dositheus the Cilician (4.15.5). This Dositheus, not to be confused with the Samaritan precursor of Simon Magus, is said at 3.43.26 to have been the "coryphaeus" or ringleader of a number of sects—the Encratites, Apotaktikai, and Eremites—whose austerities were inspired by hatred of the creation rather than by a pious desire to render the flesh obedient to the spirit. Macarius is not setting his face against the ascetic movements of his day, but as these movements gathered numbers, he was not the only one who thought it necessary to check their aberrations. Since

---

8 See Robertson (2007), 128–129. *Hypostasis* is a versatile noun which can mean "foundation," "concrete entity," or "finite determination of an essence." In Trinitarian parlance, it is the equivalent of "person" in English. Further definition would be contentious, but it is agreed that the Father is the first *hypostasis*, the Son the second, the Spirit the third, and that each of these *hypostases* contains the undivided *ousia*, or essence, of the one God.

9 Pseudo-Anthimus, *To Theodore* 8 (Mercati [1991], 91). The locution "three *hypostases*" is first used by Origen, *Commentary on John* 2.75, then (it appears) by Porphyry as the title to Plotinus, *Enneads* 5.1, to be taken up by Arius in his letter to Alexander of Alexandria, preserved by Athanasius, *On the Synods of Ariminum and Seleucia* 16.

10 For this formula see Basil of Caesarea, *Letters* 214.4 and 236.6, trans. Behr (2004), 295–299; Zachhuber (1999), 61–92.

11 This form is often preferred because it resembles the Greek for "madman."

MACARIUS AND THE CHRISTIAN TRADITION 7

he names Isauria, Pisidia, Lycaonia, and Galatia as the localities in which these false evangelists had prospered (3.43.25), it would seem that he is a native of Asia Minor, and that Dositheus is a local gadfly rather than a Gnostic enemy of the Church universal. Macarius therefore prefaces his assault on the Asian heretics with another reference to the Manichaeans, who were anathematized throughout the Christian world, though it is only Macarius who gives the impression that they preached with peculiar vigour in this one province.

The refutation of heretics by public debate was now an established custom, at least in literature. Origen's interrogation of Beryllus of Bostra is commended by Eusebius,[12] while the *Dialogue with Heraclides*, another dialogue featuring Origen, was rediscovered in the twentieth century. Stenographers were present to record the acts of the council that deposed Paul of Samosata from the see of Antioch in 269. In the fourth century Manichaeans became the most common defendants in these staged assizes: Mani himself is worsted before an audience of his Persian compatriots in the fictitious *Acts of Archelaus*, and more veridical records survive of the erudite wrangling between his African followers and Augustine.[13] Disputation with pagans, on the other hand, is not so well attested, even in fiction. We possess a text, embedded in the *Ecclesiastical History* of Gelasius of Cyzicus, in which the Nicene faith is defended by a simple believer against a "philosopher,"[14] but even this bully is not so much a pagan as an Arian, and we cannot say whether any version of the dialogue would have been known to Macarius. It may be that he is the first to imagine a pagan interlocutor who is not content to publish written strictures on the New Testament, as Porphyry and Celsus had already done, but insists on being answered in one of those histrionic contests that had been the regular sport of sophists, and their means of livelihood, since the second century. In the tract *Against Hierocles*, attributed to Eusebius of Caesarea, a Christian mimics the tropes that had been employed in the composition and advocacy of Philostratus's *Life of Apollonius of Tyana*;[15] in the *Apocriticus*, it is not this showpiece of ungodly eloquence that is impugned, but the Gospel itself. It will not be not enough for Macarius to show his skill in persiflage if the Hellene's criticisms go unanswered.

---

12 Eusebius, *Ecclesiastical History* 6.20.
13 Augustine's anti-Manichaean writings are translated in NPNF ser. 1, vol. 4; see also *Acts of Archelaus*, translated in Vermes and Kaatz (2001).
14 [Gelasius], *Ecclesiastical History* 2.11–24.
15 English translation in Jones (2006).

Neither the criticisms nor their refutation would have held the attention of a pagan audience; for Christian readers, on the other hand, more than one end could be served. The catholic Church professed to have received its doctrines through an uninterrupted chain of witnesses from the apostles. To those who accepted this tradition, the apostolic writings were perspicuous, and required no interpretation until their meaning was perverted by some heretic. On this principle, Origen repeatedly joins issue with Heracleon the Gnostic in his *Commentary on John*; on the same principle, questions that must surely have been put to every bishop at some time by his congregation are treated by polemicists of the fourth century as though they could proceed only from a heretic. Macarius follows the trend, ascribing every question in the *Apocriticus* to his hostile interlocutor; too often we wonder whether it is he who has given the invidious tone to an otherwise innocent request for elucidation. The ordering of texts is not dictated by a systematic theology (there was no such thing in his time), although passages on the same topic are often gathered into small clusters. We can give a more logical shape to his apology by dividing it into three parts: a preamble in vindication of the apostles, a nucleus of replies to Christ's detractors and an epilogue concerning the fruits of Christian obedience in the next world.

The apostles

Opponents of Christianity have often begun by pointing out the apparent inconsistencies of Paul, and it is only the kinder critics who detect a cleft palate rather than a forked tongue. The conventions of ancient rhetoric were not kind, and Paul's resolution to "be all things to everyone"[16] is interpreted by the Hellene as a recipe for unbridled tergiversation. Did he not circumcise Timothy in defiance of his own strictures on the practice in his letter to the Galatians?[17] Did he not claim the privileges of a Roman from the Romans, then appeal to the Jews as a Jew?[18] How could he tell the Corinthians that it is better for a man not to touch a woman, yet declare in a private letter that it is heresy to forbid marriage?[19] How could sacrifices be

---

16 1 Cor. 9:22; cf. *Apocr.* 3.37.6.
17 See *Apocr.* 3.30.2 on Acts 16:2. Cf. Gal. 5:2; yet at Gal. 2:3, some witnesses read "I circumcised Titus."
18 See *Apocr.* 3.31 on Acts 22:3 and 22:27.
19 *Apocr.* 3.6, citing 1 Tim. 4:1 and 1 Cor. 7:25. Cf. also 1 Cor. 7:1.

abominable to a God who cares nothing for oxen,[20] or the altar a source of pollution to one who opines that an idol is nothing in the world?[21]

Macarius, in common with many of his coreligionists in the ancient world, is prepared to accept that dissimulation may be a pious expedient where it serves to advance the Gospel.[22] When Timothy was circumcised, this temporary capitulation won the trust of some who were not yet ready to hear the Gospel in its purity (3.37.6). If another excuse is needed, would we not applaud the general who elected to live for a time among his enemies in order to acquire a better knowledge of their designs and their mode of fighting (3.37.5)? There may be an allusion here to some historical episode, but it is one that has now been forgotten, unless this passage is to be read as a gloss on David's treasonable conduct as a captain of mercenaries among the Philistines (1 Sam. 27:5–12). Another simile drawn from the martial sphere acquits Paul of subterfuge in calling himself a Roman: a man who is handed over to the enemy, as Paul was handed over by the Jews, cannot be blamed if he begins to regard his new hosts as his own people (3.38.3). Paul's amphibianism has amused the infidel more than it has troubled Christian scholars,[23] but Macarius forgets that he was already in the custody of the Romans when he tried to appease his former coreligionists by describing himself as a Jew. His logic cannot be faulted, on the other hand, when he observes that Paul's commendation of celibacy is quite consistent with his reluctance to enforce it. When he expresses a preference for virginity, he disclaims any "word from the Lord"[24]– implying not (Macarius tells us) that he was speaking without authority, but that Christ himself did not enjoin this counsel of perfection as a universal ordinance, as he would have done had marriage been a sin like murder or theft (3.43.6–12).

The case against sacrifice must be handled delicately, as a Christian must not appear to countenance Porphyry's view that God has created foods but forbidden us to eat them. Among professing Christians this was the heresy of the Encratites and the Manichaeans, as Macarius observes (3.43.25). To

---

20 1 Cor. 9:10, cited by Macarius himself at *Apocr.* 3.40.18.
21 *Apocr.* 3.35, citing 1 Cor. 8:4 and 10:20.
22 See Jerome, *Commentary on Galatians* (*PL* 26.338c) on this text; Origen, *Homilies on Jeremiah* 20.3.2–3 on Jeremiah 20:7 ("Oh, Lord, thou hast deceived me"). Origen's medical simile is adopted by Macarius at *Apocr.* 3.37.4.
23 Sherwin-White ([1973], 273) asserts without proof that "Paul was certainly not the only citizen of the eastern provinces" who resorted to this appeal against "summary justice."
24 1 Cor. 7:25, cited at *Apocr.* 3.43.4

obviate this misreading, he sets out Porphyry's taxonomy of offerings in some detail (3.42.4), citing the *Philosophy from Oracles* by name and in a manner which proves that, whatever the Hellene's intellectual linage, he is something more than Porphyry's dramatic incognito (3.42.6). Once it has been established that the object of the sacrifice is to feed demons (3.42.15), the eating of meat without the intention of worship is seen to be innocent. Paul says that an idol is nothing in the world[25] because there is nothing that could be styled an *eidōlon* in Greek that is not properly something else, whether this be an element of the cosmos, the wood or stone that is fashioned by human artifice, or simply a phantom of the imagination (3.42.12–15). Nevertheless, because the recipient of the worship given to the idol is a demon,[26] the worshipper's genuflexions to a fictitious deity lead him into real sin.

More charitable readers than the Hellene have been at a loss to reconcile Paul's statements on the authority of the Mosaic Law.[27] Though spiritual, it was given not to prevent sins but to increase them.[28] Where it is absent sin is not imputed (Rom. 5:13), yet those who are not guilty of any formal trespass inherit from Adam the death that he incurred as the wages of sin (Rom. 5:14; cf. 6:23). Where it is present, it cannot be obeyed, yet to err in one point is to be guilty of all (Gal. 5:3). The Hellene triumphs in these contradictions, which had not escaped the notice of such heretics as Marcion and Mani.[29] Macarius replies that the Mosaic Law is grounded in natural law, and that if human nature were not now fallen and prone to err, the Law would be neither a cause of sin nor a necessary instrument of restraint (4.18.12). Nature can teach us to recognize sin, but not to avoid it; where there is no written law to reward good works and rebuke the transgressor, we are barely conscious of our imperfections (3.41.2–5). So long as they remain unobserved they remain unexpiated: the Law is therefore given, not to relieve our shortcomings, but to expose them and to punish them with a severity that ennobles virtue and at the same time makes us feel the want of it (3.41.7–10). Sin, or rather the imputation of sin, is multiplied not because the Law lacks any good thing but because it is only the perfectly good who can obey it perfectly. Christ, as God incarnate, is the one human being who has displayed this obedience. Now that he has done this on our behalf it

25 1 Cor. 8:4.
26 Cf. Athenagoras, *Embassy* 25–26.
27 See e.g. O'Neill (2003); Räisänen (2003).
28 See *Apocr.* 3.34 on Rom. 5:20.
29 See *Apocr.* 3.33.34. On Marcion, see May and Greschat (2002).

would be hubristic to emulate him (3.40.3; 3.41.12–13); Paul's admonition that he who offends in one point is guilty of all is addressed to those who have failed to grasp that the sins for which Christ suffered were their own (3.40.3).

If Paul at times seems weak in logic, Peter can be charged with caprice and cowardice in his acts. He hid himself for fear of Herod Antipas;[30] he shunned the Gentile Christians at Antioch lest the Jews should refuse to eat with him;[31] no sooner had he said "Thou art the Christ, the Son of God" at Caesarea Philippi than he drew from his Master's lips the reprimand "Get thee behind me, Satan."[32] Yet the same man caused the deaths of Ananias and Sapphira for nothing more than retaining a little of their own property.[33] Macarius replies that this impeachment of the apostle's acts betrays a false estimation of his motives. He fled from Herod only because he knew that God was reserving him for a more conspicuous death in the "Queen City" (3.29.3); we may assume that the apologist has in mind the words of Jesus to Peter at John 21:18, which "showed in what manner he would glorify God" (Jn. 21:19). In justifying Peter's conduct at Antioch, Macarius ignores his altercation with Paul, who roundly accused him of dissimulation;[34] he is therefore free to argue that it was not through pusillanimity that Peter ate with the Jews, but with the object of converting them—an object that could not be achieved if he gave them the least occasion of offence (3.29.6–10). The unanimity of Paul and Peter, he adds elsewhere, was demonstrated in their common martyrdom, which took place not (as the Hellene thinks) in defiance but in fulfilment of God's plan (4.14; cf. 4.4). At Caesarea Philippi Peter gave proof of his discernment by his use of the definite article—not merely "Thou art Christ," but "Thou art *the* Christ, *the* Son of God" (3.27.18). For this he received a testimony from Christ that made him conscious of his deserts and Satan seized his opportunity, inducing him to tempt his Master in the sincere belief that he spoke from love. Christ, who perfectly understood the necessity of his own death, was neither tempted nor deceived, and any reader of the text will see that it was to Satan, not to

---

30 See *Apocr.* 3.22 on Acts 12:3ff, though Macarius at 3.29.3 seems to read more obloquy into the Hellene's remark than was intended. The Hellene's question is not why Peter fled, but how, if Christ foresaw his flight and subsequent death, he could have enjoined him at Jn. 21:15 to "feed my sheep" (*Apocr.* 3.22.2–3).
31 See *Apocr.* 3.22.4 on Gal. 2:12–13.
32 See *Apocr.* 3.1.9 on Mt. 16:18–23.
33 See *Apocr.* 3.21 on Acts 5:1–11.
34 Gal. 2:13.

Peter, that he addressed his malediction (3.27.4–8). Envy wrought Satan's fall[35] where charity caused an apostle to stumble, and there was no further stumbling after Peter received the Holy Spirit. He acted from zeal, not petulance, when he pronounced a fatal curse on Ananias and Sapphira, as he perceived that, if he allowed them to treat as theirs the property they had vowed to Christ, their example would corrupt the Church (3.28.4–9).

Jesus, God and man

Historians of early Christian exegesis have been wont to contrast the Antiochene school, which sought to divine the intention of the biblical author at the time of writing, with the more scholastic Alexandrian school, which required that the text should speak not only to its own time but for all time, and that every word should be replete with meaning for the reader.[36] If a thoroughbred specimen of either school exists, it is not Macarius, who simply adopts in every case the hermeneutic stratagem that resolves his difficulty. He thus performs what we might call an Antiochene manoeuvre when he credits both Paul and Peter with a calculated tempering of their words and acts to the prejudices of a group that would otherwise have refused their ministry. There is Alexandrian precedent—by which we mean, as often, that there is precedent in Origen[37]—for his argument that a noun with the definite article has a more specific reference than the same noun without the article (3.27.18, as above); Macarius, however, is comparing the augmented noun in the text with the unaugmented form that Peter might have chosen, whereas Origen reserves his casuistry for the occasions on which both the augmented and the unaugmented forms are present in the text. Antiochenes are often described as literalists, and Macarius adopts the most literal reading of the words "Get thee behind me, Satan"; for us, as for the Hellene, this would not be the natural reading, as the rebuke is obviously addressed to Peter. None of his glosses on Paul or on the Acts of the Apostles involves the typically Alexandrian trope of allegory,[38] which eschews both the literal and the natural reading in the hope of imbuing the text with a sense more palatable or

---

35 *Apocr.* 3.27.9; cf. Wis. 2:27.
36 The distinction is not without merit, but has given rise to numerous misconceptions, many of which are exploded by Young (1997), 161–185.
37 Origen, *Commentary on Romans* 3.7.9, trans. Sanday and Headlam (1907), 58.
38 For the term "tropic" see *Apocr.* 2.20.2, 3.24.10. The term "allegorical" occurs at 3.10.14.

more edifying than any that might have been derived from it by more workaday methods.

Macarius cannot dispense with this expedient when he has to explain the more hyperbolic utterances of Christ. The Creator who has fixed the bounds of all things cannot have wished his disciples to exercise their faith by the deracination of mountains; when he promised that faith as big as a mustard seed could achieve this feat,[39] he spoke not of any mountain but symbolically of "*the* mountain"—that is, the towering pride of Satan (3.25.9). Again, when he said that those who believe would eat deadly foods and live,[40] his meaning was that they would be immune to the blandishments of sin (3.24.5–9). Here, however, the more ingenuous reading is almost tenable, for the saints have displayed uncommon powers of healing (3.24.10–14). We see another instance of this dual exegesis in the interpretation of Christ's hard saying that no one enters the Kingdom of heaven unless he has eaten the flesh and drunk the blood of the Son of Man.[41] Macarius follows Origen,[42] though without naming him, in his application of this verse to the metaphorical eating and drinking of the Word in Scripture (3.23.9–10). Without explicit reference to the eucharist, he goes on to quote the statements "this is my body" and "this is my blood" from the speech of Christ to his disciples at the Last Supper.[43] Here again he does not embrace what we might call the literal inference that the bread and wine of the eucharist are the body and blood of the Saviour; his argument is a subtler one, and grounded once again in the economy of nature. Christ sustains all life through the elements of the first creation (3.23.14 and 21); having made for himself a body from those elements (3.23.18), he voluntarily yields it to the death by which it becomes the sustenance of the new creation (3.23, 18, and 24–25). We are no longer in the realm of allegory, since the subject of the word "body" is now literally Christ's body; but the verbs "eat" and "drink" contain an elusive metaphor, which is not parsed anywhere in the *Apocriticus* by a full explanation of the reasons for his death and its consequences.

---

39 Matthew 17:20, quoted at *Apocr.* 3.17.

40 Mk. 16:18, quoted at *Apocr.* 3.16. This verse is now regarded as an accretion to the gospel of Mark.

41 Jn. 6:53, quoted at *Apocr.* 3.15.

42 Origen, *Commentary on John* 10.102–105. The reference to the breasts of god in this passage of Macarius may owe something to Song of Songs 1:2, on which see Gregory of Nyssa, *Oration on the Song of Songs* 1.

43 *Apocr.* 3.23.13–14, citing Mt. 26:26–28 and 1 Cor. 11:24.

On one question that divided Churchmen of the fourth century,[44] Macarius speaks with firm conviction: the crucified man was none other than the Word of God. That is to say, he is not a coupling or conjunction of a divine with a human agent, but one agent who is both human and divine. The miracles that accompanied his death suffice to prove that there was no separation of his divinity from his humanity; and since the Divine cannot perish, it is evident (to everyone but the Hellene) that when he declared, "the poor you have always with you, but me not always,"[45] he was speaking of his bodily separation from the disciples (3.14.20). As in exegesis, so in Christology it has been common to set Alexandria against Antioch, the Christ whose Godhead swallows up his frailties against the Christ who is at once all that is divine and all that is human.[46] Few Alexandrians fall so clearly on one side of this antithesis as Macarius. He will not allow that Christ was subject to any mortal passions but contends that he allowed himself to seem weak because his enemies would otherwise not have dared to crucify him (3.9.4–5). Again he was so far from suffering any real trepidation in Gethsemane[47] that he called his passion a cup and was barely willing to postpone the pleasure of drinking it (3.9.11); but Satan, who had left him "for a season" only (Lk. 4:13), would not have returned had he not been led to believe that Christ was a passible man like others (3.9.8). Christ's cup was the necessary corrective to the eating of the fruit of the tree of knowledge; but for his Passion, the conquest of the passions would not have been vouchsafed to the elect (3.9.6–9).

Christ was no Apollonius of Tyana, duping the world by sorcery in order to gather laurels that profited no one but himself (3.8.10). The Hellene wonders why he did not show himself to his enemies after the Resurrection (2.14), forgetting that had he done so the Jews would have questioned the reality of his death and their hatred would have been redoubled (2.19.4–9). Needlessly perplexed by a verse which means "you are of your father the Devil [διαβόλος],"[48] Macarius takes it to mean "you are from the father of the Devil," and explains that the Greek διαβόλος (slanderer) signifies

---

44 See Behr (2011).
45 Mt. 26:11 and parallels, quoted at *Apocr.* 3.7.
46 See Sellers (1940); Grillmeier (1975), 345–391. For criticisms see Young (1971), 103–114; Edwards (2009), 138–145.
47 Mt. 26:37–39 and parallels, quoted at *Apocr.* 3.2.
48 Jn. 8:44, quoted at *Apocr.* 2.32.1. John Chrysostom, *Homilies on John* 67.1 is more willing to admit that Christ was subject to the fear of death, which is not a sinful passion.

MACARIUS AND THE CHRISTIAN TRADITION   15

in this case not the Devil but the serpent who deceived Adam (2.32.9), so that "father of the διαβόλός" is a sobriquet for Satan (2.32.7). "Prince of the world" is another of his appellatives,[49] and while it may not be true that Christ has dethroned the visible tyrants of this world,[50] he can say with truth that "the prince of this world has been cast out" because the fleshly appetites which collude with him have lost their sway in the hearts of the elect (2.20.11). This passage makes it clear that the Jews are not the sole oppressors of the Church, and if a pagan asks why the Scriptures cannot speak the truth more plainly, one can ask in return what truth was ever spoken in a society whose most cherished authors openly promote rapacity, fornication, violence, and false notions of the gods.

There are sayings of Christ which are patient of exegesis at two levels. The statement that his mission is to put a sword between members of the same family[51] can be understood as a commendation of the monastic life, but according to the higher or "noetic" sense (as Macarius terms it in this case)[52] the father of the household represents the Mosaic Law, the daughter the flesh, the stepmother the synagogue and the mother circumcision, while the bride who is severed from them is an emblem of the Church (2.7.12; cf. Ephesians 5:32). According to a principle espoused by orthodox thinkers after Nicaea, we must also differentiate what is said as man from what is said as God, though we must thus fall into the error of imagining Christ the man and Christ the Word as different subjects. When he exclaims, for instance, "Who is my mother and my brethren?"[53] he intimates that, as the only-begotten Son of God he has no familial link to any being but the Father. At the same time he aligns himself as man with the apostles, as his spiritual kindred, in contradistinction to those who are merely his mother and brethren after the flesh (2.8.8). When, though bearing witness to himself, he appears to deny that he can do so,[54] we are to understand that he testifies as God, but has no right as man to vouch for this testimony (2.11.4). Even when he speaks as man, he does

---

49   Jn. 12:31, quoted at *Apocr.* 2.15.

50   At *Apocr.* 2.20.9 Macarius says that Christ could not speak openly of the powers of the air who govern the human world. Cf. Eph. 6:12, 1 Cor. 2:8–9, and Caird (1954).

51   Mt. 10:34–38, quoted in a lost passage of Book 2.

52   Cf. Origen, *Against Celsus* 6.70 and Clement of Alexandria, *Who is the Rich Man Who Shall Be Saved?* 5.2 (referring to the *nous* of the text, or its deeper, intellectual meaning, which a Platonist would have styled its *dianoia*).

53   Mt. 12:48, quoted in a lost passage of Book 2. According to Tertullian (*On the Flesh of Christ* 7.1), this verse had been adduced by Apelles to prove that Christ's flesh was illusory.

54   Compare Jn. 5:31 with Jn. 8:14–18. Again the Hellene's question is lost.

not conceal his Godhead:⁵⁵ thus, accommodating himself to the ignorance of a man who has addressed him as "good master," he answers, "Why do you call me good? No one is good but God,"⁵⁶ not so much denying that he is God as stimulating the inquirer to ask himself how one who is merely a man could deserve the epithet "good" (2.20.9–10). If he appears to betray a human failing, that too is evidence of divinity: he denounces those who beg him to heal a lunatic as a faithless generation⁵⁷ because he can read the mind of his suppliants, and knows that they regard the moon as the cause of lunacy, thus traducing the handiwork of God (2.10.6).

The device known as typology, which finds anticipations of the New Testament in the Old, allows Macarius to see the Cross in the horns which God revealed to the prophet Habbakuk in a vision.⁵⁸ He does not comply with the Hellene's demand for evidence that Moses also spoke of Christ,⁵⁹ as Christ himself asseverates (3.10), and the suggestion that Ezra failed to restore an accurate transcript of the works of Moses to the Jews is not so much answered as shouted down.⁶⁰ Macarius takes greater pains to demonstrate that no contradiction or error can be imputed to the Gospels. Where they appear discordant in their accounts of the Passion,⁶¹ the reason is that each has reproduced only a handful of details from an ensemble, or selected one individual as the mouthpiece of a crowd (2.17). We need not be perturbed that only one evangelist records the miraculous flow of blood and water from the side of Christ,⁶² which mirrors and counteracts the creation of Eve, the instigator of sin, from Adam's rib.⁶³ If the same miracle is described in Matthew as the healing of two demoniacs and in Mark as the healing of one,⁶⁴ the reason is that Mark speaks of the shared *ousia* or nature of the demons and Matthew of their numerical manifestation.⁶⁵ Christ's walking

---

55 For this hermeneutic strategy cf. Athanasius, *Apology against the Arians* 3.31–34.
56 Mk. 10:18, quoted in a lost passage of Book 2. Cf. Origen, *On First Principles* 1.2.13 for a comment resembling that of Macarius.
57 Mt. 17:15, quoted in a lost passage of Book 2.
58 Hab. 3:4, cited at *Apocr.* 3.8.9.
59 *Apocr.* 3.3., citing Jn. 5:46–47.
60 *Apocr.* 3.10.2, responding to 3.3.1. The Hellene may be parading his knowledge of the apocalypse known as 4 Ezra as well as the book called Ezra in the Septuagintal canon.
61 See *Apocr.* 2.12 on the contradictions between Mt. 27:33/Mt. 27:46 and Mk. 15:36, Lk. 23:46, and Jn. 19:19.
62 Jn. 10:33–35, quoted at *Apocr.* 2.13.
63 *Apocr.* 2.18.3. Cf. Augustine, *Tractate on John's Gospel* 120.2.
64 *Apocr.* 3.4.1, contrasting Mk. 5:1–12 with Mt. 8:31ff.
65 *Apocr.* 3.11.3. Gregory of Nyssa (*On the Making of Man* 16.16–18) asserts that all

on the waves[66] is a sign that he has as much power in the moist as in the dry element (3.13.9), and it is because this miracle recapitulates every taming of the waters since the First Day that the lake is called a sea (3.13.3–6). Again we notice that the exegesis is underwritten by the economy of nature; Christ makes another parabolic use of his creatures when he casts the demons into the Gadarene swine[67] as an illustration of the manner of life into which the soul is bound to fall when it neglects the divine commandments (3.11.20). Some of the Hellene's errors arise from his failure to grasp the logic of a continuous text: had he perused the whole sequence of temptations in the wilderness, for example, he would have understood that Christ refused to throw himself down from the temple,[68] not because it was a sin, but because to do so at Satan's behest would have been to worship him (3.26.7). To be carried down by angels at his own desire, on the other hand, was to manifest his omnipotence as God.

World without end

We have twice observed an appeal the "economy of nature" in the *Apocriticus*. This is underwritten in Macarius, as in all Christian authors, by the presupposition that one world implies one God. The Hellene protests that a ruler must have subjects, and hence that there must be other gods over whom the first God can exercise his monarchy (4.20); Macarius retorts that to be God is to rule not only in one but in every order of being, and that other beings who are styled gods in Scripture[69] are not so by nature but by divine adoption (4.26.6). As though dissatisfied with this long rebuttal of a short challenge, he fills the *Apocriticus* with digressions on the grandeur and harmony of the physical cosmos, assuming (as it seems) that because he is praising infinite bounty the reader's patience will be as inexhaustible as his ink. It is true that those who had books and were able to read in his time enjoyed more leisure than the modern reader; furthermore, all precedent had taught them that in a Christian apology the proofs from Scripture ought to be reinforced by liberal exercises in natural theology, to show that

---

human nature is comprehended in the creation of the inner man at Genesis 1:26; in his *Letter to Ablabius* he maintains that since the noun "man" denotes an *ousia*, it should properly be used only in the singular. See Zachhuber (1999), 213–218.

66 Mt. 14:25 and parallels, quoted at *Apocr.* 3.6.
67 Mt. 8:31 and parallels, quoted at *Apocr.* 3.4.
68 As Satan enjoins at Mt. 4:6, quoted at *Apocr.* 3.18.
69 See Ex. 15:11; Ps. 82:1, 6; 1 Cor. 8:5.

the world bears witness to the unity of God and the ubiquity of his love.[70] Constantine, in his *Speech to the Assembly of the Saints*, and Eusebius in his encomium on the thirty-year reign of the emperor, had been equally unwilling to shorten the inventory of God's labours, while Athanasius's treatise *On the Incarnation* is prefaced by another *To the Nations*, in which polytheism, idolatry, and infidelity are all refuted by appeal to the manifest working of divine providence. We may regret the prolixity of Macarius—all the more if we have to translate him—but he says no more than is warranted by the taste and faith of his own contemporaries.

Yet a Christian also holds that there are truths which cannot be known until God chooses to reveal them. The Bible speaks in ciphers of the last days, or at least in terms that cannot be appropriated literally today. Where Paul had said that it is not for the pot to accuse the potter (Romans 9:21), Macarius adopts a grander image: it is not for us to tell God how he will turn the wheel of fortune. The Gospel has been preached to all the nations,[71] and if the end has not yet come as Christ predicted, we may be sure that it has been deferred for the good of the elect (4.13.11). That "the fashion of this world passes away"[72] does not mean that no relic of his handiwork will remain, but that we live in a state of perpetual vicissitude, as empire tramples empire and the rich of one generation are the paupers of the next (4.11.4–5). There will indeed be a new heaven and a new earth, but the decrepitude of the old one is no judgment on the Creator, any more than the decay of a house through negligence can be laid at the door of the architect (4.16.9). The end is the consummation, not the ruin of God's design, for whereas the old creation was for the sake of the human race, the new heaven will be humanity itself and God will set his throne in the hearts of the elect (4.16.1–24.26). This equation of heaven with what is best in our humanity may be another borrowing from Origen;[73] on the other hand, Macarius invokes a notion of human solidarity that was later employed by Gregory of Nyssa[74] when he contends that Paul did not expect to be taken alive into heaven, but used the pronoun "we" to express his sense of brotherhood with all other Christians, even those who were not

---

70 Cf. *Apocr.* 4.26

71 *Apocr.* 4.13, citing Mt. 24:14 in response to *Apocr.* 4.3.

72 1 Cor. 7:31, cited at *Apocr.* 4.1.

73 *Homilies on Genesis* 1.2. Volp (2011) argues that Macarius is only partially an Origenist in his eschatology.

74 On the so-called *Tunc et ipse Filius* (a short dissertation on 1 Cor. 15:28) see Zachhuber (1999), 207–212; Ludlow (2000), 89–95.

yet born.[75] It is clear, then, that Macarius believes in a future assumption of the living as the apostle foretold it at 1 Thessalonians 4:16–17: it is not clear how he interprets the blast of the trumpet, but the ascent of the saints to the clouds is for him a symbol of their elevation to the angelic state (4.12.17).

The dictum that only the sick need a physician[76] does not indicate that the scope of redemption is limited, since only the angels are free of the malaise that we have inherited from Adam (4.18.10–14). God is the sun who illumines without receiving illumination (4.26.10), and if we shut our eyes to him he is not to be held accountable for our blindness (4.30.31).[77] In the parable which likens the Kingdom of heaven to a pearl,[78] the pearl is the concealed divinity of the incarnate Word (4.7.8); in the parable of the mustard seed,[79] the Word itself is the germinating seed which uproots the weeds of sin within us (4.17.7). The Hellene is offended by Paul's assurance that the elect are pure because they are washed;[80] this is not a charter for unrepentant and flagitious sinning (4.25.14), but an assurance that our infirmities will be forgiven if we rely not on the Law but on its master (4.25.11; cf. 3.41.12). Baptism initiates a work of regeneration which is carried on (though not to perfection in this life) by the Spirit (4.25.20–22). Although it is from Christ's fullness that he makes up our deficiencies, his humanity makes it possible for him to sympathize with our fallen state (4.17.5; 4.18.7)—another index, if we care for such labels, of the apologist's Alexandrian Christology. The peroration, or rhetorical conclusion, to the whole apology is a rebuttal of the customary objections to the possibility of a future rising from the dead. The god who created everything from nothing does not dwell in the inanimate works of our hands; he speaks to us not through images but through angels, who assume a human shape because they would otherwise be invisible, not because He who sent them is circumscribed by any form (4.27.3–4). By the power through which he creates from nothing he is able to create us again (4.30.22–23), and those

---

75 *Apocr.* 4.12.19, citing 1 Thess. 4:17 in answer to *Apocr.* 4.2.
76 Mt. 9:12 and Lk. 5:31, cited at *Apocr.* 4.10.
77 At *Apocr.* 3.14.10 God is called the noetic sun, i.e. the light of the intellect. Cf. Malachi 4:2 and Jn. 8:4, but these biblical texts appear to have been conflated with the Socratic conceit attested by Plato (*Republic* 509c) and Xenophon (*Memorabilia* 4.3.14), that the difficulty of seeing the sun directly for its brightness suggests the frailty of the seer, rather than deficiency in the object of sight. See also Emperor Julian's *Hymn to the Sun*.
78 Mt. 13:45–46, cited at *Apocr.* 4.8.1.
79 Mt. 13:31–32, cited at *Apocr.* 4.8.1.
80 *Apocr.* 4.19, citing 1 Cor. 6:11.

who ask how bodies that have been devoured by beasts will be redeemed (4.24.3) do not understand that all change in the world occurs only for the benefit of humanity (4.30.11). Taking up a trite motif from previous apologists,[81] Macarius observes that in the present world the cycle of death is also the cycle of life (4.30.8–10). Our assurance of a life without death is grounded in the condescension of the eternal Word to our condition; not all, however, are destined to enjoy it (4.30.27–37), but only those on whom God sets his seal (4.30.28) because they have grown into his likeness by obedience to his statutes and imitation of his living Word.

---

81 See Ps.-Justin, *On the Resurrection* 5–6, ed. Heimgartner (2001), 155–168.

III. THE HELLENE

Jeremy M. Schott

A. MACARIUS'S USE OF A SOURCE OR SOURCES

Since the rediscovery of the *Apocriticus* in the nineteenth century, scholars have recognized that Macarius almost certainly constructed the Hellene's objections based on a work of anti-Christian polemic. The scholarly consensus that Macarius has based his Hellene upon an independent source has become so well established that it is worth recounting the arguments in its favour. Richard Goulet's magisterial study of Macarius offers a useful synopsis of the arguments in favour of the idea that Macarius used a source.[82] Adolf von Harnack contended that Macarius must have used a non-Christian source because he could not imagine a self-respecting Christian affecting such a "violent and punishing tone."[83] This, in itself, is not a strong argument, as authors of dispute texts often cast their imagined adversaries as sharp and cantankerous. Moreover, that the Hellene is a formidable, fearful opponent is crucial to Macarius's portrayal of the debate.[84] In each narrative prologue, Macarius presents the Hellene as a snickering bully and himself as a meek respondent in need of Christ's aid.[85]

Others have pointed to stylistic differences between the Hellene's critiques and Macarius's responses.[86] It can be countered, however, that the acerbity and terseness of the Hellene's speeches is due to Macarius's pen, for Macarius wished to contrast the beauty of simple Christian rhetoric with Hellenic bombast.[87] Harnack's 1911 study made the first attempt at a systematic comparison of the style and vocabulary of Macarius and the Hellene. He concluded that the Hellene's objections are marked by

---

82 Goulet (2003), 66–75.
83 Harnack (1911), 97.
84 Also noted by Goulet (2003), 67.
85 E.g. *Apocr.* 2.23.1; 2.28.1; 3.prol.1; 3.23.1; 3.36.3; 4.prol.1; 4.11.1; 4.19.1; 4.25.1.
86 Duchesne (1877); Wagenmann (1878).
87 As argued by Salmon (1882), 768.

a "poetic" vocabulary, neologisms, and rare words.[88] Goulet has shown, however, that the vocabulary Harnack found characteristic of the Hellene is in fact found *throughout* the text (Goulet 69–71). It thus becomes quite difficult, if not impossible, to decide whether these stylistic elements derive from Macarius, or whether the vocabulary and style of the source has subtly "infected" Macarius's own writing.

More secure evidence of Macarius's dependence on a source comes from a comparison of scriptural quotations and exegeses in the Hellene's and Macarius's portions of the text. Early German scholarship recognized that a number of the Hellene's quotations of the New Testament reflect a "Western" text."[89] In addition to quotations that reflect a "Western" text, the Hellene employs variants not found in any manuscript.[90] In his replies, Macarius often repeats the variants quoted by the Hellene. Significantly, however, Macarius *never* quotes anything approaching the "Western" text when he is not recapitulating the Hellene. The simplest explanation would be that Macarius has incorporated the Hellene's variant quotations from a source text, rather than inventing them himself, for if Macarius himself was familiar with the Western text, one would expect to find evidence in his many biblical citations that are independent of the Hellene.[91]

In at least two cases, moreover, Macarius finds himself having to *correct* the Hellene's biblical quotations. The Hellene quotes John 12:31—"Now is the judgment of the world; now the Ruler of this world will be cast out" (2.26.1)—following the text of Codex Bezae in the omission of the pronoun (τουτοῦ) in the first clause and in the reading of βληθήσεται ἔξω (will be cast out), rather than ἐκβληθήσεται ἔξω (lit: "will be outcast out") of the received text. Macarius repeats the Hellene's version of the quotation (2.31.1), but remarks: "or as it is in some copies 'will be cast down [κάτω].'" In the exegesis that follows, Macarius does not, in fact, make use of the variant adverb ("down" vs. "out"); rather, he seems simply to have mentioned the variant because he was struck by the Hellene's own variant reading, and wished to adduce, or show that he could adduce, another.

Even more striking is the Hellene's quotation of the *Apocalypse of Peter*. As part of his attack on Christian eschatology, he says:

---

88 Harnack (1911), 96–97. For a helpful tabular presentation of Harnack's word lists see Goulet (2003), 69–71.
89 Goulet (2003) identifies 2.26.1; 3.2.1; 3.18.1–2; 3.19.1; 4.19.2; 4.7.3; 2.23.6 as the most secure examples; see also Hausschildt (1907), 19, n.1 and Beatrice (1996).
90 For a list see Goulet (2003), 292–303.
91 See also Goulet (2003), 98.

For the sake of completeness, let us also consider what is said in the *Apocalypse of Peter*. It intimates that the heaven together with the earth will be judged, in this way: "The earth," it says, "will present everyone to God on the Day of Judgment and that it will itself be judged with the heaven that surrounds [it]." (4.6.1)

He also quotes a second passage:

And furthermore, that [book] has the passage, which is full of impiety, that states: "And every power of heaven will dissolve and the heaven will be rolled up like a book scroll. And all the stars will fall like leaves from a vine and as leaves from a fig tree." (4.7.1)

In his reply (4.16.1–3), Macarius replicates the Hellene's quotations. He rejects the *Apocalypse of Peter* as unorthodox (4.16.3), but nonetheless notes that the Hellene's second quotation is itself a quotation of Isaiah 34:4, and argues that Mt. 24:35 expresses the same concept.

… let us examine the subtle phrase in the *Apocalypse of Peter* that speaks about the heaven and earth as though they are things being put on trial: "The earth will present all those judged to God on the day of judgment and will itself be judged with the heaven that surrounds [it]." But that it is not because of a fault of heaven or any wrong of the earth that they are going to be judged is obvious, while the report of the divine words is not false, and this is evident and especially unambiguous. For although we should reject the *Apocalypse of Peter*, we are compelled by the prophetic and evangelical voice to [consider] the *Apocalypse of Peter*, even against our will, for the prophet says, "The heaven will be unrolled like a book scroll and all the stars will fall, as leaves from a vine, as leaves fall from a fig tree" (Is. 34:4) and the Gospel says: "The heaven and the earth will pass away, but my words will not at all pass away." (Mt. 24:35)

Macarius is thus in the position of having to reject the Hellene's quotation, yet simultaneously respond to the underlying critique of eschatology. To do so he must find canonical parallels to the apocryphal passages. It is possible that Macarius has crafted a Hellene who quotes apocryphal texts in order that he may himself adduce canonical parallels. The more likely and more economical solution, however, is that Macarius's source knows and quotes the *Apocalypse of Peter*, Macarius does not know the text himself,[92] but can identify the embedded quote from Isaiah and, in turn, adduce the Matthean parallel.

---

92 It is numbered among the rejected books by Eusebius, *Church History* 3.25.4.

24 MACARIUS, *APOCRITICUS*

The strongest evidence that Macarius has drawn from a source to create the Hellene are the several moments in which Macarius's replies seem to misunderstand, either in whole or in part, the Hellene's critiques. If Macarius had crafted the Hellene from whole cloth, one would expect a point-for-point correspondence between each question and answer. This, though, is not the case.[93]

In Book 2, the Hellene develops a critique of Christian cosmology and theology based on John 8:43–44. Both the Hellene (2.27.1) and Macarius 2.32.1) quote the received text: "You are unable to hear my word, because you are of your father, the Accuser." The final clause consists of two genitives in apposition (ἐκ τοῦ πατρὸς τοῦ διαβόλου). The Hellene's critiques consist of two *reductiones ad absurdum* concerning the being named "Accuser" (διάβολος). Firstly, the passage assumes that the Accuser is blameworthy, but if the being named "Accuser" is so named accidentally, rather than essentially, then it is the accused, who prompted accusation, not the accuser, who acts unjustly (2.27.4–6). Secondly, is the Accuser impassible or passible? If the former, then he would not accuse (for he would not be moved by any of the passions that would prompt accusation). If the latter, he ought to be pitied as a being who has suffered wrong, just as the sick are pitied when they may complain of their woes (2.27.7).

In his reply, however, Macarius seems utterly to misunderstand the Hellene's points. He offers a convoluted reading of the two nouns in the genitive case in John 8:43 as possessives: "you are of the father of the Accuser" (2.32.1). He then leverages this reading into a tortured exegesis. The Accuser is the Antichrist who dupes humanity into following the "anti-god," a "deceitful angel" (2.32.6, 9). Macarius is interested in using his reading to set up an analogy: as Christ the Son is to God the Father, so is the Accuser to *his* Father, the anti-God (2.32.6). Macarius thus attempts to answer the first of the Hellene's charges—the Accuser is unjust and blameworthy because he leads people to the anti-God. This, of course, misses the point of the Hellene's critique, which had asked why a being could be blameworthy for being an *accuser*. Macarius simply ignores the second critique.

Another example of incongruity between critique and reply comes in the Hellene's quotation of and objection to Mt. 19:24: "It is easier for a camel to

---

93 In what follows I provide some of the clearest examples; for a complete list and discussion see Goulet (2003), 71–73.

pass through a needle than a rich man into the Kingdom of heaven" (3.5.1). He claims that this saying values poverty over the cultivation of the virtues. Macarius responds (3.12.1–16) with a long excursus in the right use of wealth and the virtue of charity. His response repeats many commonplace early Christian arguments concerning wealth, but he does not address the Hellene's specific point, which is that the renunciation of wealth entails the renunciation of civic euergetism and other civic duties, destabilizing the social order and, in turn, removing opportunity to cultivate the civic virtues (3.5.5).

Macarius also appears to misunderstand aspects of the Hellene's objection to the story of Jesus's walking on water (3.6.1–4, discussing Mk. 6:48; Mt. 14:25). According to the Hellene, the miracle account is nothing more than a "children's story" or a "deceptive stage play," because the details of the narrative are fabulous. The Sea of Galilee is too small a body of water to develop a raging sea storm, and too small to require an all-night crossing, as the narrative suggests when it states that the disciples set sail "after dinner" and fought the storm until Jesus appeared "at the fourth watch of the night." This means that the disciples are supposed to have sailed all night because, as the Hellene observes, "the fourth watch is the tenth hour, after which three further hours remain," but the Sea of Galilee can be crossed easily "in no more than two hours."

The Hellene's aim is to impeach the story as full of incongruities and physical impossibilities. Macarius does attempt a reply to the Hellene's chronology, but has to argue that the "fourth watch of the night" means "the fourth hour from the beginning of the night" (3.13.2). This exegesis runs counter to common Christian exegeses of the passage.[94] It seems unlikely that Macarius would invent an exegesis more intuitive than his own so that he might refute it with a more convoluted interpretation. He also ignores the Hellene's appeal to physics—that the Sea of Galilee is too narrow to provide enough fetch for prevailing winds to develop a tempest. Instead, Macarius takes the Hellene to be making a semantic argument, that the "Sea" of Galilee is not properly named a sea:

---

94 The "watches" could be read allegorically (e.g. Origen, *Commentary on Matthew* 11.6 [ANF 9: 435–436]) or historically (e.g. Jerome, *Commentary on Matthew* 14.25). Jerome's exegesis, which combines historical and figurative exegesis, is fairly standard: "Guard duties and military watches are divided into intervals of three hours. So, then, when he says that the Lord came to them at the fourth watch of the night, he is showing that they were in danger through the whole night. Then, at the end of the night and at the consummation of the world, he will bring help to them" (*Commentary on Matthew* II 14.25 [Scheck (2008), 174]).

For this is all we are required to find out: whether the body of water they crossed was a "sea" or not a "sea." And because even if the place happened to be a lake, it was a wide sea in respect of the way it behaved, whipped into waves like a sea by the winds and bearing the hulls of fishermen like a sea, it is possible to understand straightaway the accuracy of what is said. For all waters are named "sea" by *catachresis*,[95] even if they come from rivers or streams, either from the disturbance that comes from the winds or from the turbid drink that is found in it, or the saltiness it has by virtue of its location and not by nature. (3.13.2–3)

In fact, Macarius quickly turns from answering the Hellene's objections, taking the objection as an opportunity to interpret the pericope as a Christological demonstration (3.13.7–27). Within this exegesis, Macarius also devotes considerable attention to parsing Peter's disbelief (e.g. "If it is you [i.e. Jesus] order me to walk upon the waters" [Mt. 14:28]). Again, the Hellene's critique is not at all concerned with the actions of either Jesus or the apostles in the pericope, merely the contextual incongruities of the story. The Hellene does level charges against Peter's ignorance, but at a different point in his critique than that to which Macarius is responding here (3.20.1–22.5). To speculate, we might imagine that Macarius goes into such detail about Peter at this point in the text because his source *did* go on at this point to mock the apostle's behaviour, and that Macarius responds to the critique, but edited the critique out when he adapted his source.

Macarius also seems to misunderstand the philosophical details of several of the Hellene's arguments. In Book 4, the Hellene mocks Christian eschatology, represented for him in Paul's statement in 1 Cor. 7:31 that "the form of this world is passing away" (4.1.2). His argument crafts a *reductio ad absurdum*, drawing upon logic characteristic of any late Platonist or Peripatetic: the form of the cosmos cannot pass away because this would imply that the demiurge either destroys that which was rightly created, or must correct what was wrongly created. Either case entails the absurd conclusion that the demiurge is not perfectly good (4.1.3). Alternatively, the Hellene jabs, if the things of the created order are thought to be "causes of grief and pain," then the demiurge should be castigated as evil (4.1.4).

Macarius does not address the logic of these arguments, but instead develops a lengthy diatribe on the various connotations of the word "form" (σχῆμα) (4.11.4–20). He attempts to address the Hellene's argument

---

95 *Catachresis* refers to a figure of speech wherein a word's semantic range is stretched or extended beyond its usual bounds; in Macarius's example, "sea" is taken to refer to all bodies of water.

at 4.11.22–23, but construes the Hellene as equating "eternal" and "unchangeable." The Hellene's position entails only that the good cosmos created by a good demiurge must be eternal (e.g. 4.1.3–5), not, as Macarius seems to think, that it must *therefore* be ungenerated (4.11.22–23).

Finally, although both Macarius's and the Hellene' arguments develop based on Aristotle's treatment of names and beings in the *Categories*, they at times seem to have divergent theories of names and naming. The Hellene argues:

> For if you say that angels stand beside God, being impassible, immortal, and incorruptible with respect to their nature [τὴν φύσιν], which we term "gods" on account of their nearness to the Godhead, what does this dispute about the name amount to, besides the conclusion that the difference is only one of nomenclature? ... Certainly nothing is changed or detracted from the title "god" by the difference in names. Now, whether one names them "gods" or "angels," the difference is no great thing, since their divine nature [τῆς φύσεως αὐτῶν ... θείας] is testified to when Matthew writes as follows: "And Jesus, replying, said, 'You err, not knowing the Scriptures or the power of God, for in the resurrection they will neither marry or be given in marriage, but they will be as angels in heaven.'" [Mt. 22:29–30] Therefore, as it is agreed that the angels participate [μετέχειν] in divine nature ... (4.20.3–21b.1)

The Hellene's point is that "angels" and "gods" are two different names that refer to beings that share the same definition of essence (λόγος τῆς οὐσίας). He is, in other words, claiming that "angel" and "god" are polynyms, that is, different words that have the same referent [e.g. "lift" and "elevator" in contemporary English]. Polynymy is not discussed in Aristotle's *Categories*, but it was inferred by later commentators, for example Porphyry, who explains that "polynyms are things that have several different names, but one and the same definition [i.e. of essence] (λόγος [τῆς οὐσίας]) ... Polynymns seem to be opposite of homonyms."[96]

When he replies to the Hellene, Macarius does not grasp the specificity of the Hellene's point.

> ... it must reasonably be asked whether the nature of things is accustomed to be preserved in homonymy. For we have found that it is not the thing that has acquired its true nature from the name, but the name from the thing, as [one predicates] of fire that it is hot, as well as of what is near fire, for both are hot. But both do not have the essence of heat, but the one is hot by nature, while the other is so by position [τῇ θέσει], and the one has heat in itself, while the other

---

96 Porphyry, *Commentary on the Categories* 69.1, trans. Strange (1992).

28 MACARIUS, *APOCRITICUS*

derives heat from another—and so the word [i.e. "hot"] does not at all indicate for us a single nature from homonymy. (4.26.1)

Macarius misreads the Hellene, thinking his opponent is drawing an unwarranted conclusion about essence/nature[97] based on homonymy. Macarius understands homonymy correctly: "When things have only a name in common and the definition of essence which corresponds to the name is different, they are called homonyms."[98] He is also correct that the same word (e.g. "hot" or "god/divine") can be predicated essentially of one being (i.e. "God") but only relatively (i.e. "by position")[99] of others. But this is not the Hellene's argument. The Hellene's point is simply that "angel" and "god" are two names that are applied to beings that are impassible, immortal, and incorruptible. He does not claim that they possess this nature *essentially* or that "god" (or "angel") is a name that is predicated essentially. Instead, the Hellene claims that angels and gods are beings divine by "participation" (τὸ μετέχειν), an ontological relationship described by predications made "by relation" or "by position."

B. IDENTIFYING THE HELLENE?

Since the rediscovery of the *Apocriticus* in the 1870s scholars have shown much greater interest in the identity or identities of Macarius's sources than in the text itself as a whole. Four polemicists are regularly considered among the most likely suspects: Celsus, Sossianus Hierocles, Porphyry of Tyre, and the Emperor Julian. Points of contact and parallels to these and other authors are indicated throughout the notes that accompany the translation. Rather than resolving the question of the Hellene's identity,

---

97 Macarius regularly uses "nature" (φύσις) and "essence" (οὐσία) as equivalent; see discussion in Goulet (2003), 184–185. Some conflation of "nature" and "essence" was common in later Platonic readings of Aristotle. In Aristotle, φύσις designates an internal cause or principle of motion and rest (e.g. *Metaphysics* 192b20–23), while οὐσία (most often rendered "substance" in English translations of Aristotle) designates an existing entity; for Aristotle, the individual members of a species are what are primarily termed οὐσίαι (e.g. *Categories* 2a13–18). For later Platonists in the tradition of Plotinus, φύσις and οὐσία were synonymous insofar as both were used to refer to the Platonic Forms that structure reality—φύσις referring to forms in virtue of their causal role and οὐσία to a form's definite ontological existence (see e.g. Plotinus, *Ennead* III.8 [30]).
98 Aristotle, *Categories* 1a1, trans. Ackrill (1992).
99 Aristotle places "by position" (θέσις) among what is predicated πρός τι, that is, "in relation" (*Categories* 6a37; 6b12).

what follows aims merely to lay out the main arguments for and against identifying specific polemicists as Macarius's sources, as well as offer a short discussion of the *strongest* points of contact between the Hellene and each possible source. Richard Goulet's study of the *Apocriticus* offers an almost-comprehensive collection of parallels to each of the key suspects, and readers wishing to undertake further study should begin there.[100] Those wishing to undertake more detailed study are encouraged to consult the primary sources as well as the secondary literature referenced in the notes and bibliography.

i. Celsus

Celsus's *True Account*, written in the 170s and preserved in fragments in Origen's voluminous reply, *Against Celsus*, written eighty years later, seems the least likely candidate. The parallels between the Hellene and Celsus are too broad and too commonplace to suggest more than a shared polemical tradition. The list of these points of contact includes:

- Christianity is marked by internal strife and heresy (*C.Cels.* 3.10, 12; *Apocr.* 1.1).

- Christ made post-resurrection appearances only to disreputable women, when he should have revealed himself to those in power (*C.Cels.* 2.63, 55, 70; *Apocr.* 2.25).

- Christ should have defended himself when placed on trial, or performed miracles, or caused himself to disappear like other holy men (*C.Cels.* 1.67, 2.35, 3.26, 1.8, 2.23, all of which are listed by Goulet as parallels with *Apocr.* 3.1).

- Both attack Christ's request that he might be spared from the Passion (Mt. 26:41; Mk. 14:35; Lk. 22:46). This is one of the closer parallels, as both Celsus (*C.Cels.* 1.24, 2.76) and the Hellene (*Apocr.* 3.2) argue that this is worthy neither of a god (Celsus) or child of god (Hellene), nor a wise man (Hellene and Celsus).

- Christ manifested himself in a remote part of the world (Celsus: *C.Cels.* 6.78) and to only a few people (Hellene: *Apocr.* 3.4.7), when he should have made himself manifest to the entire world. Celsus's critique, however, is situated within a series of criticisms directed against the notion that the "Spirit of God" entered into Jesus (*C.Cels.* 6.75–79), while in the Hellene's

---

100 Goulet (2003), 261–291.

polemic it appears in the midst of an attack on Jesus's casting of the demon "Legion" into swine (Mt. 8:28–34 and parallels).

- Both Celsus (*C.Cels.* 6.16) and the Hellene (*Apocr.* 3.5) criticize Mt. 19:24 ("It is easier for a camel to pass through a needle than a rich man to enter the Kingdom of God"). The Hellene, however, includes the critique among a set that attack *logia* of Jesus, while Celsus quotes the passage to make the specific argument that such an ethic derives from Plato.

- Both Celsus and the Hellene attack the idea that the Creator would destroy creation. But while the Hellene develops this critique within a set of objections directed against Pauline eschatological statements (*Apocr.* 4.1–2), Celsus attempts to situate Christian eschatology in comparison with the Stoic concept of cyclical conflagrations (*C.Cels.* 4.69) and attacks what he sees as the Creator's wanton destruction of his creation in the Flood narrative of Genesis 6 (*C.Cels.* 6.58).

- Both Celsus (*C.Cels.* 3.44, 6.13) and the Hellene (*Apocr.* 4.9) mock Scripture for privileging ignorance over wisdom. Again the parallel is rather loose: Celsus and the Hellene base their attacks on different scriptural passages, and the Hellene develops this critique within a set of objections related to soteriology, while Celsus develops a familiar *ad hominem* lampoon of Christians as the dregs of society.

The remainder of the parallels that can be adduced between the Hellene and Celsus are similarly loose. While there are important thematic points of contact, the very different contexts in which Celsus and the Hellene develop and deploy each of these themes strongly mitigates against identifying Celsus's *True Account* as Macarius's source.

ii. Sossianus Hierocles

Certain of the Hellene's arguments have been taken as evidence that the *Apocriticus* was originally written in a third-century milieu. The Hellene's references to persecution and martyrdom as present realities have been taken as references to either the Decian or Diocletianic persecutions. The reference to Christian buildings has also been construed as reflecting a later third-century context, when other literary sources indicate an increase in church building during the last quarter of the third century.[101]

In a long essay of 1906–1907, T.W. Crafer contended that these chronological hints, together with the content of the Hellene's polemic,

---

101 Harnack (1911), 107–110; Digeser (2002), 475.

THE HELLENE 31

pointed to Sossianus Hierocles, who, at the outset of the Diocletianic persecution in 303, was governor of Bithynia. Hierocles wrote a two-book polemic he called *The Lover of Truth*, and presented his anti-Christian arguments publicly at Diocletian's court. The work has been lost. The Latin rhetor and apologist Lactantius, who was present at court, describes the treatise briefly. In addition, a text traditionally ascribed to Eusebius of Caesarea, *Against Hierocles*,[102] targets the noteworthy feature of the work (also noted by Lactantius)—an extended rhetorical comparison (*synkrisis*) of Jesus and the second-century philosopher and holy man Apollonius of Tyana.[103]

There are many elements of the Hellene's polemic that accord with Lactantius's description of Hierocles's work. Both "attempt to prove the falsity of Holy Scripture on the basis that it entirely contradicted itself,"[104] both are familiar with the Scriptures,[105] and both single out Peter and Paul as "disseminators of falsehood."[106] Based on these points of contact, Crafer and, more recently, Digeser argue that the *Lover of Truth* is Macarius's source.[107] There are, however, significant reasons to doubt this identification. The noteworthy feature of Hierocles's work—as *Against Hierocles* and Lactantius agree— was the comparison of Jesus and Apollonius. Macarius's Hellene, however, mentions Apollonius only twice.

- At 4.5.2, the Hellene mentions Apollonius as an example of the sort of miracle working holy men referred to by Mt. 24:4–5 ("See that no one leads you astray, for many will come in my name saying, 'I am the Christ,' and they will lead many astray."). Here, though, the Hellene is challenging the *logion* as absurd, since, he claims, none of these figures has appeared in the three hundred or so years since the advent of Christ.

- At 3.1.1, the Hellene asks why Jesus did not simply avoid crucifixion by disappearing from his trial, as Apollonius does in Philostratus, *Life of Apollonius* 8.5, 10.

Even granted that Books 1 and 5 of the *Apocriticus* are lost, and that portions of Book 2 are missing as well, the extant *pinakes* of Books 1 and

---

102 On the disputed authorship of *Against Hierocles* see Johnson (2013), Borzì (2003), Hägg (1992).
103 *Against Hierocles*, 1.2.
104 Lactantius, *Divine Institutes* 5.2.13, trans. Bowen and Garnsey (2004).
105 Lactantius, *Divine Institutes* 5.2.14.
106 Lactantius, *Divine Institutes* 5.2.17.
107 Crafer (1906–1907); Digeser (2002).

2 make it clear that no *synkrisis* of Jesus and Apollonius appeared in these books. An extended comparison of Jesus and Apollonius is also not in keeping with the basic structure found throughout the Hellene's polemics: arguments developed out of apparent contradictions and absurdities in the Gospels and Paul. Goulet also points out that Lactantius's description of the structure of the *Lover of Truth* does not square with what we find in the *Apocriticus*.[108] According to Lactantius, Hierocles concluded his work with an encomium praising the gods and the monarchy of the highest god. Although the final book of the *Apocriticus* is lost, it seems that Macarius's Hellene only addresses the issue of God's monarchy and the existence of the lesser gods within a set of broadly theological objections in Book 4 (4.20–21a). According to Lactantius, moreover, Hierocles's praise of God's monarchy was an *epilogus*, or peroration to his composition. Macarius's Hellene, by contrast, discusses God's monarchy specifically to challenge Christian ontological doctrines concerning God, and to accuse Christians of failing to follow Moses's command in Exodus 22:28 ("You shall not speak ill of the gods and you shall not speak badly of the one ruling your people.").

In addition, the author of *Against Hierocles* contends that, apart from the comparison of Jesus and Apollonius, the remainder of the *Lover of Truth* merely parroted other polemicists.[109] What parallels there may be between Macarius's Hellene and Hierocles—especially those concerned with the self-contradictory nature of Scripture—are also found in other polemicists whose extant fragments have more points of contact with the Hellene: Porphyry of Tyre and the Emperor Julian.

iii. Julian

The emperor Julian the "Apostate" (332–363), wrote a three-book polemic *Against the Galileans*. Julian probably composed the work in the winter of 362–363, the period Julian spent in Antioch in preparation for his spring invasion of the Sassanian Empire. *Against the Galileans* is known only from fragments preserved by Cyril of Alexandria in his *Against Julian*,[110]

---

108 Goulet (2003), 126.
109 The statement in *Against Hierocles* that anyone seeking a comprehensive response to anti-Christian polemics should consult Origen's *Against Celsus* need not be taken to mean that Hierocles copied Celsus, specifically; it is, rather, an assessment of the *comprehensiveness* of *Against Celsus*.
110 Masaracchia (1989), 9; see also Libanius, *Oration* 18.178.

The extant fragments of Theodore of Mopsuestia's *Against Julian* also preserve important fragments of Julian's work.[111]

As in the case of Celsus, many of the parallels between the Hellene and *Against the Galileans* involve thematic similarities. Both Julian and the Hellene, for instance, attack Christianity as fragmented by heresy (Julian, fr. 48 and *Apocr.* 1.1) and critique literal readings of Scripture while also denigrating allegorical interpretations (Julian, fr. 17 and *Apocr.* 3.4, 15). Both also note discrepancies among the canonical Gospel narratives (Julian, fr. 50, 79 and *Apocr.* 2.24). Several of the most interesting parallels show the Hellene and Julian concerned with similar topics and the same biblical passages, though in most instances the surrounding contexts are different.[112]

- Both question Jesus's actions when on trial. Julian asks why Jesus performed no miracle when brought before Herod (Julian, fr. 104). The Hellene asks why Jesus said nothing worthy of a holy and wise man when brought before the High Priest and Pilate (*Apocr.* 3.1.1).

- Both level a critique based on traditions concerning Ezra/Esdras. Julian suggests that "Esdras has added material based on his own opinion [to the books of Moses]" (Julian, fr. 34). The Hellene's claims are similar, but broader: "After all, nothing written by Moses is extant. For all his writings are said to have been burned in the temple, while whatever is written under the name of Moses was written 1,180 years after Moses's death, by Esdras and those of his circle" (*Apocr.* 3.3.1). The Hellene's polemics appear to be based on 4 Esdras/4 Ezra 14:21–48, where Ezra is commanded to gather scribes and produce books under God's inspiration because "thy law has been burned" (2 Esdras/4 Ezra 14:21).

- Both impugn Jesus's agony in Gethsemane. Julian focuses specifically on Luke 22:45–47, and in particular on verse 43 ("Then an angel from heaven appeared to him and gave him strength"), gibing that "Although he was God, he was strengthened by an angel" (Julian, fr. 95). The Hellene points to a contradiction between Matthew 10:28 and Luke 12:24 ("Do not fear those who kill the body") and Jesus's telling the disciples, "Be watchful and pray that the test passes us by" (*Apocr.* 3.2.1–2; cf. Mt. 26:41; Mk. 14:35; Lk. 22:46). The Hellene's quotation is an amalgam or paraphrase of this synoptic passage, while Julian quotes the Lukan version but omits

---

111 Text and commentary: Guida (1994).
112 For a complete synopsis of parallels see Goulet (2003), 279–287 and, more recently, Bouffartigue (2011), 415–417.

precisely the phrase quoted by the Hellene ("Why are you sleeping? Get up and pray" and the rest [Julian, fr. 95.6–7]).

- Both cite Exodus 22:28 ("You shall not speak ill of the gods") to accuse Christians of failing to heed Moses's own commands concerning respect for the traditional gods. Julian cites the passage in order to accuse Christians (and certain Jews) of disobeying Moses's instructions and of failing to acknowledge other tutelary deities:

    When the Lawgiver decreed that they must not serve all the gods, but one only, whose "lot is Jacob and [whose] allotted portion is Israel" [cf. Dt. 32:9], he did not say this only, but, as I recall, he also added, "You shall not speak ill of the gods" [Ex. 22:28]. But the coarse and reckless masses thought that following the command not to worship [other gods] entailed blaspheming [them], which indeed is the only thing you [Galileans] have taken from them. (Julian, fr. 58.11–17)

    The Hellene cites Exodus 22:28 as part of an argument concerning the name "god." The Hellene's argument is that Christians refuse to acknowledge that traditional deities can be called "gods," despite the evidence of Scripture and the fact that Christians acknowledge angels (4.23.1–3).

These comparisons show that Macarius's Hellene and Julian deployed some similar polemics. Importantly, however, enough remains of *Against the Galileans* to show that even where the polemics are similar, the contexts in which they are deployed are often different. Macarius's source, moreover, engages in detailed critiques of the Gospels and the Pauline corpus, while the remains of *Against the Galileans* reveal a work concerned with demonstrating that Christians have deviated from Judaism, and offers extended rhetorical comparisons (*synkriseis*) between "Hebrew" and "Hellene" wisdom. *Against the Galileans* is structured as a retorsion[113] of Eusebius of Caesarea's *Gospel Preparation*. Where Eusebius set out to define Christianity as a natural theology that rightly eschewed Judaism and Hellenism, Julian aimed to "question those who are neither Hellenes nor Jews, but are of the Galilean heresy, as to why they choose the doctrines of the Jews over ours, but also why they do not even adhere to them, but forsake them and follow their own peculiar path."[114] As Jean Bouffartigue has recently argued, the points of contact between Julian's polemics and

---

113 A retorsion is the rhetorical technique of "turning back" an opponent's arguments against him or her.

114 Julian, *Against the Galileans* (fr. 3 [Masaracchia]); the passage in Julian is almost certainly a verbal allusion to Eusebius, *Gospel Preparation* 1.2 [4d–5c].

the Hellene show that both stand within the same general trajectory of anti-Christian literature, though *Against the Galileans* itself was probably not Macarius's source.[115]

iv. Porphyry

Since Harnack, Porphyry has been the polemicist most often connected with Macarius's Hellene. To some, identifying Porphyry as the source of the Hellene is precluded by Macarius's allusion to Porphyry's *Philosophy from Oracles* in Book 3 (3.42.6). Macarius would not have cited Porphyry by name against the Hellene, the argument runs, if he was using a Porphyrian text as his source.[116] In itself, however, this argument is not conclusive. Harnack, for example, argued that Macarius cited Porphyry against the Hellene because he was drawing from an epitome of *Against the Christians* and was unaware that Porphyry was its author.[117] Goulet argues that, if Macarius has drawn on Porphyry, he has heavily redacted his source; the reference to Porphyry might thus be an ironic "wink" on Macarius's part.[118] If Macarius has borrowed from Porphyry, this may also be his way of demonstrating contradiction in Porphyry's thought, much as Eusebius of Caesarea had quoted Porphyry's *On Abstinence* against Porphyry's *Philosophy from Oracles.*[119]

The Hellene's objections have more points of contact with known *testimonia* to and fragments of Porphyry than either Hierocles or Julian. In particular, there are a number of parallels between the Hellene's polemics and polemics that Jerome ascribes to Porphyry.[120] Both Porphyry, as reported by Jerome, and Macarius's Hellene:

- Claim that *daimones* are able to dupe Christ. Commenting on Matthew 8:28–34, the Hellene chides that Christ was "made womanish" by the pleas of the *daimones* and gave in to their demand to be sent into the swine (3.4.1–5). Jerome writes that Porphyry argued that *daimones* tricked Christ by feigning their torment.[121]

---

115 Bouffartigue (2011), 415–417.
116 Barnes (1973), 428–429 has been the most influential.
117 Harnack (1911), 141–144.
118 Goulet (2003), 148–149.
119 Eusebius, *Gospel Preparation* 7–10.
120 On the methodological issues surrounding Jerome's references to Porphyry see two excellent treatments by Magny (2010) and (2011).
121 Jerome, *Against Vigilantius* 10 = Harnack 49b.

- Accuse the apostles of being con artists who duped wealthy women out of their property. Jerome includes Porphyry among those who claim that the apostles preyed on gullible rural poor and women. He offers a polemical paraphrase:

> Paul subjected the whole world from the Ocean to the Red Sea. Someone might say, "They did all this for profit." Thus indeed says Porphyry: "Being poor rustics, because they had nothing they worked some signs by means of magical arts. But it is no great thing to work signs, for even the Magi in Egypt worked signs against Moses, and Apollonius did them, and Apuleius did them—and they worked an infinite number of signs." I concede to you, Porphyry, that they worked signs by means of magical arts, in order that "they might steal wealth from wealthy women, whom they had duped." For this is what you say.[122]

Jerome seems to quote from Porphyry most directly in the last clause, where he retorts what in its original context was a charge that the apostles duped wealthy women.

In the Macarian parallel, the Hellene attacks Matthew 19:24 ("Sell your property and give to the poor and you will have a treasure-house in heaven"):

> Hence, it seems to me that these statements are not Christ's, if, that is, he taught the Rule of Truth, but of some poor men wishing to take the property of the wealthy with vain talk ..." Sell your property and give to the poor and you will have a treasure-house in heaven," when read to noble women persuaded them to distribute all the wealth and property they had to the poor ... (3.5.4–5)

- Attack the evangelists for describing the Sea of Galilee as a "sea" rather than a "lake" and discredit the pericope of Christ's walking on water based on this geographical point. It is interesting, too, that Jerome's response, like Macarius's, is based on putative knowledge of Hebrew vocabulary. Commenting on Genesis 1:10, Jerome writes:

> It must be noted that all accumulations of water, whether they are salty or fresh, are denominated "seas" according to the idiom of the Hebrew language. In vain, then, does Porphyry calumniate the evangelists who, in order to concoct as miracle for the ignorant that the Lord had walked upon the sea, called Ganessaret a "sea" instead of a "lake," since all lakes and accumulations of water are denominated "seas."[123]

---

122 Jerome, *Tractates on Psalm* 81 = Harnack 4.
123 Jerome, *Questions on Genesis* 1.10 = Harnack 55.

THE HELLENE

The Hellene notes that "those who describe the true character of these places say that there is a not a "sea" there, but a small lake in the territory of Galilee by the city of Tiberias." He then castigates the evangelist (Mark):

> And he calls it a "sea," and not merely a "sea," but one disturbed by a storm and terribly raging and tossed frighteningly by the disturbance of the waves, in order that, from this, he might introduce Jesus as if having performed a great sign ... (3.6.2–3).

- Impugn the apostles and other Christian leaders based on Matthew 17:20 ("If you have faith like a mustard seed, truly I say to you, you will say to this mountain, 'Get up and throw yourself into the sea,' and nothing will be impossible for you)."

In his *Commentary on Matthew*, Jerome writes: "The dogs of the Gentiles bark at us in their volumes, which they have left in memory of their own impiety, maintaining that the apostles did not have faith, because they were unable to move mountains."[124] The Hellene remarks: "It is clear, then, that he who is unable to move a mountain with his command is not to be considered worthy of the brotherhood of the faithful" (3.17.2).

- Accuse Peter of unjustly causing the deaths of Ananias and Sapphira (Acts 12:3–18). Writing to encourage the noblewoman Demetrias to the ascetic life, and extolling the necessity that elites engage in the ascetic redistribution of their wealth, Jerome remarks: "The apostle Peter never prayed for the death of Ananias and Sapphira, as the stupid Porphyry [other manuscripts read: "stupid philosopher"] accuses."[125]

The Macarian parallel appears in a sequence of charges levelled against Peter (3.19–22). The Hellene remarks: "This Peter is also convicted for committing injustice in other ways. For he put to death a man named Ananias together with this wife, Sapphira, when they did not turn over the full value of their property, but set aside a small amount for their own needs, committing no injustice" (3.21.1).

- Impugn Peter and Paul for the dispute over circumcision recorded in Galatians 2:11ff. Jerome refers to Porphyry in the preface to his *Commentary on Galatians*. Jerome himself famously resolved this embarrassing passage by arguing that Paul was merely dissembling a controversy with Peter for the benefit of both Jewish and Gentile believers. He singles out Porphyry as one who disagrees:

> Not at all understanding this, that wretched criminal and Batanaean Porphyry, in the first book of his work written against us, objects that

---

124 Jerome, *Commentary on Matthew* 21.21 = Harnack 3.
125 Jerome, *Letter* 130.14 = Harnack 25b.

Peter was reprimanded by Paul for not putting the right foot forward in preaching the Gospel, wanting to inure them with the stain of error and of great shamelessness for this, and to accuse them both in common of fabricating lies in their doctrines, since among these princes of the Church there was a disagreement.[126]

Macarius's Hellene, for his part, refers to Paul's dispute with Peter at the end of a series of charges against Peter. He strings together several Pauline passages with Galatians 2:12:

Paul, too, condemned Peter, saying: "For before some came from James, he ate with the Gentiles. But when they came, he separated himself, fearing those of the circumcision, and many Jews joined him" [Gal. 2:12]. But in this there is a major and serious condemnation—that a man who was an interpreter of the divine mouth live in hypocrisy and act obsequiously with people, and even take a wife, for Paul also says this: "Do we not have the authority to take a sister as a wife, as even the rest of the apostles and Peter?" [1 Cor. 9:5]. Then he adds: "For such people are pseudo-apostles, doers of trickery" [2 Cor. 11:13]. (*Apocr.* 3.22.4)

The charges against Peter conclude the Hellene's set of objections. His next round of questioning consists of a focused attack on Paul's inconsistencies and duplicity, and opens with a further assault on the apostles' apparent inconsistencies concerning circumcision (3.30.1).

Philosophically and theologically, the Hellene fits a Porphyrian mould. He articulates a theology of religious iconography that accords with what we know of Porphyry's.[127] His theory of naming—that the various ethnic names given to deities as well as the generic term "god" are used polynymously (4.20–21a.3–5)—is consistent with Porphyry's interpretation of Aristotle's *Categories* and the theory of names articulated in his *Letter to Anebo*.[128] The Hellene critiques Christian notions of God's omnipotence using arguments similar to Porphyry, who levelled the same criticism in

---

126 Jerome, *Commentary on Galatians* prol. = Harnack 21a (see also Harnack 21b, c, and d, all passages from Jerome that mention the same critique).

127 Compare *Apocr.* 4.21.1–4 with, e.g., Porphyry, *On Abstinence* 2.34–35; 4.6 and *To Marcella* 17, where Porphyry emphasizes that proper worship involves the cultivation of the worshipper's virtue and *On Statues*, passim, where Porphyry argues that traditional representations of the gods represent, but do not embody, divine nature.

128 On polynymy see Porphyry, *In Cat.* 69.1, trans. Strange (1992); for Porphyry's conventionalist critique of Iamblichus's naturalist/essentialist theory of divine names see 2.10a (Sodano [1958]).

a fragment of Didymus the Blind's *Commentary on Job*.[129] The Hellene, like Porphyry, also assumes that the demiurge must of necessity create a perfect cosmos and do so following an eternal paradigm.[130] It should be stressed, however, that these are philosophical and theological articulations common among many later Platonists,[131] and could point to a source text in the Porphyrian tradition, rather than Porphyry himself.

C. CONCLUSIONS

As this brief summary makes clear, it is not possible to determine the identity or identities of Macarius's source(s) with certainty. In addition to the fact that one cannot discern a point-for-point correspondence between any known anti-Christian treatise and Macarius's Hellene, Macarius's fingerprints can be found everywhere in the Hellene's speeches. Goulet has shown convincingly that one cannot assume that Macarius has merely "pasted" quotations into his text. Macarius's own vocabulary and thought has "infected" his source, while that of the "source" has similarly tinged Macarius.[132]

As has become quite clear in the preparation of this translation, determining where Macarius ends and his source(s) begin(s) is fraught with difficulty. A maximally sceptical position would eschew all attempts to identify Macarius's source or sources. On this estimation, Macarius's redaction of his sources precludes considering the Hellene as anything other than Macarius's creation. At the other extreme, one might be tempted to conclude that Macarius has quoted directly from a source. Current scholarship embraces neither of these extremes. The balance of the evidence suggests that, among known anti-Christian polemicists, the most *likely* source is Porphyry.[133] Of course, Macarius may have used an otherwise unknown source. The nature of the intertextual relationship between Macarius's source(s) and the text of the *Apocriticus*, however, also means that one cannot take the Hellene's critiques to be verbatim

---

129 See extended discussion of these parallels in Goulet (2011), 223–225.
130 Compare *Apocr.* 4.2.3 and Porphyry *apud* Proclus, *Commentary on the Timaeus.* 332.10–15.
131 Compare for example Celsus in Origen, *Against Celsus* 7.62; Sallustius, *Concerning the Gods and the Universe* 16; Julian, *Letter* 89B.
132 Goulet (2013), 76–89.
133 Goulet (2003), 149 and idem (2011), 229.

"fragments" of Porphyry, Julian, or any other writer. Again, a maximally sceptical position would resist any use of the *Apocriticus* as a source of late ancient philosophical anti-Christian polemic. This is extreme scepticism, however; Macarius's Hellene is *at least* as "real" an example of philosophical anti-Christianity as, for instance, the polemical questions Augustine answered in *Six Questions Explained in Answer to the Pagans*.[134] Augustine's correspondents claimed that some of their pagan friends had posed questions based in part on Porphyry's *Against the Christians*, though Augustine doubted whether they really derived from the great Platonist.[135] Ultimately, the *Apocriticus* would better illuminate the history of late ancient philosophy and religion if we decentred the question of the precise identity of Macarius's sources. The Hellene of the *Apocriticus* embodies the *kind* of anti-Christian polemics one would expect of a late ancient Platonist, and Macarius's responses offer a window into how a later fourth-century Christian intellectual of middling ability attempted to engage them.

---

134 This is the title Augustine gave the treatise that accompanied his *Letter* 102 to Deogratias. On the possibility of a Porphyrian origin of some of the *quaestiones* to which Augustine responds in *Letter* 102 see Bochet (2011).

135 Augustine, *Retractions* 2.31; *Letter* 102.8, 28, 30.

IV. MACARIUS AND THE *APOCRITICUS*

Jeremy M. Schott

A. THE TEXT

Like many incomplete and fragmentary works, that translated in this volume has a curious history. We have translated the edition of Goulet, taking account also of the text of Volp.[136] Neither of these modern editions, however, is based on autopsy of the sole manuscript that preserved significant portions of the *Apocriticus*. That manuscript—a fourteenth-century paper codex of 125 folios—was discovered in Athens in 1867 and published (posthumously) in an edition by Charles Blondel in 1876.[137] The "Athens manuscript" (A) has since disappeared.[138] *Vaticanus graecus* 1650 (the "Vatican manuscript," or "V"), from the eleventh century, contains Acts and the Pauline and Catholic Epistles, as well as several paratexts: rubrics indicating lectionary readings, a list of readings appropriate for the dedication of a church, the portion of Athanasius's thirty-ninth festal letter that recounts the books of the Canon (along with a stichometry),[139] and—serendipitously—the *pinakes* of *Apocriticus* Books 1–3.[140] Volp and Goulet base their editions on Blondel, collated against alternative readings proposed by subsequent scholars.

The most influential of these has been Adolf von Harnack, who drew

---

136 Goulet (2003); Volp (2013), unfortunately, Volp's edition was published too late in our process to take complete account of the published edition; however, Professor Volp generously made his manuscript available for our consultation.

137 Blondel (1876).

138 In 1867, the manuscript was in the possession of a curator of the National Library in Athens, apparently as a private possession, since upon the curator's death his wife sold the manuscript. When Georg Schaulkhauser attempted to locate the manuscript for his 1907 study of Macarius, the library was unable to locate it or the party to which it was purportedly sold (Schaulkhauser [1907], 20). Richard Goulet was likewise unable to locate the manuscript in 1971 (Goulet [2003], 235).

139 That is, a list of the number of lines contained in each book.

140 Mercati (1941), 49–71; Goulet (2003), 243–244.

42 MACARIUS, *APOCRITICUS*

fifty-one passages from the *Apocriticus* in his edition of the fragments of Porphyry's *Against the Christians*.[141] Harnack argued that Macarius drew the Hellene's polemics from an epitome of Porphyry's anti-Christian work. Harnack's assessment has greatly shaped subsequent scholarship on the *Apocriticus*; nearly all literature on the text has focused on the identity or identities of Macarius's "Hellene," while a mere handful of studies are dedicated to the text as a whole. Indeed, until the French and German translations that accompany Goulet's and Volp's editions, respectively, the complete text had never been translated into any modern language. Apart from the present volume, the only English translations of Macarius are of passages adduced by Harnack as Porphyrian fragments.[142]

The work appears not to have been widely known in the late antique and Byzantine periods, and is mentioned only sporadically before the discovery of the Athens manuscript in 1867. Nicephorus, the iconodule[143] Patriarch of Constantinople from 806 until his deposition in 815, is the earliest extant witness. Nicephorus quotes from and discusses the *Apocriticus* in the *Epikrisis* (often titled *De Magnete* in scholarly literature), one of the patriarch's responses to an iconoclast *florilegium* of patristic texts that the iconoclasts planned to deploy at the upcoming Council of Constantinople of 815.[144] He reports that the iconoclasts drew in particular on a set of passages from Book 4 in which Macarius rebutted the Hellene's defence of traditional religious iconography with what they took to be a rejection of icons.[145] As part of his critique, Nicephorus quotes a passage from the otherwise lost Book 1, which tells of "Berenikē," a "Queen of Edessa" who commissioned a bronze sculpture to honour her miraculous healing

---

141 Harnack (1911) and idem (1916).

142 Crafer (1919) translates only the Hellene's critiques, while summarizing Macarius's responses; Crafer also rearranges the order of the text, placing each response after each objection. Hoffman (1994) translates only the Hellene's portions of the *Apocriticus* and, despite the title does not translate other fragments of *Against the Christians*, while Berchman (2005) translates the Hellene's portions of the *Apocriticus* along with the other fragments and *testimonia* included in Harnack's edition.

143 "Iconodules" ("image-servers") or "iconophiles" ("image-lovers") argued for the legitimacy of figurative representations of Christ and the saints against "iconoclasts" ("image-destroyers") in the disputes over the veneration of icons that fractured the Byzantine world in the eighth and ninth centuries. For a comprehensive study of the period see Brubaker and Haldon (2011).

144 For text, translation, and commentary on the *Epikrisis* see Featherstone (2002), 65–112.

145 *Apocr.* 4.21 (the Hellene's explanation of iconography); *Apocr.* 4.27–29 (Macarius's rebuttal).

MACARIUS AND THE *APOCRITICUS* 43

by the power of Christ's cloak. The passage is an interesting amalgam of traditions, as discussed below.

Nicephorus's text is interesting in its own right for the light it sheds on the use of *florilegia* in Middle Byzantine culture. The first iconoclastic council of 754 had made use of patristic *florilegia*, and the compilation of *florilegia* for use in doctrinal disputes dates, at least, to the Arian controversy and was put to use by Cyril, Nestorius, and Theodoret during the Christological disputes of the fifth century. But the period of disputes over icons also saw an increased interest in discovering (and sometimes forging) new sources, as well as probing the *authenticity* of the works from which *florilegia* were produced.[146] So too in the case of Nicephorus's reading of Macarius. The Patriarch writes that both the *Apocriticus* and Macarius are previously unknown to him and that "having expended great effort and taken many pains in seeking [a copy of the work], we only just managed to find the one we have now in our hands for examination."[147] It is not clear whence Nicephorus obtained his copy: the patriarchal library, a monastery, or a private party. Nor is it clear whether Nicephorus had a complete text; Featherstone speculates that he could merely have obtained a copy of Book 4, with the fragment of Book 1 added.[148]

After Nicephorus in the ninth century, there are no extant references to the *Apocriticus* until the sixteenth century, when the Spanish Jesuit Francisco Torres drew on the *Apocriticus* in several counter-reformation treatises published in Rome between the 1550s and the 1580s. Torres's references and quotations were studied extensively by Georg Schaulkhauser, whose study informs Goulet's and Volp's recent editions.[149] Torres read a manuscript of the *Apocriticus* housed in the collection of St Mark's Library in Venice. The manuscript first appears in an inventory of 1474, and is referenced in others from 1524, 1543, and 1546, but is absent from the library's catalogue of 1637.[150] The variant readings in the passages shared between Torres's quotations and the Athens manuscript suggest that the manuscript studied by Blondel in Athens was not that lost from Venice. Torres, furthermore, knows the author of the *Apocriticus* only as "Magnetes" and "beatus Magnetes," and claims that he is a "most ancient" writer. Neither does he know the title *Apocriticus* or *Monogenēs*,

---

146 Brubaker and Haldon (2011), 44–50, 52.
147 *Ekphrasis* 2 (Featherstone [2002], 78).
148 Featherstone (2002), 80, n.2.
149 Schaulkhauser (1907).
150 Schaulkhauser (1907); Goulet (2003), 233.

44   MACARIUS, *APOCRITICUS*

calling the work an *Apologia*. Consequently, Torres appears to have known an acephalus manuscript.[151] The fourteenth-century catalogues list the manuscript as damaged and lacking *pinakes*.[152] The manuscript known to Torres, then, is neither that known to Nicephorus, nor that discovered by Blondel, nor the Vatican manuscript that contains the *pinakes* of the first three books. Torres's quotations and references are nevertheless significant: he is the only witness to Book 5 of the *Apocriticus*, preserving a short quotation concerning Abraham's faith. He also preserves a quotation from Book 4 that fills a *lacuna* in the Athens manuscript (4.30.24).

B. TITLE, AUTHOR, PROVENANCE, AND DATE

The *pinakes* preserved in the Vatican manuscript do not agree as to the title of the work. In that for Book 1, it is titled Μονογενὴς πρὸς Ἕλληνας, while those of Books 3 and 4 present a dual title, Ἀποκριτικὸς ἢ Μονογενὴς πρὸς Ἕλληνας. Ἀποκριτικὸς πρὸς Ἕλληνας would give us "Response to the Hellenes," a standard enough title for a Christian apologetic text. Μονογενὴς πρὸς Ἕλληνας is more difficult. Goulet concludes that the more difficult reading is most likely the original title.[153] Μονογενὴς can mean "unique" and in Christian theological literature can refer to the second person of the Trinity as "Only-begotten." The title might then be translated either as "A Unique [Discourse] to the Greeks" or "The Only-begotten, to the Greeks." If this is the case, the multivalence of μονογενὴς is certainly intentional, and the author seems to point to it at several points in the text. Regardless of the original title, we have referred to the text by its more familiar title, *Apocriticus*, throughout this book.

The extant manuscripts of and *testimonia* to the *Apocriticus* yield little about the identity of its author. The authorial voice does not identity itself as "Macarius"; rather, the name appears, together with the demonym "Magnesian," in the *pinakes* preserved in the Vatican manuscript. In the eighth century, Nicephorus recognizes the author as "Macarius" and identifies him as "hierarch by rank."[154] The manuscript Nicephorus used seems to have indicated Macarius's rank, for the patriarch writes that, "this

---

151 That is, a manuscript lacking a heading indicating the title of a work; Goulet (2003), 43, n.4.
152 Schaulkhauser (1907), 98–103.
153 See extended discussion in Goulet (2003), 42–47.
154 Featherstone (2002), 78–79.

is shown not only by the text of the work [συγγραφή], but is also presented more expressly by the image of Macarius imprinted with reverence on the outside covers of this ancient book (it shows him wearing the stole of a hierarch)."[155] The iconoclast *florilegium* to which Nicephorus is responding likewise understood the name of the author to be Macarius; Nicephorus writes that "The title of the citation, then, runs thus: Saint Macarius [τοῦ ἁγίου Μακαρίου], from the fourth book of *Responses*."[156]

Several manuscripts, including the title of the *pinax* to Book 1 in the Vatican manuscript, read τοῦ μακάριου μάγνητος. This can be translated as "the blessed Magnesian," or, if μάγνητος is taken as the genitive of a personal name, "of the blessed Magnes [or Magnetes]. This is apparently the understanding of the sixteenth-century Jesuit Francisco Torres (or, when Latinized, as often in bibliographic references, "Turrianus"), who quotes from "Magnes" and "the blessed Magnetes" (*beatus Magnetes*) in several of his treatises.[157] Goulet, expanding upon the work of Georg Schalkhausser, argues convincingly against any effort to follow Torres in assuming that μακάριος is an adjective rather than a proper name.[158] As Goulet explains, "the addition of an article is easier to explain than its suppression"; the Vatican manuscript (influenced perhaps by the iconoclast *florilegia*'s construction τοῦ ἁγίου μακάριου as well as the authorial genitives of other patristic works [e.g. τοῦ μακαρίου X]) has "corrected" what appeared to a medieval copyist as a confusing name.[159] Furthermore, the *pinakes* to Books 3 and 4 as preserved in the Athens manuscript, as well as several manuscripts that excerpt a passage from the *Apocriticus* on the eucharist (3.23.25), designate the author Μακάριος Μάγνητος, or simply "Macarius of Magnesia."[160]

The text of the *Apocriticus* itself presents precious little in the way of explicit evidence that might situate Macarius in time and place. The meagre evidence there is has suggested three possible locales: Mesopotamia, Syria, and Asia Minor.

The first, Mesopotamia, is the least likely, as the only evidence to support it is a short fragment from Book 1 giving an account of "Berenikē" a "queen of the Edessenes" and a bronze sculpture she is supposed to have

---

155 Featherstone (2002), 78–79. For Nicephorus, "hierarch" is synonymous with "bishop."
156 Featherstone (2002), 76–77.
157 See Schaulkhauser (1907), 18–81 for a complete study of the Turrianus fragments.
158 Schaulkhauser (1907), 1, n.4.
159 Goulet (2003), 48–49.
160 Schaulkhauser (1907), 6–13; Goulet (2003), 48.

commissioned to commemorate her miraculous healing from an "issue of blood" and which, Macarius claims, is preserved in his own day. Far from proving that Macarius is familiar with Edessa and its traditions, the passage seems rather to be a conflation of a variety of traditions. In particular, Macarius may conflate Eusebius of Caesarea's account of a pair of bronze statues in Caesarea Phillipi, which Eusebius claims portray the gospel story of the woman with an issue of blood (Mk. 5:25–34), and traditions surrounding Berenikē (i.e. Veronica). In the *Acts of Pilate*,[161] for instance, Berenikē is identified with the woman of Mark 5 and is said to have cured the Emperor Tiberias with a portrait of Christ.[162] In the medieval West, Berenikē/Veronica became associated with the "Veil of Veronica," a cloth that came to bear an *acheiropoiētos*, or an icon "not made by human hands," when Veronica wiped Christ's face as he carried the Cross. Macarius may, in addition, be conflating these traditions with early accounts of the Mandylion—another *acheiropoiētos* associated with the city of Edessa—the earliest account of which is preserved in the Syriac *Doctrina Addai*, compiled around 400 CE. In short, Macarius's references to Berenikē do not indicate an Edessene or Mesopotamian context, but instead simply provide evidence for the ongoing development of these traditions. The fact that this passage is preserved only in Nicephorus's *Epikrisis*, a polemical work of the period of intense dispute over icons, should also raise suspicion as to whether the iconodule Patriarch has presented this source with complete fidelity.

Macarius also mentions ascetic practice in and around Antioch, suggesting to some that Syria may be the author's milieu:

> You can traverse the cities of the East and, collectively, the districts of Syria and learn more precisely of the matter about which I speak. For example, those who live in the royal metropolis of Antiochus are divided by their myriad attitudes about the pursuit of perfection. Some gladly welcome the conjugal yoke, while others do not accept the fellowship of a wife. Some honour a soft life, others the harsh toil of a life of little food. Some insatiably pile up material resources; others love poverty as a good. Some pride themselves exceedingly on their commerce; others rejoice by feasting on difficulties. Some eagerly desire to be with courtesans; others want to dwell together with female solitaries. (2.18.10)

To use this passage as empirical evidence of provenance is less than

---

161 The *Acts of Pilate* is an apocryphal text that dates (probably) to the fourth-century CE and purports to be Pilate's report to the Emperor Tiberius concerning the trial of Jesus.
162 *Acts of Pilate* 7, English translation available Elliot (1993), 175.

straightforward, however, since its function in the text is to provide a rhetorical demonstration in support of Macarius's elucidation of Matthew 10:34 ("I did not come to cast peace upon the earth, but a sword."). The section hinges on a series of antitheses: marriage/celibacy, ease/toil, wealth/poverty. The "sword" of Matthew 10:34 is thus "that which differentiates attitudes, but does not cause wounds" (2.18.11). Antioch serves Macarius's rhetorical aims because, in the late antique imagination, "Antioch" was a city that embodied the extremes of ascetic practice and worldly sensuality. Though some, like Goulet, read the passage as a reference to peculiarly Syrian forms of asceticism,[163] the set of ascetic virtues listed are simply too general to associate with any specific forms of ascetic practice.

Macarius does employ a *hapax legomenon* in the passage, which may give some suggestion of the date of composition. Among the antitheses he draws between the ascetic and worldly life, Macarius writes: "Some eagerly desire to be with courtesans [ἑταίραις]; others want to dwell together with/in μονηρίαις" (2.18.10). The *hapax* μονηρίαις may derive either from μόνος ("alone," "solitary") or μονή ("dwelling," "residence"). Because it stands in contrast with ἑταίραις, the common term for "courtesans," it would seem to indicate a group of women, thus "female solitaries." Goulet opines that this may be Macarius's term for συνείσακται (Latin: *subintroductae*), or female ascetics who cohabited with male ascetics, usually in urban contexts.[164] They are known especially from the Antiochene John Chrysostom, who staunchly repudiated the practice in the last third of the fourth century.[165] To opine further, it is not impossible that, if Macarius is referring to ascetic practice in a Syrian milieu, he is translating the Syriac îhîdāyâ, literally "solitaries" or "single ones." This became the usual term for translating the Greek μοναχός ("monk," "solitary"), though its usage in Syriac predates the forms of later fourth- and early fifth-century Syrian asceticism described, for example, in Theodoret's *History of the Monks of Syria.*

It is also possible, however, that μονηρίαις derives from μονή ("dwelling," "residence")—a term Macarius uses several times.[166] A contrast between "courtesans" and "monastic dwellings" is, nonetheless, a

---

163 Goulet (2003), 58.
164 Goulet (2003), 59.
165 See, for example, Chrysostom's *Instruction and Refutation Directed against those Men Cohabiting with Virgins* and *On the Necessity of Guarding Virginity*, both translated with notes and introduction in Clark (1982).
166 For example: 2.28.9, 2.31.14, 2.32.7, 3.43.10. The word appears in the Hellene's speeches as well, e.g. 3.5.3, 4.2.3.

poorly balanced antithesis. The Athens manuscript reads ἑταίραις, but one could conjecture the omission of an iota. In this case the contrast would be between ἑταιρίαις (political or social clubs) and μονηρίαις (monastic dwellings). On either of these readings, Macarius does seem to be referring to some form of relatively organized ascetic practice that one could have observed (or heard tell of) in and around Antioch (and other regions) in the last half of the fourth century and first third of the fifth.[167]

Goulet suggests that the author turns to Syria as his ascetic *exemplum* because he does not himself reside in a region in which formalized forms of asceticism were popular.[168] He contends that this helps support a provenance in Asia Minor, a region for which there is indeed less evidence of monasticism and asceticism in the late fourth and early fifth centuries. Again, though, given Macarius's commitment to his rhetorical display it is as, if not perhaps more, likely that he uses the example of Syria and Antioch for its rhetorical significance as the city of sin/city of virtue.

There are several pieces of internal evidence, however, that better suggest an Asian context. First, Macarius mentions several figures associated with the region. In a discussion of cosmology, he mentions Aratus of Cilicia (4.17.3). Aratus's *Phaenomena* was by no means an obscure work, yet Macarius also refers, twice, to a heretic "Dositheus of Cilicia," who is otherwise unknown (3.43.26, 4.15.5). In both instances, Macarius describes Dositheus in a way that suggests this heretic is a figure of prominent concern to Macarius. In a discussion of authentic versus heretical sexual asceticism he mentions the Manichaeans, Encratites, Apotactics, and Eremites, noting that they are active in Pisidia, Isauria, Cilicia, Lycaonia, and Galatia (3.43.25)—all regions in Asia Minor. To this list Macarius appends Dositheus, who, he claims, wrote an eight-book treatise (4.23.26). Macarius mentions Dositheus again in a list of heretics who claim to be "false christs"; he lists Cerinthus, Simon (Magus), Marcion, and Bardaisan—a fairly standard heresiological list to which he adds Droserius and Dositheus of Cilicia.

If, as seems likely, the μάγνητος of the titles preserved in the manuscript tradition indicate that Macarius is "of Magnesia," there are two "Magnesias" in Asia Minor that fit the bill: Magnesia on the Meander, southeast of Ephesus, and Magnesia ad Sipylum (i.e. "at the foot of Mt Sipylus"), modern Manisa, Turkey. Looking to the prosopography of late ancient Christianity,

---

167 Goulet (2003), 58.
168 Goulet (2003), 60–61.

there is at least one "Macarius of Magnesia" who may reasonably be identified with the author of our text. During his reading of the *Acta* of the Synod of the Oak (403 CE), which deposed John Chrysostom as Patriarch of Constantinople, the ninth-century patriarch Photius remarked that:

> The thirteenth session concerned the case of Heraclides, who had been consecrated by Chrysostom to the See of Ephesus, and whose deposition no one dared decree, because of the opposition of certain other bishops. Heraclides's accuser was a bishop of the city of the Magnesians by the name of Macarius.[169]

Both Magnesia on the Meander and Magnesia ad Sipylum were bishoprics under the metropolitan see of Ephesus. If, as we will argue shortly, the *Apocriticus* dates to the last third of the fourth century, Photius's Macarius may well be the author of the *Apocriticus*.[170]

The *Apocriticus* is a difficult work to date with certainty or precision. On balance, the internal evidence suggests that it is best contextualized in the last quarter of the fourth century. Mark J. Edwards's essay in this volume considers Macarius's place within the Christian tradition in detail. Here it suffices to point out that there is nothing in the *Apocriticus* that would situate Macarius firmly among Nicenes, Homoians, or Homoiousians. He comes closest to an explicitly Nicene position in Book 4, where he writes that

> For the one name of "God" applies to the Son and to the Father and to the Holy Spirit, and God is one in three subsistent entities [*hypostases*] and is so named, and the believer accepts neither Father without the Son, and the Son does not lead anyone to the Father apart from the Spirit. For behold how he spoke mystically: "But you have been washed, but you have been sanctified, but you have been justified." For he whom Christ washed, this one the Spirit made holy, while he whom the Spirit made holy, this one the Father justified, and not because Christ, washing, is not able to make holy, or the Spirit, making holy, does not have the strength to justify, or the Father, justifying, is in some way too weak to wash or make holy whom he wishes. For the Father, the Son, and the Holy Spirit are similarly competent to wash, make holy, and justify everything, but because it is fitting that the Son, as Son, make sons, and the Holy Spirit, to make holy, as Spirit, the Father, as Father, to justify what has been made holy, in order that the name of three subsistent entities [*hypostases*] be known in one essence [*ousia*]. (4.25.22)

This articulation parallels Basil of Caesarea's famous elaborations of the

---

169 Photius, *Bibliotheca* 59.
170 Goulet (2003), 50–51.

difference between *ousia* and *hypostasis*.[171] Macarius's description of the actions associated with each *hypostasis* also has strong parallels in Gregory of Nyssa.[172] Thomas Crafer, who wished to date the *Apocriticus* to the early fourth century, contended that this passage was a post-Nicene interpolation, but there is no textual basis for this argument.[173] Yet the parallels with the Cappadocians need not indicate that Macarius was dependent on their writings; the formula "three *hypostases* and one *ousia*" appears as early as the 360s.[174] Macarius's predilection for grammatical approaches to metaphysics is also noteworthy here; like Basil and Eunomius, he makes use of theories of names and naming.[175] Macarius, though, is not as sophisticated as Eunomius or Basil in this regard, instead deploying fairly basic knowledge of Aristotle's *Categories*.[176] Other significant patristic parallels in the *Apocriticus* also come from authors whose *floruits* date to the last third of the fourth century.[177] On the whole, therefore, Macarius's theology is likely to come from the same basic period as the Cappadocians—that is, between the 360s and the end of the fourth century,[178] though the fluidity with which he uses certain terms may weigh in favour of an earlier rather than a later date within this period.[179]

---

171 See, for example, Basil, *Letters* 214.4 and 236.6.

172 Gregory of Nyssa, *To Ablabius* (GNO III.1 47.22–48.8).

173 Crafer (1906–1907), 553.

174 It is referenced, for example, in the *Tome to the Antiochenes* 6 (NPNF 2nd ser., vol. 4, 485); see also discussion in Goulet (2002), 182.

175 On name-theory and the conflict between Basil and Eunomius see DelCogliano (2010).

176 See, for example *Apocriticus* 2.20; 3.11; 4.26; 4.29.

177 E.g. Eusebius of Emesa (2.18.10; 3.14.11); the *Incomplete Commentary on Matthew (Opus Imperfectum in Mattheum)* (2.20.6); Gregory of Nyssa (4.25.22; 3.9.14–17); Amphilochius of Iconium (3.9.14–17).

178 The promulgation of an amplified form of the Nicene Creed at the Council of Constantinople on 381 has been posited as a *terminus ante quem*, on the grounds that the terminology of Macarius would be more rigid if it were informed by a credal pronouncement. This argument, however, is fallacious because (a) the date of promulgation is highly uncertain; (b) it does not contain the technical terms *hypostasis* and *ousia*; (c) in content it falls well short of the Cappadocian affirmation that the Spirit is both God and *homoousios* with the Father; (d) in the fifty years after 381, no author who purports to cite the Nicene Creed in full cites any version but that of 325.

179 Goulet would situate Macarius a bit more precisely—"between homoiousianism and Nicene orthodoxy"—and suggests he may be among the "compromise" theologians who, in the years preceding the Council of Constantinople, sought rapprochement by avoiding predicating the *homoousios* of the Son (Goulet [2003], 188); Macarius's silence on *homoousios* and the fact that nothing in his work explicitly contradicts the concept could be taken as support for this position.

While points of contact between the *Apocriticus* and other late fourth-century Christian literature are the best evidence for dating the work, several pieces of internal evidence help corroborate this dating. The closest the text comes to dating itself are two references within the Hellene's first speech in Book 4. The Hellene remarks, first, that "it has been three hundred years" since Paul wrote his letters (4.2.5) and that "three hundred or more years have passed" since Jesus's warning in Matthew 24:4–5 concerning false christs (4.5.1). Taken absolutely literally, they would provide a date in (approximately) the 350s (i.e. three hundred years after Paul's writing in the 50s and more than three hundred since Jesus's ministry). One must be cautious in taking these dates too literally or precisely, however. Firstly, the reference to "three hundred years" since Paul is conjectural. The Athens manuscript reads "thirty," which, in view of the reference to "three hundred years" in the same set of objections, must be an error.[180] Secondly, these references come from the Hellene's portion of the debate and, as will be discussed below, Macarius was almost certainly drawing on a source or sources to construct the Hellene. One must decide, then, whether the references date this source or sources, the *Apocriticus*, or both.

Those who contend that Macarius's source is Hierocles or Porphyry argue that the period of "three hundred years" since Jesus's warning about false christs need only be taken as indicating approximately three centuries since Jesus's birth, not his public life.[181] The reference to Paul is more difficult. Blondel proposed the emendation "three hundred years," and we have followed his conjecture in this translation. Duchesne, and later Harnack, proposed that Macarius altered the dates of his source to reflect his own late fourth-century context, about "three hundred and thirty" years after Paul.[182] More recently, Digeser has argued that the passage could be emended to "two hundred and thirty years," rendering a date circa 300.[183] Frassinetti, in contrast, suggested the reading "three hundred and thirty years," supporting his identification of Macarius's source with Julian's *Against the Galileans*.[184] Yet, as Goulet has proved, Macarius certainly

---

180 Three hundred and thirty: Frassinetti (1949), 41–56; two hundred and thirty: Digeser (2002).
181 E.g. Harnack (1911), 330; Digeser (2002), 477–478.
182 Harnack (1911), 108.
183 Digeser (2002), 477–478.
184 Frassinetti (1949), 41–56. Early Christian estimates of the time that separates them from past events can often surprise us. Optatus, *On the Donatist Schism* 1.13 speaks of an

had a hand in redacting whatever source he used; would Macarius have allowed a blatant anachronism undo his efforts to craft a realistic, though fictional, debate? Goulet's point is well taken: these formulae probably reflect Macarius's own date and provide only a general *terminus post quem* of around 350–360 CE.[185]

There are several hints concerning date and context that merit mention, though none represents unambiguous evidence. The first is Macarius's brief passage concerning ascetic practice in and around Antioch, already discussed above. The passage really offers little in the way of details that suggest a specific date. If the *hapax* μονηρίαις does refer to something like Chrysostom's συνείσακται (ascetic women who cohabited with ascetic men), then this might imply a date in the 370s–early 380s, the period during which Chrysostom wrote against the practice.[186] But, as noted above, the term may simply refer to ascetic dwellings. But it is not at all clear that Macarius's description "corresponds well with the *specific* type of extreme asceticism that developed in Syria over the course of the fourth century."[187] Nevertheless, the description certainly does accord better with a later fourth-century context than an early fourth-century one, as Macarius's rhetoric assumes that the Christian ascetic life is reified and visible enough *as such* that his audience will be familiar with it.

A second group of hints as to the date come from several passages in which Macarius uses the emperor and imperial politics in his rhetorical arguments. In Book 4 Macarius responds to the Hellene's criticism that Paul's teachings concerning the forgiveness of sins encourages antinomianism (the notion that Christians, by virtue of forgiveness, are absolved from following moral precepts) and contradicts his claims concerning the validity of God's law (4.19.4–5). Macarius counters by defending God's absolute power and authority to grant favour as he will. He uses the example of the emperor: "Now many who have received a sentence of death from the law have, by appealing to the emperor, had it overturned, which demonstrates that the philanthropy of the emperor is stronger than

---

interval of roughly sixty years since the Great Persecution, though at least seventy must have elapsed by the time of writing; Arnobius, *Against the Nations* 1.13, asserts that Christianity has been in the world for about 300 years, though his work is commonly thought to have been composed some time between 297 and 305.

185 Goulet (2003), 58.
186 On the dates of Chrysostom's treatises see: Dumortier, (1949), 248–251; Kelley (1995), 49; Clark (1977), 175, n.46; Adkin (1992), 255–266.
187 Goulet (2003), 58, emphasis added.

[evil] deeds" (4.25.5). As Macarius continues, he elaborates by drawing an example from recent history. It is worth quoting at length:

> For yesterday and the day before, not long ago at all, some who were entangled in illicit deeds and were to be chastised with an appropriate punishment, but bowed to the imperial train, expressing the hope that his reign may be perpetual, were released from any supposition of guilt and put behind them the judicial decision. But others, free of every spot and blemish, who did not partake even of common crime and theft, nor had feigned to honour royalty, like the unpurified and ungrateful, immediately received the awful chastisement of destruction, enjoying no advantage from living without reproach nor gaining any profit from being clean of any accusation. (4.25.13–14)

The passage stands out because Macarius's comparison between the emperor and God is less than flattering. Is it in Macarius's rhetorical interest to liken God to a *fickle* emperor who persecutes those who are "without reproach?" Yes, if he aims to launch a thinly veiled polemic against the emperor. Macarius is more explicit when he counters the Hellene's claim that to be a proper monarch, God must rule over beings of a like nature. The Hellene adduces the example of Hadrian (4.20–21a.2). Macarius responds that God's monarchy consists precisely in his ontological difference from all other beings, while those who rule over beings of a like nature are tyrannical:

> That is something untyrannical, then, and just—ruling beings that are unlike himself on account of the sublimity of his essence. For one who is lord to beings of a different kind by virtue of his superiority in nature does not govern them despotically with tyrannical force, but directs them benignly by the firmness of love. But Hadrian, or some other world ruler, being a human being and reigning over humans like himself, did so by the law of domination and tyranny; not ruling over beings of a like nature by the precept of consistency [i.e. with the natural and ontological order], he rather enslaved fellow kin by constraint and violence ... In so far, then, as he plays tyrant over nature by force, he does not have authority by nature, but shows by savagery that he is more powerful than those like him. (4.26.6–8)

Those who would date the *Apocriticus* to the early fourth century read these passages as evidence that Macarius wrote during or just after the Diocletianic persecution.[188] Were it not for other evidence that points to a later fourth century theological and cultural context, this would seem a strong argument. But Macarius's subtle and not-so-subtle criticisms of

---

188 See, for example, Digeser (2002) 475–476 and Crafer (1919), xvi–xix.

the emperor as a tyrant also fit a later fourth-century political context.[189] Depending on which side of the fourth-century theological controversies one found oneself, various emperors were characterized as tyrants. Macarius's theology strongly suggests a date between the 360s and the 380s, leaving at least two likely candidates: Julian and Valens. Many Christians openly characterized Julian as a tyrant after his death. His "fickle" recall of exiled pro-Nicene bishops could perhaps be described as being "released from any supposition of guilt and put[ting] behind them the judicial decision," but probably not from Macarius's perspective as a likely pro-Nicene or compromise bishop. Valens, on the other hand, was also characterized as a tyrannical ruler who was guilty of capricious judgment.[190] Sozomen and Socrates report that, after the Council of Lampsacus deposed Eudoxius as Patriarch of Constantinople in 364, Valens, under the influence of Eudoxius, refused to confirm the Council's decree and, instead, condemned the members of the Council's delegation to exile.[191] Macarius's allusions are too vague to identify this precise historical episode with the hypothetical scenario presented in the *Apocriticus*, but it does show that the behaviour of Macarius's hypothetical emperor accords with other authors' characterizations of Valens.[192]

In sum, though it is difficult to assign a conclusive provenance and date to the *Apocriticus*, the weight of the evidence suggests that this is a work of the last third of the fourth century. Among known Macarii of the period, our Macarius is likely to be the Macarius of Magnesia who attended the Synod of the Oak in 403 CE.

C. A LITERARY ASSESSMENT

The *Apocriticus* purports to record a public disputation between Macarius and an unnamed "Hellene." The setting is a sophistical contest: the speakers perform in a theatre before an audience of notable citizens (3.prol.1). Each disputant offers an extended discourse, and is answered in turn by

---

189 Goulet (2003), 62–65.
190 Goulet (2003), 65; Socrates, *Ecclesiastical History* 4.16; Gregory of Nazianzen, *Oration* 25.10; see especially Ammianus Marcellinus 31.14.5–6, where Valens is described as often overturning judicial decisions that ran counter to his whim.
191 Sozomen, *Ecclesiastical History* 6.7.
192 Goulet (2003), 65, n.4 references Sozomen's narrative, but does not press the connection between this episode and the *Apocriticus*.

MACARIUS AND THE *APOCRITICUS* 55

his opponent. Here the similarity to real public disputations ends. Even allowing for the editing that marks other records of public disputations—Augustine's disputes with Manichaeans, for instance the *Debate with Fortunatus*—this "debate" is entirely one-sided.[193] The Hellene delivers short strings of *aporias*[194] and exegetical questions, to which Macarius offers lengthy, often tedious, responses. The Hellene never rebuts or redirects Macarius responses, nor does he answer any of the rhetorical questions posed by Macarius. Thus the disputants serve as caricatures and the public disputation is a literary fiction.

The title as preserved in the Vatican manuscript situates the *Apocriticus* within the popular late ancient genre of "question and answer" (ζητήματα καί λύσεις) literature.[195] Where other late ancient Christian "question and answer" texts adopt the dialogue form (Theodoret's *Eranistes* and Aeneas of Gaza's *Theophrastes*, for example), the fictional public disputation is Macarius's rhetorical vehicle.

Although Macarius presents the *Apocriticus* as the record of a five-day public disputation, the setting is almost certainly fictional. As in early Christian works ranging from Justin's *Dialogue with Trypho* to Zacharias's *Ammonius*, the public dispute is here a useful literary trope. Public disputes did occur and were, on occasion, recorded in late antiquity. Augustine's debate with the Manichaean Fortunatus is perhaps the best-known example. The *Debate with Fortunatus* claims to be based on stenographers' notes "in the way in which judicial proceedings are recorded."[196] As the first and final books of the *Apocriticus* are lost, there is no way of knowing whether Macarius claimed that his text is a similar record, or even the context in which the debate is supposed to have taken place. From the extant internal evidence we learn only that Macarius and the Hellene are supposed to have confronted one another in the winter (4.11.20) and that the audience was composed of "distinguished listeners" (3.prol.1). In the prologue of Book 3, Macarius addresses the work's dedicatee, "Theosthenes," and states that he will "desrib[e] in detail, as far as possible, the propositions he [the Hellene] had prepared" (3.prol.1). Macarius, therefore, claims to present his recollection of a debate, not a stenographer's record.

---

193 On public debate in late antiquity see Lim (1995).
194 That is, philosophical questions that appear to admit of no logical solution.
195 On this popular genre see the recent studies collected in Bussières (2013), Papadogiannakis (2012), and Volgers and Zamagni (2004); Volp ([2013], xix–xxiii) also places the *Apocriticus* within this genre.
196 Augustine, *Retractions* 1.16.1, English translation in Ramsey (2010).

Almost everything about the short narrative interludes that punctuate the dialogue suggests a completely fictional debate. Macarius repeatedly describes the Hellene as a formidable, even terrifying sophist, yet his speeches are rather simple rhetorically, especially when compared to Macarius's rhetorical flourishes and his penchant for amplification. The relative brevity of the Hellene's speeches compared to Macarius's lengthy responses also suggests that the former serve primarily as prompts for the latter.

Macarius's writing is not an easy read. He is prolix and florid, his theology and philosophy are underdeveloped, and as an apologist his λύσεις to the Hellene's ζητήματα are often wanting in precision and persuasiveness. But it is in part Macarius's mediocrity that makes him interesting for historians of late antique culture and literature. If, as seems likely, Macarius was a late fourth-century bishop, we have in the *Apocriticus* an example of the literary talent of an "average" Christian intellectual. He has a rhetor's education and deploys a variety of textbook examples of the figures of speech and compositional techniques taught in the late ancient rhetorical schools. He has some rudimentary knowledge of philosophy. He seems to understand some of the basics of the Aristotelean *Categories*: on several occasions, for example, he uses concepts like "definition of essence" and "homonymy" in attempts to unknot metaphysics.[197] He is aware, and makes use of a range of figurative and non-figurative exegeses—from the allegorical to the historical—but is a strong proponent of neither.

In many ways, Macarius's rhetoric is his response to the Hellene. As Goulet puts it: "[T]his work is above all that of a rhetor who intends never to depart from the canons of the rhetorical tradition ... This oratorical debate is thus less concerned with refuting pagan objections than in establishing cultural superiority over paganism."[198] While rhetorical force is part of the argument of every early Christian apology—the classic apologies of the second century, for instance, are nothing if not prime examples of second sophistic literature—Macarius regularly subordinates the content of his responses to their form. Whether this rhetorical display is effective, however, is debatable.

The *Apocriticus* offers textbook examples of the techniques taught in late antique rhetorical curricula and preserved in various rhetorical manuals

---

197 E.g. *Apocr.* 2.20.8; 3.11.3; 4.26.1–15.
198 Goulet (2003), 164. Goulet also charts the elements of Macarius's rhetoric in detail ([2003], 166–175).

from the period.[199] Macarius has a penchant for "speech-in-character" (*ethopoiia*), the device whereby a rhetor speaks in the persona of a particular historical figure, stock character, or significant object.[200] According to one influential description of the device, "Ethopoeia ... is an imitation of the character of a person supposed to be speaking; for example, what words Andromache might say to Hector."[201] All of Macarius's examples are in the character of Christ. The lengthiest examples occur in Book 2, where "Christ" explains two sayings attacked by the Hellene ("I have not come to bring peace upon the world, but a sword" [Mt. 10:34] and "Who is my brother and sister" [Mt. 12:48]). Macarius develops two extended speeches-in-character (2.18.1–5, 2.19.3–9), which together present Macarius's ascetic exegeses of these verses and lay out an ascetic ethics. In classical rhetoric, a speech-in-character was often also an exegesis. When a student composed on "What words Medea might say when she is about to murder her children," or "What words Achilles would say over the dead Patroclus,"[202] he or she was also *interpreting* Euripides's *Medea* and Homer's *Iliad*, respectively. So too, Macarius, who closes the aforementioned speeches with formulas like "This is what he [Christ] would say to those wanting to receive the heavenly armour" (2.18.6) and "Christ would probably have said these things to those who spoke nonsense" (2.19.8), uses speech-in-character as a primary exegetical method. In this, Macarius is following other late fourth-century Christians, who often deployed the technique for hortatory and exegetical purposes—particularly in homiletics.[203]

Various techniques of amplification (*amplificatio/auxesis*) are another of Macarius's favourite devices. His lengthy response to the Hellene's critique of 1 Corinthians 7:31 ("The form of this world is passing away")

---

199 Many of these treatises are now available in accessible English translations; see, for example Kennedy (2003) for translations of the *Progymnasmata*, or *Preliminary Exercises*, of Aelius Theon, (Ps.) Hermogenes, Aphthonius, Nicolaus, and Sopatros; and Gibson (2008) for those of Libanius.

200 Some rhetorical manuals distinguish between *ethopoiia* (in the character of a living person), *prosopopoiia* (the personification of something inanimate), and *eidolopoiia* (in the character of a dead person) (e.g. [Ps.] Hermogenes, *Preliminary Exercises* 20–22; Apthonius, *Preliminary Exercises* 44–46), though others do not (e.g. Aelius Theon, *Preliminary Exercises* 115–118). Goulet identifies ten instances in the *Apocriticus* (165, n.2; note that the reference to 8, 32–30 is a typographical error and should read 28, 32–30, 6).

201 (Ps.) Hermogenes, *Preliminary Exercises* 20, trans. Kennedy (2003).

202 Two examples from Libanius, *Preliminary Exercises* 1, 3; trans. Gibson (2008).

203 See for example Goulet (2003) 165, n.2; Kecskeméti (1994); see also the collected studies in Amato and Schamp (2005).

is characteristic. Here, Macarius amplifies a rather jejune reply—that "the 'form' of this world can be understood in various ways" (4.11.4)—by joining various figures into a long excursus that runs to five pages in Goulet's edition (4.4–24). "Form," he argues, can refer to the transitory honours of human society (4.11.6). Macarius then develops a series of commonplaces (*topoi*)[204] concerning the inevitable changes of fortune experienced by courtiers, generals, captains, and beggars. He further amplifies by adducing a *chreia*, or instructive anecdote, concerning the rise and fall of Croesus, Cyrus, and Tomyris. *Chreia* on the fate of Babylon and the Macedonians follow, as do commonplaces on the inevitability of old age and death. Macarius concludes with long vivid descriptions, or *ekphrases*, on the course of each of the four seasons.

As this example shows, Macarius is able to deploy a full range of common rhetorical techniques. He is likewise a competent rhetor at the level of *cola* and *commata* (clauses and phrase-units).[205] He is especially fond of *anaphora* (the repetition of words/phrases) and *isocola* (clauses of equal length) as structural and balancing elements. To give but one illustrative example, in response to the Hellene's claim that Christ should have manifested his power as God before Pilate, Macarius writes:

> For if he had subdued the governor and the high priests by force, in the way that God *shook a rock with a word, with a word rocked a building, with a word dispersed the thick air, and with a word combatted the anger of wild beasts*, he would have done an injustice. In making them accept the good by force, he would have offended justice, and he would even have seemed suspicious for this, as if he were performing novel marvels through sorcery, and been judged like one of the so-called Gorgons, *if he had frightened Pilate with extraordinary wonders, if he had scared the priests with novel signs, if he had reduced the Jewish people with portents*. (3.8.5)

But though Macarius has a rhetorical education, his work reads much more like the school exercises (*progymnasmata*) preserved from the period. He follows the rules of good composition, but does not use them (or break them) in a way that would suggest the work of a truly accomplished orator. This is the rhetoric of an educated man, even if it is not the *tour de force* of a Libanius or Chrysostom. Macarius's commitment to his rhetorical display is itself significant, and offers a window onto the influence of the

---

204 On *topoi* see, for example, (Ps.) Hermogenes, *Preliminary Exercises* 12–14, trans. Kennedy (2003).
205 For a very detailed colametrical analysis of Macarius, see Goulet (2003), 164–176.

literary culture of the "Third Sophistic" among Christian intellectuals.[206] Rather than offering a more sober piece of question and answer literature, he understands himself to operate in a social context in which a bishop's political success depended as much on his eloquence as on his orthodoxy.

---

[206] On the recent introduction of the term "Third Sophistic" to describe the flourishing of rhetorical culture in the later fourth through to the sixth century, see for example Quiroga (2007) and Van Hoof (2010).

ABBREVIATIONS AND SIGLA

A = Athens manuscript

V = Vatican manuscript (*Vaticanus graecus* 1650)

Blondel = ΜΑΚΑΡΙΟΥ ΜΑΓΝΗΤΟΣ, Ἀποκριτικὸς ἢ Μονογενής. *Macarii Magnetis quae supersunt ex inedito codice edidit C. Blondel* (Paris, 1876)

Goulet = Richard Goulet, *Macarios de Magnésie, Le Monogénès, Tome II*: Édition *critique et traduction française* (Paris, 2003)

*** = *lacuna*

< > = words or letters absent in the manuscript but editors suggest should be supplied

{ } = words or letters that stand in the manuscript but editors suggest should be deleted

[ ] = words or phrases supplied by the translators for clarity

BOOK 1

Macarius of Mag[nesia's[1]

Uniq]ue Discourse to the Hellenes

Co[ncerning the troubling] ques[tions] in the beginning of the Gospel [and their] soluti[ons][2]

1. What is the reason for the variety of heresies among Christians?
2. Why did the Lord choose the disciples, and then with them, the Traitor ...[3]
3. What is the reason for the passage: "Follow me and I will make you fishers of men"?[4]
4. What is the meaning of: "And Jesus was tempted in the desert by the Accuser"?[5]

---

1 Or "The blessed Magnesian's." For a discussion of the manuscript evidence for the name of the *Apocriticus*'s author see the Introduction.

2 The *pinax* ("table of contents") of Book 1 is preserved only in *Vaticanus graecus* 1650, fol. 187 recto. On the reconstruction of the title of Macarius's work based on the tables preserved in the Vatican manuscript, see discussion in the Introduction and, for a more detailed discussion, Goulet (2003), 41–47. A subscription in the Vatican manuscript at the conclusion of the *pinax* reads: "O Macarius of Magnesia, you have theologized everything well, just as the Holy Spirit inspired you to." As Goulet notes ([2003], 5, n.3), it is also possible to read "O Macarius of Magnesia" (Ὦ Μακάριε Μαγνῆτα) as "O blessed Magnes." For debates concerning the name of the author, see discussion in the Introduction. The subscription recalls Macarius's own claims to have received divine aid in his responses to the Hellene; see, for example 4.11.2, where Macarius writes that: "encouraged from somewhere by an invisible ally, we stood fast against the threatening tempest, opposing to it the alliance of the Holy Spirit," and 4.25.1, where Macarius says that he has "supplicat[ed] that which secretly reveals deep things from the shadows and which teaches men the clearest knowledge."

3 Cf. Jn. 6:70.
4 Mt. 4:19; Mk. 1:17.
5 Lk. 4:2.

5. For what reason did Christ come not at the beginning, but at the end of time?

6. How, after being humiliated and crucified, was Christ able to make people believe in him?

7. What is the meaning of: They were in the desert "five thousand, not counting women and children"?[6]

8. What is the meaning of the statement given to the disciples that they should teach the whole world,[7] and why did he [i.e. Christ] cure their leader, Peter, of his denial?[8]

9. What is the meaning of the statement made against[9] the fig tree: "Fruit shall no longer produce fruit, forevermore"?[10]

10. Why did Pilate come out of the *praetorium* saying[11] to the Jews: "Take him and judge him according to your Law"?[12]

Fragment of Book 1[13]

For he [i.e. Macarius], in the first discourse[14] *of his book, in response to the*

---

6 Mt. 14:21. The compiler writes "in the desert" based on Mt. 14:13 ("in a desert [or 'deserted'] place").

7 E.g. Mk. 16:15: "He said to them, 'Go out into the whole world and proclaim the gospel to all creation.'"

8 See Mt. 26:69–75 (and parallels) for the account of Peter's denial of Christ.

9 Accepting the correction "against" (κατὰ) with Goulet and Mercati, against the Vatican manuscript, which reads "under" (ὑπὸ); as Goulet notes, it is, of course, possible that the compiler of the *pinax* did in fact merely mean that the curse was uttered under said fig tree.

10 Mt. 21:19, where Jesus curses a fig tree when he is hungry, but finds no fruit on it.

11 Literally "after saying," but in the narrative of the trial in John, the Jews do not enter the praetorium (Jn. 18:28), as Goulet ([2003], 5, n.2) notes.

12 Jn. 18:31.

13 The fragment is quoted by the ninth-century Patriarch of Constantinople, Nicephorus (c.758–828 CE) in his *Critique* (commonly known as *De Magnete*, or *On [i.e. Macarius] Magnes*). Nicephorus wrote the *Critique* in response to an iconoclast document compiled in preparation for the iconoclastic Council of 815 CE that had adduced quotations from the fourth book of the *Apocriticus* as patristic support for the iconoclast position. The passages quoted in the iconoclast document are *Apocriticus* 4.20–32 and 4.26–30. The quotation of patristic texts figured prominently in both iconophile and iconodule literature in the eighth and ninth centuries; see Brubaker and Haldon (2011), 44–50.

14 "In the first discourse" = ἐν τῷ πρώτῳ λόγῳ. Each of the five books of the *Apocriticus* records a single day's public disputation between Macarius and the "Hellene."

BOOK 1 63

sixth topic,[15] *in which he examines the miracles accomplished by Christ, writes as follows, that*:

<...> at that time Berenikē, queen of a renowned land and replete with honours, who was ruling the great city of the Edessenes, and who had long since been released from streams of impure blood and had been cured quickly of a painful malady—one that many physicians had examined many times, offering no help, but only making the malady much more painful[16]—was saved by the touch of the fringe of the Saviour's [cloak], which caused the great accomplishment that is famous in song, sung even today in Mesopotamia, or rather throughout the whole world. For the woman, piously having had it cast in bronze, brought the story of this very deed to life, as if the deed had occurred just now, not long ago.[17]

---

15 I.e. the sixth topic (κεφάλαιον) or objection raised by the Hellene; according to the sequence of objections in the *pinax* preserved in the Vatican manuscript, the sixth topic concerned "How, after being humiliated and crucified, was Christ able to make people believe in him?" Goulet ([2003], 382) suggests that Macarius may have discussed the healing of the woman with an issue of blood, among other miracles, as reasons for belief despite the humiliation of the crucifixion.

16 Cf. Mk. 4:26.

17 Macarius thus identifies the unnamed "woman with an issue of blood," (Mk. 5:25–43, in which a woman suffering a bleeding disorder for twelve years is healed upon touching Jesus's cloak) as Berenikē, a queen of Edessa. Eusebius of Caesarea (*Ecclesiastical History* 7.18.1–3) describes what he claims was a pair of statues representing Christ's healing of the woman with an issue of blood (Mk. 5:25–34) in Caesarea Phillipi. In Eusebius's account, the statues, one of a man extending his hand and the other of a woman kneeling with outstretched hands, stood on pedestals flanking the entrance to what was reputed to be the woman's home. Eusebius, however, does not identify the woman as Berenikē or as a queen of Edessa. The woman with the issue of blood is named as Berenikē or Beronikē (i.e. Veronica) in the *Acts of Pilate* 7. In this text, she cures the Roman Emperor Tiberius with a portrait of Jesus. Macarius appears to conflate (or draw on a source that conflates) the "woman with the issue of blood" and the "Berenikē/Veronica" of the *Acts of Pilate* (or a similar tradition). He appears further to identify her as a queen of Edessa by conflating the tradition of Mandylion (that is, the icon said to have been painted during Jesus's lifetime and presented to King Abgar of Edessa; the earliest literary account of the Mandylion is the *Doctrina Addai*, composed c.400 CE, but drawing on earlier traditions) with Berenikē's miraculous portrait in the *Acts of Pilate*. By the medieval period, the fully developed account of "Veronica" has her offering a cloth to Jesus as he carries the cross to Calvary; he wipes his face, leaving a miraculous portrait upon the cloth. This episode in turn became one of the regular "stations of the cross."

BOOK 2

[Cont]ents of the second book [of] responses
[to the Helle]nes[1]

[1. What is the meaning of:] "The heaven was closed for three years and six months"[2] from the Gospel?

[2. Why] Jesus said: "The little girl has not died, but she sleeps."[3]

[3. How L]azarus was raised from the dead on the [four]th day.[4]

4.

5. [5]

[6. W]hat is the meaning of: "If someone [follows be]hind me and does <not> hate his father and himself he is not worthy of me"?[6]

7. What is the meaning of: "I did not come to cast peace upon the earth but a sword"?[7]

8. What is the meaning of: "Behold! Your mother and your brothers are waiting outside wanting to speak with you"?[8]

9. What is the meaning of: "No one is good except God alone"?[9]

---

1 The *pinax* ("table of contents") of Book 2 is preserved only in *Vaticanus graecus* 1650, fol. 187 verso.
2 Lk. 4:25.
3 Mt. 9:24.
4 Cf. Jn. 11:38–44.
5 Headings 4 and 5 are undecipherable; see Mercati (1941), 66–67.
6 Cf. Lk. 14:26–27; Mt. 10:37–38. Luke adds "and his own soul" (or "life") to the list of ties which must be abandoned; the list of relationships as presented in Luke and Matthew is also considerably truncated here.
7 Mt. 10:34.
8 An amalgam of Mt. 12:47 and Lk. 8:20.
9 Mk. 10:18; Lk. 18:19.

BOOK 2 65

10. What is the meaning of: "Have pity on my son, for he is a lunatic"?[10]

11. What is the meaning of: "If I bear witness concerning myself, it is not true"?[11]

12. What is the meaning of: "*Eliem' ele lima sabachthaneï*;[12] into your hands I turn over my spirit"?[13]

13. What is the meaning of: "Coming to Jesus, they did not break his legs"?[14]

14. Why, having risen, he did not appear to Pilate.

15. What is the meaning of: "The ruler of this world will be cast out"?[15]

16. What is the meaning of: "You are of your father, the Accuser"?[16]

18. 1. [17]<"if one wishes> to throw himself into <so many and such great> struggles, let him first read my command, which I firmly decreed with strong maxims and fearful injunctions on account of the toilsome[18] nature

---

10 Mt. 17:15.

11 Jn. 5:31.

12 Mt. 27:46. The scribe who composed this heading used a transliteration different from that of the received text and the text as quoted at 2.23.3 below (i.e. "*Eloeim, eloeim, lema sabachthaneï*").

13 Lk. 23:46. The heading presents Mt. 27:46 and Lk. 23:46 as though a single saying, rather than two alternatives for Jesus's last words.

14 Jn. 19:33.

15 Jn. 12:31. Here and again in 2.26.1 and 2.31.1 the quotation does not follow the received text (ἐκβληθήσεται, or "will be outcast") but the variant βληθήσεται ἔξω, or "will be cast out," a variant found in Codex Bezae. For a similar variant reading also found in Codex Bezae see 2.23.6. On the significance of variant readings generally in the *Apocriticus* see the Introduction.

16 Jn. 8:44. Here we translate ἐκ τοῦ πατρὸς τοῦ διαβόλου, as two genitives in apposition ("of your father, the Accuser"). This is how the Hellene understands the passage in the objection in 2.27.1–3. Macarius, however, reads the passage as "of the father of the Accuser" in his response at 2.32.1–3.

17 The Athens manuscript begins in the middle of one of Macarius's many apologetic *ethopoiiai* (Latin: *serminocationes*) —the rhetorical practice of crafting a speech that demonstrates a subject's character and supports the rhetor's argument. This speech-in-character (2.18.1–5) responds to the Hellene's criticism of Mt. 10:34 ("I have not come to bring peace upon the earth, but a sword"). The *pinax* of Book I (q.v.) indicates that this was the seventh topic raised by the Hellene; thus, along with the Hellene's first discourse the first six portions (just over one-half) of Macarius's first discourse have also been lost.

18 "Toilsome" translates ἐναγώνιον, which might also be rendered "competitive." The

of the matter, and let him take in hand and count upon his fingers,[19] and then let him reckon more precisely within his mind, that when one soldiers in such a battle one ought to disregard one's father and mother, and push aside the charms of one's children and wife,[20] and to spurn brotherly and familial relations, and finally, to abominate one's own life according to the flesh,[21] and to take up the armour of God,[22] and do battle against the treacherous phalanx of Beliar,[23] setting aside every corporeal thought and stripping off every earthly care for the flesh. For I do not summon corporeal beings for an incorporeal battle, nor do I arm earthly beings against spiritual beings.[24] 2. For if I did this, I would seem to be drunken with ignorance, and thoughtlessly to do what ignorant people do, and to differ in no way from little children who, building a wall upon delicate sand, pulverize the basis of their work before it begins, thus laughably erecting not a wall, but a plaything.[25]

3. Hence, lest we be laughed at as we soldier against the sly serpent and arm ourselves against invisible enemies, let us look first at the nature of this engagement and consider carefully in our mind the manner of the battle, in order that we complete the contest on the appointed day and, having protected everything with the new 'breastplate of faith,'[26] slough off this flesh like scales. 4. Let us cast off the memory of our temporal father, <for> an eternal Father will call us after our victory and an [eternal] Mother will gladly welcome us.[27] But let us despise the love of a wife and

---

description of the ascetic life as an athletic contest (ἀγών) or combat was commonplace in early Christian ascetic literature (e.g. Athanasius, *Life of Antony* 5–7; Evagrius, *Eulogius* 2).

19 For a description of a mode of counting upon one's fingers, see *Gospel of Truth* (Nag Hammadi Codices I.3.32.4–11), where integers and tens are counted on the left hand, hundreds on the right.

20 Cf. Mt. 10:37, 19:29; Lk. 14:26.

21 Cf. Lk. 14:26.

22 Cf. Eph. 6:13.

23 Cf. 2 Cor. 6:15 ("What agreement has Christ with Belial?"). In the Hebrew Bible the word "belial" (often in the phrase "sons of belial" [e.g. Dt. 13:13, 1 Sam. 2:12, etc.]) is a compound adjective meaning "without worth/worthless," but among early Jews and Christians it was also taken as the proper name of a wicked demon ("Belial" or "Beliar") as in 2 Cor. 6:15 and in the present passage.

24 Cf. Eph. 6:1; 1 Pet. 4:1.

25 Mingling an echo of Eph. 4:14 with a well-known parable in which the Gospel is likened to the stable foundation of a house (Mt. 7:24–27; Lk. 6:47–49).

26 Cf. 1 Thess. 5:8.

27 The "heavenly mother" here may be a reference to the heavenly Jerusalem; see, for example Paul's allegorical reading of "Hagar" and "Sarah" (Galatians 4:24–26 [NRSV]):

BOOK 2 67

dearest ones, for much more than these, a resplendent community that has no end, with its own good people and children, will embrace us after we have nobly gained the prize for valour.[28] Let us entirely forget our brothers and relatives, for instead of them, angels, <***>[29] and the whole family of heaven, seeing us victorious, will regard us with affection.[30] Let us not take thought at all for our precarious salvation here in this form; rather, let us abhor the fact that we live in the flesh. For a life that is pure will look upon us after we have succeeded. For he who wishes to be victorious over the battle line of sin and to be inscribed in the register of my Kingdom[31] must assume such an attitude.

5. But if one is not protected in this way or by such counsel, nor strengthened his mind with such words, but holds fast to sympathy for the body of clay[32] and is caught up in the snares of corporeal concerns, and is made womanish by the love and charm of a wife and loves his temporal and earthly father here below more than the imperishable and eternal Father, he is 'not worthy'[33] to be enrolled among my *hoplites*. Let not this one 'walk behind me'[34] on my path. This one does not withstand my enemies' battle line. This one is unable to break through the phalanx of evil. This one is already easily despoiled[35] before the engagement. This one is a pitiful sight before the battle. This one, though living, has already died in his soul and once dead, does not rise. This one cannot be healed from his self-inflicted

---

"Now this is an allegory: these women are two covenants. One woman, in fact, is Hagar, from Mount Sinai, bearing children for slavery. Now Hagar is Mount Sinai in Arabia and corresponds to the present Jerusalem, for she is in slavery with her children. But the other woman corresponds to the Jerusalem above; she is free, and she is our mother. It is also possible, that the "mother" is Christ; see e.g. Lk. 13:34 (NRSV), where Jesus likens himself to a mother hen: "Jerusalem, Jerusalem, the city that kills the prophets and stones those who are sent to it! How often have I desired to gather your children together as a hen gathers her brood under her wings, and you were not willing!"

28 Cf. 2 Tim. 4:7, though Macarius here adopts the verb ἀριστεύω ("to excel in valour"), as at *Iliad* 6.206, etc.

29 There is a *lacuna* here. Goulet notes that the parallel structure calls for a verb in order to balance the phrase.

30 Cf. Lk. 15:7.

31 Cf. Ps. 69:28; Rev. 20:12–15.

32 Cf. Gen. 2:7.

33 Cf. Mt. 10:37.

34 Cf. Mt. 10:38.

35 "Despoiled" translates the singular λάφυρον, which usually appears in the plural ("spoils"); Macarius means that the distracted soldier can be considered defeated (and consequently despoiled of his weapons and armour) before the battle begins.

wound. This one is embattled with passion before the contests. This one is a slave among slaves and the footman of slaves—hence one such as this 'is not worthy of me.'"

6. This is what he [Christ] would say to those wanting to receive the heavenly armour. But as to what honours are won by those who soldiered honourably out of yearning for the eternal Kingdom, once they had despised this life here below that is full of suffering, it is possible to see their achievement by their very deeds. As [for example] the blessed martyrs, who in that season held onto this command as a steadfast and indestructible shield,[36] bested many-faceted trials by means of preparation, and pacified the manifold war of the passions. They repelled innumerable enemy attacks. They destroyed unspeakable hordes of evils, having faith as their sword and the Cross as their weapon,[37] [the weapon] by which every shield of the tyrants was cut to pieces, by which the tribes of armed demons fell, by which the world was defeated[38] and cowered in fear, by which the missiles of evil were shattered, by which the arms of deceit were demolished.

7. For though they were cut off in the very midst of a phalanx full of fearful enemies, the martyrs spared neither father, nor mother, nor their imploring children, nor wife, but neither did they take pity on themselves by asking for mercy, but, as though urged on by a single call and one trumpet blast, they did not reject the Cross, but with it battled nobly up to the moment when they put off their corporeal garment and received the incorporeal glory of confession[39]—clearly, that is, on account of the salvific and blessed voice that says: "If someone wants to come with me, let him deny himself and take up his cross and follow me."[40]

8. This, then, is the sharpened sword that gleams with desire for the incorruptible Kingdom, by which fathers have been separated from their children and daughters have left their mothers—as Thecla left Theocleia[41]—

36 Cf. Eph. 6:16.
37 Cf. Mt. 10:38; Lk. 14:27. See also Eph. 6:13–17 (NRSV): "Therefore take up the whole armour of God, so that you may be able to withstand on that evil day, and having done everything, to stand firm. Stand therefore, and fasten the belt of truth around your waist, and put on the breastplate of righteousness. As shoes for your feet put on whatever will make you ready to proclaim the gospel of peace. With all of these, take the shield of faith, with which you will be able to quench all the flaming arrows of the evil one. Take the helmet of salvation, and the sword of the Spirit, which is the word of God."
38 Cf. Jn. 16:33.
39 Cf. 1 Tim. 6:12 with 1 Cor. 15:53–54 and 2 Cor. 5:1–4.
40 Mt. 16:24.
41 The story of Thecla circulated as a long episode in the *Acts of Paul*, but also separately

BOOK 2 69

and a brother has denied his love for his brothers. 9. Often, therefore, in various trials and contests, chaste daughters who have been persuaded by the saving teaching have been cut off from their maternal community in some way,[42] as though receiving the promise of the commonwealth above as a sword that cuts and divides. Others who were the objects of desire rejected the custom and manner of their mothers for the sake of virginity and honourable purity, gladly accepting the incisive word of instruction that is like a sword.[43] Sons of renowned men and famous residents of populous cities,[44] having rejected the custom of ancestral laws, have converted to the ascetic life, ascending through the struggle of continence to the acropolis of the heavenly virtues,[45] having been happily separated from their paternal habits by the evangelical teaching. Nor do their fathers become angry when they see this, nor are their mothers vexed or their brothers embittered.

10. You can traverse the cities of the East and, in a word, the districts of Syria[46] and learn more precisely of the matter about which I speak.[47] For example, those who live in the royal metropolis of Antiochus[48] are divided

---

as the text now commonly known as the *Acts of Paul and Thecla*. For an introduction and English translation see Elliot (1993), 350–389.

42 In the *Acts of Paul and Thecla*, upon hearing Paul preach virginity, Thecla breaks off her planned marriage to Thamyris, garnering his ire and causing a bitter conflict with her mother, Theocleia, and forcing Thecla to flee her hometown of Iconium. On the prominence of Thecla in late antiquity, especially in Asia Minor, see Davis (2001).

43 Cf. Hebrews 4:12 (NRSV): "Indeed, the word of God is living and active, sharper than any two-edged sword, piercing until it divides soul from spirit, joints from marrow; it is able to judge the thoughts and intentions of the heart."

44 The Athens manuscript reads: υἱοὶ δὲ καὶ κρίτων ἀνδρῶν καὶ ναΐδων πόλεων οἰκήτορες ἔνδοξοι. We have followed Goulet's proposed emendation of ἐκκρίτων for καὶ κρίτων; the translation of ναΐδων, as "populous" is suggested by Lampe (PGL), who cites this passage in Macarius; it appears to derive from the verb ναίω ("dwell" or "populate"). We have followed Goulet, who lets ναΐδων stand, against Palm (1959–1960), who suggests the emendation λογάδων ("elites" or "renowned men") (υἱοὶ δὲ ἀνδρῶν καὶ ναΐδων πόλεων οἰκήτορες ἔνδοξοι).

45 Macarius may be the first Christian writer to use this metaphor, though Clement (*Pedagogue* 2.3) had spoken of an acropolis of wickedness.

46 In the Athens manuscript, a marginal comment here reads "Concerning the districts of Syria."

47 Scholarly opinion is divided as to whether Macarius's account of asceticism in Antioch should be taken as indicative of the place of the text's composition. Opinion also differs as to whether Macarius is describing a formalized "monasticism" or ascetic practice more generally. On these questions see the Introduction.

48 A circumlocution for Antioch, though in fact the great city of that name was founded in 300 BCE by Seleucus, the father of Antiochus I.

by their myriad attitudes about the pursuit of perfection.⁴⁹ Some gladly welcome the conjugal yoke, while others do not accept the fellowship of a wife. Some honour a soft life, others the harsh toil of a life of little food. Some insatiably pile up material resources; others love poverty as a good. Some pride themselves exceedingly on their commerce; others rejoice by feasting on difficulties. Some eagerly desire to be with courtesans; others want to dwell together with female solitaries.⁵⁰ 11. And the salvific sword that divides them without harming them separates all of them though they live as though in a single house. For it differentiates attitudes, but does not cause wounds. It usefully cuts family ties, without being the cause of any suffering. It cleaves but makes no cut on those whom it cleaves. For it does not slice bodies, but without causing suffering it transforms one's choice of life and one's policy.

12. But if you want to take the passage noetically,⁵¹ see the man cut off from his father as the chorus of the apostles separated from the Law, while

---

49 Goulet ([2003], 385) notes that Eusebius of Emesa (*Homily* 26 [*On why the Lord said: I have come not to bring peace on earth*]) similarly employs antitheses and *asyndeton* to contrast ascetic and worldly lives.

50 "With female solitaries" translates μονηρίαις, a hapax that, standing as it does in parallel construction with ἑταίραις ("with courtesans, "prostitutes," or «female companions"), appears to indicate a type of female ascetic or a residence housing female ascetics. Etymologically, the word may derive either from μόνος ("alone," "solitary") or μονή ("dwelling," "residence"; a word that Macarius uses several times in the *Apocriticus*); if the latter, then the contrast may be between "the houses of prostitutes" and "the residences of female ascetics." Goulet ([2003], 59) suggests that that it may be Macarius' term for συνείσακται, or, in Latin, *subintroductae*, female ascetics who cohabitated with male ascetics, often in urban environments; this brand of asceticism is known especially from John Chrysostom, who staunchly criticised the practice, see, e.g. his *Instruction and Refutation Directed Against Those Men Cohabiting With Virgins* and *On the Necessity of Guarding Virginity*, both translated with notes and discussion in Clark (1982). It is also possible that, if Macarius is referring to ascetic practice in a Syrian milieu, he is translating the Syriac *îhîdāyê*, literally, "solitaries" or "single ones." This became the usual term for translating the Greek μοναχός ("monk"), though its usage in Syriac predates formalized monasticism. In Ephrem and Aphrahat, for instance, the *îhîdāyê* were ascetics who were "single" (i.e. celibate) and displayed a "singlemindedness" in their devotion. The term *Îhîdāyâ*, moreover, served as the standard Syriac version of the Greek μονογενής, and fourth-century Syriac literature also describes the *îhîdāyê* as imitating and enjoying a special relationship with the "Unique" or "Only-begotten" Son. Μονογενής, it will be recalled, is also one of the titles of Macarius's treatise (see Introduction).

51 The "noetic" sense of scripture refers to the "intellectual" significations to be discerned within the "sensible," or literal, narrative meanings of biblical passages; see, for example, Origen, *Commentary on John* 10.5.18 for this designation of the higher sense in scripture.

BOOK 2   71

"daughter" is the flesh and "mother" the circumcision, the "betrothed" is the Church, the "mother-in-law" the Synagogue, and the "sword" that cuts is evangelical grace.⁵²

19. 1. I think that is a sufficient elucidation of the passage "I have not come to bring peace upon the world, but a sword."⁵³ But we still must discuss why Christ said, "Who is my brother and sister" and then raising his hands "towards the disciples said, 'Behold, my brothers and my mother.'"⁵⁴

---

52 Goulet ([2003], 386) notes that this passage reads like a summary of an allegorical reading for which Macarius offers no further explanation. Goulet cites a catena fragment of Origen's *Commentary on Matthew* as an example of a tradition of allegorical exegesis on Mt. 10:34: "The Saviour does not give the peace of the world, which is his own [cf. Jn. 14:27], to the disciples—[a peace] which he does not cast upon those who have their minds on sensible and earthly things. But he says that a sword, the word that cuts apart, will undo the amity of soul and body, in order that the soul, giving herself to the spirit that fights 'against the flesh' [cf. Gal. 5:17] and separates believers from cheap union with unbelievers and worldly people, will be beloved by God" (Origen, *Commentary on Matthew* fr. 214). The vocabulary of Origen's exegesis ("give herself"/ἐπιδίδωμι, "union"/ἕνωσις) could be read as a nuptial metaphor, like the allegory that seems to lie behind Macarius's summary, though the former would be equating the soul with the bride, while Macarius's exegesis reads the bride as the "Church." Origen, like Macarius in the preceding passages and many other commentators on Mt. 10:34 (e.g. *Incomplete Commentary on Matthew* 25.34), also reads the "sword" in terms of the choice of life that differentiates believers from unbelievers: "When he spoke about the sensible 'sword' he did not mean to indicate the nature of the material object, but peoples' choice of life" (Origen, *Commentary on Matthew* fr. 215).

53 Mt. 10:34b.

54 Mt. 12:48–50. Pseudo-Justin, *Questions and Responses to the Orthodox*, 485.A7–C7 contains a criticism based on several of the passages Macarius addresses in his response (cf. 2.19 below) and offers a sense of the kind of argument the Hellene might have developed in his (unfortunately lost) critique. The way in which this criticism combines a critique of scriptural contradictions with a reproach of Christ's behaviour is reminiscent of other of the Hellene's attacks: "If rejecting one's parents is forbidden by Divine Scripture and he who transgresses what is forbidden is called a sinner, then how can Christ the Master be shown to be without sin, when he rejects his own parents in several places. For, on the one hand, he gives a rebuke in saying to his mother, 'What is this to me and you, woman?' [Jn. 2:4]. And on the other hand, when his mother wished to see him he called those who do the will of God his mother and brothers [cf. Mt. 12:46–50]. And again, when the womb that carried him and the breasts that nursed him were declared blessed he declared blessed those who do the will of God [cf. Lk. 11:27–28]. All of which is thought to have been said by him out of disrespect for his mother, because, when his mother was named and declared blessed, others were declared blessed by him in opposition to her. And it is clearly in opposition because he ascribes [these blessings] to opposite things. In any case, if he chose the holy virgin to play a role in so great an economy, how can the virgin be thought unworthy of a blessing, as she is according to the aforementioned passages? But if the statements are contradictory to one another, how do the statements that contradict one another cause each other's dissolution?" Harnack prints

2. Many of the Jews, especially the more rash among them, not understanding clearly the plan of his becoming human, supposed that he was a mere man and that he possessed nothing more than a human being. Hence, because they had assumed such an opinion about him and thought there was nothing more divine in him and did not want to look out from behind the curtain or "veil,"[55] [Christ], blaming their blindness, reproached their folly, which came from stupidity for daring to steal the glory of the Only-Begotten, all but calling out and bridling their unbridled tongue, saying:

3. "Who is my brother, if I am the Only-begotten? And who, moreover, is the mother who stands outside of him who is motherless? For tell me, what mother has given birth to the Creator who resides within creation?[56] Who wrapped in swaddling clothes the Craftsman who is without birth?[57] Who can be called his older or younger brother? Look how in ignorance you run riot[58] with your unrestricted tongue against what is immaculate. Look how out of season you whisper unseasonable things. Look what damage you do in your stupidity. You have grasped nothing beyond appearance, but you judge and condemn what you see—and seeing a man you think that is all he is. 4. Tell us, then, holding nothing back, who, throughout the ages, who, as you say, has known brothers and a mother, ever took a dead man from his bier, raising him up?[59] What man, throughout the ages, ever walked upon the sea, treading it as if it were dry land? What man, throughout the ages, who had brothers and a mother and relatives ever raised from the dead a man dead for four days?[60] What mere man, of the same kind as his fellows, throughout the ages, ever removed leprosy from a body like

---

this passage as fragment 53a in his edition of Porphyry's *Against the Christians*; however, he notes that this ascription is conjectural.

55 Cf. 2 Cor. 3:14 ("Indeed, to this very day, when they hear the reading of the old covenant, that same veil is still there, since only in Christ is it set aside" [NRSV]) and Heb. 10:20 (where Christ's flesh is likened to the curtain or "veil" concealing the Holy of Holies in the Temple).

56 Compare the *sermocinatio* ascribed to Christ in the Anonymous *Incomplete Commentary on Matthew (Opus Imperfectum in Matthaeum)* (PG 56: 791): "'*And who is my mother and my brothers?*' [Mt. 12:28]. I know no parents in the world, I who before the constitution of the world created the world. I know no beginning from the flesh (as Photinus thinks), I who was in the beginning with God [Jn. 1:2]."

57 Cf. Lk. 2:7, 12.

58 Accepting Goulet's emendation ἐπικωμάζετε for ἀποκωμάζετε; Goulet notes that the latter is a *hapax*, while the former appears in three other passages in the *Apocriticus* (2.32.8; 3.8.11; 3.15.5).

59 Cf. Lk. 7.11–17.

60 Jn. 11:1–44.

scales and spread over that flesh a fresh skin?[61] What man with blood in his veins, throughout the ages, ever transformed the nature of water into dry wine?[62] What man, throughout the ages, having made whole a man who was lying palsied and motionless on a bed, ever caused him to run like a deer?[63] What man, throughout the ages, ever fed five thousand hungry people in the desert with only five loaves of bread and two fish?[64] What man, throughout the ages, ever healed ten lepers and then sent them on their way to purification, using invisible power?[65] What man, throughout the ages, ever called back to health a myriad crowd suffering from every kind of illness and malady at one time, overlooking no one?[66] What man, throughout the ages, having fulfilled what yet needed completion, ever also promised to fulfil things to come?

5. But if no one [ever did these things]—for there never was, is, or ever will be a mere man capable of such things—how do you not stop yourselves when you babble that the only-begotten Son of God is a mere man[67] who has brothers? And are you not made timid by the deeds that you see him doing? Have the dead who now live not taught you that they rose from their tombs because they perceived the voice not of a mere man but of God?[68] Did not the man who was blind from birth explain to you that he saw the light not of a man, but of God?[69] 6. Even though he was blind in body he saw the one who had come with the eyes of his soul, but you who see the lightning-like flash[70] of such power do not know the one present, but as

---

61 Mt. 8:1–4.
62 Jn. 2:1–11.
63 Mt. 9:1–8.
64 Mt. 14:13–21.
65 Lk. 17:11–19.
66 Cf. Mt. 8:16.
67 The notion that Christ was a "mere man," or "psilanthropism," was associated by early Christian heresiologists with, among others, the Ebionites (see e.g. Eusebius, *Ecclesiastical History* 3.27.2) and Paul of Samosata (see Eusebius, *Ecclesiastical History* 7.30.11), see also 3.14.13 below.
68 Cf. Mt. 27:52–53.
69 For the healing of the man blind from birth, see Jn. 9:1–34. Macarius infers that the blind man identifies Jesus as God from Jn. 1:30–31 ("You do not know where he comes from, and yet he opened my eyes. We know that God does not listen to sinners, but he does listen to one who worships him and obeys his will" [NRSV]). We have not followed Goulet's conjecture of a missing preposition here (ἀπό), which would render "not from a man but from God."
70 Cf. Lk. 17.24: "For as the lightning flashes and lights up the sky from one side to the other, so will the Son of Man be in his day" (NRSV).

though stumbling about in this sightlessness think he has brothers and a mother.[71] So, as though to blind people I too say that 'He who does the will of my Father, this one is my brother and my mother.'[72] 7. For he who does the will of the Father—and I will what the Father wills—I say that this one has the goodwill of a brother and mother. For like a mother he gives birth to me, when he joins with me in doing the will of the Father, and is born together with me, not coming to be in the essence of a *hypostasis*,[73] but united [to me] in the grace of the will. For he who does the will of my Father, in communion with this action, gives birth to me and is born together with me.[74] For one who believes me to be the Unique Son of God in a way gives birth to me by faith, though not essentially, being mystically present together with the one born."[75]

8. Christ would likely have said these things to those who spoke

---

71 The belief that Mary remained a virgin forever, and hence that Jesus's siblings mentioned in the gospels (e.g. Mt. 12:46; Mt. 13:55; Mk. 6:3) were not literal siblings born of the same mother, had been argued since the time of Origen (*Homilies on Leviticus* 8.3), and was defended in the fourth century by, for example, Jerome (esp. *Against Helvidius* 16, a well-known argument based on an idiosyncratic interpretation of the term "brethren") and Epiphanius (*Panarion* 78.7.9–10). In implying, however, that Mary was not truly the mother of the Word, Macarius falls into language that would have been deemed heretical after the Council of Ephesus (431 CE) had affirmed that Mary was the *Theotokos*, or mother of God, insofar as he took his flesh from her in becoming human.

72 Mt. 12:50.

73 Cf. 1 Cor. 6:17. Macarius wishes to forestall any notion that the elect can be sons of God in the same sense as Christ (that is, hypostatically). That what Christ does in the flesh is done for the sake of humans, and that the faithful are eternally one with him through the flesh, is nonetheless a commonplace: see Gregory Nazianzen, *Third Theological Oration*; Gregory of Nyssa, *Against Eunomius* 5.5. Compare also Gregory of Nyssa, *Against Eunomius* 8.2, where the Father's "willing" of the Son is contrasted with creative acts of the human will; the former does not imply any temporal or spatial separation of essence between begetter and begotten, whereas what is willed by humans obtains in time and space.

74 Alluding perhaps to Jn. 1:13: "But to all who received him, who believed in his name, he gave power to become children of God" (NRSV).

75 Compare the *Incomplete Commentary on Matthew (Opus Imperfectum in Matthaeum)* PG 56: 791: "And holding out his hand towards the apostles, he said 'Behold my mother and my brothers' [Mt. 12:49]. He did not give this response spurning corporeal generation or blushing at human generation, but because he wanted to show that spiritual relationships must be placed before corporeal. Now corporeal relationships partake neither in our will or knowledge. Now, none of you are accustomed to think about whose son you are or whose relation; but one acquires a spiritual relative for himself intentionally through faith. For the obedience through which one wills to do the will of the Father is voluntary. He is made a son of the Father and a brother of Christ."

nonsense—not singling out Peter, Judas, or some other of the disciples by name, but saying universally: "He who does the will of the Father."[76]

20. 1. Enough concerning these matters, but let us also elucidate for you that question about the passage that says "No one is good except God alone"[77] and that which states: "The good man brings forth the good from the good storehouse of the heart."[78] See, please, how here Jesus clearly differentiates himself from men, saying: "No one is good except God alone." But Christ is unambiguously God, as John says "And the Word was God,"[79] and the Saviour himself, indicating the *hypostasis* of his own Godhead said, "I and the Father are one,"[80] so the one saying these things is incontrovertibly God. 3. For what reason, then, when he is God, did he deny being good, saying: "No one is good except God alone. Why do you call me good?"[81]

4. If you will genuinely pay attention to what is said, that which is sought by many and is a basis for vain babbling will clearly and easily be understood. A young man, fair in outward show, was sketching a constitution[82] for righteous living in the Saviour's presence, thinking that he who had become human on account of men was the equal of other men and enjoyed nothing greater than mortal ancestry. 5. But, being ostentatious, this young man often tricked many people, receiving praise from many

---

76 Mt. 12:50.
77 Mk. 10:18; Lk. 18:19. The verse troubled those who wished to uphold the Nicene assertion of the full divinity of the Son. Basil of Caesarea, *Letter* 25, contends, like Macarius here, that it is intended to differentiate the Godhead from humanity, not the Father from the Son.
78 Lk. 6:45.
79 Jn. 1:1.
80 Jn. 10:30.
81 Lk. 18:19.
82 "Constitution" translates πολίτευμα, which in classical usage refers to the institutions of a *polis* or other community (e.g. Plato, *Laws* 945d; Aristotle, *Politics* 1278b11, where it is synonymous with πολιτεία, or "polity"). The term appears in the Pauline corpus at Phil. 3:20 ("But our citizenship [πολίτευμα] is in heaven" [NRSV]). In philosophical circles, the term is used to refer to a shared philosophical way of life. In early Christian literature, the term can refer to the "constitution," "citizenship," and by extension, to the "community" of the ascetic way of life (e.g. *History of the Monks in Egypt* 11.34), as well as to the Christian community and its way of life more broadly (e.g. Eusebius, *Gospel Preparation* 12.33.3 ["the pious polity"] and *Ecclesiastical History* 5.proem.4; Basil of Caesarea, *On the Holy Spirit* 23; Gregory Nazianzus, *Oration* 33.12). We have opted for "constitution" rather than the more general "way of life" because here as elsewhere in early Christian literature the term connotes an ascetic way of life that is understood to have been prescribed or legislated by Christ.

people as though he was doing well, and thinking that the Lord was one of these many and approaching him not as God but as a man he addressed him, saying: "Good teacher."[83] Then, in response to him who had such an opinion about him, he said:

6. [84] "Why do you say that I am 'good,'[85] thinking that I am a mere man? You stumble, young man, in assuming a human opinion about me and addressing me as 'good.' For what is 'good' in the proper sense does not exist among men, but only in God. In your sense I deny that I am 'good,' if I am considered to be a man, for if you had thought that the unadulterated nature of God is in me, you would have seen fit[86] to confess that I am the nature of the good, and I would not have balked. But since you have unwittingly stolen that which is good by nature and irrationally given your suffrage to what is good by relation,[87] you will not have me as an accomplice for your theft through my agreement. 7. For do not assume that we have ever used the definition of the good in an uncritical way. Even though we have said 'The good man brings forth the good from the good storehouse,'[88] we name the man 'good' not by nature but, rather, by relation, when through participation[89] in the good he does something good. 8. For as

---

83 Lk. 18:19; Mk. 10:17.
84 Compare 2.20.6–10 and the *Incomplete Commentary on Matthew (Opus Imperfectum in Matthaeum)* PG 56: 806: "Jesus said to them, 'Why do you say that I am good. No one is good except God alone.' Was he, therefore, not himself good, when he was the Son of God? Because as he was the Son of God he was also God and likewise, as Son, from the fact that God is good, the Son of God is himself also without doubt good in so far as he is the Son of the good. And while the Jewish people had knowledge of the One God, they did not want to know Christ as the Son of God or as God. For this reason he rejects the praise addressed to him, because he called him 'good' not as God is good but as a man is good, which he would not have done if he had called him 'good' as God is good. And truly, for the Jews who venerated the One God and did not know Christ the Son of God, no one was Good except God alone. But among the faithful, in fact, just as the One God the Father is Good so too is the Uniquely-begotten Son no less Good."
85 Lk. 18:18; Mk. 10:17.
86 The Athens manuscript reads ἔκριναν, corrected as ἔκρινας. Goulet, following Palm, suggests correcting the reading to ἔκρινα, which would give the reading: "I would have decided to confess that I am the nature of the good, and I would not have balked"; the correction is plausible, but so is the manuscript, so we have followed it.
87 The term θέσις, in opposition to φύσις or "nature," often means "by convention"; here, however, Macarius appears to have in mind Aristotle's placing of θέσις ("position") within the category "relative" (πρός τι) (Aristotle, *Categories* 6a37, 6b12); Macarius also uses the term at 4.26.4 (q.v.) in his discussion of the appellations "God" and "god."
88 Lk. 6:45.
89 "Participation" translates μετουσία, a term used to describe the soteriological

fire is 'hot' and what is near fire is named 'hot,' the former is so by nature but the latter is named 'hot' by relation: it is not the case that homonymy, by stealing the truth, conveys a single notion of the fact, but that the difference of natures is wont to distinguish the homonyms.[90] So too if one names both the Creator 'good' and what is created 'good,' he makes clear that the former is good in itself but the latter by virtue of another. 9. Hence a man is 'good,' not because he has acquired this by virtue of his own nature, but because he obtains this advantage by virtue of another. God, however, is good not because he has received or obtained this from another, but is what he is by nature, unchangeably and eternally good."

10. Accept this distinction concerning the good so that Christ will not seem to have contradicted his own word when he said: "No one is good except God alone."[91] For it is God alone, he says, who is and subsists as what is good by nature, properly good, the prototypical Good, the eternal Good, the unchangeably Good; whereas what is good by relation, changeably good, unstably good, alterably good, this he rightly says of the man, as also in the case of any of the created beings, for instance a fish or an egg,[92] when he says: "You know to give good gifts to your children."[93]

---

relationship of humans to Christ. For example, Methodius of Olympus writes (*Symposium* 8.8): "... those who have been baptized in Christ having become christs by participation in the Spirit"; for a usage similar to Macarius's see e.g. Gregory of Nyssa, *Homily 4 on the Song of Songs* 124: "For virtue means not only seeing the good and becoming so through participation in this higher thing, but being preserved unchangeably in the good." The term μετουσία was rejected as a valid description of the Son's relationship with the Father by fourth-century orthodox Christians; e.g. Athanasius, *Oration 1 against the Arians* 15, ascribing such a position to the Arians: "According to you [i.e. Arians], the Son is from what does not exist ... and he is certainly called 'Son,' 'God,' and 'Wisdom' by participation." Macarius therefore knows better than to say that the divine Son is good by participation in the Father; his argument that, insofar as Christ is man, he is good by participation in the Godhead, would have satisfied his contemporary Theodore of Mopsuestia, though not those (later vindicated by ecumenical councils in 431 and 451) who maintained that Jesus of Nazareth was strictly identical with the incarnate Word.

90 "When things have only a name in common and the definition of essence which corresponds to the name is different, they are called homonyms" (Aristotle, *Categories* 1a1). Macarius also uses the example of the predication "hot" in 4.26.1 (q.v.) to explain homonymous predications of the word "god." Goulet ([2003], 386) points to a comparison here with Eusebius of Emesa, *On Faith* 25: "We must not confuse difference in nature based on shared names."

91 Lk. 18:19; Mk. 10:18.
92 Cf. Lk. 11:11–12.
93 Lk 11:13; Mt. 7:11.

21. 1. Let us next examine the meaning of the passage which says: "Have pity on my son, because he is a lunatic."[94] For it was not the moon that harassed this man, but a demon.[95] And let us not deem it trivial when we hear this also: "O faithless generation, how long will I be with you?"[96] 2. For what reason did the crowd need to hear this statement, when one person made the request, even if he was mistaken in his request? Why, then, when the father pitifully pleaded for his son on his knees[97] did he [Christ] answer, replying in a critical tone not to him alone but to the crowds as well?[98] 3. Was it not necessary, rather, to receive the petition gladly, a petition made out of compassion for the boy who was suffering? But on the contrary, he cursed the entreaty of the suppliants; for Christ seems irrationally to insult the people in an overt way.

4. But let us not attend only to the surface of what was said [i.e. by the boy's father], but let us consider the evil hidden in this matter. What then? The serpent, who is called a demon, being cunning and deceitful, was torturing the boy's body inhumanely, by depicting manifold terrifying and fearful apparitions, while he resourcefully whipped up the souls of those telling of the event, leading the unscrupulous to assume an attitude inimical to God. 5. For, approaching the boy at the turning, or rather, returning of the moon's cycle, he effected great and unendurable fury, such that he would pitiably throw him into water or fire,[99] and mercilessly harass him with great mania, so that those who saw him thought the child was suffering this not from a demon but was tortured by the cycle of the moon, based on their careful observations, for the wicked demon attacked the youth each time the light of the moon returned. And, furthermore, from this at first a secret but in a short time an open blasphemy came to develop, when those who love cavilling said that, "Based on what we have learned, the Creator did not create the cycle of the moon as a good creation, but for the ruin of the human flock. 6. For behold, the moon's natural principle is deadly and exceedingly inhumane, but as it is we must not hold the moon

---

94 Mt. 17:15.
95 Like the word "lunatic," the Greek σεληνιαζόμενος means "moonstruck." Macarius's contemporary John Chrysostom is also at pains to point out, in *Homilies on Matthew* 57.3, that this term is a libel on the Creator, and is employed by the evangelist only because he is acting as a faithful scribe to the speech of the deluded father.
96 Mt. 17:17.
97 Mt. 17:14.
98 Mt. 17:17–18.
99 Mt. 17:15; Mk. 9:22.

accountable, but rather the one who created and fashioned this thing that is so harmful and inimical to us and crafted a vessel that is the cause of destruction."

7. The demon busied himself with this so that he could savagely harass the child's body, and at the same time prompt a criminal blasphemy against the Creator among those who observed it, thus effecting a double wound with a single blow: harming the souls of a myriad crowd through one person and through what is visible firing a volley of arrows against what is invisible.

8. Since, therefore, they did not believe the moon was created for good but fancied that it was produced for harm, and the starting point for this evil lay in their observation of the boy under demonic influence, for this reason Christ strongly deemed those unhappy who were secretly ill along with the demoniac in their souls, and chastised the infirmity of their lack of faith, saying:

9. "'O faithless generation,'[100] unstable in judgment, which fancies that people are made insane by the moon, that libels the Creator through the creation, and dares blame the Maker on account of what he has made! 'Bring him here to me,'[101] for the infirmity does not belong to one, but many. 10. And once he has been healed, your souls will be healed, when you understand that the suffering of the invalid did not come from the moon but from a spirit, and after it has departed the child will be seen to be healthy, he will make your wickedness public, namely that you falsely accused the moon based in an uneducated opinion."

11. But if Matthew says that a "lunatic" was brought to Christ it was not because he was ignorant that the moon did not cause the malady that he thought it correct to write this, he expressed what he had heard as he heard it; for this is characteristic of a historian, to state [exactly] what he heard and saw, not what is actually the case.[102]

22. 1. Let it be that the question raised on this subject has been handled well, if in fact it pleases you who have been liberally educated to accept a liberal teaching.[103] But let us examine this one as well, inquiring carefully as to

---

100 Mt. 17:17.
101 Mt. 17:17.
102 Macarius does not mean that a historian reports falsehood; rather, he means that an eyewitness historical account (as he assumes Matthew's gospel is) merely reports verbatim what was seen and heard, without any interpretation or correction. Cf. Lk. 1:1–3, which claims that the gospel has been transmitted by eyewitnesses.
103 Macarius's play on words is difficult to capture in English: the Hellene enjoys

what [Christ] means in saying: "If I bear testimony concerning myself, the testimony is not true."[104]

2. For a man testifying on his own behalf is not true, but on the contrary, God, based on his works, is true when he testifies concerning himself.[105] For saying "I am the light and the truth"[106] would not accord with a man, but only with God, who is by nature life and light and immortality.[107]

3. Since, then, Christ, who was saying these things and things akin to them, was thought by the Jews not to be God but a mere man, he refutes the unfitly rendered estimate.[108] For when they decided that the inspired works were accomplished by human power, the divine portion was overturned as though it had not become human. But the mortal nature would have received no benefit if this was not the case.[109] If this opinion held sway, the risk was that the mystery of the divine economy would collapse and there would be a worse shipwreck[110] in the world and that everything would be dashed to pieces by a huge wave, if God was present and what he did divine, but these events had the testimony of a man.

4. Hence, in so far as he was human, he declined to bear witness to himself, but sought testimony from God, while in so far as he was God he did not stumble[111] in bearing witness to himself, saying "I am the light of the world and the life and the truth,"[112] for no one other than he himself[113]

---

the education of a free man (is "liberally [ἐλευθέρως] educated"), so he should accept a teaching that is "of freedom/liberal [ἐλευθερίας]." Macarius may well tap the polyvalence of ἐλευθερία here: the Hellene should accept the explanation to follow because it accords with liberal education, and he should also accept it because, as it concerns the soteriological implications of the passage in question (e.g. 2.22.3 below), the Hellene can be soteriologically "liberated" by accepting it.

104   Jn. 5:31.
105   Cf. Jn. 5:36.
106   Jn. 8:12, 9:5, 14:6.
107   Cf. Jn. 11:25.
108   As the discussion in 2.22.5–6 below makes clear, this refers to the Pharisees' estimate of him (e.g. Jn. 8:13), unfitly rendered because they reckon him a mere man.
109   That is, if God did not assume what was human, humanity would not have been drawn into corporate union with the sanctifying Word; compare, for example, Eusebius of Caesarea, *Theophany* 57–59; Athanasius, *On the Incarnation* 8–9; Cyril of Jerusalem, *Catechetical Lectures* 12.15.
110   Cf. 1 Tim. 1:19: "By rejecting conscience, certain persons have suffered shipwreck in the faith" (NRSV).
111   Macarius explains the metaphor below at 2.22.8.
112   Jn. 8:12, 9:5, 14:6.
113   Reading ἑαυτοῦ of the Athens manuscript against Goulet and Palm (αὐτῷ).

has given these testimonies, for the glory of the Almighty would have been insulted if it had received testimony from beings of an unlike[114] nature.

5. Hence, to those who were inappropriately jesting with him by saying: "You bear witness concerning yourself,"[115] he quite rightly said: "If, according to you I have borne witness as a man, the testimony is not true, but if I am not only a man but also God, I have borne witness truly, saying: 'I am the light of the world and the truth and the life.'[116] 6. For just as I perceive your estimate of me I will answer you. If as you judge, I am a mere man, the testimony that I have given is not true, but if I am God, as the divine estimate has affirmed, the word of my testimony is true. 7. I refute, then, not the saying that came from me concerning myself, but I cast aside your judgment, which pronounces Christ, who evinces prodigious powers much greater than, or rather that bear no comparison to those of a man, to be a man only. 8. If, then, you think that I bear witness concerning myself in so far as I am human, I do not do this, but I seek testimony from another. But if it is in so far as I am God, you stumble[117] greatly—for God does not stumble when he bears witness concerning himself. For who will bear witness to God when no one exists before him or with him? Who is found to be of equal age? Rather, he who is before all is one, and he speaks concerning himself and when he speaks, proclaims the truth."[118]

9. May what has been said be sufficiently clear for us, and let that be the end of this question. But if something else from the Gospels seems more perplexing, make this plain, laying it out for the audience.

23. 1. *He, becoming severe and glaring very solemnly, as he loomed at us more formidably, said*[119] *that the Evangelists were the inventors, not the historians, of the events pertaining to Jesus.*

---

114 Obliquely giving the lie to Eunomius and the "Anomoians" who maintained that the divine Son was unlike, and consequently unequal to, the Father.

115 Jn. 8:13.

116 Jn. 8:12, 9:5, 14:6.

117 For Christ as a stone that causes unbelievers to "stumble," see e.g. 1 Pet. 2:8 ("A stone that makes them stumble, and a rock that makes them fall" [NRSV]) and Rom. 9:33 ("See, I am laying in Zion a stone that will make people stumble, a rock that will make them fall, and whoever believes in him will not be put to shame.' [NRSV]), quotations of Is. 8:14 and 28:16, respectively.

118 In late ancient Roman law, witnesses of greater social standing were given greater credence (see e.g. *Codex Justinianus* 4.20.9 [334 CE]). By the later fourth century, there were also restrictions on one's ability to testify on one's own behalf (see e.g. *Codex Theodosianus* 2.21 [376 CE]).

119 Goulet translates what follows as direct discourse; it is, rather, indirect discourse, and

2.¹²⁰ For each of them wrote an account of the Passion that is not consistent, but extremely inconsistent. For one recounts that someone offered the crucified a sponge full of vinegar.¹²¹ <This is Mark.> ¹²² 3. But another recounts it differently, "Having come," he says, "to the place called Golgotha, they gave him wine mixed with gall to drink, and then having tasted it he did not want to drink,"¹²³ and a little later: "But at about the ninth hour Jesus cried out with a loud voice, saying, 'Eloeim, eloeim lema sabachthanei,' that is, 'My God, my God, why have you forsaken me?'"¹²⁴ This is Matthew. 4. But another says: "A vessel full of vinegar was lying there. Then, having bound the vessel full of vinegar to a hyssop,¹²⁵ they offered it to his mouth. Then, after he took the vinegar Jesus said, 'It is finished,' and letting his head fall he gave up the spirit."¹²⁶ This is John. 5. But another says: "And crying out with a loud voice he said, 'Father, into your hands I shall hand over my spirit.'"¹²⁷ This is Luke.

6. From this spoiled and discordant history it is possible to gather that the story is not about one sufferer but about many. For if one said, "Into your hands I shall hand over my spirit," but another, "It is finished," and another, "My God, my God, why have you forsaken me," and yet another, "God, my God, why have you reproached me?"¹²⁸ then it is clear that either this is an inharmonious fable, or it refers to many crucified people, or there was a single man who experienced a difficult death and who did not say

---

the Hellene's direct discourse begins in the next line.

120 On the Evangelists's contradictory accounts of the drink of vinegar/wine/gall compare a *testmonium* to Julian's *Against the Galilaeans* preserved in a seventeenth-century printed edition of a collection of *Catena of the Greek Fathers on the Gospel According to Mark* (Neumann fr. 14): "And they gave him wine mixed with myrrh to drink [Mk. 15:23]. Gall is most bitter to drink. What another Evangelist calls 'wine mixed with gall' this one calls 'wine mixed with myrrh.' So says Cyril in the thirteenth *kephalaion* of his *Against Julian*."
121 Cf. Mk. 15:36.
122 There is a *lacuna* here in the Athens manuscript; Goulet infers this restoration based on parallel structure.
123 Mt. 27:33–34.
124 Mt. 27:46.
125 As Macarius's response at 2.28.5 below makes clear, the Hellene reads the passage as though the vessel full of vinegar has been lifted using an implement called a "hyssop."
126 Jn. 19:29–30.
127 Lk. 23:46.
128 Mk. 15:34; the Hellene cites a variant reading—"reproached me" (ὠνείδισάς με) instead of the much more common "forsaken me" (ἐγκατέλιπές με). This variant is attested in the fifth-century Codex Bezae as well as a twelfth/thirteenth-century Old Latin version.

anything clear to those present during the Passion.¹²⁹ But if, being unable to give a truthful account of the manner of his death, these writers have entirely fabricated it, then they have also said nothing clear about anything else.

24. 1. But that they merely guessed about everything concerning his death will be shown from another passage. For John writes: "Having come to Jesus, since they saw that he had already died they did not break his legs, but one of the soldiers pierced his side with a spear, and immediately blood and water poured out."¹³⁰ 2. For only John said this, none of the others.¹³¹ Thus he also wants to provide testimony for himself, when he says: "And he who saw has borne witness and his testimony is true."¹³² 3. This seems to me to be the utterance of a bird brain!¹³³ For how can the testimony of one whose testimony concerns someone not living be true? For one bears witness about what exists, but how can a testimony be uttered about what does not exist?

25. 1. And there is another passage that can refute this teaching as unsound: that about his Resurrection, which we hear babbled about everywhere. For what reason did Jesus, after he suffered, as you say, and rose, not reveal himself to Pilate, who had punished him and said he had done nothing to merit death,¹³⁴ or to Herod, the king of the Jews, or to the High Priest of the Jewish tribe, or to many worthy of faith together, or, especially, to the Roman Senate and people,¹³⁵ in order that, being astonished at the matters concerning him, they would not with a universal

---

129 Macarius means that one experiencing a difficult, painful death may not speak coherently.

130 Jn. 19:33–34.

131 In his *Against the Galilaeans*, Julian also remarks on passages and ideas unique to John's gospel; for example, "... you say that he made the heaven and the earth—but in fact not one of the disciples dared to say this about him, except John only, and he did not say it clearly or plainly (apud Cyril, *Against Julian* 213C) and "Neither Paul, nor Matthew, nor Luke, nor Mark dared to say Jesus was God. But honest John, perceiving that a great crowd had already been infected by this disease in the cities of Greece and Italy, and hearing, I think, that the tombs of Peter and Paul, secretly, yes, but nonetheless were being worshipped, first dared to say this [i.e. that Jesus was God; Julian goes on to cite Jn. 1:14]."

132 Jn. 19:35.

133 Bird brain = κέπφος; the word refers to a type of sea bird, but was used in a comic sense by Aristophanes, *Peace* 10.67 and *Wealth* 912 (see also entry in LSJ).

134 Cf. Jn. 18:38; Lk. 23:4.

135 An echo of the official *senatus populusque Romanus*, which formally designated the "The Roman Senate and People."

decree condemn to death those who believed in him as though they were impious.[136]

2. By why, instead, did he appear to Mary Magdalene, a common woman[137] who came from some wretched little village and was once possessed by seven demons,[138] and along with this woman to another obscure Mary[139] also from a paltry village, and to a few others who were not at all notable, even though, as Matthew claims, he predicted [his appearance] to the High Priest of the Jews, saying: "Henceforth, you will see the Son of Man seated at the right hand of power and coming with the clouds"?[140] 3. For if he had revealed himself to notable men, through them all would have believed and none of the judges would have chastised <them [i.e. the Evangelists]> as fabricators of bizarre myths. For, presumably, it is acceptable neither to God nor to an intelligent man that many be subjected to the worst punishments on his account.

26. 1. But, if one also reads this pedantry written in the Gospel he will understand all too well that those statements are chimerical[141] where he [Christ] says: "Now, judgment is upon the world; now the ruler of this world will be cast out."[142]

2. For tell me, by God, what is this "judgment" that comes then and who is the "Ruler" of the world who has been cast out? For if, on the one hand, you mean the emperor, he is neither the only ruler, nor has he been cast down. For many rule the world. But if, on the other hand, [you mean]

---

136 The charge that Christ should have made post-resurrection appearances to Pilate, Herod, the high priests, and/or other powerful or well-respected people can also be found in Celsus (apud Origen, *Against Celsus* 2.63, trans. Chadwick): "... if Jesus really wanted to show forth divine power, he ought to have appeared to the very men who treated him despitefully and to the man who condemned him and to everyone everywhere."

137 Celsus also criticized Christ's post-resurrection appearance to a woman. Compare Celsus apud Origen, *Against Celsus* 2.55 (trans. Chadwick): "... but after death he rose again and showed the marks of his punishment and how his hands had been pierced. But who saw this? A hysterical female, as you say, and perhaps some other one of those who were deluded by the same sorcery ..." and 2.70 (trans. Chadwick): "... but when he would establish a strong faith after rising from the dead, he appeared secretly to just one woman and to those of his own confraternity."

138 Cf. Lk. 8:2; Mk. 16:9.
139 Cf. Mt. 28:1–10.
140 Mt. 26:64 and parallels.
141 "Chimerical" translates τερατολογία, tales that are so marvellous as to be utterly unbelievable, or even monstrous (the first term in the compound, τέρας, can mean both marvellous and monstrous).
142 Jn. 12:31.

BOOK 2   85

an intelligible and incorporeal "ruler," it is not possible for him to be cast out, for where would he be cast out, since he is ruler of the world?[143] 3. For if you say another world exists somewhere into which the one who rules will be cast, then support this with a persuasive account.[144] But if there is not another [world], since it is impossible that two worlds exist, where is the ruler cast out to, if not into the same [world] in which he exists? And how can one be thrown down into a place where he already is? Unless, to be sure, [the world] is like an earthen vessel, which, when broken, causes what is within it to be cast out of it; after all, in this case he is not cast out into a void but into another body, whether it happens to be air, earth, or something else. 4. If, once the world has been similarly broken (which is impossible), and the one in it is cast out, then what sort of space is outside, into which he will be cast? What are the characteristics of that space—its quantity or quality, height or depth or length or breadth?[145] For if these exist in it, it will be [another] world because it has them.

---

143 The Hellene's critique in this sentence is based on basic Platonic principles concerning space and place. That incorporeal beings are not in a place is a basic Platonic principle; see e.g. Porphyry, *Sentences* 1 ("Every body is in place, but none of those beings in themselves incorporeal, in so far as they are incorporeal, is in a place"). The Hellene's argument in what follows, however, does not seem to proceed from this principle. On its own, the participial clause "since he is ruler of the world" need not suggest that the "ruler" is spatially "in" the world, but merely that he is an incorporeal being (e.g. an "archon"). The reasoning of the sentences that follow, however, seems to assume that the "ruler" is located spatially within the world. In his response to this critique in 2.31.3 (q.v.). The Hellene may be equating the "ruler of the world" with the demiurge as conceived in gnostic and/or Marcionite cosmology. Platonist critics of Christianity were familiar with gnostic Christian traditions and texts; Celsus attacked Christian gnostics for positing an evil or deficient Demiurge (Origen, *Against Celsus* 5.61), while Porphyry wrote a treatise refuting the gnostic cosmological treatise *Zostrianos*, in which the "ruler of the world" is condemned to death (*Zostrianos* 9). It is thus not impossible that the Hellene has gnostic exegeses of the "ruler of this world" in view, and Macarius may be correct in thinking that the Hellene equates the "ruler" with the demiurge of certain gnostic cosmologies.

144 Platonists inferred the uniqueness of the cosmos as a consequence of its being the perfect likeness of a unique intelligible paradigm; thus Proclus commenting on *Timaeus* 31a3–4 summarizes: "If the cosmos has come into being after the Paradigm and the Paradigm is unique, the cosmos is unique" (*Commentary on Timaeus* 439.4–6 [trans. Runia and Share]). Atomists, in contrast, argued for the possibility of an infinity of worlds based on the infinity of atoms (e.g. Epicurus, *Letter to Herodotus* in Diogenes Laertius, *Lives of Emminent Philosophers* 10.45).

145 Cf. Eph. 3:18: "In order that you might be able to grasp with all the saints what is the breadth and length and height and depth ..." Macarius seems to be giving a Christian hue to this pagan diatribe: cf. Irenaeus, *Against Heresies* 2.13.1, where another reminiscence of

5. But what is the reason for casting the ruler out as a foreigner from the world? And how was he the ruler, if he is a foreigner? And how is he cast out: voluntarily or involuntarily? Involuntarily, evidently, for the statement is clear in its expression—for what is "cast out" is cast out involuntarily. But the one who does the constraining, not the one enduring the constraint, commits injustice.

6. It is right for weak women to tolerate such obscurity in the Gospels, but not for men. For if we wanted to examine such things in great detail, we could find myriad obscurities that have no reasonable explanation.

27. 1. But come, let us also hear this histrionic statement made to the Jews: "You are unable," he [Christ] says, "to hear my word, because you are of your father, the Accuser, and you want to do the desires of your father."[146]

2. Now, make it clear to us who the "Accuser" is who is the father of the Jews, for they act appropriately who accomplish the desires of their father, deferring to their father's will and honouring him. But if the father is evil, the charge of evil should not attach to the children.

3. Who, then, is this father, that by doing his desires they did not hear Christ? For although the Jews were saying, "We have one father, God," he dismissed this statement by saying, "You are of your father, the Accuser," that is, "You are from the Accuser." 4. Who, then, is this Accuser? And where does he live? And whom does he accuse that he is called by this name?[147] For he does not seem to have this as a proper name, but accidentally, as we know if we have learned as we ought.[148] For if he

---

Ephesians 3.18 introduces a satire on the Valentinian myth in which the aeons are emitted from the Godhead.

146 Jn. 8:43–44.

147 The Hellene points out the etymological relationship between διάβολος ("slanderer/false accuser," most often translated "devil" [e.g. RSV, NRSV, NIV, et al.]) and διαβολῆς ("slander/false accusation"). This is also an etymological point made by Porphyry, as witnessed by a fragment of Didymus the Blind's *Commentary on Ecclesiastes* (*Pap. Tura. Eccles.* 281.16–22). See also discussion in Goulet (2003), 145–147. For Satan's role as accuser see e.g. Zech. 3:1, Job 1:9, Jude 9.

148 It is difficult to tell whether the Hellene uses "accidently" (ἐκ τοῦ συμβεβηκότος) in a broad sense or a narrowly philosophical, Aristotelean sense. In his *Isagoge* to Aristotle's *Categories*, Porphyry defined "accident" as "items which come and go without the destruction of their subjects" (*Isagoge* 12.25–26 [trans. Barnes]); if the Hellene intends "accident" in this sense, he means that the being named "accuser" exists whether or not he is accusing, and thus is not named "accuser" essentially. But it is perhaps more likely that the Hellene uses "accident" in a broader sense that is not specifically Aristotelean; Dionysius of Halicarnassus, for instance, writes that: "[Nouns] indicate essence, while [verbs] indicate accident, and essence

BOOK 2 87

is called the "Accuser" from "accusation," between what parties did he appear and present the charge that had to be answered? 5. For the one who receives the accusation will be seen to be passive in this,[149] since the one who is calumniated will be seen as greatly injured. The Accuser himself will not appear to have acted unjustly in any way, but rather the one who has provided a cause for the accusation. 6. For as the one who places stakes in the road at night is liable, and not the pedestrian who falls, and the one who set them there receives the charge, so too the one who provides the basis for an accusation, and not the one who makes the arrest or seizes him, does more injustice.

7. But tell me this: is the Accuser passible or impassible? For if impossible, he would never have accused, but if passible, he ought to receive forbearance. For no one who is encumbered by physical ailments is judged as having committed injustice, but is pitied by all as one exhausted by troubles.[150]

{Christian}[151]

28. 1. *After this eloquent paragon of Hellenic ostentation had said all this in these declamatory terms, we, though shaken to our very soul by the clamour of his words, feared nothing. But, as we are accustomed, adamantly appealing to the Essential Word for speech, we spoke as divine grace came to our assistance, and inasmuch as the Evangelists preserved a single meaning in their differing expressions of the same history, we offered a clear interpretation, saying*:

2. No one seeks the truth in the nature of things from syllables or letters; one determines the difference of the words from the [nature of] the thing. 3. For instance, when one calls a rational being "human" and another calls it "mortal," another "articulate," and still another "man," he will say many things as respects the words, but names one substrate, and whether one

---

takes precedence by nature over accidents" (*On Literary Composition* 5.7–9). For a detailed discussion of the broad and formal definitions of "accident" see Barnes (2003), 220–224.

149 That is, the magistrate or prosecutor. The term rendered "passive" (εὐχερής) acquires the pejorative sense of "pliable" in the following chapters.

150 The Hellene's point is that, if the Accuser is impassible, he would not be subject to the movement of emotions that would prompt an accusation, while if he is passible, he ought to be pitied as a being who has suffered wrong, just as the sick are pitied when they may complain of their woes.

151 A marginal gloss in the Athens manuscript marks this as the beginning of Macarius's response.

says "mortal," "man," or "articulate," he names nothing other than the human being, and likewise in the case of a cloak, whether one says "cover," "wrap," "mantle," "robe," he does not name many things, but a single thing with interchangeable names.[152] 4. So too, the diligent Gospel writers who recorded what happened upon the Cross at that time, though some said one thing and others another, did not corrupt the history. For even though one said "vinegar"[153] and another said "wine,"[154] they did not err in any way. 5.[155] And you ought not be surprised about the sponge and the hyssop, when you hear "Having fastened a container of vinegar to a hyssop, they gave it to him to drink"[156] and again "Having soaked a sponge with vinegar, they offered it to him."[157] 6. For the "reed," the "sponge," and the "hyssop" seem to have a single mode of genesis, for each of them grows wild and is cut when grown. Now, then, it being necessary to say "reed," he said "hyssop" on account of the fact that they have the same mode of growth and cutting, and especially because they preserved the law of history and wrote nothing beyond what was said in the roiling clamour of insanity that there was at that time. 7. For the Jews were accusing them, while the Romans were the judges, each a barbarian people that did not pursue the principle of liberal education or possess the delicacy of Hellenic learning.[158]

---

152 This is a textbook description of Aristotelean polynomy: "... polynomous are things that have several different names, but one and the same account [i.e. "definition of essence/substance"], such as 'sword,' 'sabre,' and 'blade,' and in the case of clothing, 'cover' [λῶπος] and 'cloak' [ἱμάτιον]" (Porphyry, *Commentary on Aristotle's Categories* 69.1). The example of "cover" and "cloak" appears frequently in Aristotle (e.g. *Metaphysics* 1006b; *Physics* 185b, 202b). Porphyry's three words for "sword" are all Homeric/epic terms, as are two of Macarius's three words for "human" (βροτός, μέροψ).
153 Cf. Mk. 15:36; Jn. 19:29.
154 Cf. Mt. 27:34.
155 A marginal gloss in A on the passage that follows reads: "In other [copies] it says 'having placed on a lance [ὕσσῳ [soldiers] at many intervals the sponge at a different time. For many [soldiers] at many intervals, in the roiling clamour ῳ]. It is possible that the copies in which 'to a hyssop' y [soldiers] at many intervals the sponge at a different time. For many [soldiers] at many intervals, in the roiling clamor [ὑσσώπῳ] is written are mistaken. But a spear shaft is called a 'spear' [ὑσσός]. For another soldier presented the sponge at a different time. For many [soldiers] at many intervals gave him things to drink, thus pleasing the Jews."
156 Jn. 19:29. Macarius (and the marginal gloss in note 155 [q.v.]) reads the dative ὑσσώπῳ ("hyssop") as the implement with which the drink was offered to Christ.
157 Cf. Mk. 15:36.
158 The Jews and Romans are "barbarian" here in the classical sense of "non-Greek speakers"; hence their use of the awkward term "hyssop" rather than the more apropos "reed" or "spear." The remark is also a backhanded compliment of the bombast that Macarius ascribes to the Hellene.

8. But all was confused in tumult at that time: the earth was shaken as though by concussions from below and rocks were broken and crashed in their rumbling. Then, a 'palpable shadow'[159] fell, as the sun hid its own rays. No one was sober then; rather, they were darkened by the confusion of the elements, so shaken were the subterranean, aerial, terrestrial, and superterrestrial regions. 9. Finally, there was a fearful expectation that, since the whole cosmos was in revolt, it would suddenly turn the earth into the sea, night into day; that the dry land, rattled by violent motion, would be opened into gaps like furrows, and collapsing, bring up groaning chasms from the depths. There was fear that, as the mountains were crashing together, streams of unquenchable fire would suddenly flow, caused by bitter and harsh friction. Everything was in darkness, apart from the hypercosmic, undefiled realm. Creation, seeing the Creator treated with insolence within his creation, quaked immoderately, and against the mindless [offenders] prepared lashings of unendurable punishment.

10. Who then, tell me, amidst so great a tumult preserved the soundness of his wits? Who remained strong in soul? Who did not suffer mental consternation? Whose thoughts were not disturbed? Who did not slur his speech, as though drunk on wine? Who did not, after the manner of a huckster, speak meaningless words? Who did not see what was happening as a deep vision or great dream-vision?[160] Not a man, woman, old man, old woman, virgin, or youth kept his reason firm and stable, but all were speechless, as though deafened by thunder in the air, and each one in their delirium did something different, maintaining no consistency, reason, or steady state.

12. Hence, those who wrote recorded people's drunken state and their outlandish actions, both in deed and word, as they happened at that time, falsifying nothing. 13. For historians are not permitted to write anything beyond what occurred or what was said, even if the expression is a barbarism.[161] You have, for example, even the eloquent historiographer

---

159 Cf. Ex. 10:21.
160 Cf. Origen, *Against Celsus* 2.60, where similar terms are applied by Celsus to visions of the risen Christ.
161 "Barbarism" = λέξις βάρβαρος; barbarism, that is, the incorrect use or pronunciation of a word (and, often, as here [i.e. "hyssop"], of non-Greek origin), was considered a stylistic fault. In rhetorical treatises it was often contrasted with "Hellenism"/ἑλληνισμός, that is, proper usage and pronunciation (see, for example, Ps.-Herodian, *On Solecism and Barbarism* 39; Diogenes Laertius, *Lives of Eminent Philosophers* 7.59). Stylistic critique and cultural polemics were intertwined; the second-century Christian polemicist Tatian, for instance, characterized the Greek language as wholesale barbarism as part of his challenge to Greek

Herodotus himself, who though not barbarian records barbarian words in his history—the barbarian names of mountains and rivers that would have no name unless from where, he, writing his history, recorded them, working most diligently, not at purity of style, but at the truth.[162] 14. It is nothing to wonder at, then, if the Evangelists seem to record some outlandish phrasings, since it did not please them to embellish the words, but their concern was to preserve the truth of what was said. And if a woman or a man uttered an *anacoluthon* or solecism, all their concern was to inscribe this alone.[163] 15. For they perceived that the history would thus be without suspicion in the world, if the letter of the history was found not to be overwrought but uncontrived. For those writing these things were not descendants of educated men or grammarians. But even if they had been educated men, there would have been no need to conceal the narrative of these uneducated passages and to embellish what happened with clever words, but to preserve the mannerisms of the speakers as they were spoken.

29. 1. But let not this subject trouble you either, that only John says, "Coming to Jesus, they did not break his legs,"[164] while the others do not say it. For it is not the case that, since he alone says it, he is unworthy of acceptance; rather, because he diligently remembered this, he is rightly deserving of praise.

2. For in saying this he has said something else that is greater—something that maintains the mystery of the divine economy and explains the principle of the miracle, when he says: "One of the soldiers pierced his side with a spear."[165] This was in order that his opened side take on the role of the locked entrance of the walls of purification, in order that,

---

cultural hegemony (*Address to the Greeks* 1: "you have made your language a mixed thing, since you use barbarian words").

162 Herodotus's (c.484–425 BCE) *Histories* offer a simultaneous political, social, and ethnological account of the Greco-Persian wars of the fifth century BCE. Herodotus records many non-Greek words in his accounts of the peoples of the Mediterranean and Near East. His work remained an important (if dated and not always accurate) ethnographic and geographic reference for writers of late antiquity; Macarius, for instance, draws upon the *Histories* at 3.15.2 and 4.13.6.

163 In fact, ancient historians and biographers often describe the ways in which they have corrected awkward phrasing and solecisms; see for example Philostratus, *Life of Apollonius of Tyana* 1.3, where Philostratus reports that he has edited some of his sources to improve them stylistically.

164 Jn. 19:33.

165 Jn. 19:34.

as the blood poured and the water gushed, those inhabiting the territory of captivity might be redeemed by the blood, while those bearing the wounds of sins might be washed by the water.[166] 3. This, therefore, was not done superfluously, but by providence, as though established by divine forethought. For since <the font of perdition came from Adam's side,>[167] it was necessary that the starting point of salvation pour from the side. From his [i.e. Adam's] side the wound;[168] from his [i.e. Christ's] side the font. From his side the disease; from his side the cure. From his side the error; from his side the solution. From his side the suffering; from his side impassibility.

4. John, being the one witness of this because the ineffable [mystery] is one, bears witness to the ineffable. John cried out that the error that came from [Adam's] side is corrected from [Christ's] side. But this is true, even if he alone says it and the other three do not, since another tells the truth when he narrates the story of the poor man Lazarus and the pretentious rich man,[169] though the other three do not speak of it.

30. 1. Enough on that. Come—let us thoroughly examine also that matter which seems to you not to have been accomplished well. For what reason did the Saviour, after conquering the tyranny of <death> and returning from the innermost recesses on the third day after the Passion not appear to Pilate?[170]

2. In order that those who have learned how to undo fine things would not undo this success. In order that no paltry suspicion that might emerge among paltry men would steal the truth of the Lord's Passion. In order that the pliable would not think the event false. In order that the tongues of the Jews would not again spit the venom of the serpent. In order that the righting of the inhabited world would not become a universal scandal.

---

166 For the idea that the blood of Christ imparts a cathartic virtue to the waters of baptism see e.g. Ignatius of Antioch, *Letter to the Ephesians* 18.1.

167 Following Blondel (1876), Waelkens (1974), and Goulet, who suspect that a verse has been omitted here. Allusions would be to Rom. 5:14; 1 Cor. 15:22, 15:45, read perhaps alongside the reference to Eve at 1 Tim. 2:13–14. A recent marginal gloss in A here suggests <ἡ τῆς ἀπωλείας ἡ πρόφυσις>, which would be rendered "<The bud of destruction> necessitated that the starting point of salvation pour from the side." Goulet's suggestion better fits the parallel structure of the lines that follow.

168 If the emendation suggested in note 90 above is correct, there is a word play here with πηγή ("font/source") and πληγή ("wound").

169 Cf. Lk. 16:19–31.

170 A marginal gloss in a recent hand inserts a "heading" in the margin here: "Why the Saviour did not appear to Pilate first."

3. For if he had come to Pilate and his entourage immediately—immediately!—they could with cause have said, having readied a charge of sorcery,[171] that: "Pilate, thanks to some machination that pulled the wool over his eyes, nailed someone other than him to the Cross,[172] either because he was deceived or supplicated incessantly by him, which is something that often happens, unnoticed. 4. Hence, after seeming to rise through some subterfuge, he came to him, wanting him to use his authority to proclaim a resurrection that did not happen as though it had happened, and to confirm the story of this subterfuge through Roman power. Once plotted, the affair was a mockery. A serious thing became a drama. He who did not suffer strutted augustly about the *praetorium* as though he had suffered and conquered the Passion. One of those condemned to death was handed over to the Cross instead of him. There was a trick in the courtroom. By a subtle device and a type of sorcery he who had been arrested was released. Another of the condemned was bound over, unobserved. 5. And now Pilate, who just sat as judge over this scheme, now no longer acts this part in the scheme, but embraces the one responsible as a friend. Among the evils already committed against the Jews, this drama is a great innovation. Great is the laughter that has spread throughout the East. We Hebrews have incurred indelible shame, having fought against one man and failing to prevail against him.

6. See what a great intrigue this impostor has effected, both in his life and in his artful death. Having caused another to be nailed to the wood in his place, he wounded him, and persuaded the governor that he himself had endured the moment of his death, and deceived his company with enticing words, that, seeming superior to death, he returned from the subterranean realms on the third day. 7. Pilate, captivated by these words or perhaps even out of friendship, would have reported persuasively to the emperor what had not happened as if it had,[173] and then we would be compelled by the decree of imperial rule and power to believe in one charged with myriad accusations. A great scandal has seized the entire inhabited world. A great omen has enslaved the region below heaven. 8. He has subjected every authority by trickery, in order that, having made those preeminent

---

171 Celsus (in Origen, *Against Celsus* 2.44), hints that Jesus was put to death on a charge of sorcery. Origen conjectures at 2.56 that he suffered a public execution to forestall the suspicion that he had feigned his death. Cf. Athanasius, *On the Incarnation* 22–23.

172 This was in fact alleged of Simon of Cyrene: see *Second Treatise of the Great Seth* (Nag Hammadi Codices VII.2.56.9).

173 Tertullian (*Apology* 5.2) claimed that Tiberius had presented such a letter to the Senate.

among men his obedient servant, he could easily subject those under their authority. We have irrationally entered combat with an unbeatable evil. We thoughtlessly dared to fight this fearful one. Our battle line, lacking proper preparation, has become disordered. The failure of our misstep cannot be remedied. We ought to have judged what he said and ruminated on this statement of his, when boasting to those present he blurted: 'Behold, the Son of Man will be handed over into the hands of the high priests and elders, and they will flog him and crucify him, and on the third day he will rise.'[174] 9. For he said these things in confident assurance of his invincible and potent sorcery, knowing that it was easy for him to make a company of soldiers disappear and veil a whole community of people and make a game of the judge's sentence and prevail over everything with a word of powerful artifice by secret machination. Behold, then, how he reveals by his works what training in sorcery can accomplish. Hence we receive irremediable accusations from every race of men. We have prompted indelible hate from this false accusation that we have abused the common benefactor and crucified the Saviour of every race. 10. Now we do not have clear air, our vision is not free, nor are we allowed to see. We are the shame of our fathers, black eyes upon our ancestors, and unsightly blemishes upon our forebears.[175] 11. Who will be seen to have compassion for us given such a state of affairs? Who, taking pity on us, will share in suffering the ill of this error? The East and West seethe against us for what was done. Report of the matter quickly seized the North and South. Every region[176] of the inhabited world was driven into confusion when it learned that a man who was crucified and died (or so we thought) was raised on the third day, and sang [his own] praises not in neglected or obscure places, but in the halls of rulers and judges. What are we to do? Where will we wretched people take refuge, trapped as we are—woe is us!—in the midst of a drama such as this?"

12. Because of such and similar nonsense that might come from the Jews, he did not go to Pilate upon rising from the dead, lest what was well done be judged a plot or trick designed for evildoing. But neither did he come to the high-ranking men among the Romans, lest he seem to need support and allies in order to confirm the account of the Resurrection.

---

174 An amalgam of Mt. 20:18–19; Mt. 16:21; Lk. 18:32; Mk. 10:34; Mt. 17:22.
175 Cf. Eph. 5:27; Jude 12.
176 Referring either to the four points of the compass or to the five zones demarcated, e.g. in Cicero's *Dream of Scipio* (*On the Commonwealth* 6.21), of which one, the equatorial, is too hot to be inhabited, while two others (the poles) are too cold.

But he appeared to women unable to aid or persuade anyone about the Resurrection, then to the disciples, who were also powerless and themselves obscure among most people because of their humble condition. 13. He did all these things fittingly and entirely well, in order that the account of the resurrection would not be proclaimed with the help of world leaders but established by being confirmed by simple men who appeared to be nothing as respects the life that is according to the flesh. Thus the proclamation would not be human, but divine.

31. 1. Now, since these passages have been legitimately defended, it is time for us to interpret the critical passage that reads thus "Now is the judgment of the world. Now the ruler of this world will be cast out"[177]—or as it is in some copies: "will be cast down"[178]—"and when I shall be raised up, I will draw all to myself."[179]

2. Here, he calls humanity "world" tropologically,[180] referring not to heaven, the parts of heaven, the earth, or the sea, or the other parts of creation. For the one called "ruler" does not rule over these, but over men on account of their free capacity, while over beings without souls he has no power on account of their lack of free capacity. 3. But he names the "ruler," not the "demiurge," as they fancy, nor the lawgiver,[181] but an arch-demon, a sower of evil and an inventor of wickedness, who became ruler over the pliable through their pliability, and enslaved beings with free capacity by means of cunning trickery. He did not rule them through force or domination;[182] rather, he laid hold of the rational flock—which he here calls "world" metaphorically—through counsel and varied trickery. For the human being is fittingly called a "world," since it is the adornment of

---

177 Jn. 12:31.
178 The difference being between the preposition ἔξω ("out/outside") and κάτω ("down").
179 Jn. 12:32.
180 Cf. Jn. 3:16, 17:14–23 etc., where "the world" could be read as a synecdoche for "humanity."
181 "They" are gnostics and Marcionites who, respectively, equated the "ruler of this world" in Jn. 12:31 with the malevolent demiurge (see for example the *Apocryphon of John*; Tertullian, *Against the Valentinians* 22) and the inferior "lawgiving" Creator god (see for example Tertullian, *Against Marcion* 2.12). Support could be gathered from Paul, who speaks of Satan as the god of this world at 2 Cor. 4:4. It is possible that the Hellene has gnostic conceptions of the "ruler" or "archon of the world" in mind in his critique at 2.26.2–4 above (q.v.).
182 That humans yield to Satan of their own accord had been a Christian platitude since Origen (*Homilies on Genesis* 1), though Irenaeus treats this deception as a form of violence at *Against Heresies* 5.21.3.

the world,[183] an august creation, and an honourable creation created for honour.[184]

5. He says that the ruler will be cast out of *this* world,[185] by means of a just judgment that liberates those tyrannized by inhuman tyranny, saying, "Now judgment is upon the world," that is, "Now I will show that I am the magistrate[186] of this oppressed world. Now I will cast down[187] the ruler of this world, who does not rule and hold power justly, who until now has wielded power by means of the arms of disobedience and deceived faith, this aerial being hidden from all, invisible and incorporeal, and who wishes to murder the incorporeal soul. For I have not called him the 'universal' ruler or the ruler and dominator of all. 6. For he would be just if he held power over all; he would be invincible if he commanded all beings; he would be genuine if he gave orders to all; he would be without a master if he enjoyed universal domination. But in fact he rules only recently, originating in evil. Now, beginning with an evil teaching, he rules not the whole, but *this* world, or rather a portion of this world."

7. For the world that consists of everything is vast, and incomprehensible to human beings, but since a portion of the world was seized by tyranny, he says that the whole world has suffered. For as when one limb of the body hurts we say that the whole person hurts and suffers, so too since a portion of the world was ill from trickery he teaches that the whole world suffered. And, just as when the hem of a cloak is frayed the entire cloak is said to be worn, so too when a person is pricked by the sting of sin[188] he says that the world is wounded and shares the hurt.

8. This is because, if one speaks of the universal world, he will exhaust much time and, though he thinks to speak about the whole of the thing, he will not even explain the beginning of everything. What, in truth, will he explain about the world, in a true way, when he cannot even offer an

---

183 Cf. Ps. 139:14. The word play is difficult to capture fully in English. The "world" or "cosmos" (κόσμος) is a beautifully ordered whole, while "cosmos" can also refer to any type of adornment—thus the human being is the adornment (cosmos) of the beautiful whole that is the cosmos. For the human being as the "adornment of the world" (κόσμος κόσμου) compare Methodius of Olympus, *On the Resurrection* I.35.4.

184 See, for example, Methodius (*Symposium* 1.35.4) for an example of the commonplace that the human form is an epitome of the world.

185 I.e. human beings.

186 Following Goulet in reading δικαστήρ ("judge/magistrate") against the Athens manuscript's δικαστήριον ("tribunal").

187 Here Macarius uses the variant reading ("cast down") mentioned above at 2.31.1.

188 Cf. 1 Cor. 15:56.

accurate account of the nature of phaenomenal things? He will not describe the earth or the sea in a true way. He will not understand springs and rivers—not as respects their complete nature. 9. But if one who speaks about these things cannot speak more clearly, how can he provide a true account when he speaks about things beyond them? How [will he speak truly about] the subtle air, the broad and wide bosom of living winds that is held between heaven and earth just like a vessel able to hold myriad bodies, or the finer aether that lies above, illuminated continuously by the fiery luminaries, or the heaven that hangs above them, or the circumference of the circular vault, the multiform shimmering and shining of the stars, and the invisible region of the inhabited world,[189] and the inexpressible cohesion of life, or the preeminent beings that have been allotted the invisible territory and way of life, such as the innumerable class of Thrones, the unutterable order of Lordships, and the indescribable glory of the Potencies,[190] the great, unexplainable crowd and mass of Powers,[191] or the <***> throng of those called First-borns,[192] or the ardent service of the Seraphim,[193] or the course of the cherubimic chariots?[194] For the world is all of these things, when conceived as consisting in various essences of bodies. These things fill out the universal and invisible world.

10. But here he speaks about human nature as a portion of the world. For the divine instruction is wont and accustomed to name and describe the whole from the part and the part from the whole, just as one might say when speaking about life in a philosophical way: "The world is crucified for me and I to the world."[195] Here he does not mean that the heaven or the earth or the sea are crucified—for these constitute the world and portions

---

189 Macarius appears to believe, with Cicero (*Dream of Scipio* 21,), that the southern temperate zone, though inaccessible, is peopled. Lactantius, *Divine Institutes* 3.24, did not concur. Cf. Augustine, *City of God* 16.9.
190 Col. 1:16; Eph. 3:10, 6:12.
191 Rom. 8:38.
192 Heb. 12:23; cf. Job 38:7. Christ is πρωτότοκος ("firstborn") of all creation at Col. 1:15, the verse preceding Paul's enumeration of the angelic orders.
193 Is. 6:1–3.
194 Cherubim appear at Genesis 3:24, but are usually supposed to have been the creatures who descended in a chariot before Ezekiel (Ez. 1:10; cf. 41:18–19) and are seen again as satellites to the throne of God at Rev. 4:6. A fixed hierarchy of nine orders of celestial beings arranged in three hierarchically descending groups of three of was recognised in the next century by the author who styled himself Dionysius the Areopagite (*The Celestial Hierarchy* 6–9). Goulet finds a parallel to the catalogue of Macarius in Eusebius, *Commentary on the Psalms* (PG 23: 1084.18–23).
195 Gal. 6:14.

of the world, and to say this would be unlearned—but that corporeal evil is nailed up and that for him corporeal glory does not live and that he does not exist or live for the sake of corporeal concerns, but he is crucified in that he does not live by the dictates of worldly teaching and opinion, and in that he does not live according to a corporeal rule, nor does the way of life of the flesh grow within him.[196]

11. If, then, the habit of the flesh is named "world," and if Paul, as he suffered evil, has crucified this, then it is reasonable that the Saviour has justly called the tribe and race of men, borne hither and thither by disorderly impulses, a "world," which he prophesied will be judged, when the Cross was planted in the ground, and he predicts that he will cast out the one who rules this [world] through sin, and threatens to depose him from power. 12. Whoever this "ruler" is, he sows pleasures insane and illicit, revelry and drunkenness. For, since humanity allowed his error to command it,[197] it was necessary that this [ruler] rule by leading those he persuaded over to his own will. 13. But Christ, wanting to vindicate those who in their frailty had been overpowered and subdued by the demon, says: "Now judgment is upon the world. Now the ruler of this world will be cast down and when I shall be raised, I will gather all to myself."[198]

14. For having bound his congenital nature to the cord of the body,[199] and in so far as he was man interweaving the human essence with divinity, he rose up from the toilsome and bitter life here below, as if from a great and cavernous depth, being lifted up into realms high above. For as if bound by a cable to the salvific body, the flock of men here below went up together with him into the heavenly realms.

15. Now, casting down the ruler of the world means nothing other than that he be deposed him from his ruling authority, not signalling here a spatial fall, but the stripping of the honour he enjoyed when he was worshipped by men through their miserable deeds. 16. For just as today an emperor, by deposing one who governs a territory unjustly, puts an end to his rule, depriving him of all his authority, and everyone gossips

---

196 Cf. Gal. 1:16, Eph. 2:3, Rom. 8:9, etc.
197 Literally "bore the injunction of his error." Error takes the place of Satan in the *Gospel of Truth*, a second-century Valentinian text preserved in the Nag Hammadi compilation (*Nag Hammadi Codices* I.3.18.21).
198 Jn. 12:31–32.
199 This conceit may be inspired by Neoplatonic speculation on the chain of gold (*Iliad* 8.19–21) by which Zeus undertook to pull all his fellow-deities up to heaven; see Lévêque (1969).

that such a man was "put down" by the emperor, not from some residence above the ground or high in the air, but from dignity and power. And it happens that the same man, though he remains in the same residence within the territory in which he lived when he held authority and was haughty to all and inspired fear in everyone, once he has been deprived of rule is cast down and assumes the condition of the lowly. So, too, he who exercised power over the world by means of soul-destroying evil and abused free people as slaves, having been seized by him who is master and judge by nature, is deposed, having his haughty brow humbled, in this not enduring not a spatial deposition from a peak, but being stripped of the authority for power that he had. 17. For as one condemned by and receiving an accusation from the emperor is no longer of service, nor is his word valid even if he should walk within the imperial halls, so too the Accuser, once stripped of the despotic control that he insolently held through false pretence, is cast out from the rule, which, when he had it, he boasted of, and is no longer strong enough or able to do anything, even if he continues to live in the very midst of the world. 18. He, therefore, who before this was a strong and powerful ruler—though Christ was of course stronger and more powerful—this powerful one became weak, having been "cast out" in a certain way, from power.[200]

32. 1. With this having been explained as far as we have been able to speak about it, it is time to explain for you that troublesome statement made by Christ to the Jews: "You are not able to hear my word, because you are of the father of the Accuser."[201]

2. From here on, if you please, attend closely to what is about to be said concerning the passage at hand, since these points ought to be made concerning this key passage: namely, who the father of the Accuser is here, and why the Jews are accused in respect of this and fell from their inherited

---

200 Cf. Mt. 12:29, Mk. 3:27, and Lk. 11:21 on the binding of the strong man.
201 Jn. 8:43–44. When the "Hellene" cites this verse at 4.27.1 above it is translated "of your father, the Accuser." The verse contains two genitives (ἐκ τοῦ πατρὸς τοῦ διαβόλου); the familiar translation "You are of your father, the Devil/Accuser" (RSV), like most patristic authors, takes the two genitives as standing in apposition. Macarius, by contrast, reads the second genitive as a possessive, thus "You are of the father *of the Accuser*," and argues below at 3.27.3–4 that the former reading would require the personal pronoun (i.e. "your"), and while this is not philologically correct, it serves his exegetical purposes well in what follows. Origen offers a detailed critique of this way of reading the verse (which he admits is "ambiguous") in *Commentary on John* 20.21.

noble birthright and were cut from their "natural root,"[202] and were grafted without discernment on to that which is unnatural.

3. For truly great and exceedingly difficult is the discourse that explains the Accuser and the father of the Accuser. For the Accuser is not the father of the Jews. For if the passage intended this meaning, it would have been written: "You are of *your* father, the Accuser," yet it has not been written in this way, but rather "You are of the father of the Accuser," as though the Accuser has a father. 4. For the Accuser is not the Accuser on his own account, but because of another. That is, once the accusation was planted in him, he began to accuse and come to blows with the laws of proper order, with the result that the father became accuser in the son and the son a most forceful sophist full of cunning and accusation in the father.

5. It is possible to understand this by juxtaposing something greater, as when Christ says: "I am in the Father and the Father [is] in me."[203] Now, just as those who believe in Christ become heirs of the Father of Christ, being established as heirs of the Father through the Son, so too those persuaded to go over to the opinion of the Accuser are through him made associates of the father of the Accuser. 6. For the Accuser knows how to do nothing other than tear man away from divine grace and bring him over to his own parent,[204] in order that, as Christ leads those who are holy to God the Father, so the Antichrist[205] [leads] those he has persuaded to the anti-god.

7. You wish to inquire closely, then, who the father of the Accuser is. Being fond of inquiry, you have certainly heard of the region and garden of Paradise and its husbandman, and of course its watchman and worker, too. And you have also heard of the serpent and the accusation that came from the serpent. You know, since some speak of it,[206] the dramaturgy

---

202 Cf. Rom. 11:16, 21.
203 Jn. 14:10.
204 "Parent" translates γεννήτωρ, a term which could have Trinitarian meaning when applied to the Father as "begetter" of the Son by, e.g. Athanasius (*Oration Against the Arians* 1.14), but also means "parent" more generally; Cyril of Jerusalem applies to term to the Devil in *Catechetical Lectures* 2.4 ("parent/father of evils"). Macarius is exploiting both the common and theological valances here as he sets up his parallel between Son/Father: Accuser/father of the Accuser.
205 The designation "antichrist" (antagonist of the Messiah) is given at 2 Jn. 7: "Many deceivers have gone out into the world, those who do not confess that Jesus Christ has come in the flesh; any such person is the deceiver and the antichrist" (NRSV).
206 Macarius likely means the account in Genesis 3 and other biblical references and allusions to it (e.g. Rom. 5:12; 1 Tim. 12–14, etc.), but he may also refer to non-Christian references to the Gen. 3 narrative in polemical literature (e.g. Celsus apud Origen, *Against*

that occurred there. You know of the sly-talking[207] tragedy of deceit that occurred there. You know the sophisms. You know the words spoken there. You know the cunning banter of those words and the pageant of destruction that followed. You know of the change in things for the worse. You know—if you have studied the full account of this narrative—how the founder of human nature, having heedlessly accepted the serpent's accusation, was cast out of that divine ambit, was pushed out of that blessed way of life, and was exiled from the divinely inspired realms, having become a foreigner to that garden of blessed abundance.

8. Thenceforth the disastrous drama mockingly befell the race. Thenceforth the rational shoot fell. Thenceforth, having been plucked, we yet wander. Thenceforth a tyrannical army rose up close upon us. Thenceforth, there were murderous and inhuman feelings. Thenceforth our customs and schooling were those of a flock of irrational beasts. Thenceforth the currency of freedom was stolen and the fraudulent denarius of slavery appeared.[208] Thenceforth, the soul received the bruises of iniquity. Thenceforth the mind was blemished. Thenceforth rational thoughts, suffering as they were, became dulled. Thenceforth we bore incurable pocks. Thenceforth the vision of [our] thought became confused. Thenceforth there were the bruises and broken bones of evils. Thenceforth the cloud of confusion thickened. Thenceforth death's missiles were forged. Thenceforth Hades,[209] opening itself wide, was enriched. Thenceforth the Accuser and the father of the accuser imposed themselves menacingly.

9. Naturally, then, the "Accuser" is the serpent who accuses man to

---

Celsus 6.28; Julian, *Against the Galilaeans* apud Cyril of Alexandria, *Against Julian* 89A–89B, 93D–94A).

207 "Sly-talking" translates πολύφωνος, literally "many-voiced"; it is used, for example, to refer to Homer's skill in portraying a variety of characters' speech (e.g. Dionysius of Halicarnassus, *On Literary Composition* 16) and can also mean simply "having many voices" (e.g. Plutarch, *On the Decline of Oracles* 409e) or "loquacious" (e.g. Lucian, *How To Write History* 4). The description of the serpent's use of deceptive speech suggests that Macarius means to indicate that the "tragedy" was caused by the serpent's cunning use of wheedling words. Goulet, for his part, takes the adjective to mean "involving many agents," that is, that the account of the serpent's deception of the first humans is like a staged tragedy involving multiple actors.

208 Cf. Origen, *Homily 1 on Genesis*, where human beings are said to have exchanged the image of God for the brand of the devil.

209 Macarius equates Hades with the Sheol of the Hebrew scriptures (e.g. Is. 14:15) and the abode of the wicked in the parable of the rich man and the beggar (Lk. 16:23). Christ foretells, however, that the gates of hell shall not prevail against his Church (Mt. 16:18), and an allusion at 1 Peter 3:19 to his sojourn with the spirits who fell in the days of Noah

God and God to man, and naturally he has this appellation based on what he did.[210] But the father of this Accuser is clearly the deceitful angel[211] who sits and dwells in him,[212] an incorporeal power that has been separated from the governance of the Almighty, about whom one of the ancients spoke, saying: "He raised his neck proudly before the all-powerful Lord; he ran before him in defiance."[213] Having irrationally broken the bond of friendship and finding the serpent to be a persuasive servant, he sowed the seeds of accusation in him,[214] or rather, in some way taking him as a subordinate, making him an accuser as if by generating him.[215]

10. Since, therefore, the Jews turned their noses up at the Son of God, unconvinced by the things said about him and not accepting his Father through him, but instead were persuaded by deceptive teachings and removed themselves from the Kingdom of God as if led by the evil of the serpent, as though they had inclined to the apostate[216] father of the serpent and were fighting with him against the lordship of God, for this reason Christ, because of what they were doing and because they were wickedly deciding not to be beloved friends of Christ[217] and through him, of God,[218] but dupes of the Antichrist and through him, the anti-god, said to them: "You are unable to hear my word, because you are of the father of the Accuser."[219]

11. Enough on that topic. But, if it please you, we will end this discourse

---

became the germ of the popular legend of the harrowing of hell, which by Macarius's time had already assumed its classic form in the *Gospel of Nicodemus*.

210 Like the Hellene, Macarius makes the etymological connection between διάβολος ("slanderer/accuser") and διαβολή ("slander/false accusation"), cf. 2.27.4 above.

211 In the verse under discussion (Jn. 8:44), the devil is said to have been a liar from the beginning.

212 As Christ the Word, imitating the God of the Exodus, is said to dwell among humans for their salvation (e.g. Jn. 1:14).

213 Job 15:25b–26a. Macarius here reads ἐνώπιον ("in front of," "before"), a reading found in Origen and Didymus the Blind, rather than the received reading ἔναντι ("in the presence of") (Goulet (2003), 65, n. a). For examples of other patristic writers who identify the διάβολος/"Accuser" see Eusebius, *Ecclesiastical Theology* 3.4.8.

214 According to the distribution of roles in chapter 27, Adam will be the one calumniated, the devil his calumniator, the serpent a passive recipient of the calumny.

215 In his response to Celsus (*Against Celsus* 4.65), Origen also addresses the origin of the διάβολος/"Accuser" and his angels; here, though, Origen is responding to Celsus's raising the problem of the origin of evil for a monistic philosophy.

216 So called by Irenaeus (*Against Heresies* 5.21.2, perhaps also 5.1.1) because he caused the secession of a third of the stars from heaven (Rev. 12:4).

217 Cf. Jn. 15:14, 21:17.

218 Cf. Ex. 33:11; Is. 41:8; Jas. 2:23.

219 Jn. 8:43–44.

with dignity, as having been sufficiently discussed. But again, at another time, if some other troubling topic should occur to you, with the aid of the divine gift, we will discuss it, meeting once again.[220]

---

220 As each book records a day of the public debate, this marks the conclusion of the second day. On this narrative structure see the Introduction.

BOOK 3

Macarius of Magnesia's *Apocriticus* or *Unique [discourse]* to the Hellenes concerning the questions in the Gospel and their solutions[1]

Contents of the third volume of discourses in response to the Hellenes

1. Why did Jesus endure being crucified with contumely?

2. What is the meaning of: "If it is possible, let the cup pass by"?[2]

3. What is the meaning of: "If you believed in Moses, you would believe me"?[3]

4. What does the passage about the swine and the demons mean?[4]

5. What is the meaning of the passage that says it is "easier for a camel to pass through a needle than a rich man [to pass] into the Kingdom of God"?[5]

6. What is the meaning of: "Around the fourth watch of the night he came out upon the sea"?[6]

7. What is the meaning of the passage "You have the poor always, but me you do not have always"?[7]

---

1 The *pinax* ("table of contents") of Book 3 is preserved both in A and in *Vaticanus graecus* 1650, fol. 187 verso. The title as preserved in the Vatican manuscript thus situates the *Apocriticus* within the popular late ancient genre of "question and answer" literature (see further discussion in the Introduction).
2 Mt. 26:39.
3 Jn. 5:46.
4 Mt. 8:28–34 and parallels.
5 Mt. 19:24 omitting "eye" (τρήματος).
6 Mk. 6:48; Mt. 14:25.
7 Jn. 12:8 omitting "with you" (μεθ'ἑαυτῶν).

8. What is the meaning of the passage "Unless you eat my flesh and drink my blood, you will not have life"?[8]

9. What is the meaning of: "And even if they drink deadly poison, it will not at all harm them"?[9]

10. What does the passage about the mustard seed mean?[10]

11. What is the meaning of: "Throw yourself down"?[11]

12. What is the meaning of the statement "Get behind me, Satan," which is made to Peter?[12]

13. What does the passage about "seventy times seven" mean?[13]

Here begins another subject of discussion taken from Acts and the Apostle[14]

14. Why did Peter kill Ananias and Sapphira?[15]

15. Why did Peter escape from the locked prison?[16]

16. Why did Paul circumcise Timothy?[17]

17. Why did Paul say he was Roman when he was not Roman?[18]

18. What is the meaning of: "No one soldiers on his own provisions"?[19]

19. What is the meaning of: "he is bound to do the entire Law"?[20]

20. What is the meaning of: "For the Law came in so that the transgression might increase"?[21]

---

8 Jn. 6:53.
9 Mk. 16:18.
10 Mt. 17:20; Lk. 17:6.
11 Mt. 4:6; Lk. 4:9.
12 Mt. 16:23; Mk. 8:33.
13 Mt. 18:22.
14 The "Apostle" is, of course, Paul.
15 Acts 5:1–11.
16 Acts 12:5–19.
17 Acts 16:3.
18 Acts 22:25–27.
19 1 Cor. 9:7.
20 Gal. 5:3.
21 Rom. 5:20.

21. What is the meaning of: "I do not want you to be in communion with demons"?[22]

22. What is the meaning of: "In the latter times, some will apostatize from the faith"?[23]

Prologue. 1. *Once he had gathered a theatre-full of distinguished listeners, the celebrated [rhetor] contrived this third contest for us, which we will make clear for your incomparable wisdom, O Theosthenes,[24] describing in detail, as far as possible, the propositions he had prepared. For after we had gathered in a tranquil spot, we toiled in debate the whole day. 2. He, then, began to roll out the plumed crests of Attic oratory[25] for us, so that for a little while even this most competent crowd was disturbed, as they watched a fearful windbag full of arrogance. In this, therefore, he frightened us, as if he was charging quickly down a hill, since he was shaking from the force of his tongue. This was the beginning of his speech addressed to us.*

I. Why did Jesus allow himself to be crucified with contumely?

1. 1. For what reason did Christ, when brought before the High Priest and the governor, not utter anything worthy of a wise and divine man, something able to instruct the judge and those present and improve them,[26] but allowed [himself] to be struck with a reed, spat upon, and crowned

---

22 1 Cor. 10:20.

23 1 Tim. 4:1.

24 Macarius's addressee, Theosthenes, is otherwise unknown. The theophoric name means "Might of God," and so can also be read, like the "Theophilus," or "Lover of God," to whom the gospel of Luke is dedicated (Lk. 1:3; Acts 1:1) as a general address to all Christian readers.

25 For the metaphor cf. Aristophanes, *Frogs* 925. Macarius repeatedly describes the Hellene's rhetoric as particularly impressive and withering; in fact, the Hellene's rhetoric consists primarily in series of pointed historical, theological, and philological ζητήματα, or *quaestiones*, for which, in the tradition of "question and answer" literature, one would expect concise λύσεις, or *solutions*; Macarius's own rhetoric is in fact much more self-consciously stylized and florid than the Hellene's, see also discussion in the Introduction.

26 Compare Theodore of Mopsuestia, *Against Julian* fr. 9 (Guida): "But Jesus, when brought before Herod, performed no sign, even though the latter said he wanted to see and hear something, since he [i.e. Jesus] knew that it would do no good. For he did not merely perform signs, nor did he do them as a proof and so that he would inspire wonder, but in order that those who believed might be saved. For it was clear that it was not for this reason that

with thorns? Why did he not do as Apollonius,[27] who, after speaking freely to the Emperor Domitian, disappear from the imperial court, and after a few hours, appear most manifestly in the city of Dicearchia, which is now called Puteoli?[28]

2. Even if Christ had to suffer according to God's commands, it was necessary that he endure punishment, but not that he endure the Passion without speaking freely,[29] that he utter something powerful and wise to Pilate the judge, and not be humiliated like one of the common street thugs.

II. Why did he say: "If it is possible, let the cup pass"?[30]

1. What is more, that statement is also full of obscurity, or indeed stupidity, which was spoken by Jesus to the disciples: "Do not fear," it says, "those who kill the body,"[31] when he himself, in agony and staying awake with expectation of dangers and begging that the Passion pass him by, said to his

---

[Herod] was seeking a sign, but because he was maddened against him and was looking to discover something to merit his anger."

27 The comparison of Christ with Apollonius of Tyana was maintained, to the great advantage of the latter, by the sophist Hierocles: the trial of Apollonius is ridiculed in chapters 38–44 of the tract *Against Hierocles*, still commonly attributed to Eusebius of Caesarea.

28 In Philostratus's *Life of Apollonius of Tyana* 8.5, 10, the hero disappears after delivering an *apologia* to the Emperor Domitian in Rome and appears a few hours later to his friends around 175 kilometres away in the Campanian city of Dicearchia. The city of Dicearchia, founded as a Greek colony, became the Roman colony of Puteoli in 194 BCE (Livy, *History* 34.45), though Philostratus uses the Greek name of the city. The polemicist Celsus also criticized Christ for failing to demonstrate his power by miraculously disappearing from the cross (apud Origen, *Against Celsus* 2.68) and compares Christ to Aristeas the Proconnesian, whose miracles also included disappearance/reappearance (apud Origen, *Against Celsus* 3.26; Celsus and Origen know of Aristeas from the account in Herodotus, *Histories* 4.14–15).

29 "Frank speech," or παρρησία, refers to open, honest, candid communication of those unencumbered by social trappings and affectations; it is the kind of communication that can take place among friends who enjoy the same social status, or the bold speech of those who would speak truth to power. Παρρησία was the fatal virtue of such philosophers as Socrates, Musonius Rufus, and the heroes of the *Acta Alexandrinorum*. Peter and John evince frank speech, for instance, before the Sanhedrin in Acts 4:13, while Paul claims he can speak frankly to Philemon (Phil. 1:8); in Athenagoras, *Plea for Christians* 11.2, it signifies the philosophical candour that he demands from his pagan interlocutors.

30 Mt. 26:39. The Hellene does not here discuss this passage, but Macarius does in his response below (3.9.1).

31 Mt. 10:28; Lk 12:4.

closest members of his circle: "Be watchful and pray that the test passes us by."[32] 2. For these statements are not worthy of a child of God, nor indeed of a wise man who despises death.[33]

III. Why he said: "If you believed in Moses, you would believe in me."[34]

3. 1. But it seems to me that the statement "If you believed in Moses, you would believe in me, for he spoke concerning me"[35] is a great load of stupidity. After all, nothing written by Moses is extant. For all his writings are said to have been burned in the temple, while whatever is written under the name of Moses was written 1,180 years after Moses's death, by Esdras and those of his circle.[36] 2. But even if one grants that the writing is by Moses, it is not possible to show that the Christ is anywhere called "God," or "God-*Logos*," or "Creator." For that matter, who said Christ would be crucified?[37]

---

32 Compare Mt. 26:41; Mk. 14:35; Lk. 22:46, though the Hellene's quotation does not accord with any of these variants.
33 Compare Celsus's accusation based on Mt. 26:39 (apud Origen, *Against Celsus* 2.24, trans. Chadwick): "Why then does he utter loud laments and wailings, and pray that he may avoid the fear of death, saying something like this, 'O Father, if this cup could pass by me'?" and Julian, *Against the Galilaeans* (apud Theodore of Mopsuestia, *Against Julian* fr. 8.1 [Guida]): "But Jesus prays like a person unable to bear his circumstances peacefully [Lk. 22:42; Mt. 26:39, 41], and although his is God is encouraged by an angel [Lk. 22:43]. And who proclaimed this to you, Luke, about the angel (if, in fact, this ever happened, for those who were present with him praying at that time did not see it, for they were asleep)? Thus 'rising up from prayer he found them asleep from grief and said, "Why are you sleeping? Rise up and pray,"' and what follows; then, '"and as he was speaking, behold! There was a great crowd and Judas [Lk. 22:45–47]." Thus John did not write this, for he did not see it.' So says Julian."
34 Jn. 5:46.
35 Jn. 5:46.
36 The Hellene's polemic is based on 2 Esdras 14:21–48, where Ezra is commanded to gather scribes and produce books under God's inspiration because "thy law has been burned" (2 Esdras 14:21, RSV); ninety-four books are produced, twenty-four of which God commands Ezra to make public, and these twenty-four were often assumed to be a rewriting of the canon of the Hebrew Bible. Compare Julian, *Against the Galilaeans* (apud Cyril of Alexandria, *Against Julian* 168a): "Julian claims that Ezra has added material based on his own opinion [to the books of Moses]."
37 Denial of a prophetic basis for the crucifixion was an anti-Christian commonplace. Compare for example Justin, *Dialogue with Trypho* 90; Celsus apud Origen, *Against Celsus* 1.50, 2.28, 7.14.

IV. What the passage about the swine and the demons means.

4. 1. But if you are willing to address this story as well—the statement seems utter huckster's nonsense, where Matthew says that two demons encountered Christ as they were leaving the tombs, and then, fearing Christ, passed into many swine and died.[38] 2. But Mark did not hesitate to invent an inordinate number of swine. Here is what he says: "He said to him, 'Go out from this man, unclean spirit.' And he asked it, 'What is your name?' And it replied, 'My name is Legion, because we are many.' And they begged him not to cast them out of the territory. 3. But there was a herd of swine being tended there, and the demons begged of him whether they might be allowed to go into the swine. And after they went into the swine, they ran madly towards the cliff and into the sea, about two thousand of them, and they drowned, while those tending them fled."[39]

4. Oh what a yarn! O what nonsense! O what an absolute farce! A crowd of two thousand swine ran into the sea, and died by drowning. And who upon hearing this—that the demons begged that they not be sent into the abyss, then that Christ, once asked, did not send them there, but sent them into swine—would not say, "My, what idiocy! My, what a comic error! To accept the petitions of deadly demons who do great harm in the world, and give them exactly what they want! 5. But the demons wanted to dance through life and make of the world an endless child's game.[40] They wanted to confuse earth and sea and make the whole universe a mournful theatre. They wanted to whip the elements into confusion and weaken all of creation by harm.[41] Of course it was not necessary to throw those who treat man wickedly into the place of the abyss, where they begged not to go—those chiefs of evil—but, to help them commit another offence having been made womanish by their pleas!

6. For if this is really true and not, as we are demonstrating, a fiction,[42]

---

38 Cf. Mt. 8:28–34. Here and in the ensuing discussion, the Hellene and Macarius cite the text as though it spoke of "demons" (δαίμονες) rather than of "demoniacs" or "men troubled by demons" (δαιμονιζόμενοι), as in the received text.

39 Mk. 5:8–14.

40 Possibly an allusion to Heraclitus (Fr. 52 Diels-Kranz), where *aiōn* (eternity, the ages) is said to play chess with a child.

41 For a more detailed discussion of the harm done by evil demons (δαίμονες) to the material world (plagues, earthquakes, etc.) and their efforts to dupe humans, see Porphyry, *On Abstinence* 2.40.

42 A marginal gloss by a later hand in A inserted here reads: "The Jews raised swine contrary to the Law, selling the meat to the Roman soldiers; on account of this the Saviour,

the passage accuses Christ of great evil: driving the demons out of one man, to send them into irrational swine and to frighten the swineherds and make them flee breathlessly in terror and work the city into an uproar because of what happened. 7. For is it not just to relieve not only one, or two, or three, or thirteen people from harm, but every person, and all the more so because he testified that he had come into life for this purpose?[43] But simply to release one [person] from invisible bonds, and invisibly send others into bondage, and auspiciously to free some from fear, but throw others irrationally into fear—this is rightly not called correct action but evildoing. 8. Not only that, but also by accepting the petitions of enemies to inhabit and plunder another territory, he acts like a king who destroys his subjects, [a king] who, because he is unable to drive the barbarian from every territory, sends him from one place to another, rescuing one territory from the evil one and donating the other to him as a boon?[44]

9. If, then, Christ too, because he was at that time unable to free the territory from the demon, sent it into a herd of swine, he does something truly wondrous and able to impress whomever hears of it, but which [in fact] effects something full of wicked suspicion. For someone of good sense, upon hearing these things immediately—immediately!—judges them, and gauging the account on its own merits pronounces a just judgment on the affair, saying: 10. "If he does not free everyone under the sun from harm, but [merely] banishes those who cause harm into different territories, and gives heed to some but does not attend to others, then it is not safe to take refuge with him or be saved by him. For he who has been saved mocks the condition of him who has not been saved, and he who has not been saved is the accuser of him who has been saved." Hence, in my estimation, what

---

acting as an advocate for the Law, permitted the demons to enter into the swine." Macarius's response is made in response to the Hellene's argument at 3.4.11 below, and differs from Macarius's response at 3.11.9–11 below. "Fiction," translates πλάσμα, which in other third- and fourth-century Hellenic exegetical texts suggests a narrative that is purely entertaining and contains neither historical truth nor deeper allegorical meaning; cf. Porphyry, *On the Cave of the Nymphs in the Odyssey* 4 passim, and Julian, *Against the Galilaeans* apud Cyril of Alexandria 39a, 115e.

43 Cf. Lk. 5:32 and Jn. 17:18.

44 Perhaps an allusion to Valens's policy of allowing Gothic peoples to settle in Roman territory as *foederati*, or peoples granted subsidies of land and supplies in exchange for providing troops. Contemporaries lamented the strain that these sanctioned migrations placed on the land and existing populations (see e.g. Ammianus Marcellinus, *History* 31.4.1–13).

this story reports is a fiction.[45] 11. But if it is not a fiction, but akin to truth, it is truly enough to cause gaping laughter. Come! Let us examine this clearly: how, in the land of Judaea, was there ever such a throng of swine, which have always been considered the most unclean and hated of domesticated animals by the Jews? And how, too, did all those swine drown, when there is no deep lake or sea there?[46]

V. What is the meaning of the passage that says it is "easier for a camel to pass through a needle than a rich man [to pass] into the Kingdom of God"?

5. 1. Let us leave these things for infants to judge, but let us examine another, more obscure statement, where it says: "It is easier[47] for a camel to pass through a needle than a rich man [to pass] into the Kingdom of heaven."[48] 2. If, then, a rich man who stays away from sins during his life—murder, theft, adultery, poisoning, unholy oaths, grave robbing, profanation of temples[49]—will not enter into the so-called Kingdom of heaven, what good is it for just men to practise justice, if they happen to be rich? And what harm is there for poor men if they do every unholy act of evil? For virtue does not lead man to heaven, but poverty and lack of property. 3. For if wealth bars the rich man from heaven then poverty, conversely, brings the poor man in. And it is proper for one who has learned this teaching to take no account of virtue whatsoever, but to cling to the basest poverty, as though poverty is such that it saves the poor man and wealth shuts the rich man out of the inviolate abode.

4. It therefore seems to me that these statements are not Christ's, if,

---

45 The Hellene terms the pericope of the demons and the swine a "fiction" (πλάσμα), that is, a fiction concocted with wicked intent. Compare Julian, *Against the Galilaeans* 39A, apud Cyril of Alexandria, *Against Julian* 39A, where the emperor writes that "the knavery of the Christians is a fiction (πλάσμα) made-up by men motivated by evil-doing."

46 The Hellene is not deliberately misreading Mk. 5:8–14 and Mt. 8:28–34, which clearly situate this pericope on the shore of the Sea of Galilee; rather, he wishes to emphasize the shallowness of the Sea of Galilee as reiterated below at 3.6.2.

47 In A, a marginal note in a later hand reads: "The Hellene's objection is useless; for he who performs one virtue perfectly is not able to perfect the rest [at the same time], for the virtues are situated one after another like a staircase, and vice versa."

48 Mt. 19:24. Julian also criticized this apophthegm: "The eye of a needle and the camel. Not the animal, so the impious Julian supposes, which is stupid and idiotic, but rather the thick rope that one finds on every ship. This it is the word that experts in sailing normally use" (apud Cyril, *Against Julian* fr. 17).

49 Cf. Rom. 2.21–23; 1 Cor. 6:9–10; Gal. 5:19–21.

that is, he taught the Rule of Truth,[50] but of some poor men wishing to take the property of the wealthy with vain talk.[51] 5. One must acknowledge that today, not long ago, these words—"Sell your property and give to the poor and you will have a treasure-house in heaven"[52]—when read to noble women persuaded them to distribute all their wealth and property to the poor and, when they themselves became needy, to ask to be put on the dole, passing from a state of freedom to unseemly begging, from well-being to a pitiable mien, and finally, they found it necessary to go to the homes of those who have [wealth].[53] This is the first, or rather the highest outrage and calamity—that they should flee from their own property on the pretext of piety and then beg from others because of the necessity of their want.[54] 6. It seems to me that these are the utterances of a sick woman.

50 The Hellene uses the phrase "Rule of Truth" (ὁ τῆς ἀληθείας κανών) in the sense of a universal moral standard; for this usage compare Philo of Alexandria, *Allegorical Interpretation* 3.233, Clement of Alexandria, *Stromateis* 7.3, Hierocles of Alexandria, *Commentary on the Golden Verses of Pythagoras* 14.8. Among philosophers, the term was also used to refer to universal metaphysical, physical, and theological propositions; compare Plotinus, *Ennead* 1.3.5.17. In early Christian heresiology the phrase is synonymous with "orthodox" doctrine (cf. Epiphanius, *Panarion* 59.5 [Holl 369:21]) and Macarius seems to use the phrase in this sense at 3.27.12 below (though see textual note).

51 Celsus's polemic against Mt. 19:24 (apud Origen, *Against Celsus* 6.16, trans. Chadwick) is sometimes adduced as a parallel to the Hellene's arguments: "Jesus's judgment against the rich, when he said 'It is easier for a camel to go through the eye of a needle than for a rich man to enter the kingdom of God,' was manifestly borrowed from Plato ... Jesus corrupts the Platonic saying where Plato says that 'It is impossible for an outstandingly good man to be exceptionally rich' [*Laws* 743a]." The Hellene's point is that, if Jesus preached the "Rule of Truth" (e.g. some version of a universal ethic) the apophthegm must have been invented by his poor, jealous followers; Celsus's argument, by contrast, is that Jesus plagiarized the apophthegm from Plato.

52 Mt. 19:21.

53 Compare Porphyry, *Against the Christians* fr. 4 (Harnack), apud Jerome, *Tractates on the Psalms* LXXXI: "Paul subjugated the whole world from Ocean to the Red Sea. Someone may say, 'They did this all for profit,' for this is what Porphyry says, '[these] rustic, poor men; they worked some sign by magical arts. But it is nothing to do great signs; did not the magi in Egypt do signs against Moses, and Apollonius did them, and Apuleius, and infinite numbers [of people] have done signs.' I concede to you, Porphyry, that they did signs by means of magical arts, so that 'they might obtain [things] from wealthy women whom they misled.' For this is what you say. But for what reason did they die? For what reason were they crucified?"

54 Compare Julian, *Against the Galilaeans* apud Theodore of Mopsuestia, *Against Julian* fr. 6 (Guida): "If all were persuaded by you, Jesus [e.g. to follow the injunction of Mt. 19:21; Lk. 12:33], who would be the buyer? Who praises this teaching, which no city, no people, not a single household would be able to endure if it were to hold sway? For how, if everything

VI. Why does it say: "Around the fourth watch of the night he came out upon the sea"?[55]

6. 1. But come, let us open up[56] this passage from the Gospel for you as well, which is laughable because it is written so unconvincingly,[57] but which recounts an even more laughable story, the one in which Jesus, after sending the disciples to sail across the sea after dinner[58] appeared to them himself at the fourth watch of the night, as they were terribly harassed by the surge of the storm, heaving all night long against the strength of the waves.[59] For the fourth watch of the night is the tenth hour of the night, after which three further hours remain.[60]

2. Now those who describe the true character of these places say that there is not a "sea" there, but a small lake in the territory of Galilee by the city of Tiberias, which is sailed across easily by small wooden boats in no more than two hours, and does not offer enough room for waves and storms [to develop]. Mark, therefore, straying outside the truth, spins the ludicrous

---

were sold, would any household or home still be worth anything? In addition, the fact that if everything in the city were being sold you would not find any buyers is evident and need not be mentioned." Photius (*Epist.* 187), quoting from the eighteenth book of Cyril's *Against Julian*, preserves the same fragment, adding a few additional lines before what is quoted by Theodore: "Hear a fine and statesmanlike precept: 'Sell all that you have and give to the poor; provide yourselves with bags which will not age [Lk. 12:33].' Who has a more statesmanlike command to offer than this?"

55 Cf. Mk. 6:48; Mt. 14:25.

56 The verb here, ἀναπτύσσω, describes the act of "unrolling" a scroll for reading and, metaphorically, "opening up" or "unfolding" a passage of written text by means of exegesis or literary criticism. Cf. Porphyry, *Cave of the Nymphs* 4, and perhaps also Lk. 4:17, where "unrolling" may refer both to Jesus's unrolling of the scroll containing the Book of Isaiah and his interpretation of the text.

57 The adverb ἀπιθάνως, "unconvincingly," here attacks the narrative as unbelievable because it is inaccurate or untrue in its contextual details (e.g. by presenting a raging storm on a tiny body of water); "unrealistically" might convey the sense better, yet it would risk importing a modern "realist" literary aesthetic not present in ancient literary criticism.

58 Cf. Mk. 6:35–44; Mt. 14:15–21.

59 Cf. Mt. 14:22–24; Mk. 6:45–48.

60 The Hellene and Macarius calculate "watches" and "hours of the night" differently. Here, the Hellene is presented as understanding the "night" to consist of four watches of three hours each, with Jesus appearing at the beginning of the fourth, and final, three-hour watch before daybreak. Below, at 3.13.2, Macarius equates the fourth watch with the "fourth hour of the night"; he also reads the Hellene as saying that Jesus arrived at the fourth hour before daybreak, when in fact he argues that he appeared three hours before daybreak. This inconsistency is an indication that Macarius is likely drawing upon a source for the Hellene's arguments rather than crafting them wholesale.

yarn that, after nine hours had passed, Jesus came to them at the tenth (that is, "at the fourth watch of the night"),[61] and found the disciples [still] sailing across the lake. And he calls it a "sea," and not merely a "sea," but one disturbed by a storm and terribly raging and tossed frighteningly by the disturbance of the waves, in order that, from this, he might introduce Jesus as if having performed a great sign, by stopping waves both large and lawless, and having saved from the depths of the sea the disciples who were in danger but a moment. 4. From children's stories such as these we have learned that the Gospel is [merely] a deceptive stage play.[62] Which is why we examine each passage in great detail.[63]

VII. What is the meaning of the passage: "You have the poor always, but me you do not have always"?[64]

7. 1. At any rate, since we have found another incoherent little phrase spoken by Christ to the disciples we have decided not to pass it in silence—where he says: "You have the poor always, but me you do not have always."[65] 2. The reason for the statement was this: a woman brought a vial of myrrh and poured it upon his head.[66] But as they were chattering about the inappropriateness of what she had done, he said: "Why do you trouble this woman? She has done a good deed for me, for you have the poor with you always,

---

61 Cf. Mk. 6:48.
62 Compare Porphyry, *Against the Christians* fr. 55 (Harnack), apud Jerome, *Questions on Genesis* 1.10: "It must be noted that every aggregation of water, whether it is salty or sweet is termed a 'sea' in the idiom of the Hebrew language; in vain, then, does Porphyry accuse the evangelists of using the word 'sea' instead of 'lake' for Genezareth, so as to fabricate that miracle for the ignorant, wherein Christ walked upon the sea, when every lake and aggregation of water is termed a 'sea.'"
63 As Goulet (2003), 393 notes, the Hellene's critique is based on a fairly detailed comparative criticism of the synoptic gospels and John. The synoptics (Mk. 6:45–52; Mt. 14:22–33) do not mention the Sea of Galilee by name, though Mark 6:19 states that the disciples are sailing across to Bethsaida. In Matthew (14:13–21), the pericope is preceded by the feeding of the five thousand (Mt. 14:13–21); the parallel at John 6:1–15 begins by noting that "Jesus went to the other side of the Sea of Galilee, which is the Sea of Tiberias." The Hellene's polemic thus requires this comparative work, a knowledge of Palestinian geography, having read/heard Christian synoptic exegeses of these passages, or any combination of these. If, however, Macarius has fabricated the Hellene's objections himself, then the objection sounds much like other common ζητήματα ("questions") found in Christian "question and answer" literature; see also discussion in the Introduction.
64 Cf. Jn. 12:8.
65 Cf. Jn. 12:8.
66 Cf. Mt. 26:7; Jn. 12:3.

but me you do not have always."⁶⁷ 3. For they were muttering not a little: should not the myrrh, rather, get a good price and be given to the poor who were hungry to meet their expenses? On account of this, as if it were an inappropriate remark, he uttered this mischievous statement, saying that he would not always be with them—he who reassured them elsewhere, saying to them: "I will be with you until the end of the age."⁶⁸ But when he was vexed about the myrrh he denied that he would be with them always.⁶⁹

After the master of Hellenic cleverness uttered these things against the divine teachings of Christ, since no one responded, he was silent for a moment. But we, experiencing the same thing as he who set fire to the smashed stumps of the many-headed Hydra,⁷⁰ which immediately grew back many in place of the one when each dragon's head had been severed, experiencing the same thing for a moment we were similarly hard pressed. For after we persuasively and once and for all untangled three of his propositions, or four or five, this fellow imitating the mythic Hydra, put forward myriad questions after one had been untangled, indefinitely extending [his] speculation into difficult [passages of Scripture]. For instance, presently having put forward questions on such topics, he asked us to reply to each one. But, after recollecting everything that had been said, we spoke, beginning with the first question.

8. 1. For what reason did Christ perform no wondrous sign when he was brought before the High Priest and before Pilate, nor display a reputable attitude, nor offer any high-flown speech or anything akin to wisdom, but was observed in a humble attitude, offering an abrupt, simple speech,

---

67 Mt. 26:10; Jn. 12:8.
68 Mt. 28:20.
69 Jerome references a Porphyrian critique of inconsistency in Jesus's statements (Porphyry, *Against the Christians* 70 [Harnack], apud Jerome, *Against the Pelagians* 2.17): "[Jesus] said that he would not go, yet did what he earlier said he would not. Porphyry barks at this, accusing him of inconstancy and changeableness, not knowing that everything scandalous must be ascribed to the flesh." In the reference in Jerome, Porphyry's criticism is directed against John 7:8–10: "'Go to the feast yourselves; I am not going up to this feast, for my time has not yet fully come.' So saying, he remained in Galilee. But after his brothers had gone up to the feast, then he also went up, not publicly but in private." Harnack (1916) prints the passage from Jerome as a parallel to this section of the *Apocriticus*, though only the mode of argument is parallel, not the details; the focus on inconsistency in Jesus's statements was a feature of Porphyry's *Against the Christians* as well as Julian's *Against the Galilaeans*.
70 Herakles, with the help of Iolaus, killed the Hydra in the second of his twelve labours. Each time Herakles smashed one of the heads with his club, Iolaus cauterized it, preventing a new head from growing (see Apollodorus, *Library* 2.5.2).

and a sore sight? 2. So that he would not void the prophecies about him and render the sacred tablets[71] false and make useless the labour of the holy men, which they piously endured as they proclaimed the account of the [divine] economy, and wrote of the mystery[72] of his coming, and long before proclaimed the manner of his Passion. 3. As the eloquent and great Isaiah somewhere says, "We have seen him, and he had no form or beauty, but his form was without honour,"[73] and elsewhere, "A man being beaten, who knows how to bear weakness,"[74] and elsewhere, "He was led like a sheep to the slaughter, like a mute lamb,"[75] while elsewhere in the person of Christ he says: "I gave my back to whips, my cheek to blows, but my face was not turned away from the shame of those spitting on me."[76] But it is possible to find myriad other things said about him by the prophets.

4. If, then, as you yourself say, when he was standing before the High Priest and the governor he had offered them portentous words, astonished them with divine signs, terrified them with a novel sight, or had by performing some sudden portent caused them to fall face down on the ground, then he would have rejected every prophetic judgment and had no regard for the foreknowledge of the divinely inspired men of earlier times, rendered the words of the famous memorials[77] invalid, annulled the divine declarations of the Holy Spirit, and, to put it simply, he would have set aside every notion about him, if he fulfilled the [divine] economy of his death with a sign from on high, subjected the universe to the constraint of fear, and mastered those present with a supercilious terror.

5. For if he had subdued the governor and the high priests by force, in the way that God shook a rock with a word, with a word rocked a building, with a word dispersed the thick air, and with a word combatted the anger of wild beasts, he would have done an injustice.[78] In making them accept

---

71 I.e. the Scriptures.
72 Cf. Ignatius, *Ephesians* 19.1; Justin Martyr, *Dialogue with Trypho* 40.1.
73 Is. 53:2b–3a.
74 Is. 53:3b.
75 Is. 53:7b.
76 Is. 50:6.
77 The "famous monuments" or "famous stelae" (ἀοίδιμαι στῆλαι) is a metaphor for the Hebrew Bible; Macarius's use of the word "stele" likens the scriptures to stone monuments inscribed with deeds, dedications, etc. See also 3.12.10 below, where Macarius uses the phrase "the monument of the Sacred Writing."
78 Cf. Irenaeus, *Against Heresies* 5.1.1, which stresses that the incarnate Word used only "persuasion," not "force," in redeeming humanity, as the latter would have run contrary to "justice."

the good by force, he would have offended justice, and he would even have seemed suspicious for this, as if he were performing novel marvels through sorcery,[79] and been judged like one of the so-called Gorgons,[80] if he had frightened Pilate with extraordinary wonders, if he had scared the priests with novel signs, if he had reduced the Jewish people with portents. 6. In this, falsity would fight against truth; in this, the wonders done by him would introduce a foul opinion among men, that the deeds he did were not based on discernment, but in shadow and fakery; in this, everything done well and long ago on land and sea, in city and field, would all be thought and judged a dream and not a waking vision;[81] in this, Jeremiah, who names him a spotless lamb led [82] as if he were a sacrifice, would be overturned, and again he would be lying tremendously when he describes him as the God-Word inscribed among men.[83]

7. For he who does things foreign to humanity does not dwell among men, but would have his own specific place separated from them. In this, he

---

[79] On the charge that Christ was a sorcerer see Matthew 12.24; Justin, *First Apology* 30; Arnobius, *Against the Nations* 1.51, etc.

[80] The Gorgons were female creatures with serpents for hair whose gaze was so terrifying it turned those who looked at them into stone; the best-known Gorgon in the Greek mythological tradition is Medusa, who was killed by Perseus.

[81] A "waking vision (ὕπαρ)" was reliable while a mere dream (ὄναρ) was considered unreliable and without inherent relation to reality; cf. Homer, *Odyssey* 19.547; Plato, *Statesman* 278e. The distinction between "waking vision" and "dreams" was also important in early Christian discussions of the visions of the prophets; see for example Eusebius, *Commentary on Isaiah* 1.1: "Now, he [i.e. Isaiah] says *vision* (Is. 1:1); this is not common sight gained by human eyes, but epoptic prophetic vision of events in much later times; for just as if someone could see the approach of wars and the sacking and enslavements of besieged lands represented in color on a great tablet, in the same manner he seems to have seen things in a waking vision, not a dream (ὕπαρ ἀλλ' οὐ καθ' ὕπνους), when the Spirit of God illuminated his soul."

[82] A marginal gloss in A that begins here reads: "Not for this reason alone did the Lord not utter divine words nor perform wonders when he was before Pilate, but because if, on the one hand, the Lord did such things, as I said, and they did not believe, he would have made their crime greater, while on the other hand, that [crime] which was done by a few would have to no good end been done by many. For this reason he spoke to the Jews earlier in parables, not because he had evil intent, but in order that he not make their sin greater. And indeed, O champion of truth, what did the splitting of the rocks, the opening of tombs mean [cf. Mt. 27:51–52] ... were these small wonders? But not ... those with hearts of stone. Macarius." As Goulet ([2003], 89, n.1) remarks, if the phrase "as I said," refers to 2.30.5ff, then the gloss may indicate an emendation, though if we take the phrase "O champion of truth" as a remark *against* Macarius, then this note may have been written by another Macarius in reaction to the author. The former seems the more likely scenario to the present translators.

[83] Jer. 11:19a, 30:9 LXX.

who says, in the person of the Only-begotten, "They gave gall for my food and for my drink they gave me vinegar,"[84] is being completely untruthful.

8. For who, struck by the flash of such a [divine] manifestation, would dare to ready vinegar and prepare gall? Who would not tremble, seeing him [appear] severe and terrible and adding a dreadful aspect to his words, seeing him speaking one moment and then immediately disappearing the next, at one moment visible and the next suddenly invisible? Who, tell me, seeing a character full of portents would not cringe? Who would ready a cross, wood, a thorn, or sharp nail? Who would have dared to subdue him who cannot be subdued? Who [would dare] to subdue as a man him who was speaking and acting as more than a man?

9. But, if the wood had not been set in the ground, and no nail point had been sharpened, then he would not have defeated the Passion that came through the wood, nor, after being pierced by evil, would he have healed, nor would Habbakuk have predicted anything clear when he says he has horns in his hands[85]—that is, the nails of the Cross or its "horns"—nor would Moses be trustworthy when, long before, he described him as a "life suspended."[86] All would be false which in fact is true to the very word, all the things laid up long before in these works of piety,[87] and it would be necessary to look for and expect another Jesus. For him proclaimed beforehand in the Books[88] has not come, since he did not keep to the precise manner in which they spoke, but became human by appearing as a strange spectacle.

10. For if, like Apollonius, he had made sport of life through the sorcerer's art, speaking solemnly to the emperor within the very imperial halls themselves, he would at the same time have uprooted the plants for the gardeners,[89] and truly the world would have been led astray in its judgment and the whole of creation would have been wrapped in the darkness of deceit, blindly serving a sorcerer-philosopher who could whisk away his body through evil and conceal the title of piety with an apparition. No

---

84 Ps. 68:22.
85 Hab. 3:4.
86 Cf. Dt. 28:66.
87 Arguments from prophecy were as regularly deployed against pagans as against Jews: cf. Justin, *First Apology* 31–32; Constantine, *Oration to the Saints* 19–21.
88 I.e. of scripture.
89 Allusion to Philostratus, *Life of Apollonius* 6.42. Macarius satirically overturns the claim of Philostratus to have proved, against Moiragenes, that Apollonius was not a sorcerer. Cf. Origen, *Against Celsus* 6.41; Eusebius, *Against Hierocles* 37.

longer, then, would God or the Son of God be thought to do these things, but one of those who live the life of a superstitious sophist.[90]

11. So that no such scandal would mock the salvific Passion, and that no suspicion of the practice of sorcery would sully the mystery[91] of the [divine] economy, as man he bore being subjected to outrageous things with patience, being ashamed of nothing. For he had the Impassible dwelling within and did not admit of any principle of shame. 12. For as a vessel full of fire does not admit of the cold that is applied to it externally but repels it, since it is heated from within, so too Jesus, having God within him, [like] a divine, inexhaustible, and unquenchable fire, considered the coldness of outrages as nothing, and upon seeing these calumnies, was not turned from his purpose. 13. For, just as someone who is old enough feels no shame when he sees children laughing at him, so too Christ deflected the mockeries of the Jews, as if they came at him not from men but from infants. And just as a rock covered with the droppings of myriad reptiles takes on no scratch, no spot, no mark, supporting serpents with its physical firmness though it is not scratched by them at all, so too Jesus, when the coils of the Jews raged against him after the manner of reptiles, remained firmly unblemished like a rock, admitting no mark of shame.

14. But, it was necessary, moreover, that he restrain his divine powers before the Passion, in order that after the Passion or even during the Passion itself, as he broke Hades asunder, rent the earth, resurrected a mass of inanimate bodies, and revealed an assembly of the departed, he might reveal who was suffering and Who was within him. 15. For if, in a single moment, creation had been thrown into confusion by the one who was seen[92] to suffer, then unambiguously it would have been God and the Creator within him that rocked the cosmos and extinguished the mad celebrations of the mindless. For it is not before an engagement but once it is met that a soldier makes known to the enemy what kind of soldier he is; for what could be greater than to pass through Hades for three days?[93]

---

90 Macarius may be aware that Lucian had stigmatized Christ as a "crucified sophist" at *Passing of Peregrinus* 13.

91 For the use of the term "mystery" to describe the divine economy see e.g. 1 Tim. 3:16.

92 Macarius's use of the verb δοκέω ("to seem" or rather "be manifest") here need not indicate a docetic Christology; rather, as the previous sentence and what follows makes clear, Macarius means to differentiate between the human and divine in the person of Christ.

93 The primary scriptural bases for the "harrowing of hell" are Ps. 16.8 and 1 Pet. 3:19–20, where Christ is said to have "preached to the spirits in prison, who formerly did not obey, when God's patience waited in the days of Noah," and 1 Pet. 4:6, where "the gospel was preached even to the dead." By the second century, some read in these passages a sojourn in

16. It is truly right and in good order, therefore, that Christ perform no novel marvel when brought before Pilate, so that he should not, as if donning a frightening new theatrical mask, stir up the evil of wild beasts against him, but rather provoke [them] into the struggle of battle by his humility and, loving the good, conquer their madness with intelligence and might. 17. Hence he who appeared humble in the engagement appeared most awe inspiring after the engagement, when the earth could not bear him, nor the heaven endure to watch the combat, but the former tried to shrug him off, causing earthquakes as it fled from under him, while the latter, so to speak, closed the eye of day and no longer permitted the sight of what was happening.[94]

9. 1. Up to this point, I have given you answers concerning the Passion, but concerning how he agonized about the Passion and feared those who were coming for him, I will explain this point to you more clearly, even if the passage seems contradictory and unclear. For by saying "Do not fear those who kill the body,"[95] though he ostensibly fears death and is frightened to such an extent that he begs off dying through prayer, saying "Father, if it is possible, let the cup pass,"[96] he seems to contradict his own precepts and invalidate [his own] ethical prescriptions. For if he establishes that others must not fear death, while he himself, when in dire straits, prays it be taken away, what he says is greatly lacking in clarity.

2. But one must not look superficially at the letter, but rather hunt for the deeper meaning of the [divine] economy hidden in the letter. Just as wise physicians do not judge a plant based on its manifest unpleasantness alone, but discern with understanding the aid lying hidden within the herb and, holding it in high regard for this reason, prescribe it, in the same manner must we, as we apply ourselves to the divine teachings, pay attention not only to the unpleasantness of the letter, but also search for the unseen plan, seek out the concealed profit. We must examine what it means, then, when he says: "Father, if it is possible, let the cup pass from me."[97]

3. Having taught the disciples to despise death and having protected them with sturdy weapons of endurance, he himself shudders with

---

Hades to release the patriarchs, prophets, and or other righteous souls who lived before the Advent (e.g. Tertullian, *On the Soul* 55; Celsus apud Origen, *Against Celsus* 2.43).
94 Cf. Mt. 27:45–56.
95 Mt. 10:28.
96 Mt. 26:39.
97 Mt. 26:39.

cowardice and trembles in the face of death because of, as I said, the abundant correctness of the [divine] economy. And what it is that caused him to have doubt, hear truly.

4. The Enemy, fearing that Christ was truly God and Child of God, with delays hindered the crowd of the Jews from taking the field and did not effect the appointed moment of the Passion; the fear seized him that he would be utterly destroyed, as if struck into obscurity, if in attacking one he thought a man he was coming to blows with God. 5. For seeing him call the dead from their tombs and back to life, and the blind led out from their dark prison into the enjoyment of brightness and light, seeing suffering driven from men in one moment and illness fleeing at his word alone, seeing the sea becoming firm for him like a road that carries travellers, seeing the winds stopping from their great clashing and becoming mild, seeing heaven on high opened as a testimony to him, hearing a voice thundering out from the aetherial tear, hearing "beloved son" and "Only-begotten" called out sonorously from on high,[98] and having ruminated about these things on each occasion, he did not dare to arm his own battle formation, since he was astounded by what had been said.[99]

6. And if the Lord's Passion had not happened, the whole world would have remained without correction, the universe would have been condemned to the utmost ridicule, the trespass of disobedience would have remained indelible, and the wounds of the trespass would never have been purified nor the bruises of the curse relieved.[100] Faults worse than what went before would have grown. Human nature would have been completely destroyed. There would have been a tragic scene even more dire, if he who came to extend impassibility through the Passion to the people present[101] had not suffered it because of the Demon's knavery.

7. Hence, so that this evil would not become more grievous than every evil, beyond every sorrow and calamity, he made his humanity evident, feigned fear, faced the Passion, agonized over death, faked the specifics of suffering, and acted out human humiliation, in order to provoke this

---

98 Cf. Mt. 3:16–17.

99 Or possibly "by the things spoken of" [i.e. in this paragraph].

100 Cf. Is. 53:4–5, where the "suffering servant" endures wounds on behalf of the transgression of the people of Israel.

101 The manuscript reads τοῖς παροῦσιν ("to the people present"); Goulet conjectures τοῖς πάσχουσιν, as better fitting the style of the passage, thus giving "if he who came to extend impassibility through the passion to those who suffer had not suffered it because of the Demon's knavery."

[enemy] and trumpet him on, like a beast from its cage, with the clamour of his voice.

8. For since there are two things which caused humanity, once defeated, to fall (obviously the tree and the food of the tree) and he had conquered the fall that came from the food by fasting, but had conquered by feigning being hungry[102] (for when he was not hungry, the Tempter was silent and hid the knavery of his own evil, but when he who was fasting desired to eat, the Tempter ran upon Christ as if upon one suffering and when he attacked him he was defeated and withdrew far off, as is written: "He stood apart for a time"),[103] since, then, he withdrew when defeated by his fasting, that Devil who previously wanted to deceive Christ with food like Adam and did not dare to attack because he bore the bruise marks of blows, for this reason the Unique and only combatant who always conquers and is never conquered faked being afraid, in order that he might lure this one [i.e. the Devil] into battle once again, as he had first roused him to an engagement by being hungry and, being victorious, beat down the one who had previously been victorious through [his use of] food.

9. Now, once he had purified the sickness engendered through the food through his athletic[104] fasting, he was bravely eager to destroy the deceit that had come via the tree, righting the fallen tree—or rather him who recklessly ate from it—by means of a tree, in order that, once the Cross was rooted or fixed in the earth, the general upon it might, firing his arrows, overthrow the tyrant who was stationed on [that] other tree, so that from a tree he might kill the enemy in the tree. 10. Thus, because he was eager and needed to hurry the cross along, the Saviour cries for pity, and does so with a most affected cry, and begs the Father with insistent supplications, not in order that the cup might [actually] pass him by, but that it might come quickly.

11. And he did well to name the Passion a "cup" and not a "passion," for what was happening brought joy and not grief, and the Passion was sweet nectar and most delicious, which the Saviour, after drinking it, served to

---

102 See Clement, *Stromateis* 3.7.59.3 for the Valentinian tenet that Christ did not truly feel hunger. See also Eustathius of Antioch, who argues against the "Arians" that if the incarnate Christ truly used material organs for digesting food then he must *a fortiori* also have possessed a "true," and not a "noetic" soul (*Against the Ariomaniacs* 4).

103 Lk. 4:13.

104 For the comparison of the Christian ascetic to an athlete see 1 Cor. 9:24–26; Heb. 12:1; Origen, *On Prayer* 30.2; Eusebius, *Ecclesiastical History* 5.1.42; Gregory of Nyssa, *Life of Moses* 2.36.

believers once he had breathed out his life. For if this were not the case, he would not have said "cup." 12. For, being eager that the cup be prepared quickly on account of him who does not see and does not understand the, if I may say, unseen [nature] of the [divine] plan, he says "Let it pass," so that once he [i.e. the Devil] heard Christ's pitiful voice he would attack with his own troop even more quickly than was necessary and, being repelled, experience the utmost defeat, and so that, baited by the humbleness of his words, he would perish, like a dragon pierced by a hook.

13. An experienced fisherman does this when he wants to catch a plump fish from the depths; by placing a small worm around the hook he catches one tricked by the gluttony of his stomach. So too Christ, when he wishes to draw out by its throat the arch-evil, villainous, and deceitful dragon that is hidden in the sea of life, wraps his body around the hook of his Godhead after the manner of a worm, and speaking through it, tricks the intelligible[105] and spiritual serpent. 14. Hence, long ago in the human person of the psalmist, he indicated this, saying: "But I am a worm and not a man."[106] 15. This worm, now united to the divine Word and swimming in the sea of mortal life, urged the dragon's mouth upon himself and caught him, though seeming to be caught [himself]. This very worm secretly dealt the fatal wound. This worm, having crept secretly, unobserved into inaccessible tombs, raised the mute bodies of the dead. This worm, having circled Hades with his coils, choked the guards surrounding it and, seizing the rulers there, bound them fast. 16. This worm, having entered into the archives of the tyrant, shredded the records of sins, completely destroying all of the records in which people's faults had been registered.[107] This worm made the Devil's coffer disappear, which he had made, fashioning it from

---

105 That is, belonging to the incorporeal realm which is evident only to the intellect, not the senses.

106 Ps. 21:7a LXX. There are close parallels to Macarius's extended exegesis of Christ as "worm" in the fourth-century writer Amphilochius of Iconium: "'I am a worm and not a man': on account of the fact that he fulfils the scripture 'You will catch the dragon with a fishhook' [Job 40:25] and just like a good fisherman draws him in, lowering the resplendent Godhead into the very depths of life, like a hook hidden by the worm of the body" (*De recens baptizatis* [*Orat.* 7 = Datema 166–171]), see also idem, *In illud: Pater si possibile est* (*Orat.* 6 = Datema 147–149) for a lengthier parallel in which Amphilochius, like Macarius, adduces Ps. 21:7 and Job 40:25 to explicate Mt. 26:39; also compare Gregory of Nyssa, *Catechetical Orations* 24.33–36. The reading of Ps. 21:7 in terms of the incarnation can be found already in Justin Martyr, *Dialogue with Trypho* 98.1. See also discussion in Goulet (2003) 206–209.

107 Perhaps an allusion to Colossians 2:14 ("... erasing the record that stood against us with its legal demands. He set this aside, nailing it to the cross" [NRSV]).

the wood of the tree of disobedience, and in which he hid the mantle of human glory. This worm was born without intercourse and coition. 17. It is mystical, unique,[108] unutterable. Through this worm the mystical hook captured the Ogygian[109] dragon, about which one of the chosen saints prophesied: "You will draw out a dragon with a hook."[110]

18. This response from us is enough for you, and the explanation of Christ's begging off the Passion on account of the universal plan is completely clear.

10. 1. But the third topic we must address for you is that concerning Christ's saying to the Jews: "If you believed Moses, you would believe in me, for he wrote about me."[111] That Moses wrote about Christ, the whole world knows clearly when they read him saying in one place that a prophet will be raised up in his place, in another that he [i.e. Christ] makes man with the Father, in another telling mystically of the Passion with a bush,[112] in another writing about and indicating the Cross in the form of a rod, and in yet another that a golden jar—his pure body—contains imperishable food—the heavenly Word—and myriad additional things of the same kind and consistent with these.[113]

2. But while you say that the writings of Moses suffered during the Captivity and were rewritten inaccurately by Esdras, it will be found that they were rewritten with complete accuracy. For it was not that one person spoke to Esdras and another to Moses, but the same Spirit taught both and dictated the same things clearly to both. And the same architect put the Mosaic Law back together just like a house destroyed by enemies, harmoniously organizing each section[114] according to the rule of wisdom.

3. But it is possible for you, if you have a truth-loving attitude, to know

---

108 Unique = μονογενής ("*monogenēs*"), also the subtitle of the *Apocriticus*.

109 The adjective "Ogygian" derives from Ogyges, a mythic king of Thebes during whose reign occurred a flood (see e.g. Pausanias, *Description of Greece* 9.5.1), and came to signify "mythically ancient," much as the modern English phrase "antediluvian."

110 Job 40:25a. Since Leviathan appears as a *drakōn* (serpent) in the Septuagint, he is easily identified with the "old serpent" (i.e. Satan) of Revelation 12:3–9. Cf. Origen, *Fragments on Job* (Pitra 386: 34–42).

111 Jn. 5:46.

112 On the burning bush of Exodus 3:2 as an adumbration of Christ's suffering, see Clement of Alexandria, *Pedagogue* 2.8.75.

113 Cf. Dt. 18:15; Gen. 1:26; Ex. 3:2; Num. 17:10; Heb. 9:4; Ex. 16:33; Heb. 9:4.

114 κεφάλαιον = "section," "chief point," or "chapter"; Macarius likens Esdras redaction of the text of the Mosaic Law to one who rebuilds a house originally desgined and built by another.

clearly that he who was crucified was the Word of God, God the Word, and Christ, which the divinely inspired words declared from the outset, and every prophetic tablet mentioned, since David sings in psalmody and says: "The Lord saved his Christ."[115] But about Christ being the Word, Isaiah says: "A law and a word of the Lord will come forth from Zion, and he will judge amidst the nations and he will put many nations to shame."[116] 4. But about Christ being Lord God, David says, "God is Lord and has become manifest to us,"[117] and again that the Word, being God, was anointed as ruler, in so far as he is human, he says: "On account of this, God, your God, anointed you."[118]

5. But why is it necessary to offer you many hackneyed testimonies, which the four corners of the world[119] accepted when they learned of them? So, then, since Moses wrote many luminous testimonies about Christ, but the Jews did not want to accept these [testimonies] about him, though they had read them, he [Christ] rightly said to them: "If you believed Moses, you would believe in me, for he wrote about me."[120]

11. 1. Since this explanation is quite clear, let us inquire into another subject—that of the swine possessed by demons that drowned in the sea and the swineherds who immediately fled.

2. Do not be disturbed because Matthew refers to two demoniacs but Mark only one. For Matthew says there were two demons, not, in fact, that two men were possessed by demons,[121] while Mark says there is one man, but many demons in him, so that the two whom Matthew mentions are certain leading and grievous demons, but that with them other demons also besiege the man. 3. Or perhaps the former, by saying there are two men, introduces the number of the subsistent entities, but Mark, not taking thought of the number, predicates about the essence that has been affected.[122] For the common parlance of liberally educated people

---

115 Ps. 19:7a (LXX).
116 Is. 2:3d–4a.
117 Ps. 117:27a.
118 Ps. 44:8b, quoted at Heb. 1:9; cf. Acts 4:38.
119 Cf. Mt. 24:31; Mk. 13:27. Irenaeus argues that there are four gospels to match the four corners of the world (*Against Heresies* 3.11.8).
120 Jn. 5:46.
121 The received text refers to two "demoniacs" that encounter Jesus, while the Hellene and Macarius read (perhaps by simple synecdoche, rather than a misreading or variant text of Matthew); see 3.4.1 above.
122 The terms ὑπόστασις ("subsistent entity") and οὐσία ("essence") seem to be used in

has this habit: for instance, when he who shepherds guards a flock, one says in reference to the essence, "The shepherd carefully watches over the sheep," and by saying this he does not refer to one [sheep], for they are many in number, but since, though there are many sheep, they possess a single essential nature, he says "sheep" in reference to the definition of the essence.[123] But at other times, [one says], "The shepherd watches over the sheep," in reference to the definition of the number.[124]

4. But in other ways, too, the plural is customarily referred to in the singular: "The barbarian met the king," instead of "the barbarians" or "the barbarian nation"; and "the king gathered the troop," instead of "the troops," and it is possible to find myriad related [examples].

5. Hence it is not necessary that we wear ourselves out on account of these [passages], if one said there was one demoniac but the other two, for the one, as I said, mentions the essence, since what was being tyrannized was human nature, while the other refers to the subsistent entity as happening to be not one but two in number.

6. It remains necessary to examine why the demons, who had already long harassed the rational [nature] with innumerable tortures when their essence was enflamed by the ray of the Godhead, begged not to be cast into the abyss, and why Christ acceded to their request, allowing them to be sent into the very swine into which they wanted [to go]. 7. The demons, I think, fearfully being melted by the fire which lit them up when they caught sight of the Saviour, wanted, as they were burning with the heat, to run into the water in any way [possible] and be relieved of the burning that was pressing upon them. But since, as they were incorporeal in nature and unable to submerge in the bath of the waters in their naked form, they sought the herd of swine as a means of access, so that entering through them they might release the burning heat. 8. Cunningly, the demons did not seek other herd animals as vehicles, but those forbidden in the Law of Moses, pretending to honour the letter of the legislation

---

the sense defined by Basil of Caesarea, *Letter* 214.4: "... as the common is to the particular, so is *ousia* to *hypostasis*."

123 "Definition of essence" translates ὁ τῆς οὐσίας λόγος; Macarius seems to use this phrase in its Aristotelean sense here, as defined in *Categories* 1a1, and defines the secondary substance "man" as described, for instance at *Categories* 2a14–19. Macarius also appears to equate "definition of essence" and "definition of nature" at 2.20.8 above.

124 This argument may cast light on the curious reasoning of Gregory of Nyssa in his *Letter to Ablabius*, where, in defending (his own or Basil's) earlier analogy between three men and the persons of the Trinity, he contends that one should not speak of "men" in the plural, but only of "Man."

that was despised by those inhabiting Palestine at that time. 9. Do not assume that the herd of swine was Jewish; rather, they belonged to the Roman armies that had received the cities of the East from the emperor as the Romans say, as a *sedeton*.[125] For at that time cohorts and legions of Roman power settled within these districts, since the Jews had made a treaty with the Romans. 10. For from the time of Augustus, who took a census of the whole inhabited world,[126] and the time of Tiberius, and still yet from the times before them, the Jews were subjects of the Romans and their whole territory was subject to tribute. For example, the emperor appointed as King of Judaea Herod, the son of Antipater, who was serving in the temple of Apollo at Ascalon,[127] and sent Pilate, who was also a Hellene,[128] as governor and judge, and Romans had received every position of authority over the Jews; thus for a long time the yoke of servitude hung over them because of their wickedness. 11. Hence, at that moment in time, there were flocks of herd animals belonging to Roman owners, while Roman managers who answered to their masters kept their property in good order. Thus the demons, being enemies yet enforcers of the Law, drove the swine into the water because they were burning.

12. But when Mark portrays Christ questioning the demon, saying "What is your name?"[129] as if he does not know, Christ does not interrogate the loathsome creature because he is ignorant about what the demon is called, but in order that it might accuse itself with its own words as an apostate from the Kingdom above. He asked "What is your name?" and it answered, "Legion." 13. For it was not so then, but it was a legion before, when it guarded the power of the Kingdom above, as has been written: "Am I not able right now to call upon my Father, and he will send me twelve

---

125 Macarius transliterates the Latin word *sedes* ("home," "base-camp") into Greek; Macarius's description of cities in Palestine serving as military bases better describes the deployment of Roman forces after the Bar Kochba revolt through the reign of Diocletian than the time of Jesus. Before the Jewish War of 70 CE there were few standing troops in Judaea/Palestine, while in the aftermath of the Jewish War Legio X Frentensis was stationed in Judaea and joined by Legio VI Ferrata c.120 CE; the former was stationed in or near Jerusalem and Caesarea and the latter at the town of Legio, along the road leading from Caesarea into the Galilee. Diocletian relocated most troops in Palestine to the southern portion of the province as part of his innovative defence-in-depth strategy.
126 Lk. 2:1.
127 Cf. Eusebius, *Ecclesiastical History* 1.6.2, 1.7.11; *Gospel Demonstration* 8.1.44.
128 Pontius Pilatus was Roman, not Greek; Macarius here uses the term "Hellene" in the sense of "gentile," or "pagan."
129 Mk. 5:9; Lk. 8:30.

legions of angels?"[130] But this legion deserted and was wrapped up in the wickedness of apostasy, finding a hiding place within humans by means of its craftiness. It was truly a craven and wretched legion—not a legion but a brigand,[131] pillaging the region around the earth, and committing piracy and subjecting those captured to desperate calamities. 14. In order, then, that Christ might teach those who heard for what sort of "service"[132] the legion fell, he says: "What is your name," not so that he could learn it, for he knew, but so that those present could.

15. For the demons, so thoroughly tortured as they were, appealed to the ancient name of their rank so that they might obtain mercy, in order that they might recall their old military service, as if to a great and philanthropic king who is well inclined, all but saying: "We were once legion. We were troops of your impartial power. As you remember that station which we once occupied,[133] have mercy, and do not send us into the abyss. 16. We were your legion, but are now evil brigands; then we served, but now we plunder; then we lived near your palace, but now we live near the subterranean regions; then we occupied a pure vantage point, but now we are cast about with flotsam and filth. We ask to receive an appropriate residence, so that we might no longer torment rational beings. 17. For since we have been given foul stench as our penalty, we seek something that rejoices in foul stench as vehicles. We request to be sent into a herd of swine, since we are justly cast out of the incorruptible country. We eagerly desire not to assume a herd of sheep or horses or cattle—for these are pure and unpolluted animals—but a pack of stinking, disorderly swine, so that we might teach those who reside here by means of this deed and make plain the character of our disgustingness. 18. Everyone whose mind is strong and whose thinking is sound will fear to imitate this swinish and filthy way of life, when they learn that demons have come to such depths of destruction. But also, one will know the turn we have taken by the ugliness of our form, and not be eager to make a similar choice with his life. 19. In order, then, that we might become a living reminder and a great example and a universal lesson, give us the

---

130 Mt. 26:53. The host swells to myriads of myriads at Revelation 5:11 (cf. Hebrews 12:22). Later Christian writers were content to refer to a *stratia* (host) without further enumeration: see e.g. Clement, *Stromateis* 5.7.7.

131 Macarius here illustrates his own assertion that the singular can stand for a collective plural.

132 The term λειτουργία ("service") refers sarcastically to both the poor martial and the poor ministerial "service" of the fallen angels in heaven.

133 Cf. Revelation 12:4–7.

swine to lead us into the sea, so that all might learn that we do not even have authority to rule over vile [animals] unless we are commanded and receive that office from the divine Spirit, [and] so that the whole world will look down upon us because of this, since we have no authority over the swine nor do the permitted[134] herd animals fall under our tyranny."

20. Because of this wise policy, I think, the Saviour did not cast the demons into the abyss but into a herd of swine and through them into the sea, [thereby] helping every individual and duly teaching, and made evident to men the place of the demons' correction, while making clear the lesson of that one should not be zealous to live the life of a filthy herd animal. 21. For if, as you propose, he had sent them into the abyss, it would have been unclear to everyone because unseen, ambiguous because unperceived, and suspicious because incorporeal. Someone might have suspected that, having disobeyed Christ, they did not go down into the abyss, but into neighbouring or even into far-off inhabitants, and by fleeing, effected worse harm. 22. Now this was not the case, but it was made clear and evident to all that the demons went into the sea when the swine were destroyed, and departed from the human abode.

12. 1. Accept this as a sufficient response about this story, but I will readily take on the next question: that concerning the passage "Sell your property and give to the poor and you will have a treasure-house in heaven."[135] 2. I will give you an account of this pericope from the beginning. A rich man came to Christ with an august air, but a crooked and twisted attitude, and spoke mischievously, saying: "What must I do to inherit eternal life?"[136] He answered him not as a teacher, but as a kindly father, saying gently: "Keep the commandments."[137] And he asserted that the commandments are the <starting point> for eternal life,[138] preparing him through the commandments for a higher vantage point, then, leading him into the Kingdom of heaven itself by means of wealth—if, that is, by earnestly adopting a better, more philosophical [way of life],[139] he at once exchange

---

134 I.e. "kosher."
135 Mt. 19:21.
136 Lk. 18:18.
137 Mt. 19:17.
138 Cf. Galatians 3:24. "Starting point" = ἀφορμή, that is, a prompt or basic tenets, the contemplation of which will lead to higher contemplative and ascetic practice; compare the title of Porphyry's introductory treatise, "Starting Points Towards Intelligibles" (ἀφορμαὶ πρὸς τὰ νοητά), known commonly by the Latin title, *Sententiae ad intelligibilia ducentes*.
139 That is to say, a way of austerity in accordance with fixed intellectual principles.

the lesser for the greater and dole out his heaps of corruptible things to the poor so that he might receive what is incorruptible.[140] 3. For it is not wealth, as you for your part claim, that shuts the rich man out of the Kingdom; on the contrary, it brings him in, if acting soberly he manages it well. For just as a soldier, when he uses his full array of armour finely and well, becomes honoured, illustrious, and renowned through it, and through it enters the Kingdom majestically, through it illuminates the interior of the palace halls, through it becomes distinguished for his powers of command, through it is considered unconquerable in the cities; but if he wears it badly and carries it not as it ought to be, through it becomes easy for every enemy to defeat, and through it is cast outside the city walls as a traitor, through it becomes easily captured by enemies, through it is exiled because he appears impure, through it vengeance is enacted upon him and he is cut off from life, and in this no one blames the armament, but rather him who did not use the armament well; 4. just as no one upon seeing someone resplendent in armour says that the armour produces the glory, but the diligence of him who makes use of the arms. No one, therefore, who has any sense ever praises someone's possession or conditions, but the one who has acquired them, if he uses them wisely, since it is not <grammar, rhetoric, or> stone that makes a grammarian, a rhetorician, or sculptor celebrated, but the artisan who knowledgeably shapes the material receives praise, and the grammarian, by diligently practicing grammar becomes famous in respect of his possession of knowledge [of grammar], and the rhetor, likewise, and the builder and the physician, but if on the contrary, each should neglect his proper knowledge and by inattention fall into the chorus of those who lack inspired talent, we would not judge the rational or practical art to be the cause of their ill repute, but rather each one's inattention and disdain [for his art].[141] 5. Someone, too, who has wealth and manages it well is a participant in the Kingdom of heaven, but one who uses it badly is shut out from it, and suffers this not because of wealth, but with good reason because of his own depravity.

6. Now someone who does not bear poverty as he ought does not receive praise on account of his poverty; for there are many poor people, and not all are praised, but each is [judged] appropriately according to his own proficiency. Wealth, therefore, does not harm the rich man, but the ignoble

---

140 Cf. Lk. 16:9; Rom. 15:27; Clement of Alexandria, *Who is the Rich Man Who Shall be Saved?* 30–32.
141 Cf. Origen, *On First Principles* 1.4.1.

disposition of the rich man shows wealth to be unprofitable and useless. Nor does poverty lead the poor man into heaven, but the attitude of the poor man makes poverty profitable for the soul. For nobility of virtue and disposition makes success shine for both the rich man and the poor man.

7. As a dose of medicine that has a single power, if given to the afflicted and to the healthy does not effect a singular condition in those who take it, but alters the feeling of some for the worse but makes the bodies of others better, since it is not the power of the medicine that does this, but those who take it prove the dissimilarity of the dose because of the dissimilar status of bodily condition, so too is the definition of virtue one and the same, yet it leads many rich people to a better condition, while many others it leads to a worse and mean condition, and likewise makes many poor people clients and friends of God, while it makes others hated and despised by God, and does this to them not by its own power—for in that case, being one it would either help all or harm all—but as it finds each person with his own disposition, and it bestows its effects just as he is capable of receiving [it, i.e. wealth].

8. Now no one who has forsaken wealth out of desire for the Kingdom of heaven has met with shame in eternal life or by leaving behind his own goods has not achieved his aim, for by giving what he had, he received what he did not have.[142] Leaving behind the intolerable burden of earth, he received a glory that is easy and light.

9. For the sake of this topic I will describe one rich man for you, being silent about many more because of the multitude of passages that demonstrate that wealth here in this world has been a launching point for heavenly wealth. For all that, passing over the many I will mention but one, for this one will be the critic and accuser of the many. 10. This patient and long-suffering man, whom you have certainly heard mentioned often in the monument of the Sacred Writing as the Toparch of the East and called "Job,"[143] who was indeed wealthy and foremost and second to no man of his day. He wielded the sceptre of monarchic rule with a right soul, and by the steadfast deliberations of his thoughts respected the rule of the Almighty, and elevated the polity with thoroughbred nobleness, and magnified his life by blameless conduct, doing what is just in every case both in word and deed, and bore his wealth as though he were not wealthy,[144] maintained a

---

142 Cf. Mt. 19:29; Mk. 10:29; Lk. 18:29–30.
143 Cf. Job 1:1–3.
144 Cf. 1 Cor. 7:29.

BOOK 3

humble attitude both day and night. Not selling his possessions and doling it out in bits to the poor, but giving the essence of the possessions themselves and unselfishly filling up the laps of the needy, and by his clothing the naked with sheep's wool, by this giving to the poor from his table the morsel which he ate and not another, by this mandating that his dining room be shared in common by strangers, by sitting alongside the powerless like one of them in a spirit of friendship and bemoaning their gnashing of teeth [in sorrow], and finally having forsaken all his assets and enjoyment because of longing for eternal life and having judged the possessions of this life all to be fleeting on account of the undefiled dwelling that is in heaven, he loved the dunghill.[145]

Having put off wealth he fondled his abscesses like gold and saw his worms as the most valuable pearls.[146] 11. He loved the stench more than every inhalation of royal incense. To him the heights of the dunghill were a sweet and pleasant dwelling. And neither wealth kept him out of the Kingdom, nor did poverty turn him from the virtue that is according to God, but in wealth he was beloved of God and in poverty he was beloved of virtue. And being a rich man he became rich in virtues, and when he became a poor man he loved the Creator. For him, poverty became wealth and wealth magnified the glory that one who uses his will according to reason receives from God—for wealth served and poverty obeyed his will. This man conquered evil in poverty and in wealth humbled the haughty brow of arrogance; this man in weakness destroyed the reign of temptations and in wealth turned back the trials of the passions; this man seemed well pleasing to God both in wealth and in poverty.

12. On account of this, having borne the stripes of the adversaries[147] in the skin of his flesh without yielding, he took the renowned prize for his toils; on account of this, fighting nobly against the threatening troop of Beliar, he drove away the incorporeal battle line of spirits with potsherds.[148] 13. That man, living on a dunghill because of poverty built a towered citadel admired for piety; that man, having lost the fine odour of his body and sitting in stench, breathed in the fine odour of immortality. And becoming

---

145 Contrast what was said above of the demons, who are forced to accept filth as their habitation.
146 Job 2:7–8, 9c.
147 Possibly the adversaries are Job's comforters, but cf. Job 6.15–21. No doubt Job is also assimilated here to the suffering servant of Isaiah 53.5.
148 Cf. Job 2:8.

a rich man he was well born, and becoming a poor man he became even more well born.

14. Do not think, therefore, that the Lord said, "It is easier for a camel to pass through a needle than a rich man [to pass] into the Kingdom of heaven"[149] unconditionally. For many are found in the Kingdom who are rich, but with cause he threw out the rich man from the heavens, saying: "Those having possessions will enter into the Kingdom of heaven with difficulty."[150]

15. Those, therefore, who have and do not give or share in common in sympathy with those who have not, circumscribing wealth for their own enjoyment alone and never speaking in a friendly way with the poor nor consoling a pitiable poor person nor lightening the need of someone lamenting, but turning their attention away from those who deserve mercy, and turning away from the sufferings of the despised as from pollution— these are foreigners to the Kingdom of heaven.

16. No one looks to the tribunal without advocates, no one carrying the marks of accusation goes up to the bar, no one appears before the king if he is in fact surrounded by charges, no one goes off to a festival soiled, no one introduces festivities with burdens, no one enters kingdoms carrying signs suggestive of tyranny. The poor are the advocates of the rich;[151] without them wealth is useless before God; it is a sign of wickedness and must be cast away to be found free. Possessions paint a suspicious portrait of accusations, and it is better to put it away economically and to worship the Divine with frank speech.[152] Surplus becomes a blemish and mark upon men, and it is necessary to ameliorate them thoughtfully and press on towards the blessed hearth. The protection of goods is a heavy burden and it is just to shake off that burden and march unencumbered into the festal assembly above. Possessions become the accusers of arrogance and it is useful to reject them quickly and without them ride into the Kingdom of heaven, if one believes that the Kingdom of the Holy One is in heaven.

149 Lk. 18:25.
150 Mk. 10:23; Mt. 19:23.
151 Cf. again Lk. 16:9 and Rom. 15:27.
152 "Frank speech," or παρρησία, usually connotes the bold/frank public speech, or the kind of candid conversation that can occur between social equals (see e.g. 3.1.2 above), and the privilege accorded philosophers to address social superiors with whom they would not normally be allowed to speak freely. Macarius's usage here also recalls 1 Jn. 5:14 ("This is the frankness/boldness we have towards him [i.e. the Son of God], that if we ask anything that is according to his will he listens to us."), where παρρησία connotes the authenticity of Christian worship of the divine.

BOOK 3

But if one does not believe, why does he trouble himself when he reasons in vain without faith?

13. 1. But, after developing such a discourse for you about the rich man, let us in turn add this discussion about why Christ, after sending the disciples out in the evening to attempt to cross the expanse of the sea, himself appeared at the fourth watch of the night and came upon them as they were being tossed by the waves in a tempest.

2. He did not appear to them at the fourth watch counting backwards from the end of the night, but forwards from the beginning—that is, at the fourth hour from the beginning of the night. But if, as you say, we are forced to say that it was the fourth hour before the end of the night, this is no obstacle to the question, if in fact Christ appeared to the apostles at the break of dawn.[153] For this is all we are required to find out: whether the body of water they crossed was a sea or not a sea. 3. And because even if the place happened to be a lake, it was a wide sea in respect of the way it behaved, whipped into waves like a sea by the winds and bearing the hulls of fishermen like a sea. It is possible to understand straightaway the accuracy of what is said for all waters are named "sea" by *catachresis*,[154] even if they come from rivers or streams, either from the disturbance that comes from the winds or from the turbid drink that is found in it, or the saltiness it has by virtue of its location and not by nature.[155]

4. But let the children of the grammarians or the theorists of rhetoric etymologize all this. Let us, rather, seek an answer by examining the nature of this matter: whence those who were entrusted to write the Gospel learned and received the tradition of describing lakes in their writing not as "lakes" but as "seas." For it was either by being moved by the divine Word, or following dogma, or by learning such a thing from someone who had been so instructed that they deemed it appropriate to write "sea" and not "lake." What then? We must now tell you what you ask.

---

153 On Macarius's misreading of the Hellene's interpretation of "watch" and "hour" see 3.6.1 and note 60 above.

154 *Catachresis* is defined by Quintilian (*Institutes* 8.6.34–36) as the rather forced application of a word to something else which does not otherwise have a proper term; a common example given in the *artes rhetorici* was the term πυξίς χαλκῆ (Lat. *pyxis*), or "bronze box," to refer to boxes made of any material (*Commentary on Dionysius of Thrace's Art of Grammar* (*Scholia Londonensia* 459).

155 It is one of Macarius's tricks to give his own turn to a commonplace. Here he takes the antithesis of θέσις and φύσις (convention and nature), but uses θέσις in the sense of "location."

5. He who gave an account of the creation of the cosmos, being a divine man and inspired by God, surpassing by a superior beauty[156] the nature of all the members of his race, having drunk from the ever-flowing font of wisdom, enriched by the great stream of understanding, when he wrote the inexhaustible account of the beautiful[157] and came to the concept of the wet essence heard clearly that all collections and assemblages of water were called "seas" by God.[158] 6. If, therefore, the blessed and truly reverend mouth of the Creator, the Undisturbed Beauty, the Unfading Good, who is without beginning and alone possesses immortality,[159] during creation named every gathering of water a "sea," how could the Evangelists dare to set aside the word of the Creator and call a lake what was earlier named a "sea" by God? Hence, preserving the doctrine that was in the mind of the Creator, they have called the lake a sea by *catachresis*.

7. It remains, now, that we suitably examine the passage in question and consider Christ's miracle closely, so that we not lessen that august story by the meanness of our speech, but see the ineffable truth within the matter.

8. At this time Jesus, making his mark on the earth with prodigious wonders—for having seated five thousand people in the desert as if in a great city,[160] having not even one morsel that would contribute to bodily life, he supplied them with abundant servings of food, ministering abundant victuals as if supplying them from the storehouse of his own power, and to confirm the account of this happy event visually, he filled twelve baskets with the leftovers,[161] and made the disciples carry them so that those present would see the truth of the sign that had happened there unambiguously—and having done these things he knew to transfer the miracles to the sea in order that even that would be marked by divine deeds.

9. For since he had astounded the dry land with miracles and had favourably shown friendship towards the people who live upon it, he also knew that he had to fill the wet places with grace, whether it was a sea or a lake topographically speaking, and to strike the disciples with amazement at his wonders while they were upon it. 10. For he knew—quite clearly he

---

156 Cf. Philo, *Life of Moses* 1.3.9.
157 Literally, "of Beauty." The Greek word κόσμος, like the Latin *mundus*, can also signify adornment.
158 Cf. Gen. 1:10.
159 Cf. 1 Tim. 6:16.
160 Possibly a quiet salute to the monks who had made a city of the desert at Athanasius, *Life of Antony* 14.
161 Mt. 14:20; Mk. 6:43; Lk. 19:17; Jn. 6:13.

knew—that human nature was laying blame in secret and whispering with a brigand's tongue, saying in ignorance: "Does he who makes the earth his servant so that it produces signs also have the same power to work miracles at sea? Is he who saves and without toil feeds those who frequent him on dry land able to perform portents in wet places?"

11. With good reason, on account of these overweening thoughts, without at all ceasing from performing wonders on the earth, he was eager to tread the paths of the sea and sent the disciples out first in order that, being already forewarned when they encountered a violent winter storm and were unable to complete the voyage by nautical skill and were greatly embattled by the force of the winds, they might reject every human ally and turn to an incorporeal aid. 12. The boat, then, was battered on its bow, as a sudden violent wind blew into their eyes and they ceased rowing because of the sweep of the waves, and the stern of the boat was getting swamped, and on top of all this a moonless night and deep darkness that stifled their sight made the sailors give up hope of salvation. For the nature of all the elements was not a little disturbed, since they saw that the Creative *Logos* was being ignored—which had become man for the sake of men.

13. Then, therefore, the reins of the winds were let loose even more than was seasonable, in order that, as they were overpowering the seamen with fear, they might reveal Christ walking upon the waters as if travelling along a safe thoroughfare, so that, when they saw him moving swiftly over the fluctuating essence and not sinking they would come to the thought that he was the one whom the prophetic tablet proclaimed, saying "he who walks upon the sea as upon solid ground,"[162] so that they might understand the prophecy from what they saw. 14. For Jesus, having made his body light by virtue of his divinity, carried its weight over the waters without getting wet, or rather, by gathering together the fluctuating essence of the waters, he condensed it to make it like a flat path. Traversing the sea in one or other of these ways, he fulfilled the prophecy. And the sea, knowing that God was in the man, made the backs [of the waves] firm, and carried the Creator, and denied [their] nature, not by abandoning its definition [as water], but assisting the Maker in a way contrary to [its] nature.[163]

15. But rational men, seeing the portents of myriad deeds, did not know Christ because of the hardness of their disposition.[164] Therefore,

---

162 Job 9:8b.
163 Cf. Psalm 66.6, Psalm 77.16–20, Job 26.12–13 etc.
164 Cf. Mt. 13:15, Mk. 8:17, Acts 28:27, all echoing Is. 9:6.

after making a blessed prayer to the Father[165] and, in so far as he was a man, richly entreating [him], and in so far as he was God, he [Christ] did not delay from overtaking those who were being overcome by the winter storm, but coming over the waters he frightened the crew—for he who was walking appeared to be a man, but by treading upon the wet essence he revealed a thing strange for a man.[166] Firstly, then, strong fear confused them; secondly, the sight troubled them immoderately; and thirdly, the struggles of the journey were overpowering them. 16. But at the same time as he spoke to them, with his word he calmed the upheaval that was pressing upon them, sending the ray of his utterance, which was brighter than the light of the sun,[167] to the apostles, saying "It is I," and "Do not fear."[168] He dissipated the unease that had come upon them, as if it were a cloud, saying: "I am he who a little while ago provided food to the five thousand when you were serving them. I am he who once called you when you were out at sea. I am he who said to you, 'Follow after me and I will make you fishers of men.'[169] I am he who holds the reins of the sea and all the elements. I am he who accommodates the hungry crowds on land and who has pity on those in peril at sea."

17. But Peter, upon seeing that the wet essence did not move at all, for as the Saviour walked upon it, it seemed frozen solid, determined that it was held together and held down by a strong wind. But not genuinely believing, doubting with uncertainty, and thinking that what had been said came from a phantom,[170] he said, "If you are he who a short time before was with us helping those others; if you are he who soothes chronic suffering with his word, he who gives fatherly gentleness to those in need; if you are he whom we have yearned for, on whose account we rejected the world, order me to come to you upon the waters."[171]

18. Saying these things hastily and ignorantly, he received judgment for his "if" at once, and got the sentence for his "if" not long after. For when he saw the Master walking easily upon the waters, he doubted that it was he who was doing this, as if some other had the authority to walk upon

---

165 Cf. Mt. 14:23.
166 See Mark 6.49–52.
167 Cf. Constantine, *Oration to the Saints* 1.
168 Cf. Mk. 6:50.
169 Cf. Mt. 4:9; Mk. 1:17.
170 Mt. 14:26; Mk. 6:49.
171 Cf. Mt. 14:28.

BOOK 3   137

water—{he yielded ground by what he had said}.[172] 19. Hence the Saviour, wanting to right him as he was stumbling and to make a parry against the unbelief he was suffering, said succinctly, "Come,"[173] in order that through this "come" he would not be able to walk on the waters but that he who did not believe in the Unique [Son] would come to faith. For it is not allowed to man to walk on water, nor did the prophet say, "*those* who walk," but "*he* who walks upon the sea,"[174] bearing prophetic witness about one, not about many, that this miracle belongs to God, and that the wonder does not pertain to men. 20. Hence Christ, in a timely way shaming Peter who was, if I may say, stumbling at exactly the right time for it, taught him who had disbelieved first in saying "If it is you," second in being emboldened to go upon the waters as an equal of God, and third, in wanting to prove false the prophecy that says "He who walks upon the sea." For if Peter had been able to walk, [the prophecy] would have lied when it said "*he* who walks upon the sea," and not "*they* who walk."

21. Hence the sea all but swallowed up the slave who in youthful exuberance made himself equal to the Master, eager that a fellow slave who was being unruly be punished, but Christ, taking pity on the one in peril, taking him by the hand, saved him who was drowning because of the unsound rudder of his tongue,[175] and persuaded him not to put forward utterances of his tongue akin to those of the Devil. 22. For as the Devil, doubting, said "If you are the Son of God,"[176] so Peter, disbelieving, said: "'If it is you, order me to walk to you on the waters'[177] so that I am fully convinced." And he doubted the wonder, though he beheld the thing itself, and doubted the clear fact, though he saw the very deed itself. 23. Christ, then, wanting to help him amply, says: "Come! If for you the things you have seen with your own eyes offer weak evidence in our favour, come out upon the waters. Once you are sufficiently persuaded by them that it is we,[178] form a firm conviction thanks to the wet [element]. You desire

---

172 The phrase within braces stands here in A, and if it is to make sense, must involve a military metaphor.
173 Cf. Mt. 14:29.
174 Job 9:8b.
175 Cf. Jam. 3:4–5.
176 Cf. Mt. 4:3, 6.
177 Mt. 14:28.
178 Apparently a more grandiloquent form of "It is I" (Mark 6.50), which can also be rendered "I am" or "I am the one who is," and is the Greek translation of God's response to Moses' request for God's name in Ex. 3:14; the phrase is also spoken by Jesus of himself in the Gospel of John (e.g. 6:35, 8:12, 8:58, etc.)

impossible things, wanting to receive the same authority as the Creator. Come out upon the waters, not treading the waves like us, but receiving a genuine principle of faith in us from them. 24. O Peter! Great is the struggle, and you need the help of a fourth watch. Night plunges the sea into blindness, but the cloud of ignorance hangs over you. The boat is troubled by the deep darkness, but you are harassed by lack of faith even more than the boat. The blowing of the wind has stirred up the sea, but the pettiness of your rashness makes you shudder. Your body is composed of a fourfold blending[179] and their definition lacks unity, being pulled apart by doubt. 25. You do not know what you are saying. You speak as if in a dream, saying: 'If it is you.' Did a sea serpent give you these things to say? O what a change our brief absence caused! The chorus leader of the disciples has his soul buffeted by the waves of an unseen spirit. The first of the apostles is swallowed by the depth of unbelief. <When you left the boat, your body sank, but when you failed to believe in us, your soul was swallowed>."[180] 26. And Christ nobly took him by the hand, before he suffered anything worse. For as it seemed, Peter's shipwreck was twofold: his soul was tortured in a sea of ignorance, while his body was plunged into the salty sea. These things being so, Jesus took hold of him, saying: "You of little faith, why did you doubt?"[181]

27. Therefore, it happened at the fourth watch of the night. For four main things vexed the sailors: the lack of visibility in the air, blasts of wind, a moonless night, and a shrieking sea. It happened to the sailors at the fourth watch, for the quartet of the elements raged against them.

28. But if you would like us to explain the present passage according to the rule of anagogy,[182] passing over, a bit, the statement of the letter, then let us examine what is most luminous—that is, of course, the noetic[183] sense)—saying that the "sea" is salty existence, night is human life, the boat the world, the sailors in it the race of men who pass through the whole of life as if through the whole night, the contrary wind is the great opposition

---

179 That is, of the elements.
180 This sentence appears in A at 3.13.26, between "twofold" and "his soul." We follow Goulet (who follows Palm) in relocating the sentence here, where it fits contextually; see Goulet (2003), 127.
181 Mt. 14:31.
182 Anagogy is the elevation of the reader's mind to a higher understanding of the scriptures; in the minds of those who employ the term, it is often contrasted with allegory on the grounds that the latter denies all value to the literal sense. Cf. Origen, *First Principles* 4.3.6; Methodius, *Symposium* 7.4; Epiphanius, *Panarion* 66.56.
183 Cf. Clement of Alexandria, *Excerpts from Theodotus* 8.2, etc.

of the Devil, while the fourth watch is the coming of the Saviour. 29. The intelligible night—that is human life—is divided into four "watches" from the beginning. In the first watch, the Patriarchs appeared, bettering life with the beacon of faith. Then the Law, having come at the second watch, captained the boat. The prophets, seen at the third watch, fought as allies with the sailors. But Christ, sojourning at the fourth watch, halted the seamen's troubles and restrained every attack of their enemies, shining the brilliance of his love of humanity upon the sailors at the completion of the night.[184] 30. Knowing this, the Apostle subtly penned this mystery: "The night is advanced, but the day draws near."[185] For thus is the fourth watch of the night understood, when Christ, appearing, effects the bright day of the knowledge of God.

31. It is possible to understand this ineffable mystery from another divinely inspired writing. You have certainly heard, I suppose, about Elijah, the chorus leader who returned home from this cursed life in a chariot of fire. He heard the subject of the present matter clearly from the divine voice, in the passage where it says "Stand before the Lord tomorrow and behold, there will be a strong wind that destroys mountains and shatters rocks; the Lord is not in the wind. And after the wind there will be an earthquake; the Lord is not in the earthquake. And after the earthquake there will be fire; the Lord is not in the fire. And after the fire a voice like a subtle breeze";[186] the Lord is in the subtle breeze. 32. For hear clearly in this passage also the time of the four manifestations. For the "strong wind" alludes enigmatically to the Patriarchal doctrine of piety, which destroyed the mountain of demon worship and mercilessly shattered stone statues with the zeal of faith—such as Abraham and those of his time. But it says that after the wind the Mosaic Law will be like an earthquake, which shook the inhabited world as it spoke its commandments, at one time all of Egypt, at another time Horeb and Mount Sinai, as it has been written, "The mountains leapt like rams"[187]—that is, they were shaken, at one time the

---

184 Macarius's reading of the "four watches" in terms of a periodization of salvation history can be compared with Hilary of Poitiers's mid-fourth-century *On Matthew* 14.14: "The first watch was that of the Law, the second of the prophets, the third of the Lord's coming in the flesh, and the fourth of his return in splendour" and with Chromatius (early fifth century CE), *Tractate on Matthew* 52.5 (CCL 9a:457–458), who delineates the four watches thus: Adam-Noah, Noah-Moses, Moses-advent, advent-consummation.
185 Rom. 13:12.
186 1 Kings 19:11–12.
187 Ps. 113:4a.

desert by many fears during the forty years, and at another time the territory of the Canaanites and of the Palestinians. 33. But after the earthquake it says there will be the broiling and bright fire of the vision of the prophets, as Jeremiah says: "Are my words not like fire? says the Lord."[188] But after the fire there will be a voice like a subtle breeze—clearly here it trumpets the utterance of the angel Gabriel, which proclaimed the good news to the virgin Mary—or perhaps the "subtle breeze" is the salvific body, and the "voice" the <Divine> Word teaching within it. 34. For it quite fittingly says that the Lord is not in the wind, nor in the earthquake, nor in the fire, but in a subtle breeze—that is in a subtle and pure body.[189] Reasonably, then, the passage established that the Lord is in the fourth manifestation, just as he saved the sailors when he appeared to the apostles at the fourth watch.

14. 1. Finally, let us examine why he says "You have the poor always, but you do not always have me,"[190] and why after the Resurrection he says, at the conclusion of the Gospel: "I will be with you every day until the consummation of the age."[191]

2. Naturally, a change in the speaker is apt to mark a change in the times. For when he was about to suffer and was fulfilling the plan of [his] death, he said with good reason that the disciples would not always have their teacher. But once he has crushed the insignia of death and conquered the principle of the corporeal condition, mystically having changed what is corruptible into what is incorruptible, at that same time having made what is corruptible stronger than corruption and having adorned what is transient with his own beauty, undone every anxious anticipation of fear, transitioned what is mortal from mortality into immortality, transferred what is earthly from the earth into something non-earthly, taken what was under tyrannical slavery into a kingdom of freedom, elevated the tainted life into an untainted way of life, and in general having made man divine, as God he says that his unlimited power will be with the disciples everywhere and is not confined, not by time, not by place, not by the density of a body,

---

188 Jer. 23:29–30.
189 This means the body of the resurrection, on which see Jn. 20:26 and Origen, *Against Celsus* 2.62. The teaching that the "pneumatic body" of 1 Cor. 15 would be more tenuous than the one humans wear on earth was widely regarded as an Origenist heresy by the end of the fourth century; many would also have thought it heterodox to hold, with some Valentinians, that the body of Christ before his death was already pneumatic or "spiritual" rather than psychic or "ensouled."
190 Jn. 12:8.
191 Mt. 28:20.

not by quantity, not by quality, not by colour, not by darkness, not by what has occurred, not by what will occur, not by any present affair. 3. For after his Passion, he spanned everything—present, future, and past; quantity, quality, colour, darkness, density of the body—having limited the very things that are called limits, since the entire universe was within him and nothing was outside of him.

4. For as if having fastened an inextinguishable, unquenchable, grand, miraculous, and great beacon of fire upon the Cross, marking with it his hidden divinity, traversing everything everywhere in a single timeless moment, he impressed his seal upon earth, heaven, the entire cosmos, and the hypercosmic beings: thrones, powers, eminences, the Seraphim themselves, and anything higher than these,[192] if there is any; he marked all things through the Father. 5. What need is there to mention the inner recesses, nether regions, subterranean places, and invisible spaces, since being everywhere with the lightning flash of his divinity, he spread out the absolute power of his own authority?

6. Never mind that he led the thief, once he believed in him not as a man, but as God, into sumptuous paradise at the very moment he believed— the paradise that he planted and rooted ineffably from the beginning.[193] For it is not as some myth-makers contrive their sophistries, spitting out the utterances of rotten old women, belching the smoke of foul smelling cookery, imitating the rage of rabid dogs,[194] forging an attitude like enemies of Christ, being sharers and advocates of Jewish insanity, battling against the meaning by abbreviating the passage, construing wickedly what was written well. They say, "Truly today I say to you," and then, having abbreviated it they say "You will be with me in paradise"[195] *at some time*, as though the promise to the thief is projected into a future time.

7. Who will accept this wondrous account when it is rendered in this way? And who having a sound mind and healthy reason will offer a doctrine full of statements so base that they open upon life a tavern

192 For biblical references to these hypercosmic beings see e.g. Eph. 6:12; Is. 6:2.
193 Gen. 2:8, where God "plants" paradise; compare also Col. 2:7, where the faithful are said to be "rooted" in Christ.
194 Cf. Phil. 3:2 and the death of Lucian of Samosata, as described in the *Suda*; Lucian is said to have been killed by dogs because he "wrestled against the truth [i.e. Christianity]" by mocking Christians in his satirical *Passing of Peregrinus* (*Suda* 683). Lucian's death by dogs in turn recollects the death of Euripides by dogs in the late antique *Vita* prefacing Byzantine copies of his works (see Lefkowitz [1979]).
195 Lk. 23:4. We follow Goulet in deleting the phrase "instead of 'I say to you, *today* you will be with me in paradise,'" which stands here in A as a gloss.

keeper's doctrine? Such statements belong to dogs that eat one another![196] Such common talk belongs to poisonous snakes![197] Such myths belong to hissing serpents! These daring statements steal truth with sophistries. These are cunningly sharpened words for the subversion of the beautiful. These audacities circumscribe[198] Christ in the Passion!

8. And who—for let us question those who are so empty minded—cleaved the earth and opened the gloomy prison of death?[199] Who broke the bonds that had encircled abominable Hades for long ages? Who prevented the solar rays from lighting heaven?[200] Who, faster than a sneeze, raised from their tombs the dead who had been loosed from their souls long ages ago, as if they had slept but a short time?[201]

9. At all events, is God the Word, who was never separated from what is crucified, and is capable of these things, and can do things greater than these most easily, not powerful enough to do things much lesser than these? For it is much greater to close heaven and hide the light and to open Hades and summon to life those residing there, than to open paradise and bring in the thief.

10. And this too would be irrational: if the sun, which has received authority over the day, takes hold of the inhabited world all at once and illuminated with a single ray the boundaries of the whole cosmos, but the Intelligible Sun, who is all-shining, without shadow, who rose ineffably from the Father upon the universe, who came into being non-temporally but contains temporality within [him], who is authentically "true light" and cannot be hidden, who "coming into the world illuminates all men,"[202] is hypercosmic beauty, indescribable, and uncircumscribable,[203] were *not*

---

196 A quiet confutation of the Hellene's assertion in the following chapter that no dog would eat the flesh of another dog.

197 A comparison more often applied to heretics: cf. Irenaeus, *Against Heresies* 1.30.15 and Epiphanius, *Panarion*, passim.

198 Christ is circumscribed in body, uncircumscribed in spirit, according to Gregory Nazianzen, *Letter* 101.

199 Cf. Mt. 27:51–53, where at the moment of Jesus's death: "The earth shook, and the rocks were split. The tombs also were opened, and many bodies of the saints who had fallen asleep were raised. After his resurrection they came out of the tombs and entered the holy city and appeared to many."

200 Cf. Lk. 23:44–45.

201 Cf. Mt. 27:52–53.

202 Cf. Jn. 1:9. Or "illuminates every man coming into the world."

203 Cf. Clement of Alexandria, Fr. 39 (Stahlin), though the adjective is more common after Nicaea: see for example, Theodoret, *On the Trinity* 28, etc.

present everywhere, but being on the Cross, were not in paradise, not in heaven, not at the boundaries of the universe, not in the Father who begets the Unique [Son] impassibly and without any intermediary.[204]

11. And [do you maintain that] man, when he sleeps, travels the earth by means of his imagination, seizes cities, crosses rivers, travels to every place by means of the sleepless thought of his soul,[205] but that Christ, overcome upon the Cross in respect of his body, has become inferior to man? Does not the Maker, the fashioner, the framer of man possess paradise? Did he not embrace the world? Does he not hold the reins of the universe?[206] {Does he not command the reins?}[207] Being in the Father, does he not captain heaven and things beyond the heavens? O what folly! O what blasphemy! The power of the Cross does not make better the condition of all in common if he does not have the strength to grant the requests of the faithful at the very same moment.

12. And before the Cross, <he supplied> what was needed for purification to the leper who believed,[208] similarly to the blind man and to the paralytic [he supplied] what was needed for salvation, to the deceased Lazarus, when his sisters believed, [he supplied] what was needed for resurrection, and healing myriad other symptoms and afflictions he anticipated the word of those who believed, but upon the Cross, where the completion of the whole divine plan [was occurring], where the conclusion of the mystical struggles [were happening], where the succession was truly [taking place], he who believed could not at that very moment receive the radiant guarantee of faith?

13. But what do the advocates of this unlearned way of thinking say? In so far as he is God, he has power and authority to bring the thief

---

204 In contrast to the cosmos, which was considered to have been created *through* the Son himself, see e.g. Heb. 1:2, and the Creed of the Council of Nicaea (δι' οὗ τὰ πάντα ἐγένετο ["through whom all things came into being"]).

205 For a similar account of the soul's imaginings during sleep see *Letter of Aristeas* 213–214.

206 Goulet (2003), 396 suggests a comparison with Eusebius of Emesa, *On the Son* 19 (I.58, 18–22 Buytaert): "Before the body he governed heaven, and when he came in the body, he did not turn away his hand. Before the body he held the limits of the sea and the earth, and when he was present in the body he did not withdraw the rudder. If he had done this, the sea would perhaps have been changed into earth and everything would have collapsed in confusion."

207 Goulet, following Duchesne and Blondel, suspects that this doubled phrase is a gloss that has been interpolated into the main text.

208 Mt. 8:1–4.

into paradise, but in so far as he is man, he does not. 14. If we indeed happen to meet them, against them it must be said: O you who reek with the drunkenness of unlearning! O sons and descendants of thunderstruck stupidity! In whom, now, did the believer believe? In a mere man,[209] or one who was both God and man? Unless you want to separate Christ from God and God from Christ, in order that when they believe they may believe separately in Christ—that is, in the man—and separately in God the Word which was incarnated and deigned to take on the properties of human beings. 15. Come! May this idea never come into the mind of any believer. For Christ is not one thing and the Unique[210] Son of God another, but Christ *is* the Unique [Son] of God and the Unique [Son] of God *is* Christ. Hence, Christ is not one thing and Jesus another, but Jesus is Christ and Christ is Jesus.[211] Hades thus bristles at the name of Christ;[212] it cannot endure to hear [the name] "Jesus."[213]

16. The multitude of names, however, does not introduce a multitude of Sons, but the Son is one, having many names. Even if, then, someone calls "Jesus" for help, he will not be disappointed; and even if [he calls] "Christ," he will not stumble; and even if [he calls] "Son," he will never sin; and even if [he calls] "Unique [One]," he will not be scandalized.

17. According to this way of thinking, the thief, when he believed, saw paradise together with him in whom he believed. For if, when an aromatherapy[214] made of wood or herbs is placed in part of a house, the scent of the aromatherapy wafts everywhere through every part of the

---

209 The notion that Christ was a "mere man," or "psilanthropism," was associated by early Christian heresiologists with, among others, the Ebionites (see e.g. Eusebius, *Ecclesiastical History* 3.27.2) and Paul of Samosata (see Eusebius, *Ecclesiastical History* 7.30.11); see also 2.19.5 above.

210 On the valences of the term μονογενής ("unique") in Macarius, including its use as the title of the work, see the Introduction.

211 In this section Macarius has in mind Christologies that would see not merely two natures, but two persons or subjects in Christ (e.g. a theologian like Diodore of Tarsus, cf. n.211 below); among anti-Christian polemicists, compare Julian, *Against the Galilaeans* 327a–c; 333b–d, passages in which Julian criticizes Christians for being unable to agree on the subject of various utterances in John's gospel, cf. especially 333d: "but if the Only-begotten/Unique Son is one thing, while the Divine Word is another, as I have heard from some of your sect, it seems that even John did not venture that [idea]."

212 Cf. *Acts of Pilate* 22.

213 Cf. Phil. 2:10–12.

214 "Aromatherapy" translates φάρμακον ("drug," "potion"); the term "aromatherapy" is an anachronism, but the concept is not—Macarius would have the reader understand the crucified body of Christ upon the cross as wafting salvation much as a medicinal aromatic

house by means of its uncircumscribed character, how indeed then would the mystical, great, and miraculous aromatherapy, hung upon the Cross as if in a great house—clearly the whole world—not overpower everything with the scent of the Godhead, by the strength of its sweet smell[215] and its life-giving power penetrating the East, West, North, and South, and the whole zone of the inhabited world? 18. No principle, then, confined Jesus after the Resurrection, nor any place, time, quantity, quality, breadth, length, height, or depth.[216] But even if someone calls upon Christ in the Western regions, or in the East or even in the very innermost recesses, it is possible to find Christ there before the call. For the bodily organ exists undivided from God the Word; the "strap" of that reality cannot be undone, as John said.[217] 19. By this principle, then, he also led the thief into paradise, and by this principle he was present with the apostles, and by this principle he is not separated from the faithful until the consummation.

20. Nevertheless, before the Passion he spoke the truth, when he said, "You have the poor with you always, but you do not always have me"[218] when the mystical death of the divine economy was about to separate him from the disciples corporeally. But when a woman having filled a jar with valuable myrrh poured it all upon his head, and when there were strong murmurs from the grumblers that it was necessary, rather, to feed the poor from [the proceeds] of the myrrh and not to anoint with myrrh him who became poor for our sake, the worker of betrayal kindled this murmur, he who valued the myrrh made from plants at three hundred denarii but, in his drunkenness, [valued] the heavenly myrrh emptied[219] upon the earth at thirty pieces of silver.[220]

---

compound hung within a house was understood to disperse "bad air" and provide therapeutic benefits; on scent in late antiquity see Harvey (2006).

215 Cf. 2 Cor. 2:14–16; Jn. 12:3.
216 Cf. Rom. 8:38; Eph. 3:18.
217 Cf. Jn. 1:27. The preceding line of thought (3.14.13–18), culminating in this sentence, can be contrasted with an excerpt of Diodore of Tarsus preserved in a Syriac compendium entitled *The Blasphemies of Diodore, Theodore, and the Impious Nestorius*: "Who is it that, at the time of the crucifixion, promised that the thief would be with him in paradise? The one who died, was buried, and arose not on the same day, nor even on the one that followed? It is not possible both that he, dead, was buried, and that he, living, led the thief into paradise …" (*Blasphemies* 16 [trans. Behr 179]); Macarius's reply can be read as a response to an exegesis, such as Diodore's, that would see two persons or subjects within Christ, and ascribe different words and actions to different subjects.
218 Jn. 12:8.
219 Cf. Phil. 2:7 on the self-emptying, or κένωσις of the incarnate Word.
220 Jn. 12:4–5; Mt. 26:15.

21. But it is not fitting to bring the theme of Judas's tragedy onto the stage now, for the struggles of your questions trump this and the solution to your principle conundrums is pressing. Therefore, since you have received a sufficient speech on this subject, if the beginning of some other line of questioning suggests itself, bring it out into our midst—for the work of responding profits us not a little.

{Hellene}

He, smiling a little and chiding us, answered, saying: As overbold contestants who announce their [coming] victory right up to the beginning of the contest incite many to run in the stadium, you seem to me to take on the same attitude when you want us to pursue another inquiry with you, as if beginning from the starting post. Speak to us then, my good friend, beginning with this.

15. 1. That statement of the Teacher is well known, which says: "Unless you eat my flesh and drink my blood, you do not have life in you."[221] For truly this is not [just] something savage and absurd, but the greatest absurdity of absurdities and the most savage of all savage customs—that a human taste human flesh and drink the blood of those of the same species and same family,[222] and by doing this have eternal life. For what excess of cruelty, tell me, will you introduce into life by doing this? What other accursed evil will you invent beyond this pollution? 2. Ears cannot bear, not the act, I say, but even the mention of this new and strange impiety. The apparitions of the Furies[223] never imputed this against those who lived abnormally, nor would the Potideans have accepted this, if an inhuman famine had not wasted them away; the feast of Thyestes, such as it was, was brought on by enmity among brothers; Tereus the Thracian was fed such food against his will; Harpagos feasted on the flesh of his nearest and dearest only once he had been deceived by Astyages. All of these endured such a disgusting thing involuntarily.[224]

---

221 Cf. Jn. 6:53.

222 Christians were accused in the second century of "Oedipal unions" (i.e. incest) and "Thyestean banquets" (i.e. cannibalism): Justin, *Dialogue with Trypho* 10; Athenagoras, *Embassy* 3; Eusebius, *Ecclesiastical History* 5.1.14. It is impossible to determine whether these charges are merely calumnious or were inspired by a misunderstanding of Christian practices.

223 The Furies often punished the killing of a blood-relative, as in the *Eumenides* of Aeschylus; they were also portrayed as stewards of cosmic boundaries in Heraclitus, Fr. 94 (Diels-Kranz).

224 On cannibalism during the siege of Potidea see Thucydides, *Peloponnesian War* 2.70; Thyestes was surreptitiously fed the flesh of his sons by Atreus as revenge for Thyestes's

BOOK 3

3. No one, in truth, who lives in peace ever prepared such a meal in his life. No one has been given such a foul teaching by a teacher. And even if you peruse accounts about Scythia, and even if you go through the long-lived Ethiopians, and even if you traverse the region encircling the Ocean, you will find lice-eaters and root-eaters, and you will hear of snake-eaters and mouse-eaters, but everywhere they abstain from human flesh.[225]

4. What, then, is this teaching? Even if it contains something more mystical and profitable allegorically,[226] the scent of the statement harms the very soul when it enters through the ears, troubling it with its foul odour, and destroys the entire principle of the hidden meanings, causing man to be dizzied by this misfortune.[227] Nor would the nature of irrational creatures ever abide this, even if they saw an unendurable and inexorable famine. Nor would a dog taste the flesh of a dog, nor any other creature taste the flesh of its own species.

5. Certainly, many teachers introduce strange new ideas, but no teacher has invented a piece of tragedy[228] more innovative than this! No writer of history, no philosophical man, not one of the barbarians, not one of the Hellenes, from the beginning of time. See, then, what you are disposed to persuade the simple to be irrationally convinced of; see how it incites evil not only in the country but also in the cities. 6. Hence it appears to me that neither Mark, Luke, nor Matthew himself recorded this,[229] since they determined the utterance not to be appropriate but strange, unbefitting, and

---

adultery with his wife Aerope (see for example Apollodorus, *Library* 2.10–15); Tereus was similarly tricked into eating his son by his wife, Procne, as vengeance for his rape of her sister, Philomela (see for example Hyginus, *Fabulae* 45); for the story of Astygos see Herodotus, *Histories* 1.107–120.

225 Lice-eaters: Strabo, *Geography* 11.2.19; root-eaters: Strabo, *Geography* 16.4.9, Diodorus Siculus, *Library* 3.23. But the Hellene forgets that anthropophagi, or man-eaters, were well known to the geographers (Strabo, *Geography* 4.5.4).

226 Cf. Plato, *Republic* 378d–e and *Phaedrus* 229c–230a, echoed by Origen, *Against Celsus* 4.38 and 4.45. Porphyry retaliates by accusing Origen of an infelicitous application of "Stoic" allegory to the Mosaic scriptures (Eusebius, *Ecclesiastical History* 6.19).

227 The argument that Christians used allegorical exegesis to ameliorate ethically and philosophically irredeemable texts can be found in Celsus (apud Origen, *Against Celsus* 4.48) and in Porphyry's well-known polemic against Origen (*Against the Christians* fr. 39 [Harnack], apud Eusebius, *Ecclesiastical History* 6.19.1–12).

228 The term "tragic" connotes the grandiloquent expression of false views concerning the government of the world, as in e.g. Plato, *Republic* 413b; Plotinus, *Enneads* 2.9.13.8; Irenaeus, *Against Heresies* 1.11.4.

229 The Hellene's criticism depends on sufficient familiarity with the gospels to know that Jn. 6:53 has no parallels in the synoptics.

something deviating far from civilized life. And you yourself, when you read this, ought not to approve it,[230] nor indeed should anyone else raised with a liberal education.

16. 1. But consider this passage closely as well, where it says: "But such signs accompany those who believe; they will lay hands on the weak, and they will become well; and even if they drink deadly poison, it will not harm them."[231] 2. Those, then, chosen for the priesthood and especially those who contend for the episcopacy or presidency must use this mode of judgment and be administered the deadly poison, so that he who is not harmed by the poisonous drink may be selected over others, but if they do not have the courage to accept this method, they confess that they do not believe in the <words> spoken by Jesus. 3. For if it is the particular characteristic of faith to conquer the evil poison and cast out the suffering of the sick, then he who does not do these things either has not genuinely believed or he genuinely believes but that in which he has faith is not powerful but feeble.

17. 1. Consider a statement similar to and in keeping with the former: "If you have faith like a mustard seed, truly I say to you, you will say to this mountain, 'Get up and throw yourself into the sea' and nothing will be impossible for you."[232] 2. It is clear, then, that he who is unable to move a mountain with his command is not to be considered worthy of the brotherhood of the faithful.[233] Hence, you clearly stand accused not only because the rest of the Christians are not numbered among the faithful, but also because none of the bishops or presbyters is worthy of this name.

18. 1. But come, let us also discuss this passage: for what reason, when he who was tempting Jesus said, "Throw yourself down from the Temple," does he [i.e. Jesus] not do this, but says to him, "Do not tempt the Lord your God,"[234] which makes it seem to me that he said this out of fear of the

---

230 The Hellene may be satirizing Paul's fondness for the verb δοκιμάζειν ("examine") and its cognates: see e.g. 1 Cor. 3:13, 9:27, 11:28; 2 Cor. 13:5; Gal. 6:4.

231 Mk. 16:17–18. This text is now regarded by textual critics as an accretion to Mark's gospel. On its currency in the fourth century see Burgon (1871).

232 Mt. 17:20, 21. Macarius quotes this passage somewhat differently at 3.25.1, 8 (q.v.). See Goulet (2003), 397 for synoptic comparison.

233 Compare Porphyry, *Against the Christians* fr. 3 (Harnack), apud Jerome, *Commentary on Matthew* 21.21: "The dogs of the gentiles bark against us in their books, which they have left behind in memory of their own impiety, asserting that the apostles did not have faith, because they were unable to move mountains."

234 Mt. 4:6–7. Julian also criticized the Temptation narrative as contradictory (Theodore

danger of falling. 2. For if, as you say, he performed many other wonders and indeed even raised the dead with his word alone, it is necessary that he show forthwith that he was strong enough to save others from dangers by pitching himself down from the heights above and suffering no damage to his body at all, and especially because a passage written somewhere speaks about him saying "They will carry you upon their hands; you will not even strike your foot upon a stone."[235] Hence it would have been just, in truth, to show to those present in the Temple that he was God's child and able to save himself and his own from every danger.

19. 1. These longwinded, indiscriminate statements are, as it were, greatly displeasing and kindle a battle of contradiction against themselves. For if, as though navigating a three way intersection,[236] one wishes to explain this passage from the gospels which Jesus uttered to Peter, saying "Get behind me, Satan, you are a scandal to me, because you do not consider the things of God, but the things of men,"[237] then in another place "You are Peter, and upon this rock I will build my Church,"[238] and "To you I will give the keys of the Kingdom of heaven"[239] <***>.[240]

2. For if he accused Peter to such an extent that, casting him behind he called him "Satan" and a "scandal" for having no divine thoughts whatsoever, and cursed him in this way, since he sinned mortally, with the result that he no longer wanted him in his sight but tossed him behind into the crowd of those rejected and unacknowledged, then what condemnation do we need to look for against the chorus leader and first of the disciples beyond this one? 3. If one ruminates very soberly on these things, and then hears, as though Christ has forgotten the words he spoke against Peter, "You are Peter and upon this rock I will build my Church" and "To you I

---

of Mopsuestia, *Against Julian* fr. 10, 11 [Guida]): "Why do you [i.e. Julian] marvel that 'although there is no high mountain in the desert, the Devil is said to have led him up an exceedingly high mountain'? ... But how,' he says, 'did the Devil lead the Lord up to the pinnacle of the temple when he [i.e. the Lord] was in the desert?" Theodore's reply suggests that Julian's critique focused both on the temporal and geographic contradictions within the Temptation narrative as well as Christ's status as God (see idem, fr. 12).
235 Ps. 90:12; Mt. 4:6.
236 The use of the term τρίοδος ("three-way intersection") here is a metaphor for the three quotations that the Hellene wants explained, while the verb ἀφηγέομαι can mean both "explain" and "lead the way."
237 Mt. 16:23.
238 Mt. 16:18.
239 Mt. 16:19.
240 Goulet, following Harnack, suspects a *lacuna* here.

will give the keys of the Kingdom of heaven,"[241] will he not laugh greatly with his mouth gaping? Will he not chuckle as if at the theatre? Will he not speak contemptuously? Will he not whistle at it even more vigorously? Will he not say more loudly to those seated next to him: "Either he is drunk on wine when he calls Peter 'Satan' and he speaks while he is having an epileptic fit, or when he makes this man key master of the Kingdom he describes dreams [he has] in the imagination while asleep"?

4. For what sort of man is Peter to be able to support the Church—he who was indecisive on countless occasions because of the weakness of his judgment? What firm thought was he ever found to have, or where did he show the unshakeableness of his thought—he who, when he heard a servant girl say the mere word "Jesus" was horribly terrified and denied three times, though there was no pressing need for him to do so?[242] If, then, anticipating Peter's stumbling on the principal point of piety, he called him "Satan," it is absurd that later, as if being ignorant of what he had done, he would give him the authority of chorus leader over matters of importance.

20. 1. But that Peter is accused because he stumbled many times is clear also from that passage where Jesus said to him: "I say to you: not up to seven times, but up to seven times seven you shall forgive the sin of the wrongdoer."[243] 2. But he, though he received this precept and law, cut off the ear of the high priest's slave, who had wronged him not at all, and reproached him, though he had not committed any sin. For what sin did he commit if, when ordered by his master he went along with the ambuscade sent against Christ at that time?

21. 1. This Peter is also convicted for committing injustice in other ways. For he put to death a man named Ananias together with his wife, Sapphira, when they did not turn over the full value of their property, but set aside a small amount for their own needs, committing no injustice.[244] For what injustice did they commit, if they did not want to donate all of their property? 2. But indeed, even if he thought this act unjust, it was necessary that he remember the precepts of Jesus, who taught to sympathize with four

---

241 Mt. 16:18–19.
242 Cf. Mt. 26:69–75.
243 Mt. 18:22.
244 Compare Porphyry, *Against the Christians* fr. 25b (Harnack), apud Jerome, *Letter* 30, *To Demetrias* 14: "The apostle Peter never prayed for the death of Ananias and Sapphira, as the stupid Porphyry accuses." Other manuscripts of *Letter* 30.14 read "a stupid philosopher" (*stultus philosophus*) in place of "the stupid Porphyry" (*stultus Porphyrius*).

hundred and ninety incidences of wrongdoing[245], and to grant forbearance at each instance, if what was committed was really a sin. Rather, it was necessary that he consider this along with other things—that by swearing that he did not know Jesus he not only lied, but perjured himself by despising the coming judgment and resurrection.

22. 1. This chief of the chorus of the disciples, taught by God to despise death, who fled when he was caught by Herod, became the cause of punishment for those who were guarding him. For after he fled during the night, when day came there was confusion among the soldiers as to how Peter got out, and when Herod searched for him and did not find him, he judged the guards and ordered them to be put to death, that is, beheaded.[246] 2. It is marvellous, then, how Jesus gave the keys of heaven to Peter, who was such a person as this; how he said "Tend my lambs"[247] to someone befuddled in such confusion and plagued by such great troubles, if indeed the "sheep" are the faithful who enter into the mystery of perfection, while the "lambs" are the gathering of those still being instructed, fed as yet on the tender milk of teaching.[248] 3. For all that, it is recorded that, after tending the sheep for only a few months, Peter was crucified,[249] although Jesus had said the gates of Hades would not prevail against him.[250] 4. Paul, too, condemned Peter, saying: "For before some came from James, he ate with the Gentiles. But when they came, he separated himself, fearing those of the circumcision, and many Jews joined him."[251] But in this there is a major and serious condemnation—that a man who was an interpreter of the divine mouth[252] should live in hypocrisy and act obsequiously with people,

---

245 "Seventy times seven", as at Matthew 18.22.
246 Cf. Acts 12:3–18.
247 Jn. 21:15.
248 Cf. 1 Cor. 3:2; Heb. 5:12–13; 1 Pet. 2:2. For an exegesis of "sheep" and "lambs" as "children" and "adults" or "catechumens" and "baptised," respectively, see Clement of Alexandria, *Pedagogue* 1.5.14. The parenthetical comment on the exegesis of "sheep" would suit the Christian interlocutor better than the Hellene.
249 Cf. Jn. 21:19 and the more circumstantial account in the apocryphal *Acts of Peter* 38–40. This places his death in Rome, though the only evidence for his sojourn in that city in the New Testament is 1 Peter 5:13, where Babylon is commonly taken as a cipher for Rome by collation with Rev. 17:5. Ignatius, *Romans* 3 is the first witness to Peter's ministry in the capital.
250 Cf. Mt. 16:18, though Christ is speaking of the Church, not of Peter himself.
251 Gal. 2:12.
252 The phrase here, "of the divine mouth" or "of the mouth of God" (τοῦ θείου στόματος) recalls an oft-quoted line of Aeschylus, in which Thetis accuses Apollo of falsely prophesying

and even take a wife, for Paul also says this: "Do we not have authority to take a sister as a wife, as even the rest of the apostles and Peter?"[253] Then he adds: "For such people are pseudo-apostles, doers of trickery."[254] 5. If, then, Peter is reported to have been wrapped up in such wicked things, how can one not shudder to think that he who was tied to myriad absurdities, as it were, possesses the keys of heaven and looses and binds![255]

After the pious doctrine had been thus knocked about and the foundation of the Christian ramparts had been shaken a bit, we looked for the support of an ample response, then raised it up against the enemy like a fortified tower in which we could place our confidence. Though we absorbed the many arrows of [his] words, we remained unhurt, and endured while the great quiver of [his] shrewd sophistry was emptied. And indeed, once this array and he who wielded it tired of aiming his erstwhile bow full of sharpened missiles against us, we slowly whetted the panoply of [our] moderation against him and fired a first volley, as it were, against him, speaking before him and those with him concerning the flesh of Christ, that the Saviour has not said something strange and awful when he says: "Unless you eat my flesh and drink my blood you will not have life."[256]

---

the happiness of her children, but then murdering her son; the pertinent line reads "And I supposed the divine mouth of Apollo was without falsehood [τὸ Φοίβου θεῖον ἀψευδὲς στόμα]." The passage is from a lost work, but is quoted by Socrates in Plato's *Republic* as an example of inappropriate poetic characterizations of the gods (*Republic* 383b), but it is also quoted by Athenagoras (*Embassy* 21.6) as evidence that the Greek gods are fickle and emotional, while Eusebius of Caesarea quotes the entire passage from the *Republic* as support for the argument that Plato agrees with Christians in condemning traditional Hellenic religion (*Gospel Preparation* 13.5). Thus, in using this phrase, the Hellene stresses that no one as unreliable as Peter is fit to mediate the word of God, and/or *may*, if the allusion to Aeschylus/Plato is deliberate, wish to hint that Peter's god is a liar.

253 See Gal. 2:13 on hypocrisy; 1 Cor. 9:5 on Peter's wife.
254 2 Cor. 11:13.
255 Compare Porphyry, *Against the Christians* 21a (Harnack) (apud Jerome, *Commentary on Galatians*, prol.): "Not at all understanding this, that wretched criminal and Batanaean Porphyry, in the first book of his work written against us, objects that Peter was reprimanded by Paul for not putting the right foot forward in preaching the Gospel, wanting to inure them with the stain of error and of great shamelessness for this, and to accuse them both in common of fabricating lies in their doctrines, since among these princes of the Church there was a disagreement." Also, compare parallels to this passage, all preserved in Jerome: *Against the Christians* 21b, 21c, 21d (Harnack). According to Cyril, *Against Julian* 320Cff, Julian also criticized Peter for hypocrisy based on Paul's comments in Galatians.
256 Jn. 6:53.

BOOK 3   153

23. 1. Consider for me then—for let us now discuss this—the newborn and just-birthed infant who has left its dark and humid abode. Unless it eats the flesh and drinks the blood of its mother it will not have life or grow up among men, but depart into the shadow of death. But if it partakes of these physical sources and nourishes itself abundantly upon kindred flesh, when it reaches manhood thereafter it is deemed worthy of a better regimen and class, is inscribed among men, has a share both in education and in the dignity of citizenship, learns letters, and hence finally ranks among men of distinction, sometimes among the great, having assumed the trials of generalship, captaining ships, or of a great city council. And the cause of such and so many goods is eating the flesh of the one who gave birth and drinking the blood of the mother.

2. And do not hope to say that this is not blood, but milk. For it is by nature blood, in truth of a life-giving nature, that has collected in the breast, then been metabolized into the whiteness of milk from the fact that the nipple, situated high on the chest, mixes it together with air and transforms what is red into something clear. 3. For how the air loves to endow a nature that draws near [its own] quality, [for instance], sometimes what is white when one finds it in its bare state is made black by the attack of flame, while at other times the air chills what is yellow when it is covered, making it white and transparent. Again, it compresses dark water in a well or in the deepest springs, turning it into white snow and clear ice. 4. In this way, the life-giving blood collected in the breast of the one giving birth[257] unites in some manner with the neighbouring air, and being coagulated and continuously congealed there, it is whitened and takes on the quality of milk. 5. For the creative nature did not place the spheres of the breasts atop the chest by chance or without purpose, as some sort of mysterious receptacles or containers, but with the intention that, having received without stint the congealed blood from the veins, they might sweeten it to make it clear, drinkable, and white, refining the thickness of the flesh within it. And this is nothing marvellous, when even what is salty and troubled in water, when borne through underground passages of the abyss is cleansed as though through the "breasts" of the springs.[258]

6. If, therefore, the children of the physiologists offer us a sufficient

---

[257] Compare Gregory of Nyssa on the breasts of Christ, *Commentary on the Song of Songs* 1.
[258] To the preceding description of the metabolization of breast-milk compare for example Galen, *On Venesection* 5 (K164–165) and especially Aristotle, *Generation of Animals* 4.8.

answer to these [questions] and give an accurate teaching about these matters which you make much of, how does there seem to you to be anything disturbing in Christ's evangelical statement? What horrible or strange thing, as you surmise, did he teach when he said: "Unless you eat my flesh and drink my blood, you do not have life in yourselves"?[259] 7. From where, tell me, does the newborn draw nourishment? Is it not from the blood of her who bore him, and of her flesh, just as has been demonstrated, not by the invention of persuasive words or by a device,[260] but by the unadulterated Rule of Truth?[261]

8. If, therefore, Christ gave to whomever received him the power to become children of God,[262] having given birth to them by some mystical principle and wrapping them in ineffable swaddling clothes, explain from where, exactly, the children born of God will draw life and take nourishment? Is it not clearly from tasting the mystical flesh and drinking the blood of her who gives birth to them? 9. She who gives birth to them is none other than the Wisdom of God, for she prepared her own table for her own children and mixed her own wine for her own offspring, abundantly pouring out the two Testaments as if from two breasts.[263] She, therefore, providing nourishment to the newborns from her own flesh and from her own blood, makes them adults and renders them disciples of the Kingdom of heaven, then enrolls them in the community of the angels above.[264] Leading them into the pure council house and filling them with immortality and every beatitude, she makes them like the Father, giving them incorruption. 10. Therefore, the flesh and blood of Christ, or rather, of Wisdom (for Christ and wisdom are the same)[265] are the words said allegorically of the New and Old Testaments, which one must attentively eat and digest, remembering

---

259 Jn. 6:53.
260 Cf. 1 Cor. 2:4, where Paul writes: "My speech and my proclamation were not with plausible words of wisdom, but with a demonstration of the Spirit and of power" (NRSV).
261 Compare the usage of this phrase at 3.5.4 above and 3.27.12 below.
262 Cf. Jn. 1:12.
263 On Christ as a mother who nourishes the Church from her breasts, cf. Irenaeus, *Against Heresies* 3.24.1 and especially Clement of Alexandria's extended meditation on Christ, milk, and motherhood in *Pedagogue* 1.6 and *Who is the Rich Man Who Shall Be Saved* 37.
264 Cf. Mk. 12:25, where those resurrected are described as being "like angels in heaven" (NRSV).
265 Cf. Mt. 11:19; Lk. 11:49; 1 Cor. 1:21–4. Prov. 8:22, where Wisdom proclaims herself the companion of God in creation, was often applied to Christ in this period, though the orthodox insisted that if Wisdom herself was said here to be created, this could be true of Christ only in his incarnate form.

them distinctly in the intelligence, and obtain from them life not temporary but eternal.[266]

11. Thus Jeremiah, when he received into his mouth the words given by the hand of Wisdom, he ate them and after eating them, received life.[267] Thus Ezekiel, after eating the small scrolls full of words, was sweetened and cast off the bitterness of the present life.[268] Thus each particular saint, both long ago or afterwards, whenever he ate the flesh of Wisdom and drank her blood—that is, the knowledge of her[269]—and received the revelation into himself, he lived forever, and living, will never cease.

12. For it was not to the disciples alone that he gave his own flesh to eat and likewise [his own] blood to drink—for he would have committed an injustice in doing this, supplying eternal life to some at a certain season, but not serving it to others. But to all holy men and prophets together he allegorically gave the same victuals. 13. When he in his final days gave bread and drink to the apostles, he said: "This is my body and my blood."[270] But in order that I may further clarify the story and clearly answer the question about this passage, let me unfold for you the [nature of] this feeding by means of a discourse drawn from physics—if, in fact, you want to put away your preconceived ideas. For you shall learn about the mystery[271] at once. 14. What, then, is it that we say? All we humans have been born having taken the body from earth and in a way "eating" the flesh of it, not [the earth] itself, and by drinking its blood we do not perish. The flesh and blood of the earth are its dry and moist fruit, from which we live when we eat and drink sufficiently, though we do not grieve the earth when we consume its flesh and blood. For harvesting grain and wine from it we nourish ourselves, living happily upon it.

---

266 On the milk of Christ's breasts as teaching and knowledge, see Clement of Alexandria, *Pedagogue* 1.6. On the milk as Christ's breasts as the text of the Old and New Testaments cf. the fifth-century *Life of Syncletica* 21; see also Krueger (2006), 145–146.
267 Cf. Jer. 1:9.
268 Cf. Ezek. 3:1–3.
269 On feeding on Christ as knowledge of the Word cf. Origen, *Commentary on John* 10.8.103–111. Wisdom invites all to partake of her bread and wine at Prov. 9:5.
270 Mt. 26:26–28. At 3.15.6 the Hellene had asserted that the other evangelists had not recorded Jesus's statement in Jn. 6:53 ("Unless you eat my flesh and drink my blood, you do not have life in you"); thus Macarius may quote from Matthew here in order counter that claim.
271 The Christian sacraments (baptism and the lord's supper) are not described as mysteries in the New Testament, but this usage becomes ubiquitous in the fourth century: Eusebius, *Gospel Demonstration* 9.6; Cyril of Jerusalem, *Catechetical Homilies* 19.1; John Chrysostom, *Homilies on Matthew* 23.3.

15. Well then, turn for me your ear to the design of the mystery and direct your discursive faculty towards what you will hear. What then? The Unique Son created earth in the beginning, and having taken some earth he made humanity, and having taken the body from humanity, he became human. If, then, the body is defined as earth by the principle of its ancient origin, and earth is Christ's creation by the principle of creation, being truly his own creation, and from this [earth] bread and wine were given, and from it comes the body of the human being, and Christ put on this body, then it is fitting that, having taken bread and wine, he said: "This is my body and my blood."[272] 16. For this is not a *type* of the body or a *type* of blood, as some people whose minds have become insensible have rhapsodized, but the *true* body and blood of Christ, since the body is from earth and likewise the bread and wine come from earth. 17. How, then, could anyone else have dared to say "My flesh is food, and my blood drink,"[273] since no one is revealed to be the Creator and Maker of earth, nor does this creation and work properly belong to anyone, unless it belongs to the Son of God alone?

18. Thus he meant: "This is mine, for the creation of the earth is mine and no other's; for all have come into being after the earth, having taken their body from me, but I, before the earth [existed], made it, taking [nothing] from anyone; from what is my own, then, I extend my grace to you. From the earth, bread was given you as nourishment, but the earth is my handiwork; likewise the body and this my 'lump' is from the earth.[274] Therefore, I give bread and the cup from the weft that I have woven, the Holy One using the earthly as a seal, when I declare that 'this is my body and blood.'[275]" 19. For if it were Abraham or another of the righteous saying "My flesh is food and my blood drink," he would have boldly and greatly

---

272 Mt. 26:26–28.
273 Jn. 6:55.
274 An allusion to Rom. 11:16 ("If the dough offered as first fruits is holy, so is the whole lump" [RSV]) as well as 1 Cor. 5:6 ("Do you not know that a little yeast leavens the whole lump?" [NRSV]), passage often read Christologically and soteriologically in terms of the Son's assumption of humanity (i.e. the "lump"); cf. e.g. Gregory of Nyssa, *Against Eunomius* 2.12.
275 This is Macarius's exegesis of liturgical formulae recited by the celebrant during the *anaphora* (the portion of the liturgy in which the wine and bread are ritually transformed into Christ's blood and body), specifically, during the recitation of the "institution narrative," in which the celebrant recounts the Last Supper (cf. Mt. 26:26–28; Mk. 14:22–24; Lk. 22:19–20; 1 Cor. 11:23–25), thus Macarius here has Christ speak in the person of the liturgical celebrant (and vice versa).

lied, giving as a free gift of his own what was another's, and he would have caused great harm, having given bread and the cup to anyone recklessly, saying: "This is my body and this is my blood." For it was not his, but the property of another.

20. But nor do the things eaten grant life to those who eat them, since they do not have the living Word in their composition. But the [body made from] earth, called the body of God, leads those who eat [it] into eternal life. Christ, therefore, gave his own body and blood to the faithful, having placed within it the life-giving medicine of divinity.[276] 21. Therefore, saying that the flesh is bread and the blood wine, he taught us reasonably that the body is of the earth and so too is bread, and that each one derives [its] essence [from the earth]. 22. But the common bread formed from the earth, even if flesh takes existence from the earth, does not promise the possession of eternal life, but grants to those who eat it temporary relief, which is extinguished quickly without the Holy Spirit. But the bread produced in the blessed earth of Christ, united with it by the power of the Holy Spirit, makes the human being immortal with only a taste. 23. For the mystical bread, containing the Saviour's call, which has come to be inseparably united with his body and blood, unites him who eats it with the body of Christ and makes him a member of the Saviour.[277] 24. For just as the writing tablet that has received the power of the teacher through the letters written upon it grants [that power] to the learner and through it elevates him, joining him to the teacher,[278] so too the body, which is the bread, and the blood, which is the wine, since they have derived incorruption from the undefiled divinity, immediately provide [the same] to him who partakes, and through it brings him up to the pure abode of the Creator itself. 25. Therefore, when eaten, the flesh of the Saviour is not destroyed, nor is this blood exhausted when drunk, but he who eats comes to an increase of divine powers, while what is eaten cannot be expended, since it is of the same kind as, and inseparable from, the Unexpendable Nature.

24. 1. Accept, then, if you will, this grand explanation of a grand doubt. But let us examine this next point, not considering the "sickness" or the

---

276 For the sanctified eucharistic bread as a φάρμακον, or "medicine," see e.g. Ignatius of Antioch, *Ephesians* 21.
277 Cf. Eph. 5:30; Rom. 12:4–5; 1 Cor. 6:15, 12:27.
278 Cf. Gregory Thaumaturgus, *Panegyric for Origen* 6, where Gregory describes the soul of the learner being "knit" to the soul of the teacher, and thus to the *Logos*.

"deadly poison" in an overly corporeal way,[279] since we do away with the principle of faith when we find myriad unbelieving people and strangers to God and piety who have become strong enough to resist deadly poisons. 2. For if both believers and unbelievers confute the power of poisons, how will we call some unbelievers and others believers, when they have all equally conquered the evil of these harmful things? For either we call all unbelievers or we call all believers. 3. In fact, it is possible to see many unbelieving atheists put suffering to flight after merely making a sign upon the sick. What then? Shall we name them believers from this fact, or rather Empirics who banish illness swiftly by their expertise?[280] 4. We must not, then, be deceived into determining the faithful with our senses, from the fact of one's drinking poison, nor into accepting the accurate [discernment] of the pious based on their curing of diseases. For then all will equip themselves to drink poisons and thumb their nose at them by effective artifice, and demand from men the honours of faith. In this way some, having conquered sickness with skill, boast of being saviours[281] of men.

5. Hence, one must not accept the Saviour's statement so hastily, but deem it worthy of a necessary test. For if the deadly poison is not harmful to believers, then it is clearly invisible and effects an invisible and incorporeal death. This poison is not blended from serpents; this poison is not provided by human skill, since it does not bring harm to believers. 6. I will cite the Christ-proclaimer Paul as one who teaches about this poison, where he says somewhere, clarifying this nicely: "Whoever of us has been baptized into Christ, has been baptized into his death; has been entombed together with him in baptism."[282] See that the deadly poison does not harm believers, for it killed the sin that was acting the tyrant and, through faith, saved man who was ruled tyrannically. 7. For if anyone drinks this poison in faith, he inwardly puts to death the ancient beast of transgression, himself still living, and incurs no harm himself but puts to death the ancient yet still living beast, though he is not himself harmed, but returns again to a better condition of life. That which, therefore, is harmful to unbelievers is

---

279 On the inferiority of the corporeal to the intellectual or spiritual sense of scripture, cf. Origen, *First Principles* 4.2.4. Macarius, according to his custom, is adapting a metaphor which Ignatius of Antioch used of *false* teaching at *Trallians* 6.
280 The Empirics, who despised philosophy, were in turn despised by such practitioners as Galen, *On Anatomical Procedures* 2.3.
281 The term σωτήρ ("saviour") may denote one who, like the god Asclepius and his acolytes, offers deliverance from bodily rather than spiritual evils.
282 Rom. 6:3–4.

harmless to believers. 8. In this way, as a rock placed in the road such that those travelling are not splashed with mud is an aid for those who see it and an ally on their journey, but for those who do not see it is a blow, calamity, and black eye, so the false step of the Jews has become the wealth of the Gentiles and their discomfiture the wealth of the world.[283] Thus the lustrous Cross that lights the earth with divinity has become an irremediable shadow for unbelievers, but a clear and untroubled light for believers.[284]

9. Clearly, then, he [i.e. Christ] says that these signs invisibly accompany believers, who drink poison in faith and are not at all harmed, but in truth also impose hands upon the sick. 10. Which, taken figuratively, has an evident deeper meaning: for "hands" figuratively indicate nothing other than practical actions,[285] while he names the change of seasons "sickness," from their unevenness of rains and from the great disorder they effect in life, the radical changes that come upon the earth and sea. Often, then, the season is "sick" with drought, it is ill with deluges and snow beyond measure. Thus the seasons often appear "sick" when the air is troubled by the battle of the elements. Believers, therefore, applying themselves in these conditions, do not lack efficacy in their actions, nor do they fall short of their expectations. 11. For example, Polycarp, who managed the episcopacy of the Smyrnaeans, when the season of the harvest was greatly ill since the sky, hiding not even the smallest cloud, sent unquenchable flame from the air, scorching beyond measure from above the land lying below, up to the point where it dried the moisture from the springs, that divinely inspired man, as the distress was pressing down upon men, arriving and seeing the residents so wasted and applying his hands through prayer to the season that was in a way "sick," suddenly made all well. But again, when the land was choked by rain and the inhabitants were wailing piteously, the same man, again projecting his hands into the air, relieved the danger, "healing" the hateful situation.[286] 12. And indeed, before he was bishop, while he was managing the affairs of a widow,[287] whenever he applied his hand, all

---

283 Cf. Rom. 11:12.
284 Thus the "poison" of Mk. 16:18 is, for Macarius, faith in the cross/crucified Christ, sacramentalized in baptism; cf. 1 Cor. 1:23 and especially 2. Cor. 2:16.
285 Cf. Aristobulus apud Eusebius, *Gospel Preparation* 8.10.8.
286 For Polycarp's intercession for the Smyrnaeans during drought see Pionius, *Life of Polycarp* 29–31.
287 In *Life of Polycarp* 3–5, the widow Callisto is told by an angel to purchase the young (slave?) Polycarp from his masters, and he subsequently becomes the manager of her household, but the extant manuscripts of the *Life of Polycarp* do not include healing miracles among the services Polycarp performed for Callisto.

was well. What need is there for me to point out to you the manly deeds of Irenaeus of Lyon, of Fabian of Rome, or Cyprian of Carthage?[288]

13. But leaving them aside, I will give an account of those of our time. How many—we know not how—by extending their hands in prayer[289] to the Overseer, have invisibly healed the invisible distempers of passion that terribly oppress men's souls. How many, placing their hands upon catechumens enflamed by the ancient bruises or distempers of sin, have made them well by having them pass through the mystical and divine bath into the new grace of health?[290] 14. For to drive away bodily affections is not the most pressing concern of believers, since these are wont to teach a man rather than to trouble the constitution of his soul; when anything, on the other hand, is wont to harm the discursive faculty and enslaves the thinking power of the rational faculty, it is the driving away of this by counsel and persuasion that is of benefit to the soul.

25. 1. Since, as I think, the response to this passage has been persuasive for the audience, I will explain the next proposition, concerning the passage: "If you have faith like a mustard seed, you will say to this mountain, 'Rise and throw yourself into the sea,' and your word, once spoken, will not be without power."[291]

2. It is the custom among teachers to teach their students to do perfectly that which they themselves know and are accustomed to do. But if the teacher tells his students to pursue something that he has not [himself] done, he does not do the work of a teacher, but of a cheat, when he requires them to do things which he has not been found doing. But the learner will not accept that which the teacher does not do, for it is not permitted for a student to do something other than what he sees the teacher saying or doing. 3. Now what corporeal mountain did Christ move? What sensible hill did he rattle? What ridge in Palestine did he shake and when, so that

---

288 Irenaeus, Bishop of Lyon (fl. 260–c.202 CE); Fabian, Bishop of Rome (fl. 236–250 CE); Cyprian, Bishop of Carthage (fl. 249–258 CE); in Greek patristic literature, Macarius could have read of the miraculous descent of a dove signalling the choice of Flavian as bishop in Eusebius, *Ecclesiastical History* 6.29.2–4.

289 Cf. 1 Tim. 2:8, which describes prayer with hands lifted, a common Greco-Roman gesture of supplication.

290 Baptism was followed by the laying on of hands, which was usually understood to convey the Holy Spirit (see e.g. Acts 19:4–6; Tertullian, *On Baptism* 8); here, Macarius appears to conflate the post-baptismal imposition of hands with the laying on of hands for the healing of physical ailments.

291 Mt. 17:20, 21:21.

the disciples seeing him doing so were zealous to do it [too]? 4. But if he himself manifestly never did any such thing, how did he say to his closest disciples: "You will say to this mountain, 'Rise and throw yourself into the sea'"?[292] How is it consistent to speak of moving a mountain rooted forever by the power of the Creator into the sea? 5. For even if a believer were able to do this, still the precept of consistency[293] does not allow the overturning of the art of the All-wise Power, as the Scripture says: "He made the universe firm, which will not be shaken."[294] 6. Now, the apostles are recorded to have brought the four corners of the world under their own power thanks to [their] exceeding faith;[295] and their faith was not comparable to that of a mustard seed, but to that of a great mountain higher than the clouds, so great that they were able to subjugate cities from one end of the earth to the other by faith alone. But they never moved a sensible mountain spatially, not Parnassus, not Olympus, not Ida, not Gargaros, not Taurus, not Bosphorus, not Mount Sinai.[296] But they rolled away many intelligible mountains from many [people], driving away the mountain-dwelling demons that threatened men. 7. Thus, for example, one of the prophets, fighting against the intelligible mountain, said, in the person of God: "'Behold I stand before you, the <corrupted> mountain that corrupts all the earth,' says the Lord."[297]

8. But in order that what has been said may be clearer to you, I will explain the subject from the beginning. At that time, after Jesus made the grievous demon flee from the child who was called a "lunatic,"[298] after he had come down from the sensible mountain, when the disciples were

---

292 Mt. 21:21.

293 Goulet (2003) translates this phrase (ὁ τῆς ἀκολουθίας θέσμος) as "the law of coherence/consistency" (*la loi de la cohérence*); Macarius also uses the phrase at 4.26.7 to describe the "precept of consistency" that a human ruler should exercise over other humans, rather than "constraint and violence," thus the phrase connotes "consistency" with the ontological and natural order as well as the "coherence" of the literary text, something difficult to convey in a single English word.

294 Ps. 92:1e.

295 That the apostles had subjugated the known world by faith, rather than force, was a common claim in early Christian literature by the fourth century; see e.g. Origen, *On First Principles* 4.2; idem, *Against Celsus* 2.30; Arnobius, *Against the Nations* 2.1, 12; Eusebius, *Gospel Demonstration* 3.7; idem, *Theophany* 3.1–2.

296 The lesser-known mountains here (Gargaros, Taurus, and Bosphorus) are all allocated in Asia Minor, as is Mount Ida (e.g. the Phrygian Ida in the Troad); this may suggest that the work was composed somewhere in Asia Minor, see Goulet (2003), 55; Hauschildt (1907), 4.

297 Jer. 28:25 (LXX).

298 Mt. 17:14–18.

saying to him, "How were we unable to free the child from the demon?"[299] he spoke to them thus: "On account of your small faith. Truly I say to you, if you were to have faith like a mustard seed, you could say to this mountain"[300]—not simply "mountain," but with the deictic pronoun—"this one that was just now removed by me from him who was ill." 9. For if he had said without the pronoun: "You will say to *a* mountain, 'Rise and throw yourself into the sea,'" then he would be thought to speak about a corporeal mountain. But here, when he says it with the pronoun, he indicated that he spoke about the demon and about the heights to which it swelled up against the knowledge of God.

10. Now, Jesus had already cast down many such arrogant ones like great mountains into the sea, removing them from human life and company, when he hurled those called "legions" along with the swine over the cliff into the sea.[301] Here, then, he spoke allegorically of the crest of the demon that was raised up against men.

26. 1. And it is necessary that you genuinely accept this explanation, but next we must inquire about the passage in which the Devil perversely speaks about Christ, where he says: "Throw yourself down."[302] May it be amenable to you now, if it is possible, to examine the nature of this matter.

2. The story contains a temptation by and battle with a demon. But it is never permitted for a combatant to accept the advice of his adversary—for he would seem weaker for having peacefully accepted the word of his opponent. Rather, he must in all ways hate and abominate his antagonist. 3. For even if it certainly would have been a great accomplishment for Christ to throw himself from the pinnacle [of the Temple],[303] fighting according to the rules of the adversary and arch-evil demon brings the athlete much blame. 4. Hence, even if this had been written about Christ, Christ did not have to do it based on the Devil's recalling it. For the event would have been cooperative—with the one saying, "Throw yourself down," and the other throwing himself without hesitation. But if it were cooperative, it was necessary that that which was done by cooperative sentiment should be amicable. 5. And see, furthermore, the uproar inherent in this action;

---

299 Mt. 17:19.

300 Up to this point Macarius is quoting Mt. 17:20, 21, what follows is Macarius's exegesis of the passage given in part in Jesus's voice.

301 Cf. Mt. 8:28–34; see also Macarius's discussion of this passage at 3.11ff above.

302 Mt. 4:6.

303 Cf. Mt. 4:5.

see the confusion [produced] by so great a fall—a prophetic passage was put in motion by the Devil, and hearing this statement Christ fulfilled it, as if persuaded by a zealous teacher or rhetor! O what foolishness! O what a failure! The athlete agreed amicably to the terms of his adversary before the combat! The dragon hisses, the beast calls, forging mad words full of error, while Christ gladly receives them and warmly embraces these words as a mandate.[304]

6. Observe closely what a basis for damage clearly emerges from this. For if Christ took this advice as good, he would have accepted what came next as good, hearing what is evil as good, and bringing it to completion. 7. This is the statement that followed: "If you fall down and worship me."[305] For the Saviour would not have been able to reject this if he had given in obediently to what went before. For after the Devil said clearly to him, "Make these stones into bread"[306] and "Throw yourself down," he would have had to worship the Devil when he asked and not reject him, as he was constrained by his previous obedience. 8. For he who was fully persuaded that the two foregoing [commands] were good would clearly, persuaded that the third was good, have worshipped, denying the nature of the divine essence. For all the effort and artifice of the Devil lay in presenting two persuasive demands to Christ so that, once he had made him submissive to them, he might find him ready and obedient. But understanding the greatness of his evil, Jesus immediately repelled the volleys of these temptations.

9. For even if the passage he quoted to him was prophetic, because of the evil that followed he did not do it, lest he be destroyed by his own missiles fired by Beliar and receive a mortal wound. Because it is in every way clear that the prophetic saying belongs to the Saviour and was spoken about him, but it is also manifest and evident that the Devil, like an enemy who strips a soldier's quiver, fired arrows from it against the King of the Ages, planning to slaughter him with his own weapons. 10. Hence Christ, seeing his own armaments ranged against him, rejected this, lest weakened by them he worship the impious one. For this reason, my friend, Christ did not throw himself down from the Temple.

---

304 The vocabulary likening Christ's rhetorical contest with the Devil to a combat or athletic contest echoes similar language in Macarius's narrative descriptions of his present rhetorical contest with the Hellene.
305 Mt. 4:9.
306 Mt. 4:3.

164 MACARIUS, *APOCRITICUS*

27a. 1. So much for that particular question, but now the matters concerning Peter must be investigated, for they truly require an interrogation and much explanation. Has he who is the foundation of the apostles been shaken by so great a tumult? Has the leader of evangelical operations been confounded by such a nauseous cloud? 2. If Peter has been called by Christ a "scandal," "Satan," and a "stumbling block,"[307] if Peter is convicted of unpardonable sins, then the whole chorus of the Apostles has been reproached, and the root of faith must all but be uprooted. It is necessary, therefore, to look at the time and place in which these things were said, so that we may search out the deeper meaning[308] of the matter.

3. In Caesarea Philippi, he [Christ] asked the disciples who the people were saying he was, and they said to him: "Some say John, others Elijah, others one of the prophets."[309] Then he said to them: "But who do you say I am?" Peter answering said: "You are the Christ, the Son of the living God."[310] 4. Christ, seeing Peter thus illuminated by the Father's grace and so great a divine revelation coming into him, gave him the promise of unhesitating faith and exalted him with a weighty blessing, saying: "'Blessed are you, Simon son of Jonah, because flesh and blood did not reveal to you' the ineffable mystery of so great a matter, nor one of the angels nor a leader of the incorporeal worthies, no servant of the hypercosmic powers, but the ineffable Good and Everlasting itself, the Immortal Source of our creation, 'the Father who is in heaven.'[311] Hence, receive a name worthy of grace and be 'Peter,' who appears to the whole world like an unconquerable rock,[312] who has received an unshakeable will and an unmoveable reasoning power, since today you have borne witness to the unshakeableness of the blessed essence."

5. It was natural, then, that the deceptive beast, upon hearing these statements and what Peter said when he bore witness to the Saviour, should, with all possible haste, strip Peter of his worthiness by means of a machination, and at the same time overturn this witness of Christ and

---

307 Mt. 16:23; Rom. 9:32.
308 "Deeper meaning" translates νοῦς, the "mind" or deeper sense of an historical event or scriptural passage; see, for example, Origen, *On First Principles* 4.2.4; Eusebius, *Commentary on Isaiah* 1.42.36; 1.85.97, etc.
309 Mt. 16:13–14.
310 Mt. 16:15–16.
311 Mt. 16:17.
312 The pun on the name "Peter" (Πέτρος) and the Greek word for "rock" (πέτρος) is not evident in English translation.

BOOK 3   165

divert the plan of the Passion with sophistical cunning. For he knew—he clearly knew—that the Passion of Christ meant the destruction of his tyrannical evil. And therefore he planned to put obstacles in the way of the Cross. 6. Hence, sowing words of uncertainty in Peter, he said: "I implore you, Lord, may this never happen to you!"[313] 7. Hence Jesus, knowing that the utterance was not Peter's but that the statement was a suggestion of Satan, said: "Get behind me, Satan!"[314] And in order that he [i.e. Satan] might now recognize his proper name and get far from the leader of the disciples, he said: "Get behind me, *Satan*," for everything in front of you has been cut off. 8. He said this to Satan, but to Peter he said: "'You are a scandal to me, because you do not think of the things of God, but of men,'[315] because you are persuaded by the suggestion of the arch-evil Belial." And as far as the statement to Peter, "Get behind me, Satan," that is enough.

9. For by receiving a punishment worthy of his fault, he [Peter] helped the disciples by providing a great deterrent against ever again whispering petty things against the greatness of the divine plan. For if he who shortly before transcended the very arch of heaven with the urbane and resplendent eye of faith and passed beyond the flaming streams of the Seraphim and saw the nobility of the only-begotten Son together with the Father, which outshines the incorporeal servants in beauty, and in this was helped sufficiently in his soul and gave a genuine statement of confession in faith, is so suddenly led by the suggestion of slanderous counsel to express unhelpful compassion that would lead to the harm of the world and the common detriment of all, saying in a tragic way what is not allowed and hastily exclaiming: "I implore you, Lord, may this never happen to you," then he justly receives this blow from Christ.

10. What might each person who errs imagine they could believe, when they see Peter disclosing to the audience that the one present is the Son of God, but also wanting this one to live <in the world> for a long time as though a man and that the Holy One tarry on earth for an inappropriate amount of time and not accomplish the plan of the Passion, come to the aid of human poverty, and succour the poverty of those laid low, and that he not arrive at his high vantage point[316] and in the most direct way take up his proper throne of dominion, but on the contrary, persuaded by

---

313 Mt. 16:22.
314 Mt. 16:23.
315 Mt. 16:23.
316 The cross as a beacon upon a high vantage point is an image favoured by Macarius, cf. 3.14.4; 3.24.8 above.

Peter's statement, be fond of dwelling in a deep chamber and to welcome this insolent regimen which is truly a painful and accursed life, and wait a long time for common death, and on account of Peter's advice, beg off that which was impending and full of the planned salvation?

11. Hence he with justice greatly blamed him who greatly believed and greatly afflicted the marvellous Peter who had greatly stumbled. For when he said, "You are the Christ, the Son of the living God,"[317] [Jesus] led him up to the summit of dignity, making him the key master and seneschal of the Kingdom above. For it was fitting that he who knew the king seated augustly within the immaculate palace halls receive the power to close and open, so that he could explain the might of the All-powerful to all entrants as one who knows, and, as one well acquainted with these [places], justly shut out those unfit for the blessed vision. 12. For he who gazed upon the root of immortality and saw the ever-flowing font of life also fittingly received the authority over entering and exiting these [places]. For Peter's utterance, made as it was with the [definite] articles, secured the complete accuracy of divine doctrine, disclosing the unshakeable strength of monarchy and protecting the unadulterated Rule of Truth.[318] 13. For when Peter said not "You are *a christ*," but "*the Christ*," and not "You are *a son*," but "*the Son*," and not "You are of *a god*," but "of *the God*," and not "You are of *a* living [god]," but "of *the* living [God]," proclaiming everything with the article, he disclosed more resoundingly the singularity of the blessed essence, disclosed the particularity of the unique nature. What he said was truly a revelation from the heavenly Father; truly it was a unique statement that testified to the Unique Son.[319] 14. For since there are many "christs,"[320] but only one who is called this in the truest sense, with the article, and many "sons" and many "gods," but one alone is truly living and Son of

---

317 Mt. 16:16.

318 A reads "image [εἰκόνα] of truth"; compare with the usage of the phrase at 3.5.4 and 3.23.7 above.

319 The wordplay is difficult to capture in English; Peter's singular/unique (μονογενής) statement describes the singular/unique (Μονογενής) Son. As the title of Macarius's work was also likely "*Monogenēs*," this suggests that Macarius understands his own work likewise to be a "unique" doctrinal statement concerning the Unique Son; see also Goulet (2003) 44–47 and the Introduction to the present volume.

320 The Greek "christ" translated the Hebrew "messiah," or "anointed," and was applied, for instance, to the Israelite kings in the Septuagint, while early Christians often read passages referring to plural "christs" in terms of righteous humans' soteriological mimesis of/participation in Christ (e.g. Ps. 104:15 [LXX]): "Do not touch my christs [i.e. "anointed ones"], and Origen's exegesis at *Against Celsus* 6.79).

God, whenever he has the article, and angels are often called "sons of God," without the article,[321] being honoured by the title, but only one is Unique, to whom alone the article is authentically applied, so too there are many gods and <many creators> and many lords,[322] but none of them is God, or Creator, or Lord, since they lack the article, but there is one Creator God and one Lord King, who has the article that confirms his singularity. 15. Peter, therefore, since he had been taught this mystery not of flesh and blood,[323] but accurately learning these things about the Father and the Son from the Holy Spirit, proclaimed and bore witness to the Godhead with the article.[324] And thus he was blessed and named "Peter," since he was preaching the immutability of the unshakeable rock.[325]

16. Then the good-hating demon, seeing that he was so great and such a person, was stirred up against him and was outraged with envy[326] and devised every machination so that he might trip up him who was secure and stable as a rock, at one time persuading him to utter, like a man, things unworthy of the promise, and at another time, urging him to show sympathy in a manner unfitting for a "rock." 17. Hence, in response to these

---

321 Cf. Gen. 6:1–2, where the reading "angels" is substituted for "sons of god" at Philo, *On the Giants* 1, but the standard text of the Septuagint reads "*the* sons of god." At Job 1:6 and 38:7 the Hebrew has "sons of god" but the Greek has "angels."
322 Cf. 1 Cor. 8:5b.
323 Conflating Mt. 16:17 with Jn. 1:13.
324 For a similar exegesis compare Cyril of Alexandria, *Commentary on Matthew*, fr. 190 (Reuss): "Peter did not say, 'You are *a* Christ or *a* Son of God,' but '*the* Christ, *the* Son of God.' For there are many 'christs' by grace who have that status by adoption, but only one who is 'Son of God' by nature. Thus he said, with the article, '*the* Christ, *the* Son of God.' And in calling him the Son of the Living God he indicates that life and death has no power over him. And even if the flesh was pained for a short while as it died, it yet rose, unable to be overcome by the bonds of death, since the Word was in it."
325 On Christ as rock see Mt. 21:42; Mk. 12:10; Lk. 20:17, all citing Ps. 118:22. For the phrase "unshakeable rock" (ἀσελεύτος πέτρα) as applied to Christ in patristic literature see, for example, Basil of Caesarea (Eusebius of Emesa?), *Homily on Penitence* (PG 31:1483.49–1484.1): "For if he is also a rock it is not as Christ is a rock, but as Peter is a rock; for Christ is the true unshakeable rock, while Peter is so on account of that rock." For the related phrase "unbroken rock" (ἀρραγής πέτρα) see for example Eusebius of Caesarea, *Gospel Preparation* 1.3.8: "[Christ] declared that the Church ... should be invincible and undismayed, and should never be conquered by death, but stands and abides unshaken, settled, and rooted upon His own power as upon a rock that is unshakeable and unbroken"; for the phrase applied to the Son as descriptive of his relation to the Father see for example Eusebius of Caesarea, *On Ecclesiastical Theology* 1.8.3.
326 On φθόνος ("envy") as the vice of the devil see Wis. 2:24 ("By the Devil's envy death came into the world").

improprieties, Christ, correcting him, stigmatized him, censuring him in a most severe voice. And so too, when he was overcome by passion at the high priests' attack and cut off someone's ear with the sword, he administered no light admonition to him as he easily healed the wound.[327] Likewise, when he erred inappropriately with his tongue, he [Christ] convicted him for uttering the words, but seeing the regret of his soul, he approved him, knowing <that> the mind is <not> strong enough to restrain with charity the mouth that chatters and runs.

28. 1. As for his judgment against Ananias and Sapphira, if you indeed want the story read to you, the deed will appear to you as a truly universal lesson full of many points. 2. For when Ananias received the affliction of wickedness into his soul he also shared it secretly with his wife. For as soon as the gifts of the Gospel were preached and the preachers led the people of their race to the rule of piety, the whole crowd was stupefied at their miracles, while the unbelievable report of their deeds confused the mind. For prodigious wonders and miraculous signs convinced the eyes of those who reported [them], while eagerness led the souls of those who listened, with the result that nearly every nation was urged to the common enjoyment of salvation, took up the desire for hypercosmic goods, rejected the things of this world for a better calculation, repudiated all things on earth that are subject to attack, and with the wings of eagerness took the heaven itself as their residence, welcoming a way of life like that of the angels.[328] 3. Thenceforth, a luminous attitude and a clear and solid sensibility showed forth; thenceforth city, field, and suburb were eager to drink from the stream of grace; thenceforth they considered the corporeal reality of property to be burdensome and damaging for souls; thenceforth life was lived in common and the possession of property was undivided;[329] thenceforth a joining of wealth and poverty, giving and receiving steered the human flock; thenceforth having as though not having and not having as though having[330] were judged the most distinguished fame. All were,

---

327 Macarius harmonizes several gospel narratives: at Mt. 26:51–52, "one of those with Jesus" cuts off the ear of the High Priest's slave, and Jesus admonishes him to sheath his sword; at Jn. 18:10–11 Peter is named (as is the slave [Malchus]); at Lk. 22:51 Jesus heals the wound.

328 Cf. Acts 2:43–47. Theologians also borrowed from Plato's *Phaedrus* the conceit that the soul has wings which will bear her to heaven, for example: 1 Clement 25:3; Cyril of Jerusalem, *Catechetical Homilies* 3.6.

329 Cf. Acts 2:44.

330 Cf. 1 Cor. 7:29. See also 4.1.2 and 4.11.8, where the Hellene and Macarius, respectively,

as it were, raised up to a life and existence of well-being,³³¹ enflamed in their souls by divine ardour, and not at all able to resist their thirst for that which is greater. That time was a heavenly festival, a spectacle of piety the like of which had never been seen. At that time, wealth was something hateful and the ownership of possessions was despised. In general, the word of the apostles' teaching shined brighter than the sun, illuminating the hidden places of the conscience itself, with the further result that all eagerly rushed to join so great a festival of good things and the multitude appeared, through the mediation of the Spirit, to have a single soul, since their life was suffused with a spiritual disposition.

5. This being the way it was and with matters steered rightly in this way, Ananias, together with his wife Sapphira, became a participant in such a great festival and these miraculous deeds. Since, then, many were giving property to the apostles in Christ's name so that poverty, on the excuse of want, would not be slow to join the community³³² of faith, but, finding the supply of necessities bountiful, would freely join the Message³³³ on a par with those who had [wealth], he [Ananias], since he had a property in the countryside, planned to sell it, and resolved that the whole value was a votive offering.³³⁴ 6. That which he deliberately gave to Christ, therefore, he no longer had authority to appropriate as his own, for such [an action] is temple robbery—to give property to God with everyone's knowledge, but like a slave to pilfer a portion of it secretly, with no one's knowledge. For no one who steals his own property is ever sought out as a thief, nor is he praised for taking in secret that over which he has authority; for the action is not wicked [in itself], it is the sentiment behind the action that is reproached.

---

take 1 Cor. 7:29 ("... those who have *wives* be as though they did not have them") as referring to wealth and property.

331 "Life of well-being" translates the phrase here, εὐδαίμονα βίος, better than "happy" or "blessed"; Macarius sees the early Church as living the Greek philosophical (especially the Stoic) ideal of εὐδαιμονία, that is, embodying the ethical perfection of the entire human person.

332 Τὸ κοινόν ("community," "commonwealth"), a mode of communal living in which property was shared in common.

333 "Message" (κήρυγμα) stands by synecdoche here for the Christian community constituted through the Apostles' "preaching" (κήρυγμα).

334 Macarius draws on the traditional Greek sacrificial vocabulary here and in what follows. A "votive offering" (ἀνάθημα) was anything dedicated to a deity and set up in a temple or temple precinct (see, for example, Herodotus, *Histories* 1.14 on votive offerings set up at Delphi). Theft of votive offerings, or other property dedicated to a deity, was "temple robbery" (ἱεροσυλία), and was considered most sacrilegious, and was theoretically punishable by death in the Hellenistic and Roman worlds.

7. Hence, in order that Ananias's audacity, if it had been conceded to him at that time, should not harm the whole gathering of believers, plunging all alike into the same sickness, Peter laid his mischievous condition bare before the eyes of all present, not that he might purify the sin that had previously been committed—for this had already been done—but in order to prevent future sickness and school the sentiments of those who had recently become believers, imitating a skilled physician who, by cutting off a disease spreading within a great body at its root, makes the whole body healthy and strong.[335] 8. The injustice committed, therefore, was not against Peter—hence neither did he receive philanthropic forbearance—but it was against the Divine itself and the shameless act was directed at shaking faith at its root. 9. Not only this, but Ananias himself, together with his wife, if the reproach of this judgment had not occurred, would have fallen into an endless pit of scandal. For he would have immediately supposed, unless he had been reproached, that Christ had no knowledge of things done in secret[336] and did not know the principle of good and evil, and from this would have forged a grievous doctrine in the recess of his soul, looking to do easy and wicked things, saying: 10. "If the deeds of men done in secret escape the notice of the Divine, what prevents anyone at all from accomplishing anything most disgraceful when there is no word, refutation, or accuser against any of this?" And so, with a mind wickedly disposed, he would have dared commit every unwonted deed, he would have pursued all the wickedness of impiety, making as a law within himself a lawless decree,[337] and making many people for a long time participants of such an accursed attitude, falling upon them like a great and incurable plague and consuming everyone.

11. Hence, so that this tragedy would not straightaway befall the faithful, Peter, knowing this, quickly cut out the sickness, cutting out future disease along with it. For just as sprouts of acanthus that make the farmer's labour difficult creep unnoticed in fields of grain, he cut it off at the root, liberating the rational land[338] from harm. 12. Hear straightaway, therefore, what it is

---

335 Compare Mk 9:47; Mt. 18:19.
336 Cf. Mt. 6:18 and Lk. 12:3 for New Testament passages on God's ability to see actions done in secret.
337 Cf. Rom. 2:14–15.
338 The "rational land" is the psychic landscape of rational human souls; for the soul as "rational land" see also Eusebius of Caesarea, *Commentary on the Psalms* (PG 23:641.20); Evagrius, *Antirrheticus* 1.1; John Chrysostom (or Pseudo-Chrysostom), *On Fasting* (PG 60:724.32).

that Peter says to Ananias, "What were you thinking," he says, "by testing the Holy Spirit?"[339] You see that he [i.e. Ananias] tested whether the Divine knew or was ignorant of his actions.[340] 13. And when he heard this, he straightaway breathed his last, forsaken by the Spirit that boils with love and frozen by the cold winter of evil.[341] For Peter did not sentence Ananias to be killed by the blow of a sword, as you say, but said only: "What were you thinking testing the Holy Spirit." His conscience, smiting his soul, killed him. 14. Justly, therefore, Ananias, who died in an unmanly way, and Sapphira, who became a pretext for calamity, sufficiently chastened the crowd of the faithful and Peter was not responsible for what happened to either of them.

29. 1. Next let us look at his [Peter's] marvellous wonders in prison, [to learn] that Herod, when he locked him up, was unable to hold him, although he strove to please the Jews in many ways and wanted to exact vengeance on him publicly.[342] 2. For having armed himself for an insane battle against Christ, without cause he killed James by the sword,[343] but earnestly wanted to kill the great one [i.e. Peter] in a great theatre. In the meantime he guarded him, in order to renew the great swarm of Jewish madness against him. But an angel from heaven, arriving silently in the very middle of the night, woke Peter from sleep and rousing him and leading him out of the prison, convinced him to be saved, thwarting Herod's mad plot. For the angel, having bound the guards with sleep, effortlessly released Peter from his chains, and unlocking the prison gate, led him out from behind bars to the gate of life.[344]

3. For he did not flee, as you say, because he feared death. He accepted the time marked for his death, although he determined first to preach Christ as king in the Queen City,[345] and then, in this [city] to submit to the famous death of the Cross. 4. First he had to be a great lamp for those in ignorance and last hang the torch of his martyrdom upon the city as though on a great lampstand.[346] For the sake of this wise matter, the universal principle of the

---

339 Cf. Acts 5:9.
340 Cf. Rom. 2:3.
341 Cf. Mt. 24:12. See also Origen, *On First Principles* 2.8.3 on the cooling of the soul.
342 Cf. Acts 12:3.
343 Cf. Acts 12:1–2.
344 Cf. Acts 12:7–10.
345 The "Queen City" is Rome; see e.g. Athenaeus, *Banquet of the Sophists*, 3.98c.
346 Cf. Mt. 5:14–16. For Macarius's likening of the crucified Christ to a beacon see 3.27a.10 above.

divine plan did not allow him who was the leader of evangelical grace to fall by Herod's wickedness, but [allowed him] to escape the Jews' mischief and assemble the brotherhood of the Gentiles.

5. Hence, he was not the cause of retribution against the guards,[347] since neither does a doe that breaks free from the stakes that hold down the net persuade a shepherd to kill his pups. Herod, then, killed the soldiers because he was insane. In this he took for a model his inward madness, not deriving his savagery from Peter, since neither does a lion, when roused by someone, derive its anger and agitation from that person, but has the violence of its anger from nature.

6. Thus Peter is found in every way doing everything, in deed and in word, for the sake of advantage. And even if he ate with Gentiles before the encounter with the Jews and refrained from eating with them after the encounter,[348] he is seen not to do this on his own account, but for the sake of those saved from among both the Jews and Gentiles alike. 7. For since the Jews, in honouring the Law, abstained from some foods but partook of others, and since it was Peter's eager desire to bring every nation to the evangelical gift, he for a time in a most economical[349] way honoured the command of the Mosaic Laws, in order that the Jews, knowing that Peter kept the precepts of the Law and loved Moses and glorified the letter, would in a timely way come to the evangelical gift of [his] call, knowing that Peter was not confused as he preached Christ and kept the Law, but approved both by rational consideration. 8. For if he honoured one and despised the other and through reverencing the Gospel turned away from the Law, then he would immediately have been abominated as an enemy of the Mosaic precept. 9. Thus it seems to me that Peter, in order that this not happen, adopting a strategic attitude for a time at the beginning of his salvific preaching, did not come to the meals of the Gentiles when Jews were watching, so that the Jews would not be shocked by knowing this and scandalized by the sight alone flee the word of the evangelical preaching

---

347 Cf. Acts 12:19.
348 Cf. Gal. 2:12.
349 "Most economical" translates οἰκονομικώτερος. The term "economy" (οἰκονομικός) may signify (a) statements or actions that are accommodating (or dissimulating) so as to be most pragmatic given political circumstances (just below, at 3.29.9, Macarius uses the term στρατηγικὴ γνώμη, or "strategic attitude" as a synonym; compare e.g. John Chrysostom's use of οἰκονομικός commenting on Paul's different answers to different constituencies in *Homilies on Ephesians* 6.3); (b) having to do with the divine, soteriological plan ("divine economy"), especially in the incarnation; and, as here (c) the coalescence of these senses in dissimulating/accommodating action or speech that furthers or fulfils the divine economy.

and completely beat Peter down with false accusations, chattering wildly that he was an apostate from ancestral ordinances.

10. Hence Peter, seeing a better way,[350] determined that it was fitting and advantageous to accept the letter [of the Law] of Moses with the Jews in the beginning, in order to gather them in the beginning by honouring the Law. Then, having kept their customs, he might persuade them little by little to follow and have a way of life only according to the evangelical rule, having abandoned the Sabbath, circumcision, and Mosaic foods. And this, most probably, was the thought that prevented Peter from eating with Gentiles when Jews were present. 11. But so that this custom would not harden him, as though he had turned away from the way life was lived among them [i.e. Gentiles], he ate with them when Jews were absent and lived with them, persuading them through meals, in a way, to accept the evangelical grace. 12. He is seen, therefore, to be profitable to each group,[351] and by living with them he made the one friends and clients of Christ, while by honouring the Law he made the other sharers of evangelical grace.

13. Now when Paul complains about "false apostles" his object is not Peter,[352] but those sent by the Jews throughout the inhabited world bearing encyclical letters, whom, because they were "sent out," they called "apostles."[353] The list of charges against Peter is long,[354] but for you and those seated with you what has been said is plenty. But if, another set of questions from the New Testament occurs [to you], without delay, declare it.

---

350 Accommodation (or dissimulation) is likewise ascribed to Peter at *Clementine Recognitions* 3.1.

351 By assimilating Peter's conduct to Paul's profession at 1 Cor. 9:21, Macarius prepares for the Hellene's assault on Paul, which follows just below.

352 Cf. 2 Cor. 11:13.

353 The word "apostle" (ἀπόστολος), literally "one sent out," derives etymologically from the verb "send out" (ἀποστέλλω).

354 Macarius ignores Paul's open accusation of "hypocrisy" (Gal 2:13), to which the Hellene has alluded. His intention in this omission may be to acquit Peter both of ignorance and of merely simulating a disagreement with Paul in Antioch, as was argued by Jerome in *Letter* 112, written to Augustine of Hippo, and in his *Commentary on Galatians* 1.2.11–13. Augustine, in his *Letter* 28, objected to Jerome's imputing dissimulation, even if pious, to scripture. Jerome states that he derived his exegesis from Origen and other fathers who followed Origen's exegesis in order to refute Porphyry's polemics concerning Paul's rebuke of Peter (*Letter* 112.3.6). It is possible that Macarius's statement that the "list of charges against Peter is long" refers to a more extended polemic concerning the Galatians incident in his source).

174   MACARIUS, *APOCRITICUS*

But he [the Hellene], *suddenly becoming circumspect and solemn, said,* You seem to me rather to imitate ignorant ship masters, who, while still swimming along on the voyage assigned to them, look to swim another sea.[355] So in truth you too, when you have still not dealt fully with the vital questions at hand, ask that we define other topics for you.

{Hellene}[356]

30 1. Now, if you are [still] confident after these questions and you have solutions to these difficulties, explain to us how Paul says, "For being free, I enslaved myself to all, in order that I may gain all"?[357] But also, how is it that he who calls circumcision "mis-cutting"[358] circumcises a certain Timothy in Lystra, as the Acts of the Apostles teaches?[359]

2. Well said for such stupid words! The stages of theatres paint living examples of such grandstanding, such comic devices.[360] Such, truly, is the stage trick of acrobats.[361] For how can he who is enslaved to all be free? How can he who complies with everyone win everyone? 3. For if he is without the Law to those without the Law, as he himself says,[362] and

---

355 Goulet ([2003], 399, note) suggests that the Hellene uses the verb "swim" (νήχεσθαι) to imply that the captain is shipwrecked, as well as impatient.

356 The Athens manuscript contains marginal glosses noting the beginning of major speeches by the "Hellene" and the "Christian," see also the Introduction.

357 1 Cor. 9:19.

358 Phil. 3:2. The word play is more vivid in Greek. The passage describes false- or anti-circumcision as harsh chopping or mutilation (κατατομή), in contrast to authentic circumcision (περιτομή).

359 Acts 16:2–3.

360 The equation of acting and theatrics with deception was commonplace in antiquity among both Christians and non-Christians. Plato had urged that the good man shun the stage, since he will never wish to exhibit any character but his own (*Republic* 380c and 395a–396a). Artemidorus writes that "to recite mimes, play the fool, act upon the stage, and deceive people all signify the same thing" (*Oneirocriticon* 1.76). On Christian critiques of the theatre see Leyerle (2001).

361 Reading παραπαίγνιον ("stage trick") with Harnack against Goulet's and Volp's παραπάλλιον ("costume change"). The first reading implies duplicity, the second tergiversation.

362 The Hellene is taking his terminology here ("without the Law" = ἀνόμος) from 1 Cor. 9:21: [ἐγενόμην] τοῖς ἀνόμοις ὡς ἄνομος, μὴ ὢν ἄνομος θεοῦ ἀλλ' ἔννομος Χριστοῦ, ἵνα κερδάνω τοὺς ἀνόμους· "[I became] like one without the Law for those without the Law, although [I am not] without the Law but am under the Law of Christ, so that I might win those without the Law." Throughout the Hellene's attack on Paul, ἀνόμος simultaneously suggests the "illegal" or "lawless" status of Christianity in the eyes of the Hellene; which could suggest that Macarius is using a pagan polemic dating before c.313 (the date by which

BOOK 3   175

is a Jew to Jews, and acquiesces similarly to all, he is truly a captive of manifold wickedness and a stranger and alien to freedom. He who occupies himself with the evil of the lawless and on each occasion makes their deeds his own is truly the promoter and servant of others' wickedness and is a famed zealot for irreverent deeds.

4. It is impossible that these are the teachings of a healthy soul. It is impossible that these words could bespeak a liberal education. Rather, these words have their basis in the thoughts of one who has a fever, they are the reasoning of a sickly person. For if he lives with those without the Law and also gladly accepts Judaism in his letters, participating in each [group] and adapting to each [group], he is mixed up with and subscribes to the mistakes of those who have no refinement.[363]

5. For he who so discounted circumcision that he reviles those wishing to accomplish it, and yet circumcises, is his own strongest accuser, saying, "If I rebuild what I have torn down, I make myself a transgressor."[364]

31 1. But this same man of ours, who is multifarious in his speech, as if having forgotten his own words says to the tribune that he is not Jewish but Roman, when he had said before: "I am a Jewish man, born in Tarsus of Cilicia, brought up at the feet of Gamaliel, educated strictly according to the ancestral Law."[365] 2. Now he who says, "I am a Jew" and "I am a Roman," clinging to each, is neither. For play-acting and claiming to be what he is not, he cunningly acts out the character that these roles imply, and having hidden himself behind a deceitful mask he belies what is clear and steals the truth, besieging the soul's resolution from all sides, enslaving the weak-minded by the magician's art.[366] 3. But he who has embraced such

---

all persecution of Christians was formally ended [see also the Introduction]). Below (3.37.6), Macarius's response exploits the multivalence of ἀνόμος when he likens Paul's method to a general's adoption of "lawless" barbarian customs.

363 Compare Julian, *Against the Galilaeans* (apud Cyril of Alexandria, *Against Julian* 106A–B): "but that the Jewish people alone was an object of care for God and his portion and chosen people is shown not only by what Moses and Jesus, but even by what Paul says; although as concerns Paul this is something rather odd. For as were the circumstances he changes his doctrines about God, just as the polypus changes its colours in relation to the rocks, sometimes claiming that the Jews alone are God's chosen portion, then again when he wants to convince the Hellenes to join him, saying: 'Do not think that God is the god of the Jews alone, but also of the gentiles; yes also of the gentiles' [Rom. 3:29; Gal. 3:28]."

364   Gal. 2:18.

365   Acts 22:3.

366   Accusations of sorcery or magic (γοητεία) were commonplace in anti-Christian polemic; compare for example Porphyry, *Against the Christians* fr. 4 (Harnack), apud

an attitude in [his] life differs in no way from an implacable and bitter enemy who, by pretending to adopt the customs of those living beyond the frontiers, enslaves all, treating them inhumanely.

4. Now if Paul, play-acting, is at one time a Jew, but at another time a Roman, at one time without the Law, but at another a Hellene[367], and whenever he wishes [becomes] foreign and inimical to each [identity], undercutting each. He has thus made each meaningless, disguising his adherence to each with flatteries. 5. Therefore he is a deceiver and manifestly a congenital liar; the statement "I speak the truth in Christ, I do not lie"[368] is extraordinary! For he who yesterday made a show of the Law but today of the Gospel[369]—such a man is rightly [deemed] criminal and unsound in his [personal] life and in his civic life.

32 1. But it is clear that he professes the Gospel out of vainglory and the Law out of greed[370] when he says: "Who ever soldiers with his own provisions? Who shepherds a flock and does not drink the milk of the flock?"[371] Then, wanting to reinforce this, he takes the Law as advocating greed, saying: "But does the Law not also say this? For in the Law of Moses it is written, 'Do not muzzle an ox that is threshing.'"[372] Then he adds an obscure statement full of absurdity, denying divine providence for irrational animals, saying: "Is God concerned for oxen, or does He speak for our sake? It was written for our sake."[373] 2. But in saying this he seems

---

Jerome, *Tractate on the Psalms* 81, where Paul is accused of practicing "magical arts" (*artes magici*) and Julian, *Against the Christians* 100A, apud Cyril, *Against Julian* 100A, where Paul is said to have "surpassed all sorcerers and charlatans everywhere." Celsus accuses Jesus as well as Christians generally of sorcery and makes the commonplace assertion that sorcerers' tricks deceive the masses (e.g. apud Origen, *Against Celsus* 1.6, 2.32, 6.14).

367 Or "at one time lawless, but at another time a Hellene," as a parody of Porphyry's contrast (Eusebius, *Ecclesiastical History* 6.19.8) between the Christian way of life and the lawful way of the Hellene.

368 Rom. 9:1.

369 In adopting the verb σχηματίζειν ("make a show," "take on an appearance"), the Hellene may be sneering obliquely at the levity of Christ, who at Phil. 27 adopts the σχῆμα ("appearance") of a man.

370 Compare Porphyry, *Against the Christians* fr. 4 (Harnack), apud Jerome, *Tractate on the Psalms* 81, where Paul is accused of profit seeking.

371 1 Cor. 9:7.

372 1 Cor. 9:8–9, quoting Dt. 25:4.

373 1 Cor. 9:10. John Chrysostom, *Homilies on 1 Corinthians* 21.5 agrees that care for beasts in the Jewish law is a foreshadowing of the universal philanthropy that will be enjoined on Christians. Origen, however—although he takes this verse as a licence to seek a second, psychic sense in the text at *On First Principles* 4.2.6—attributes a limited concern

BOOK 3   177

to me to insult the wisdom of the Creator excessively, as if it did not provide for that which was already created.³⁷⁴ For if God has no concern for oxen, why is it also written: "You subjected every flock, oxen, beasts, birds, and fishes"?³⁷⁵ For if he takes account of fish, how much more so of oxen, which plough and bear burdens? 3. Hence I admire the impostor who, for the sake of insatiable greed and to receive large contributions from his hearers, treats the Law so piously.

33 1. Then, having turned about all of a sudden, like someone who has had a nightmare and jerks up out of sleep, he says: "I, Paul, bear witness that if someone does [even] one bit of the Law, he is bound to do the entire Law,"³⁷⁶ instead of [saying] that it is entirely unnecessary to obey what is said by the Law. This great man, this sound-minded fellow, this sage, who was instructed strictly according to the ancestral law,³⁷⁷ who has mentioned Moses approvingly so many times,³⁷⁸ teaching as if soaked in wine and liquor, abrogates the command of the Law, saying to the Galatians "Who bewitched you into not obeying the truth," that is, the Gospel.³⁷⁹ 2. Then, causing terror and making it out to be a dreadful thing to obey the Law, he says: "For whoever relies on the works of the Law is under a curse."³⁸⁰ He who writes to the Romans that "the Law

---

for oxen to God at *On First Principles* 4.24. Cf. Epiphanius, *Panarion* 42.12ff against Marcion's citation of the verse.

374 The Hellene, as elsewhere, parodically adopts the word κτίστης ("creator"), which is far more characteristic of biblical than pagan usage. Celsus too, denounces the Christian teaching that divine providence cares more for human beings than for the animal creation (Origen, *Against Celsus* 4.75–76). The claims of animals to merit providential care are vindicated by Plutarch, *Gryllus* and *On the Intelligence of Animals*, and Porphyry, *On Abstinence*, Book 3, passim.

375 Ps. 8:7–9.

376 A rather free quotation of Gal. 5:2–3: "Listen! I, Paul, am telling you that if you let yourselves be circumcised, Christ will be of no benefit to you. Once again I testify to you that every man who lets himself be circumcised that he is obliged to obey the entire Law" (NRSV).

377 Cf. Acts 22:3 and, especially, Phil. 3:5, where Paul presents his pedigree as a Pharisee trained in the Torah.

378 Not easily demonstrable from the seven undisputed Pauline letters, though he certainly holds that the law is holy and spiritual (e.g. Rom. 7:12–14); Moses is discussed in the Letter to the Hebrews, ascribed in antiquity to Paul, and in the speeches ascribed to Paul in Acts. In stating that Paul mentions Moses often, the Hellene may also mean that Paul quotes from the Pentateuch, or books of Moses, as he does, for example, in the undisputed letters.

379 Loose quotation of Gal. 3:1 and 5:7.

380 Gal. 3:10.

is spiritual,"[381] and again, "the Law is holy and the commandment holy and just,"[382] places those who obey what is holy under a curse. 3. Then, turning the nature of the matter topsy-turvy, he confounds everything and makes it murky, with the result that the hearer is overwhelmed for a while in darkness, and as if tripping on two things in the night, stumbles on the Law and bashes into the Gospel in confusion, due to his guide's ignorance.

34 1. For behold! Behold the sage's statement! After myriad passages which he took from the Law for assistance, he also invalidated the judgment of his own words, saying: "For the Law came in so that the transgression might increase,"[383] and before this: "The sting of death is sin, but the power of sin is the Law"[384]; all but having sharpened his own tongue like a sword, he mercilessly cuts the Law limb from limb—he who many times urged obedience to the Law[385] and said that to live according to the Law is praiseworthy. 2. But, having reasserted this ignorant opinion as if out of habit, he has completely overturned his own judgments.

35 1. Again, forbidding food that has been consecrated at sacrifices, he teaches contradictorily concerning it that it is indifferent, saying that it is not necessary to be overly concerned nor to scrutinize [the matter], but to eat [it] even if it might be sacrificial food, as long as no one objects.[386] Now he commands, as it is reported, "That which they sacrifice, they sacrifice to demons, but I do not want you to be in communion with demons."[387] 2. While saying and writing this, he, in contradiction, writes indifferently about the food, saying "We know that an idol is nothing in the world and that there is no God except the One [God],"[388] and shortly after: "Food does not bring you to God; if we eat, we do not excel, and if we do not eat, we are not inferior."[389] Then, after such con man's nonsense as this, as if reclining in the lap of luxury, he chewed his cud,[390] saying: "Eat everything sold in

---

381 Rom. 7:14.
382 Rom. 7:12.
383 Rom. 5:20.
384 1 Cor. 15:56.
385 Cf. 1 Tim. 1:8; Rom. 7:12, etc.
386 For this proviso see 1 Cor. 8:9–13. Many Christians of the ante-Nicene period took more account of Revelation 2:14, where the eating of meats from a sacrifice is condemned without qualification (cf. Irenaeus, *Against Heresies* 1.26.3).
387 1 Cor. 10:20.
388 1 Cor. 8:4.
389 1 Cor. 8:8.
390 Reading ὥσπερ ἐν κλίνῃ κείμενος ἀνεμηρυκήσατο with Blondel and Goulet against

BOOK 3   179

the market, questioning nothing for the sake of conscience, for the earth and its fullness are the Lord's."[391] 3. O stage play such as no one has ever seen! O strange and inconsistent statement! O doctrine that worsts itself with the sword! O novel arrow that flies at and strikes the archer!

36 1. We found a statement similar to these in his letters, where, commending virginity,[392] but changing his mind again, he writes "In the latter times, some will apostatize from the faith, adhering to spirits of error they will forbid marriage and abstain from food,"[393] while in the first letter to the Corinthians, he says: "But concerning the virgins I have no command from the Lord."[394] 2. Therefore those who practise virginity do not do well, nor do those who abstain from marriage, who have trusted the guidance of someone wicked,[395] since they have no ordinance about virginity from Jesus. How, then, do some practise virginity, boasting that it is something great and saying that they are filled with the Holy Spirit like her who bore Jesus? 3. But we will no longer speak against Paul, knowing the verbal gigantomachies[396] he fights against himself. But if you have anything appropriate to say in reply to these [questions], answer without delay.

{Christian}

After the chosen warrior had whipped up such a swarm of subjects against Paul and had concluded[397] *his mass of objections, which were like bees*

Harnack's ἀπεμηρυκήσατο. Like the English "ruminate," ἀναμηρυκάομαι refers both to the chewing of partially digested food by cows and metaphorically to mental "rumination." Burn (see Goulet, 195, n.1) reads φάτνῃ for κλίνῃ, suggesting that κλίνῃ ("couch, bed") has entered the manuscript tradition via a gloss on φάτνῃ: i.e. φάτνῃ, βοῶν κλίνῃ ("stall [means] bed for cows"). Goulet's French translation captures the sense much better: "*il a ruminé, comme vautré sur son lit*" (he ruminated, like [one] slouched on his couch). The Hellene, in other words, is presenting a very visceral image: Paul, who at first recommends avoiding certain foods, but then allows the consumption of all foods, is like an overstuffed man at a dinner table whose food (like Paul's words) rises in his own gorge as he speaks.
391 1 Cor. 10:25–26.
392 Cf. 1 Cor. 7:1.
393 1 Tim. 4:1–3.
394 1 Cor. 7:25.
395 Πονηρός τις, but perhaps, as Goulet translates, an "evil being" (*un être mauvais*), that is, a demon.
396 In myth, a fight between gods and giants, but a metaphor for conflict between antithetical dogmas in Plato, *Sophist* 246a–b.
397 Reading καταπαύσαντος as suggested by Goulet, 197, n.2.

that had come to rest, with this mighty statement, we, stricken thus[398] *by the stings launched against us, fought back, refuting each one using every means necessary, saying*:

37 1. You do no justice to so great a man, a luminary in the contest and labour of piety, mocking him thus and cutting him down mercilessly with a calumnious attack if, by adopting reserve as his principle and policy, he met halfway the deficiencies of those who had lately received the word of faith, and led them to his own condition of virtue.[399] The fact is that a man who makes use of such a method of instruction is at once teacher, physician, and general. 2. A teacher who stammers along with his stammering student, becoming a stammerer for the sake of that which is better, leads his hearer towards the highest [level of] instruction, sharing in his suffering and assisting him for the sake of utility, for if he does not do this, he will not lead the boy's character towards betterment.[400] 3. And someone is a physician when he not only mixes a remedy and medicine that is appropriate for those who are sick, but also reclines together with and often shares meals with [the sick], and becomes a partner and sharer in the condition of sickness, in order that, once he has conversed with the invalid and shared food with him and has conquered the pain of the disease in every way, he might lead the sick person to a state of strength like his own.[401] 4. And a general who commands for the emperor with understanding and strength, fighting myriad nations of barbarians in order to bring all under his lord's sceptre, loves and embraces things barbarian, at one time delighting in a barbaric regimen and table, at another embracing their manners and customs, at one time not being averse to the clothes they wear, at another becoming one of them and doing that which imperial law does not permit, and generally

---

398 Here, as elsewhere, Macarius hyperbolically imitates passages in Plato where Socrates flippantly professes to have been unmanned by the vehemence of his antagonist: cf. *Protagoras*, 328 d–e; *Republic* 344d.

399 This defence is characteristic of exegeses that assessed Paul's rhetoric as tempered to the needs and expectations of his contemporaries: see e.g. John Chrysostom, *Homilies on 1 Corinthians* 21.6 (on soldiering) and 22.5 (on being all things to all).

400 Elementary instruction began with the alphabet and syllabic pronunciation. Quintilian (*Institutes* 1.1.37) describes lessons in which students pronounced sequences of nonsense syllables designed to improve diction. On elementary studies generally see Marrou (1956), 150–159.

401 Several Hippocratic treatises discuss the importance of collaboration between patient and physician. For an excellent discussion of the doctor-patient relationship in antiquity see Jouanna (1999), 112–140.

imitating the manner of barbarians, finally leads them complaisantly to the emperor, having seized a numberless throng by this device. For if the general does not act this way towards unruly nations, he pursues victory rashly, hoping to defeat many battle formations by the sword [alone].[402]

5. Indeed, in the same way according to this model, wanting to join together myriad human customs as if to establish a single political order[403] from different customs and laws, Paul contributes to this by becoming everything for everyone. He did not admire the actions of the masses, but knowing the utility of his actions he bound himself to everyone. Sometimes, he joins in the instruction of the nations like a teacher in a classroom, not remaining behind with them at their [educational level], but leading them to himself through fellowship and giving them a share of his own virtue. At other times, he is like a physician to those who lie ill with error, those who are feverish from the sharp attack of evil, sharing in their suffering and lying with them, saying: "Who is weak, and I do not suffer, enflamed by pain?"[404]

6. At other times, like a general, he more strategically subjugates the opinions of men by softening their prejudices with a sense of common feeling and by assuming their way of life in appearance only, becoming lawless for the lawless person, although he is not [in reality] lawless, just as a teacher becomes a stammerer for a stammerer, although he is not [in reality] a stammerer, so that, by eating at a common table with the lawless person, he can make the lawless person a fellow at the lawful table. 7. Thus he acts as a lawgiver with the Jews, though he does not think like a Jew, like a physician who shares in the illness of one who is ill, though he is not diseased, but healthy and strong, so as to cure the illness. In this way, for the sake of success, he does not overturn the circumcision of the Jews, like a general who imitates the customs of foreigners for the sake of victory, in order that he may by all means effect the good—not circumcision, but

---

402 Macarius's comments on the relative value of war and diplomacy may reflect the geopolitical situation of the late fourth century, as the use of barbarian recruits and mercenary forces became increasingly important for the Roman army. The most famous example of the kind of wholesale recruitment and resettlement of barbarians Macarius describes is Valens's resettlement of the Tervingi as *foederati* in 376 CE (Ammianus Marcellinus, *Histories* 31.4.1–5). Some of Macarius's contemporaries, such as Vegetius, in his *Epitome of Military Science*, were much more ambivalent as to the reliability and value of such arrangements, and argued instead for the rehabilitation of traditional Roman legionary forces.

403 Τάξις; for the usage of this term in this constitutional sense see Aristotle, *Politics* 1271B.

404 2 Cor. 11:29.

the profession of the good that comes from circumcision, in order that, by sharing in a portion of the Law, he might subordinate the whole Law to grace, and in order that, by yielding to one Mosaic command, he might enclose the whole Mosaic legislation in the Gospel, so that [further], by seducing the intelligence of wrongdoers with his assent [to circumcision], he may draw their disposition towards his own zeal.

8. Now, it is possible to find a way of thinking similar to this among wise physicians, who forbid drinking harmful drugs but on occasion prescribe them as a draught to those who are encumbered by passions and terribly afflicted, having mixed the same drugs with other kinds, in order that the compound formed by the infusion of the drug, once given to the patient, will conquer the invisible evil of the malady. And in doing this, they do not confound their own knowledge, but effect what is better from things forbidden. 9. Thus Paul, knowing that circumcision was harmful, did not teach it or preserve the tradition, but at a specific time when the Jews were more greatly distressed, he mixed it with evangelical doctrines and presented it to those inhumanely oppressed, thereby healing the disease that dwelled among the Jews.

38. 1. These responses to you have been spoken convincingly, but now we must address that which already seems to trouble the ear in its very formulation: why, when he is a Jew by race does he profess himself to be Roman?[405]

2. I will use the same example of the general so that the sagacity of the apostle may become clearly apparent. For in <all>[406] passages [of Scripture] most subjects, and especially those that seem intractable, can be explained accurately and clearly by propounding a worthy image, and especially whenever it is controversial, and even more so when what it said seems to contradict itself.

3. Paul, for instance, when the Jews plotted against him and he was going to be punished with an inexorable death,[407] since the divine preaching was not as yet going to cease—for soul-destroying evil was eager to effect this, in order to separate the races of humanity from grace and not allow Paul to run the universal racecourse of piety or be crowned by the toil of virtue, but to inflict on each a painful chastisement and to overshadow with envy the good things of the Almighty—then, so that the jealousy of

---

405 See Acts 22:3 and 22:27–29.
406 Following Palm and Goulet in adding "all" (πάντων).
407 See Acts 21:31, 23:12–21, 24:9, etc.

the demon would not accomplish this nor the opinions of the evildoers hold sway nor the success of the good collapse, he prevailed over the dangers by means of a speech characteristic of a general. He denies the race that is the enemy of the race[408] and flees [his] native [race], since he is being persecuted by it. For the one whom the Jews hated as an enemy, wanting to banish him from ancestral glory, this one they discovered to be a rival and were defeated. 4. First, then, having laid bare their injustice against him and second, having been exposed by him, they were put to shame, wounded by [his] intelligence and superior wisdom. For just as a general who has been handed over by the people of his own race and takes refuge with those to whom he has been handed over comes to be lord over his kinsfolk,[409] so too Paul, who was betrayed to the Romans by the Jews and said "I am Roman," was victorious over the Jews.[410] 5. For it was necessary, yes necessary, under Roman rule, that he who was serving the Word truly be "Roman," excelling beautifully in the "might" of the Holy Spirit.[411] Therefore he did not lie in calling himself "Roman," since he became the teacher of the Roman race.

6. For just as he who has left the hearth of the Galatians and lives and resides in Asia is called "Asian," even though he was known previously to be a Galatian by race,[412] so too Paul and anyone in a similar situation who travels back and forth under the sceptre and in the territory of the Romans is unambiguously "Roman," even if he is a Jew. He is not mistaken in calling himself a Jew, nor again does he err in proclaiming himself Roman, for of the former he is a kinsman by the circumcision of the flesh, while of the latter a relative by the doctrine of the divine preaching. 7. And when he is chastised, he rejects the reason for the chastisement, completely escaping the charge for which his very life was threatened.[413] But when

---

408 That is, the Christians. On Christians as a third *genus* see Tertullian, *Against the Nations* 1.8 (though here it is a pagan locution he purports not to comprehend). Clement, *Stromateis* 6.5.41, quotes a passage from the *Preaching of Peter* in which Christians are said to practise a third way of worship. For the sentiment see also Eusebius, *Preparation for the Gospel* 1.2.

409 The story of Coriolanus, the Roman general who led the Vosci against his own city, may have been known to Macarius from Plutarch.

410 Acts 22:3.

411 A common word play on "Roman" (ῥωμαῖος) and "might/strength" (ῥώμη).

412 Perhaps another indication of the author's provenance. The letter of the churches of Vienne and Lyons (Eusebius, *Ecclesiastical History* 5.1.17 and 44) applies the terms "Pergamene" and "Roman" to the martyr Attalus.

413 "Life" here translates ψυχή, as there is an echo of Romans 11:3, Paul's quotation of

there is bright profit in luminous doctrine he takes refuge in the Law and embraces his race. 8. Whenever, therefore, he calls himself a "Jew" based on corporeal law he honours his race, but when [he calls himself] "Roman" based on the definition of status,[414] he proclaims his nobility.

39. 1. These things having been said, come! Let us solve the next question, which concerns the passage: "Who ever soldiers with his own provisions? And who shepherds a flock and does not drink its milk?"[415] 2. For it was not because he needed to receive first fruits from men that Paul sent this opinion to the Corinthians, it was because he wanted the disciples' disposition to be thankful through these things that he with good reason mentioned military practice. 3. For as the soldier nourished by the public rations provided by subjects labours and toils for the emperor honestly, but when he is not fed by imperial grain but soldiers on provisions taken from his own resources on the one hand plots easily, undertaking impure attitudes and, on the other hand, mistreats everyone, plundering unsparingly, 4. so too he who has become the herald of the evangelical toil loves the weariness and honours the struggle whenever those he has taught enter into communion with the incorporeal gifts of the Word via bodily things,[416] whenever they zealously commit themselves to the evangelical laws in charity.[417] 5. For thus the eagerness of those who toil in the Word is enhanced whenever it sees the purpose of those it has aided sharing in their campaign and joining in their labour, whenever those they shepherd by the word of teaching, after the manner of good animals, on the one hand bear the thick fleece of beneficence and on the other hand pour out the milk of manly virtue in copious streams,[418] so that the shepherdly word, partaking of these things, delights and greatly flourishes in the teaching of good things, whenever instruction in the

---

Elijah's words in 1 Kings 19:10: "Lord, they have killed thy prophets, they have demolished thy altars, and I alone am left, and they seek my life [ψυχὴν]" (RSV), and Paul's negotiation of Jewish identity throughout Romans 11. Macarius would suggest that Paul, like Elijah, "denies" his Jewish identity in so far as he and Elijah would dissociate themselves as righteous over and against those Jews/Israelites who persecute them.

414 Here Macarius seems to indicate Paul's status as a Roman citizen as well as "teacher of the Roman race" (see 3.38.5 above), cf. Acts 22:28.

415 1 Cor. 9:7.

416 The "bodily things" are the gifts given by the community to Paul.

417 Macarius does not seem in complete control of his analogy; he likely does not think Paul is like a soldier who will pillage if not supported by the community.

418 Literally, "pour out streams of manly virtue copiously in milk," with a possible allusion to Joshua 5:6; Is. 55:1.

work of piety, having advanced sufficiently, enriches the zeal of the teacher with eagerness.

6. This man, then, inspired with discourse about God, wanting to advance his own disciples in beneficence and to make the labour of the Word worthy of public life, makes his teaching similar to sowing and those he teaches equal to a fertile and productive land, in order that, on the one hand, the teacher, as farmer, may be nourished by the "land" of his hearers and, on the other hand, that the students, after the manner of good land, may provide an abundant produce of faith, having received the seed of divine knowledge. 7. Because it is lamentable and a thing worthy of misfortune and grievous for a vine-dresser to destroy the shoots with his scythe or not to harvest the vines at the time of ripeness, the grapes in their season, but destroy the hope of [his] labour. 8. Hence the Apostle, in order that he might help many hearers, offered images of a marvellous portrait of a general and a shepherd, of a gardener and farmer, and calls upon the Law for their confirmation, making the evidence weighty based on it.[419] 9. Indeed, then, he did not seek payments, gifts, and honours for the sake of greed, as you yourself guess, but in order that he might make them thankful and courteous, since the divine also asks for first fruits and requests gifts, not because it lacks anything or needs anything—for it possesses every superabundance of wealth both among visible and invisible creatures—but wanting to enrich the thankful in grace and to exchange small things with great goods, it requests tribute and exacts payment.[420] 10. This response should satisfy you.

40. 1. It remains for us to look briefly at that passage wherein he says: "If someone does one thing in the Law, he is obliged to do the whole Law."[421] Neither censuring the Law nor reviling it, he tells you, rather, about the great precision and difficulty of the Law, which Christ, when he came, fulfilled, freeing humanity from great labour.

2. If someone wants to accomplish what has been fulfilled by the Only-begotten, as if it is unfulfilled, taking the fullness of Christ[422] to be lacking, then necessarily, since he <has not received> the grace of the

---

419 In 3.32.1, the Hellene quoted 1 Cor. 9:9 to accuse Paul of citing the Law to support a greedy demand for gifts.
420 Macarius's description of the Deity's request for offerings as a prompt for acts of thanksgiving beneficial to worshippers themselves can be compared with the Hellene's explanation of prayers and sacrifices to pagan gods at 4.21b.2–3 below.
421 Cf. Gal. 5:3.
422 Cf. Eph. 4:13.

Gospel and is enslaved to the Law, he must complete the entire code of despotic prescriptions. 3. Hence, [Paul] stigmatizes and smites publicly him who contends as an equal with the Saviour who alone fulfilled the Law on behalf of all and circumscribed the entire throng of precepts, all but saying: "How dare you, man, perfect as if unfulfilled what was fulfilled from the beginning, committing outrage against Christ by doing this? 4. For if you want to do the things of the Law and the exact ordinance of [each] thing, you accuse Christ of not himself fulfilling the Law and the prophets.[423] You pursue something awful, man, and novel, stealing for your own that which has been fulfilled by a divinely inspired rule as though it were unfulfilled and inconsistent. The stadium of exertion and racing has been closed since one has run on behalf of all and received the prize, yet you open it again and enjoin the race on those unable to reach the starting post. Pursuing this with delirious reasonings, you are obliged to perfect the whole Law."

5. For he who drives horses, when he hears of a citadel lying one hundred *parasangs*[424] distant and yearns to reach it, profits nothing by covering ninety-five *parasangs* but not covering the [last] five, for he remains outside of the city just as he was before he undertook the journey. 6. And again in the same way, he who guards a great city of thirty-five fortified gates surrounded by enemies is of no help if he secures thirty-four with gates but leaves one open out of forgetfulness; for the enemy will bring a catastrophe to the city by entering through it, the same as if they entered through all of them. 7. So too he who fulfils a myriad precepts of the Law, if he leaves one precept unfulfilled, through it he is condemned as though not having done the others. Hence, there was never anyone who could fulfil the Law.

8. Come, let us examine not the multitude of the precepts that [the Law] legislated but the keeping of only two commands, to see whether it is possible for a man to fulfil this; I speak, of course, of the Sabbath and circumcision. A child is born to someone on the Sabbath.[425] The Law commands him to circumcise this child on the eighth day.[426] The same [Law] orders him not

---

423 Cf. Mt. 5:17.
424 A *parasang* was a Persian measurement equal to thirty *stades* (Herodotus, *Histories* 2.6), or between five and six kilometres.
425 This dilemma may have occurred to Macarius because Paul speaks of himself as circumcised on the eighth day at Phil. 3:5. Counting is inclusive, so the eighth day falls seven days after the day of birth, i.e. on the same day of the week.
426 Cf. Gen. 17:10–12; Lev. 12:3.

to profane the Sabbath.⁴²⁷ 9. What, then, shall the man do? Circumcise the child? But [in so doing] he would not observe the Sabbath. Observe the Sabbath but not circumcise? But he would annul legitimate circumcision. Doing either he rejects the other, or rather fulfilling one he is condemned by the other as a transgressor.⁴²⁸ 10. If, then, it is burdensome, oppressive, and laborious for a man to fulfil the command of only two precepts, how will someone such as this fulfil the whole Law? Nor is the human ear able to listen to the multitude [of precepts], not to mention perfect them with works; nor is it possible for a man to remember the prescription of the Law, much less accomplish it in fact.

11. For the precepts seem like innumerable snowflakes, sometimes with continuous and constant sacrifices of calves, and rams every day, sacrificing some in the evening, others at dawn, sometimes a multitude of birds of different kinds, doves pigeons, roosters, and some on behalf of lepers, others for giving birth, others for purity, sometimes first fruits and tithes and offerings of leaven, stomachs, livers, shoulders, and skins.⁴²⁹ 12. The herds of four-footed animals totally consumed as whole burnt offerings are never sufficient, nor can the myriad species of birds piled together every day satisfy the altars. 13. Then there are the endless ablutions and ritual baths—one bathes when he rises from sleep, when he sees a dead body he bathes again, when he touches an unclean woman with his garment, he immediately bathes, when a weasel or a mouse touches a vessel, he breaks the vessel, when a leper stays at his house, he scrapes the walls, when a traveller from among the Gentiles comes to his home he separates himself completely for seven days, he wastes away the very nature of water with his constant drawing of it and transporting it in torrents.⁴³⁰

14. Time, space, and study are not enough to read the Law and remember the multitude of precepts; the mind is darkened, the tongue pained, and the reason worn out; [the Law] destroyed cities, suburbs, and every rural area by overpowering them; it enervated many whole generations, weakening the Jewish tribe and race, innumerable as they were, with its impositions. 15. Who, therefore, is capable of facing this and bearing the precept of

---

427 Cf. Ex. 20:8–11. In fact, Mishnah, Shabbat 19.4 appears to permit circumcision on the Sabbath. Mishnah Shabbat 19.5f, on the other hand, rules that if the child is born after twilight before the Sabbath (i.e. on Friday), circumcision should take place on the tenth day (i.e. the next Sunday but one).
428 Cf. Rom. 2:25.
429 Lev. 12:2–8, 14:1–32; Deut. 14:22–29, 18:3, 26:1–15.
430 Num. 19:14–22; Lev. 11:29–32, 14:34–57, 15:19–33.

the ordinance? One, the Lord Jesus, braved the Law, which he fulfilled, and having circumscribed it put an end to the necessity of anyone being subjected to it any longer. 16. For as the *pēchus*-stick measures height and breadth, while he who made it fulfils it, having measured it by comparing it to another [standard] measure,[431] so too the Law, being a measure of polity, life, and action, while no one measures up to it nor circumscribes it, but only he who made it and established it fulfilled it and, having measured it, sealed it up, filling out its measure by a greater measure in the charity of the Gospel, circumscribing the ancient Law. 17. The Law, then, which measures and compares many things in life, having been measured in turn by the evangelical measure, has been fulfilled. He who wants to fulfil what Christ fulfilled is greatly mistaken and errs exceedingly, since he adopts the reasoning and policy of the Antichrist.

18. The Apostle, therefore, in stating these things clearly, turns back the Galatians who had carelessly returned to slavery from freedom and wanted to fulfil again what had already been fulfilled. Paul, then, is not blameworthy if, for the sake of testimonies he mentions the Law, saying "It has been written in the Law, 'Do not muzzle an ox that is threshing'"[432] and "The Law is holy and the precept is holy."[433] For the Law is holy since it receives completion by the Holy One, and the unmuzzled ox is the throng of the apostles which all summer long threshes and winnows what he who came from the Father farmed in sowing the earth.[434] Hence the Apostle said this rightly: "These things were not written about oxen but about us."[435]

41. 1. Enough, then, has been said about this. It is right, fitting, and certainly follows that we interpret[436] that statement of the Apostle spoken expressly about the Law, where he says: "The Law came in in order that

---

431 The *pēchus* was roughly the measurement from the elbow to the tip of the middle finger. Measuring sticks might have been measured against publicly posted standards, such as the metrological relief in the Ashmolean Museum (AN.Michaelis.83).
432 1 Cor. 9:9.
433 Rom. 7:12.
434 On Jesus as a farmer or sower and the Church as the crop, see e.g. Jn. 4:35–38; Mt. 13:37.
435 Cf. 1 Cor. 9:10.
436 The verb δευτερῶσαι here might mean simply "to iterate," but δευτέρωσις is the Greek equivalent for the Hebrew *mishnah*, which denotes a periphrastic commentary on the scriptures (as exemplified by the halakhic commentary collected in the Mishnah), and was also used by early Christians to denote the exegeses of contemporary (Tanaitic and Amoraic Jewish (i.e. Rabbinic) exegetes (see e.g. Eusebius, *Commentary on Isaiah* 1.21–22; idem, *Gospel Demonstration* 6.18.36).

the transgression would increase."⁴³⁷ And let me now explain how the sting of death is sin and how the power of sin is the Law,⁴³⁸ which activates sins. 2. Nature was enduring much injustice in life; it was impossible that it be corrected, since the Law that justly chastises injustice had not been given. For he who was sinning and undertaking to do unholy works was not held to account, since the Law did not distinguish these actions or condemn the cause of the infraction. 3. Hence, transgression was easy for sinners, when they did not have the censure that comes from the Law. But neither did he who practised virtue enjoy repute, since he who was working vice was not held to account. And so it happened, given this state of affairs, that the life of men, after the manner of a boat without a captain, was sunk deep in the confusion of vice. 4. For the ignorance and misapprehension of what was taking place made for a harsh winter of forgetfulness. Someone, then, committing murder or pursuing the pollution of adultery, not having the order not to do this in his life, ventured vices as though they were the chief goods, since nothing prevented the boorishness of these deeds. 5. Many, therefore, contravening the appointed order of nature,⁴³⁹ became servants of insane vice; many, despising their innate moral character,⁴⁴⁰ were committing every possible illegality in their hardihood, since the Law was not yet administering human life, the rule of reason was not yet necessitating life to follow [its rules], the rational essence was not yet accepting the discernment of the good, being overreached by the irrationality of the corporeal passions on account of the confusion besieging free will and on account of the [human] race acting childishly in its thinking.⁴⁴¹ 6. But

437 Rom. 5:20.
438 Cf. 1 Cor. 15:56.
439 Macarius's phrase suggests natural law and the reasoning that follows suggests an equation of natural law, the rule of reason, and the Law. The concept of natural law has Stoic roots (Diogenes Laertius, *Lives of the Philosophers* 7.87–88), while Paul's own reasoning at Rom. 1:26–27, 2:14–15 and 1 Corinthians 11:14 suggests an equation of natural law with the Torah. The law of nature is expressly invoked by Athenagoras (*Embassy* 3.1) and by Clement (*Stromateis* 1.29).
440 Macarius's term here is καλοκαγαθία, the character or virtue of a καλος κἄγαθος, or a "fine and good" person; in classical Greek literature, the term refers to the character and deportment of a well-born "perfect gentleman"; in philosophical literature it refers to someone who displays good ethical character; see also Plotinus, *Ennead* 1.1.12.36, where καλοκαγαθία describes the practical virtues as distinct from the higher, contemplative virtues. In using this decidedly Hellenic term here, together with the exegesis that follows, Macarius subtly suggests that the Hellenic virtues propounded by the Hellene are impossible to realize without the aid of Christ.
441 Macarius's account of humanity's decline as the failure or forsaking of rationality

when, little by little, they looked up again,[442] as though out from the smoke of vice, and saw the pure air of dignity. Then the Law appeared as a guide and escort[443] leading towards the luminous life and guiding humanity, and indicating what is wicked and what is good to those who see it and condemning the faults of invisible deeds. It also vigorously rebuked those committing injustice, while it promised honour to those practicing justice, and allowed him who was innocent to live in freedom.

7. And the injustice of him who sins when the Law is present, is great, as the shame of being naked is great when light shines upon it, but when the Law is not present there is no injustice in doing wicked things.[444] As the crime of burglary is undetected when brightness is absent and the inability to see aids the culprit, so too when the Law illuminates [things] with the fine rays of its precepts the crime of those who err is well evident and requires much correction and retribution. But the crime goes uninvestigated when the Law has not yet appeared to prevent the accomplishment of the worst things.

8. What, then, followed this? Political life was destroyed and a sickness resembling a great plague wrecked life, the common desire to do the bad held sway since nothing then prevented it, and hatred of doing the good, from the fact that he who lived accursedly was not chastised; no one said anything of him who lived his life piously, while the actions of the sinner were held to be blameless.

9. Then suddenly a Law both severe and awesome stood against this inconsistent life, as both examiner and accuser of creatures, and at the same time a teacher and a bitter reproach. It did not wipe away the defect that

---

depends on Paul's theodicy in Rom. 1:26–27 and 2:14–15 (see also 1 Cor. 13:11); for similar treatments of humanity's descent into irrationality, which was a commonplace in early Christian literature of this period, compare, for example: Eusebius, *Theophany* 1.78 (where Eusebius likewise describes this state as "delusions of childhood"; the metaphor of the "infant" is used also at 1.70 and 1.72); Athanasius, *Against the Gentiles* 3–5).

442 Macarius may well be alluding to a well-known etymology of ἄνθρωπος ("human being") known at least since Plato (*Cratylus* 399c), that derives the noun from the phrase ἀναθρεῖ (καὶ λογίζεται τοῦτο) ὃ ὄπωπεν ("to look up at [and consider with reason] what it sees"). This etymology was also used by Christian apologists, e.g. Lactantius, *Divine Institutes* 7.13.3; Eusebius quotes the full etymology from *Cratylus* 399c at *Gospel Preparation* 9.6.16 and may allude to it at *Theophany* 1.54, as may Athanasius, *On the Incarnation* 12.2–3.

443 Compare Gal. 3:24, where Paul describes the Law as a "pedagogue."

444 Here and in the sentences that follow, Macarius interprets Rom. 5, especially 5:13 ("... sin was indeed in the world before the law, but sin is not reckoned when there is no law") and 5:20 ("But law came in, with the result that the trespass multiplied") (NRSV).

BOOK 3   191

had occurred, but magnified it and rendered an inexorable burden against it, forging a sword of chastisement,[445] and by punishing what had been done it prevented future [sin]. 10. Having no sympathy, it was merciless to those it had taken, since the Law is not an authority or a master, but an administrator and servant of the Master's will. Logically, then, the transgression increased when the Law was present, because [the Law] did not permit the sinner to live after his fault, but punished him without pity and sympathy. And so it was that sin became a sting of death, or a deathly sting, stinging with the result that man could not live or exist, and it took this power through the Law, the Law that prevents sinning, but punishes the sinner with its sentence.

11. Thus the Apostle says fittingly and wisely that sin is the sting of death, but apart from the Law it is totally incapable of anything. For as the sword is a "sting" that is able to pierce him "stung" by it, but without someone to hold it or wield it, it is an instrument of death but incapable of effecting it, so too is sin a "sting" of death for the soul, but is totally incapable of anything so long as the law has not yet taken control of it in some manner and subjected it to conscious examination.[446] 12. In order, therefore, that we would flee from the harm of sin and deflect the strength of the Law that was present in it, he [Paul] advises taking refuge with and being saved by the Master of the Law. For if sin has strength through the Law, then stronger is he who takes the Master of the Law as his aid. As sin mastered the soul through the Law and killed it without any delay or sympathy, so too man, through Christ who is seen to be the authoritative master of the Law, destroys sin.

13. Do not assume, then, that Paul, in preventing someone from living according to the Law, abrogates the Law, since neither does someone who takes a student from a pedagogue and attaches him to a teacher treat the pedagogue's effort[447] as of no account, but rather solemnifies it, because through him the learner acquired what was better. So too Paul says fittingly that the Law, which came to men at a time when it was needed and helped common life and taught nature, rests and no longer commands the generations because Christ came to better humanity and make it worthy of a better education. 14. For as the moon together with the stars is of service at night, but does not drive away the whole unpleasantness of

---

445 Cf. Rom. 13:4; Heb. 4:12, for passages that mention "swords" in the context of chastisement.
446 Literally: "handled it with knowledge."
447 Direct allusion to Gal. 3:24: "The Law became a pedagogue that led to Christ."

darkness or allow the darkness to wax completely, but makes the air less dim and softens it with its measured lights, while when the sun suddenly shines down with its hot bolts of light, the moon rests and the whole starry vault of heaven is hidden, having given ease as it ought to people at night-time—15. they are not, of course, abrogated and they do not lose the principle of their existence, but they remain, yielding the authority over the day to the sun, and no sailor, merchant, or traveller, having used starlight and moon light for his work at night looks for this light for his work any longer once the sun is present, but seeing the unquenchable brightness of the sun burning, he rejoices in it alone and welcomes its activity, 16. so too the Old Covenant of the Law, after the manner of the moon together with the prophets as stars, appeared in life, assuaging human life which was sullen in ignorance and great dejection, but when the radiant sun appeared—God's Christ surrounded by the twelve-pointed crown of the apostles—then the Law became silent and the prophets rested and only the grace of the Saviour, which fulfils everything, is active. And one must submit to this alone and not seek old things for the acquisition of virtue, for they remain ineffective and their nature ceases to work. 17. On the one hand, remembering them as good and beautiful is right, fitting, and exceedingly logical, but wanting to be under their control is entirely unstable and entirely irrational; for even if someone should want to follow them again, they will deny their service for this act, since they have ceased from their particular labour.

42. 1. Having given you as clear an answer as possible about this passage, it remains that we speak about what comes next, if it please you—why Paul on the one hand forbids eating meat sacrificed to idols, while on the other he does not forbid taking that which is sold in the market, even though those who sold in the market at that time were for the most part known to be Hellenes.

2. See in this, then, the precision of the sage, how he protects the way of life and forbids the pious from coming into contact with things sacrificed to demons, while he allows his closest and most advanced disciples[448] to eat

---

448 "Closest and most advanced disciples" translates γνώριμοι, the term for the members of the inner circle or "familiars" of a philosophical master. If a contrast between these intimates and the mass of the faithful is implied here, it mirrors Paul's distinction between the strong and the weak at 1 Cor. 8:11. On the other hand, below at *Apocriticus* 3.42.10, Macarius seems to assume that Paul's concession is made to the weakness of all, and not to the proficiency of a few.

what is sold in the market without examining it. 3. There were many and various sacrifices of quadrupeds throughout the world at that time. One type was sacrificed to aerial spirits, another to earthly spirits, and others were sacrificed to subterranean spirits. For the error that took the serpent as its deceptive servant[449] loudly hissed its tune, bewitching and overpowering the earth, air, and subterranean regions with its death-dealing spells.[450]

4. Therefore, the invisible spirits that fly through the air, which Isaiah describes as "flying serpents,"[451] demand white, clear sacrifices from among winged creatures, in so far as the air is bright and luminous until things appear in it. Other, terrestrial demons look for black and brown sacrifices taken from the flocks of quadrupeds, since the earth is by nature black and sombre, and order them slaughtered on their high altars. Others, the subterranean demons, demand that dark victims be sacrificed in trenches and be placed there together with all the leavings from the slaughtering. Still others, deceptive phantoms of the sea, demand sacrifices of dark winged animals, and order them to be cast into the sea, since the sea is black and continuously moves.[452] 5. Since, therefore, evil destroys irrational nature through rational beings, pitiably herding the multitude of quadrupeds and winged animals, the Apostle rightly forbids believers from partaking of such things.

6. But you can be convinced of these things by *The Philosophy from Oracles*, and learn precisely the explanation of the sacrifices which Porphyry, like one puffed up, transmitted esoterically to those of his persuasion with a fearful oath, as he himself thought, expressly ordering them not to declare these things openly to the masses.[453]

7. For the tragedy of this radical misfortune will be evident to you— how the schemes of deadly spirits rend the race of men every which way,

---

449 For the thesis that demons, under Satan's captaincy, were the authors of idolatry, see *1 Enoch* 6 and Justin Martyr, *1 Apology* 9, 14, 54.

450 The Greek term used here, ἴυγξ, a "charm" or "spell" is the ancestor of the English "jinx." In later Platonism, the plural designated a class of divinity (e.g. Damascius, *On First Principles* 111), but Macarius is using the term in the former sense.

451 Cf. Is. 14:29. Herodotus, *Histories* 2.75 also references flying serpents.

452 In this account of sacrifices to demons Macarius summarizes Porphyry, *Philosophy from Oracles* fr. 314 (Smith) (= Eusebius, *Gospel Preparation* 4.9 [146b–147c]).

453 Porphyry's opening remarks to *The Philosophy from Oracles* included an injunction against public dissemination; it was intended, ostensibly, only for those who had accepted the philosophical life. This reference has suggested to many that Porphyry cannot be Macarius's source for the Hellene's polemics, as using (and naming) a Porphyrian text to refute a Porphyrian text seems strained; others disagree (see further discussion in the Introduction).

like a flock without a shepherd attacked by savage wolves from the desert. It was impossible for anyone to breathe freely or find rest. The universe was harassed to the utmost, as if by a bolt of thunder or lightning. 8. Someone traversed the sea; he sacrificed a victim. Someone travelled on land; he sacrificed quadrupeds. Someone dug out a cave or dug a trench in the ground; he cast and threw a victim to the subterranean demons. But many even buried those of their own species alive, as if to bribe their way out of their own death! Amistra, the wife of King Xerxes, sent two times seven children into Hades annually, concealing them in a mound, so as to appease the demons of the earth.[454] 9. Hooks, barbs, and snares had everywhere filled the world. Neither air, nor earth, nor island, nor sea was free of their plots, and a girdle of deceit girt the inhabited world, the murky curtain of ignorance was drawn[455] and it was impossible for man to live easily free from fear. Life was full of suspicion, its state treacherous; the matter of life's circumstances itself was troubled. 10. Therefore, since the space of the world was full of confusion and the majority of life was dedicated to demons, he [i.e. Paul] ordered those who wanted the purest life to loathe the table of demons,[456] in order that they not, little by little, destroy the condition of their souls through fellowship [with the demons]. But again, seeing that it was difficult for anyone tied to the flesh to turn away from the corporeal way of life, he solemnly recommended and counselled going to the public market and purchasing goods from it with vigilance. 11. For this affair is not disturbing, nor is it reproached as meddling with demons, in so far as those who have taken on the job of butcher are ministers to a way of life that is held in common and public. But some are consecrated and chosen temple servants who pour libations to cult statues as part of mystery rites and sacrifice victims with sorcerers' mysteries.[457] He orders abstaining from their [meat] and not touching it at all.[458]

He destroys the unschooled concept of the Hellenes understanding, cuts the teaching to pieces,[459] and makes void their suffrage, saying "an idol is

---

454 Herodotus, *Histories* 7.114, cf. Plutarch, *On Superstition* 13.
455 Like the veil which concealed the holy of holies in the Temple; cf. Heb. 9:2–3, etc.
456 1 Cor. 10:20–21.
457 See Porphyry, *Life of Plotinus* 10, the story of Olympius, for a non-Christian account that casts suspicion on those who would combine the roles of priest and sorcerer. For this pejorative use of μυστήριον as a term for a pagan rite cf. *Epistle to Diognetus* 7.1; Justin, *1 Apology* 27.4.
458 Cf. 1 Cor. 8:10.
459 Echoing the verb used by the Hellene at 3.34.1 above.

nothing in the world"⁴⁶⁰. For the Hellenes devised the term "idols" as the serpent devised the term "gods."⁴⁶¹ But the understanding of the truth does not give its suffrage to such a teaching.

13. It is impossible, therefore, that the principle and definition of "idol" be maintained in the world.⁴⁶² For with good reason constructed effigies are called "statues" and not "idols." These things made of gold, silver, bronze, or iron are shapes made in silver and gold, certainly not "idols," and the dead bodies of animals are dead bodies, not idols. Souls released from bodies are rightly called "souls"; they are certainly not idols. The representations of the so-called heroes are "images"; they are not idols. The things customarily painted with colours on boards are "paintings" of bodies, not at all idols, and the so-called <visible signs> of visions are phantasms and shadows of dreams; they are not idols.⁴⁶³ So the Great Apostle proclaims the truth, saying: "An idol is nothing at all in the world." 14. A madman might wish to call the elements "idols"; but he is straightaway refuted.⁴⁶⁴ For fire, water, air, and earth are not idols but, naturally, are fire, air, earth, and water. 15. To whom, then, do the chief [priests] of the idols sacrifice victims? To demons, not idols. And he [Paul] does not want the comrades of Christ to become comrades of these demons.⁴⁶⁵ Those who sell provisions in the market serve as butchers not for demons but for public life. They do not have sorcery as their goal, but profit, which neither harms nor destroys the one who eats.

43. 1. May it be that you have fully understood this response to your question, but now attend to the next problem even more closely: that Paul, after saying many things about virginity, finally mocks those who abstain from marriages, saying that they burn and are liable to punishment and do not maintain their principles conscientiously, and that some are plagues

---

460 1 Cor. 8:4.
461 That is, Macarius suggests that the use of the plural at Gen. 3:5 is illegitimate because spoken by the serpent in order to deceive. The primary meaning of εἴδωλον (here translated "idols" because Macarius has in mind 1 Cor. 8:4) is "reflection" or "shadow," and it was seldom applied to images of the gods in classical usage. Origen (*Homilies on Exodus* 8.3) argues that an idol is nothing because it is a representation of an unreal object, such as a centaur.
462 Turrianus reads: "The truth does not teach this reckoning, for the uneducated definition of 'idol' cannot be maintained in the world."
463 Turrianus reads: "But the so-called phantasms of visions and shadows that exist in dreams are idols and appearances."
464 Cf. e.g. Gal. 4:4; Aristides, *Apology to the Greeks* 3; Athenagoras, *Embassy* 22.
465 Cf. 1 Cor. 10:20.

that appear at the end of days and bring with them infinite destruction to the world. I will, now, give an answer to your question from the beginning. 2. For his mode of expression is given to reversal and his reasoning obscure because of figures of speech that rely on counterpoint, whenever one reads one of the things said by way of a "turn" among the Apostle's statements.[466] For sometimes, when he uses strange expressions, the blessed Paul makes his discourse shadowy and obscure, as for instance when he says: "Indeed, then, he [i.e. God] grants mercy to whom he will and hardens the heart of whom he will."[467] 3. But in stating this, the Apostle was not of the opinion that some are granted mercy by God while others are not granted mercy but have their hearts hardened, but rather he holds that all are granted mercy by God and saved, saying: "He who wants all men to be saved."[468] 4. And therefore in saying "But concerning virgins I have no command from the Lord, but I give an opinion, as one granted mercy,"[469] he does not seem to say at all clearly what he is saying. For how can he who has Christ within himself speaking and commanding all things[470] <say: "I have no command"? Either, therefore, he will be seen to be a liar>—and it

---

466 Macarius's assessment of Paul's style employs a number of rhetorical terms difficult to capture in English. "Reversal" translates περιπέτεια, which connotes a "sudden change" or "unexpected turn"; "turn" translates περιτροπή, again, a "reversal" or "twist," effected by a rhetor (the "turn" at the conclusion of a sonnet is an analogue). "Figures of speech that rely on counterpoint" translates ἀντιστρόφη (antistrophe), a formal term for the rhetorical device in which the same word or words are repeated at the end of two successive clauses, as opposed to ἐπαναφορά (epanaphora), the repetition of the same word or words at the beginning of successive clauses (see e.g. Hermogenes, *On Style* 1.12). The Pauline example Macarius gives below, though it appears to be an *antistrophe* in fluid English translation, is in fact an *epanaphora* ("Indeed, then, he grants mercy to whom he will and hardens the heart of whom he will" [ἄρα οὖν ὄν θέλει ἐλεεῖ καὶ ὄν θέλει σκηρύνει]. Macarius's second example is neither an *antistrophe* nor *epanaphora* ("I have no command ..., but I give an opinion ..." [ἐπιταγὴν ... οὐκ ἔχω, γνώμην δὲ δίδωμι]), is simply a balanced parallel construction. Macarius seems to mean that Paul sometimes appears to say contradictory things because he uses rhetorical expressions that rely on counterpoint and "turns" or "twists" in his exposition.
467 Rom. 9:18.
468 1 Tim. 2:4. Before Augustine's *Letter to Simplicianus* (397 CE), it appears that all Christians understood Rom. 9 to mean that God elects those who are worthy of election; see e.g. Origen, *On First Principles* 2.8.7. The statements that imply predestination were sometimes understood as interjections by a hostile listener: see Pelagius, *Commentary on Romans* (de Bruyn, 116–117).
469 1 Cor. 7:25.
470 Cf. 2 Cor. 13:3. Goulet's text here follows Palm in supplying the words that follow to fill out what seems to be a corrupted passage; Goulet's text here differs markedly from that of Volp, which as it stands seems to be elliptical.

is wretched to follow a lying teacher—or, speaking the truth, Christ spoke in him also about virginity and he appears to have a particular reason for saying "But about virgins I have no command from the Lord, but I give an opinion,"; a command, however, I do not have.[471]

5. Since the precept of virginity is difficult to achieve and hard to come by in life, being threatened by the physical passions of the body and quickly ensnared by the senses, it quickly incurs the false imputation of crime and the cloud of accusations speedily surrounds it, so it is easily subdued by the battle against pleasure. Since, therefore, it belongs to the first class of virtue and *askēsis*,[472] but is also the height of strain and repressive toil, in order to preserve virginity and protect against boasting he says: "I have no command from the Lord." 6. For Christ, who commanded everything through Paul, did not command this, in order that he not seem to be imposing a necessity upon those who wanted to practise virginity, in case someone failing in virginity at some point blame Christ for exhorting or even requiring the eager acceptance of virginity.

7. Hence, except for this [i.e. virginity], Paul commands everything, Christ speaking [through him].[473] For instance, someone steals, he commands not to steal,[474] for this is easily accomplished and it is not hard to be satisfied with one's own property and to abstain from that of others. 8. Likewise, he commands not to commit adultery, for it is not hard for someone who has the use of the body in marriage[475] to be self-controlled and not besmirch the marriage of his neighbour. Again, he commands not to get drunk at all,[476] for it is possible to take wine sufficient to quench one's thirst and not drink immoderately or revel unbecomingly or for someone who walked easily before his intoxication to be carried as a burden because he is weighed down [with wine]. 9. Again, he commands him who has to provide unhesitatingly to him who has not, for this too is not burdensome, or miserable, or difficult: that one who has might give a bit from his possessions to him who has not. For he who is seen to be generous in beneficence is great and

---

471 Macarius adds these words to reinforce Paul's disclaimer.
472 *Askēsis* means, most basically, "training" or "practice," and came to refer to the regimen or discipline practised by those undertaking a philosophical life and, later, to the various regimes of bodily and spiritual discipline undertaken by Christian ascetics.
473 Cf. 2 Cor. 13:3.
474 Cf. 1 Cor. 6:10.
475 Macarius probably has 1 Cor. 7:4 in mind here, and thus the "body" of which one has use is the body of one's spouse, rather than one's own body, as Goulet translates.
476 Cf. 1 Cor. 6:10.

virtuous,[477] while he who is steadfast in poverty is crowned for his labours. 10. These things he commands and things like them: he forbids ;whispering rumours;[478] he commands not to sing ignoble and licentious songs,[479] he commands a way of life, food, drink, and comportment for the glory of Christ;[480] he commands forcing out wicked passions and establishing the virtue of *askēsis* with the support of temperance;[481] he commands not to be zealous for the practice of tasteless discourse and never receiving raucous company; and he commands diligently working to attain the residence that is above.

11. He commands everyone to do, accomplish, and pursue every august action, except virginity, and casts out the one who is not persuaded [by these commands] from the heavenly regions,[482] in so far as he does not accept to do what is in his power. But concerning virginity he says that he has not received a command from the Lord, for the reasons and causes we have already stated. 12. For out of consideration for humanity, the Lord did not command anyone to do anything especially difficult, but if someone intends to pursue the highest mode of life, he does not dissuade him by preventing it, but counsels and honours the choice, saying: "But concerning virgins I do not have a command from the Lord, but I give my opinion as one granted mercy."[483] 13. Do you see the wise man's great eloquence? Do you see his mode of teaching? Do you see his liberal understanding? Do you see the true leader of piety when he says: "Christ did <not> want anyone to practise virginity based on necessity or a command, but based on willingness, not legislation, for the practice of so great a matter is truly sublime and preeminent, and a source of pride greater than masculine virtue; hence, it must not be based on a command lest it be servile, but based on choice, so that it be seen to be glorious, brilliant, and noteworthy."

14. Do not, therefore, think that, in refraining from command for the sake of honour and leaving the power to choice, Paul is giving wicked and unreliable counsel, saying: "If one practises virginity without being commanded to do so he pursues a work that is neither pure nor holy." For,

---

477 Cf. 2 Cor. 8:13–14. Macarius appears to ignore the command of anonymous, silent almsgiving in Mt. 6:2.
478 Cf. Rom. 1:29; 2 Cor. 12:20.
479 Cf. Rom. 13:13.
480 Cf. 1 Cor. 10:31.
481 Cf. 1 Cor. 6:9.
482 Cf. Gal. 5:21, or, for a more efficacious measure, 1 Cor. 5:5.
483 1 Cor. 7:25.

rather, it shines in a superhuman way, as it adorns the preeminent ornament of virtue with a glory greater than is required. 15. For what is done in life based on command receives praise, but it is not really remarkable when one does what is good because of an order—for it is the zeal of the one commanding that is revealed by the command—but what does not wait for the opinion of the one who exercises lordship but happens freely without exhortation receives an encomium incomparable in glory.[484]

16. For this reason, Paul, seeing that the practice of virginity is high-flown and exceedingly exalted, did not dare to place this matter under an order, but left it free, setting it without constraint as the particular choice of each practitioner. Since, in fact, it is only his opinion, he expresses it humbly and *sotto voce*, saying: "I do not command, for I have not received a command, but I give an opinion, as one granted mercy." 17. Do you see how, when he saw the worth of virginity, he humbled himself? He does not speak as "Paul, the chosen apostle,"[485] but as "one granted mercy." Struck by the weight of virtue, he assumes a humble attitude, is silent about his apostleship, and proclaims the compassion through which he was granted mercy and lives together with Christ, saying: "I know who I was, and who I am, and what virginity is. 18. This is the distinction of angels and of archangels.[486] But I have not had angels teach me a command. As one granted mercy, therefore, not as an Apostle, I speak even with angels. For in my judgment virgins have become angels; hence, I do not teach, nor do I command, but I will softly tender my feeble counsel, since I am impoverished and poor, but nevertheless granted mercy."

19. Since, therefore, some were going to put about the profession of this great enterprise as the dogma of vaunted heresies, and were aiming to gain honour in the world through virginity (for somehow those of the heretics happened to hear and learn that virginity, having served augustly, preceded the blessed burden of the Saviour's birth and brought forth the common

---

484 Macarius's reading of 1 Cor. 7:25 as a statement on the centrality of free-will to the practice and merit of virginity was a common patristic exegesis; see for example: Irenaeus, *Against Heresies* 4.15.2; Origen; *Commentary on 1 Corinthians* 7:25; Methodius, *Symposium* 3.13; Ambrose, *Letter* 63.35; Jerome, *Ep.* 22.20; John Chrysostom, *On Virginity* 2.2, 47.4. For an excellent survey and discussion of 1 Cor. 7:25 in the early Church see Clark (1999), 303–308.

485 Cf. Rom. 1:1.

486 Cf. Mk. 12:25. On the ascetic life as an angelic life or a life aspiring to that of angels see, for example: Clement, *Pedagogue* 1.36.6; *History of the Monks of Egypt*, prol.5; Basil of Ancyra, *On Virginity* 37; Gregory of Nyssa, *On Virginity* 14.4. See also Lane Fox (1987), 336–374 and more recently Muehlberger (2008), 447–478.

benefactor of the inhabited world),[487] so that they therefore could simply entrap many of the simple in their own beastliness by forbidding either marrying or being given in marriage, as though they were they founders of a supreme and great way of life, for this reason they also invented abstinence from food; making an ostentatious show of these things they worked error, destroying the good in an evil doctrine.

20. For as those who dare to debase the value of gold fraudulently inscribe the image of the emperor so that the counterfeit will be called genuine currency on account of the image and just as the adulterated denarii (if I may call them so) are dipped in gold in order that they will have a brilliant and radiant appearance,[488] though their substance is matter without value and condemnable, so too the enflamed leaders of the heresies, by perverting the reputable and famous honour of virginity for their own wicked opinion, have in a way counterfeited the original beauty of this way of life. 21. Utterly despoiling it by means of their rule of wicked opinion, attaching a pearl to a foul-smelling necklace,[489] they have adulterated the pure essence of chastity, belittling it, adorning their own irrationality with dyed robes.

22. The blessed Paul, learning long before this the depravity of these most sordid habits, therefore said: "Some will revolt, their own conscience branded."[490] 22. He says that those lying in wait for a long time will rise up in an ambush, at first calm but in the end casting fearsome and fiery looks, "branded" because for the purpose of deceit they assume the form of those enflamed with piety, or "burned" because the dew of the Holy Spirit has not moistened them, the grace of baptism has not freed them from their crimes, the fire of the Chaldean furnace has burned them,[491] the flaming sword that whirls[492] has scorched them. 24. They discourse without purpose and expound sophistries in vain, insulting creation and calumniating God's creations, things that have come into being for pleasure and nourishment; not for excess, indulgence, and undisciplined living, but for thanksgiving and communion by believers.[493]

---

487 Cf. Ignatius of Antioch, *Ephesians* 19.1, where Ignatius writes that the mystery of the virgin birth was concealed from the "prince of this world."
488 For the numismatic metaphor cf. John Cassian, *Conferences* 1.20.
489 Perhaps an allusion to Mt. 7:6: "Do not throw your pearls before swine" (NRSV).
490 1 Tim. 4:1–2.
491 Cf. Dan. 3:25 (LXX).
492 Cf. Gen. 3:24.
493 Cf. 1 Tim. 4:3: "They forbid people to marry and order them to abstain from certain

25. Such are the disciples of the Manichaeans,[494] who have spread their doctrines abroad; the country of the Pisidians and of the Isaurians, Cilicia, and Lycaonia, and all Galatia contain such heresies,[495] the names of which it is tedious to list, for they are called "Encratites," "Apotactics," and "Eremites";[496] none are called "Christians" or take refuge in heavenly grace, but rather they are apostates and expatriates from the evangelical faith, though they claim to have raised an acropolis of piety by their abstinence from food.

26. Dositheus, for instance, the leader among them, a Cilician by race, affirms their doctrine in eight complete books and glorifies their practice by the resplendence of his writing, chattering that marriage is illicit and exceedingly contrary to the Law, saying: "The world has its origin from a union, but wants to find its end through continence."[497] He says that a drink of wine or partaking of meat is loathsome and completely abominable, truly stirring up a painful flame for those who are persuaded by him. For by such a principle, according to him, all of creation is accursed,[498] and all

---

foods, which God created to be received with thanksgiving by those who believe [εἰς μετάληξιν μετὰ εὐχαριστίας τοῖς πιστοῖς] and who know the truth" (RSV). The term μετάληψις is used as early as Justin (1 *Apol.* 67.5) to refer to "partaking" of the eucharist, and Macarius probably has this sense in mind.

494 In Christian polemic, the Manichaeans were typically derided for their sexual and alimentary asceticism; for extensive anti-Manichaean polemics see for example Augustine, *On the Ways of the Manichees* 15.31–17.52.

495 Possibly another indication of the Asian provenance of Macarius. The mention of Galatia assimilates the Encratites to the false teachers whom Paul upbraids for their advocacy of circumcision in Gal. 3:1–3, etc.

496 The groups listed here all represent forms of asceticism considered excessive by orthodox Christians. In early Christian heresiology the Encratites were usually in Syria, were said to have mandated universal celibacy and were often held to have originated with Tatian (e.g. Epiphanius, *Panarion* 47). The Apotactics, or "renouncers," were said to reject all possessions and to advocate an ascetic regime similar to the Encratites (e.g. Epiphanius, *Panarion* 61). For similar lists of "Encratite" groups compare Basil of Caesarea, Ep. 199, canon 7 (Cathari, Encratites, Hydroparastatae, and Apotactics) and *Codex Theodosianus* 16.5.7 (Encratites, Saccophori, and Apotactics).

497 Dositheus of Cilicia is known only from Macarius; he mentions him again below at 4.15.5; "continence" translates ἐγκράτεια, whence the heresiological term "Encratite/encratism."

498 Of course, such an ascetic regime did not necessarily entail the doctrine of a wicked demiurge. Tertullian of Carthage, for instance, who maintained in such works as *On Fasting* and *On Shamefastness* that the Spirit required believers of his time to adopt a more abstinent way of life than that of the primitive Christians, never embraced the Gnostic belief that the world is the product of a malign creator.

of life lies under suspicion and is harmful for everyone; hence such people take offence at the Divine, insulting the beauty of created things and in no way contribute to the common good, even if they teach the practice of virginity and the highest temperance in life. 28. Knowing these things long before, then, the Apostle secured the doctrine of the Church so that it would not endeavour to experiment with the caustic heretics.

29. May it be amenable to you that we conclude our discourse on these questions here. But if another difficulty occurs to you, let us discuss it, and join together in debate once again, given opportunity for leisure and at the convenience of the Almighty.[499]

---

[499] Thus ends the third day of debate.

BOOK 4

Macarius of Magnesia's *Apocriticus* or *Unique [Discourse] to the Hellenes* concerning the questions that raise difficulties in the New Testament and their solutions[1]

Contents of the fourth book of discourses in response to the Hellenes

1. Concerning the meaning of: "The form of this world is passing away."[2]

2. What is the meaning of: "We who are living will be taken up in the clouds"?[3]

3. Why does he say: "The Gospel will be proclaimed throughout the whole world"?[4]

4. Why does the Lord speak to Paul in a vision[5] and why does he allow Peter to be crucified?

5. What does the passage "Look! for many will come saying, 'I am the Christ'" mean?[6]

6. What does the passage about the Judgment in the apocryphal writings mean?[7]

7. What is the meaning of: "The heaven <will be rolled up> like a scroll and the stars will fall like leaves"?[8]

---

1 The *pinax* ("table of contents") of Book 4 is preserved only in A.
2 1 Cor. 7:31.
3 1 Thess. 4:17.
4 Mt. 24:14.
5 Acts 18:9–10.
6 Mt. 24:5.
7 The passage in question comes from the *Apocalypse of Peter*; see 4.6.1–4 below.
8 Is. 34:4.

8. What does the passage about the yeast, the mustard seed, and the pearl mean?[9]

9. What is the meaning of: "You have hidden these things from those who are wise and have understanding, and have revealed them to infants"?[10]

10. What does the passage "The healthy do not need a physician, but those who are ill" mean?[11]

11. What does the passage "but you have been washed, but you have been made holy, <but you have been justified>" mean?[12]

12. What does the passage about [God's] monarchy mean?[13]

13. What does the passage about the angels being incorruptible mean?[14]

14. What does the passage about the tablets being written "by the finger of God" mean?[15]

15. Why was the Divine born, having taken flesh within Mary?

16. What is the meaning of: "You shall not speak ill of the gods"?[16]

17. What does the statement about the resurrection of the flesh mean?

1. *After many passages [of Scripture] had been presented to us [i.e. for clarification] by Hellenic opinion, and we had made clear the obscurities in them with much sweat, toil, and trouble, O Theosthenes, the philologue (so to speak)[17] vehemently brought down upon us this fourth bout, which with your help we have with difficulty ventured [to undertake]. What the content of this discourse was is now to be explained.*

1. *When a crowd had again been gathered,[18] and not a small one but one*

---

9 Mt. 13:31–33, 45–46.
10 Mt. 11:25.
11 Lk. 5:31.
12 1 Cor. 6:11.
13 The principle passage in question is 1 Cor. 8:5–6; see 4.26.2 below.
14 The principle passage in question seems to be Mt. 22:29–30, see 4.21a.5 and 4.27.1 below.
15 Ex. 31:18.
16 Ex. 22:27.
17 Macarius is being ironic; compare Porphyry, *Life of Plotinus* 14.18–20, where Plotinus derides the critic Longinus ("He is a philologue, but in no way a philosopher").
18 The re-gathering of the crowd indicates the beginning of the fourth day of debate.

that was very large and full of exceedingly distinguished people, as if having resolved of set purpose to embarrass us in the sight of important persons, [the Hellene], with much laughter, tore apart the apostolic way of thinking,[19] *saying:*

{Hellene}[20]

2. How can Paul say that "the form of the world passes away?"[21] And how is it possible for those who have [possessions] to be as though they did not have them,[22] and for those who are rejoicing not to rejoice?[23] And how can the rest of these old wives' tales be plausible?[24] For how, on the one hand, can one who possesses become like one who does not possess, and how, on the other hand, is it plausible for one who is rejoicing to become like one who is not rejoicing? Or how can the form of this world pass away? 3. Who will cause it to pass away and for what reason? For if the Creator[25] causes this [world] to pass away, he will be slandered for setting in motion and changing that which has been firmly established, while if he alters the form for the better, for this too he would be denounced, on the grounds that, not having a clear vision of the harmonious and appropriate form[26] for the world when he was crafting it, and lacking[27] a better rational principle, he

---

19 The word translated "way of thinking" here is δόξα, which Macarius is contrasting with "the Hellenic opinion" (ἡ ἑλληνικὴ δόξα) above; the phrases have been translated differently to capture the contrast.

20 The Athens manuscript contains marginal glosses noting the beginning of major speeches by the "Hellene" and the "Christian."

21 Cf. 1 Cor. 7:31.

22 Cf. 1 Cor. 7:29: "… those who have wives be as though they did not have them"; the Hellene omits "wives" and takes the passage to refer generally to "possessing."

23 1 Cor. 7:30.

24 Cf. 1 Cor. 7:30–31.

25 The term here, δημιουργός, has been translated "Creator" throughout, though when the Hellene uses it here (and when Macarius replies to the Hellene) it must be remembered that it connotes the Demiurge of the Greek philosophical tradition as well as the creator god of Jewish and Christian tradition. The Hellene's assumption here of a Demiurge that creates the cosmos according to a perfect, harmonious model derives ultimately from the demiurgical myth of Plato's *Timaeus*.

26 "The harmonious and appropriate form" (τὸ ἁρμόζον καὶ πρέπον σχῆμα), compare *Timaeus* 33b1: "he gave it the form that was appropriate and akin to it [i.e. the cosmos]" (σχῆμα δὲ ἔδωκεν αὐτῷ [i.e. the cosmos] τὸ πρέπον καὶ τὸ συγγενές).

27 Accepting Harnack's conjecture of λειπόμενος for λειπόμενον; the manuscript reading would translate as "he created it lacking a better principle [λόγος], as if something imperfect." Harnack's conjecture makes sense in light of the allusions to *Timaeus* in this

created it as something imperfect.[28] At any rate, how is it possible to know that the nature[29] of the world will be changed for the better when, late in time, it comes to an end? 4. And what is the benefit of altering the order of phaenomena? For if the things of the visible [world] are causes of grief and pain, the Creator is drummed out by the sound of these [accusations], and is piped down with good cause, because he devised the parts of the world as causes of pain and violations of rational nature and, later repenting, decided to alter the whole.

5. Or maybe by this argument Paul teaches one who has [the ability] to think as though he does not, since the Creator who possesses the world, as if he does not possess it, causes its form to pass away.[30] And he tells him

---

sentence. That "lacking" modifies the Demiurge in this clause is likely if it is an allusion to *Timaeus* 29a6-7, where the cosmos is "generated according to that which is grasped by reason [λόγος] and thought [φρόνησις]."

28 The Platonic Demiurge creates the best of all possible worlds based on the model provided by the unchanging Forms (*Timaeus* 27d-29d), thus if the Demiurge alters the created order he must either alter the unalterable perfect pattern or have failed to comprehend the perfect pattern in the first place. Compare Porphyry apud Proclus, *Commentary on the Timaeus* 332.10-15, which reads *Timaeus* 29a4-5 as stating the necessity that the Demiurge both (a) be the creator of that which is most perfect and (b) create using an eternal/unchanging paradigm.

29 The Hellene's concept of "nature" seems characteristic of Neoplatonic harmonizations of Aristotelean and Platonic concepts: nature is that which endows things, including the cosmos as a whole, with an internal principle of motion and rest (Aristotle, *Physics* 2.1, 192b13), but nature expresses paradigms or principles (λόγοι) located in the World Soul or Intellect (see for example, Plotinus, *Ennead* III.8 [30].2.19-30).

30 Goulet (2003), 404 takes this difficult passage as an oblique attack on Christian ethics: if, as Paul states, the world will soon pass away, there is no need for a social order in which there are "haves" and "have nots," but for the Hellene, this is as ridiculous as the demiurge divesting himself of creation. Given the cosmological concerns of the rest of the passage, it is more likely that the Hellene is likening the Demiurge's alteration or destruction of the cosmos to a rational human giving up the capacity for reason. There may be Neoplatonic undertones here—the Aristotelean prime mover whose eternal thinking is the source of motion in the cosmos (e.g. *Physics* Θ, *Metaphysics* 1072a24-36) was equated by Neoplatonists with the *hypostasis* Intellect (e.g. Plotinus, *Ennead* II.3[52] 18.8-16) or with the World Soul (e.g. Porphyry, cited in Proclus, *Commentary on the Timaeus* 1.306.31-307.7). As noted above (note 27), *Timaeus* 29a6-7 couples "thought" (φρόνησις) with "reason" (λόγος) as that by which the Demiurge comprehends the Paradigm. Thus, according to the Hellene, for the Demiurge to alter creation would entail an internal change in its own eternal contemplation of the Paradigm. See Proclus, *Commentary on the Timaeus* 366.20-368.11 for a fairly standard Neoplatonic account of the necessity that the Deimurge's act of creation (and consequently act of contemplation) is eternal. It is also possible to read the critique as simple, though heavy, irony if the passage is translated "Unless by this argument Paul teaches one

who rejoices not to rejoice, since the Creator was not delighted upon seeing his elegant and radiant creation, but as though greatly disappointed with it, decided to change its course and alter it.[31]

2. 1. Let us leave behind this silly little expression with a bit of laughter, but examine another crack-brained and erroneous sophism of his [Paul's], where he says: "We who are living, who have been left behind, will in no way precede those who have died when the Saviour returns. For the Saviour himself, with a command, with the voice of the archangel and with the trumpet blast of God, will come down from heaven and the dead who are in Christ will rise first; then we who are living will be taken up in a cloud together with them, to meet the Lord in the air, and thus we will always be with the Lord."[32] 2. This affair is truly out of this world and sky-high; this fraud is the height of excess! This tale, sung even to irrational animals, compels them to bleat and caw a resounding clatter in response, once they learn of embodied humans flying like birds in the air or carried off upon a cloud! For this boast is the greatest of pretences, that living beings, pressed down by the weight of bodily masses, might assume the nature of winged birds and traverse the great expanse of the air as if it were an ocean, using a cloud as a vehicle.[33] 3. For even if it were possible, it is yet monstrous and contrary to the [natural] order. For

---

who has to think as if he has not, because the Creator who has the cosmos, as if he has it not, causes its form to pass away"; in this reading, the Hellene simply means to point out a ridiculous analogy.

31 There are several similarities between the Hellene's critique of Pauline eschatology and Plotinus's criticisms of Gnostic doctrines in *Ennead* II.9[33]: the created cosmos cannot be a failure or need alteration if it follows the pattern of the Forms (*Ennead* II.9.4.1–10); the creator does not repent of his creation (*Ennead* II.9.4.18–19); the fact that there are unpleasant things in the world does not entail the need to further perfect the cosmos (*Ennead* II.9.4.23–26); see also Goulet (2003), 403.

32 1 Thess. 4:15–17.

33 The Hellene's use of the term "vehicle" (ὄχημα) may suggest Neoplatonic thought and debate. In *Phaedrus* 247b, Plato described the rational soul as a winged charioteer driving a chariot (ὄχημα) on its cyclical journeys of ascent into the intelligible and descent into becoming. Neoplatonists interpreted the chariot as a physical or quasi-physical pneumatic "housing" for the soul. Porphyry, following Plotinus, contended that the rational soul would slough off its vehicle on its ascent to the intelligible realm, while Iamblichus and others argued that the pneumatic vehicle persisted (see for example Iamblichus, *De Anima* §37–§38; Proclus, *Commentary on the Timaeus* 3.234.18–234.32). The Hellene may be interpreting and impugning Paul as holding what he views as an especially ridiculous position—that material human bodies themselves will ascend using other material bodies, namely clouds, as vehicles.

creative nature³⁴ from the beginning assigned places that were adapted to creatures, and legislated corresponding abodes: to aquatic creatures, the sea; to terrestrial creatures, land; to birds, air; to luminous creatures, aether.³⁵ At any rate, if one of these [creatures] is taken from its native abode, it will be destroyed when it moves into a foreign dwelling and abode. For example, if you decide to take the aquatic [creature] and force it to live on dry land, it will die, easily destroyed. And again, if you throw a terrestrial, dry land-dwelling [creature] into the water, it will be drowned. And if you take a bird from the air, it will not survive. And if you remove an astral body from the aether, it will not subsist.

4. But the divine and efficacious Word of God has neither done this nor will he ever bring it about, though he is able to alter the destinies of created things.³⁶ For he does not bring anything about or will anything based on what he is capable of, but rather, based on what preserves things in [natural] order, he preserves the law of good order. In any case, even if he is able, he does not make the earth to be sailed, nor again does he make the sea ploughed and farmed, nor, insofar as he can,³⁷ does he make virtue into vice, nor again, vice into virtue. Nor will he arrange it that human beings become winged, or that the stars come to be below and the earth come to be above.

---

34 The term "creative nature," translates ἡ δημιουργός φύσις, as distinct from the Creator/Demiurge of the previous passages. The phrase suggests nature's production of corporeal beauty and order by virtue of rational principles (λόγος) in it, as articulated, for instance in Plotinus *Ennead* 5.8.2.31–32 and 5.8.3.1–2.

35 The division of animate creatures into aquatic, terrestrial, aerial, and aetherial and the corresponding elements in which they dwell is commonplace, see for example Plato, *Timaeus* 39e–40a and Aristotle, *History of Animals* 487a11ff. Augustine (*City of God* 22.11) states that Platonists use the argument of the order of elements to attack Christian doctrines of bodily resurrection. The Platonists of most concern to Augustine throughout *City of God* are those who, he claims, hold Porphyry in great esteem (e.g. *City of God* 8.12), which suggests that Porphyry may have used a version of this argument as well. See also discussion in Goulet (2003), 405–406.

36 The introduction of the "Word of God" may point to Macarius's editorializing of his source material—the equation of "Word of God" here with the Demiurge allows Macarius to deploy *Logos*- and *Sophia*-theologies in his responses to the Hellene (see below 4.16.5–6, 25).

37 "Insofar as he can" or "according as he is able" (καθ᾽ ὃ δύναται); the prepositional phrase would seem to suggest that the Demiurge's capacity to change vice and virtue is contingent in some respect. This would accord with the generally Platonic cosmology of the rest of the Hellene's comments in this section, as the Platonic Demiurge does not transcend or create the moral plane, but is itself contingent upon the preexistent form of the good.

5. Hence with good reason it is full of nonsense to say that humans will one day be taken up into the air. And Paul's lie is quite plain when he says "We who are living,"[38] for it has been three hundred years[39] since he said this, and nothing anywhere—not even Paul himself—has been taken up with other bodies.

3. 1. And so let this discredited statement of Paul's be silent, while mention must be made of that which Matthew said, like one enslaved in a mill: "And the Gospel of the Kingdom will be proclaimed in the whole world, and then the end will come."[40] But look! every street in the inhabited world has experience of the Gospel and all the boundaries and limits of the world possess the whole Gospel, and nowhere is the end, nor will it ever come.[41]

4. 1. Let this statement be spoken in a corner,[42] but let us see what was said to Paul: "The Lord said to Paul in a night vision, 'Fear not, but speak, because I am with you and no one will attack you to do you harm.'"[43] And having been arrested before even getting to Rome, this boaster was decapitated, he who said that, "We will judge the angels."[44] 2. And not only him, but Peter too, having received the power to "feed the sheep,"[45] was tortured, when

---

38 1 Thess. 4:15, 17.

39 On the import of this passage for the dating of the *Apocriticus* and Macarius's source(s), see the Introduction.

40 Mt. 24:14: "This Gospel of the Kingdom will be proclaimed in the whole *inhabited world* [οἰκουμένη] *as a witness to all the gentiles*, and then the end will come" (the Hellene omits the portion of the passage in italics). Goulet suggests that the Hellene wishes to conjure the image of a mill slave who looks forward to the day when his toils will end (Goulet [2003], 407); the Greek for "mill" here (μυλών) is equivalent to the Latin *pistrinum*, that is, a mill for the grinding of grain. Turning the heavy millstones was extremely difficult work, often done by mules or donkeys; it was a punishment for disobedient slaves (see e.g. Plautus, *Bacchides* 4.6.11; Euripides, *Cyclops* 240; Lysias, *On the Murder of Erotasthenes* 1.18).

41 Compare Julian, *Against the Galilaeans*. fr. 92 (Masaracchia) (= Theodore of Mopsuestia, *Against Julian* fr. 7 [Guida] and Julian, Frag. 1 [Wright]): "Such things often happened and happen, so how can they be signs of the consummation?"

42 "In a corner" (ἐν παραβύστῳ). The *parabyston* was the "out of the way" or "obscure" part of town where the eleven Athenian magistrates charged with administering the prison and executing confessed thieves, kidnappers, and so forth performed their duties (see e.g. Aristotle, *Constitution of Athens* 52.1); the term became a figure of speech to refer to things or people so wretchedly insignificant that they, like petty criminals, ought to be cast out of the public eye, destroyed, and forgotten (see e.g. Pausanias, *Description of Greece* 1.28.8; Harpocration, *Lexicon On Ten Attic Orators* 237).

43 Acts 18:9–10.

44 1 Cor. 6:3.

45 Cf. Jn. 21:15.

nailed to the Cross, and so were myriad others who held the same doctrines as them—some were burned, while others perished when they received punishment or were maimed. This is not worthy of the will of God, nor even of a pious man—that a mass of people be punished inhumanely because of gratitude towards and faith in him, when the awaited resurrection and [second] coming are nowhere to be seen.[46]

5. 1. It is possible to demonstrate that another little phrase is dubious, where Christ says: "See that no one leads you astray, for many will come in my name saying, 'I am the Christ,' and they will lead many astray."[47] And look! three hundred years or more have passed[48] and no one like this has appeared anywhere—2. unless, indeed, you mean Apollonius of Tyana, a man adorned with the whole of philosophy, but you would not find another.[49] But he [Christ] says "they will arise"[50] not about one [person], but about many.

6. 1. For the sake of completeness, let us also consider what is said in the *Apocalypse of Peter*. It intimates that the heaven together with the earth will be judged, thusly: "The earth," it says, "will present everyone to God on the Day of Judgment and that it will itself be judged with the heaven that surrounds [it]."[51] 2. But no one is so uneducated or so senseless as not to know that what pertains to the earth is in a state of disturbance and that it is not in its nature to preserve order, but rather it is irregular, while things in heaven have the same order forever and always move along the same [paths] and never change nor ever will change; for it was established as God's most consummate creation. 3. Hence it is impossible that those things deemed worthy of a superior destiny be destroyed, in so far as they have been fixed by a divine and undefiled law. And, for what reason will heaven be judged? What fault will it ever appear to have committed,

---

46 Accusing the Christian God of wrongly allowing the suffering of the martyrs was a polemical commonplace; see for example Origen, *Against Celsus* 8.39, 54, 69; Arnobius, *Against the Nations* 2.76.

47 Mt. 24:4–5.

48 On the implications of this comment for dating Macarius and his source(s), see the Introduction.

49 See above 3.1.1, where the Hellene also compares Christ unfavourably with Apollonius. On the question of possible relationships between the Hellene's comparisons of Apollonius and Christ to Hierocles's *Lover of Truth*, which offered an extended polemical comparison of the two, see the Introduction.

50 Mt. 24:11.

51 Cf. the Ethiopic text of *Apocalypse of Peter* §4.

when it preserves the order approved in the beginning by God and remains always in an identical condition? 4. Unless, that is, out of slander someone will declare to the Creator that the heaven deserves to be judged, as though the judge would endure such portentous charges against it—the judge so admirable, the charges so grave.

7. 1. And furthermore, that [book][52] has the passage, which is full of impiety, that states: "And every power of heaven will dissolve and the heaven will be rolled up like a book scroll. And all the stars will fall like leaves from a vine and as leaves fall from a fig tree."[53] 2. And with portentous falsehood and enormous pretension the boast is made: "The heaven and earth will pass away, but my words will not at all pass away."[54] How, indeed, can someone say that the words of Jesus will subsist if heaven and the earth no longer exist? And moreover, if the Christ did this and brought down the heaven, he would imitate the most impious of people, who destroy their own [creations].[55] 3. That God is father of heaven and earth is admitted by the Son when he says: "Father, Lord of heaven and earth."[56] John the Baptist magnifies the heaven and says that divine gifts have been sent from it, saying: "No one is able to do anything unless it is given to him from heaven."[57] And the prophets say that the heaven is the holy dwelling place of God, in the passage: "Look down from the holy dwelling place and bless your people Israel."[58] 4. If, indeed, the heaven that is so vast and so great, according to these testimonies, will pass away, what seat will be left for

---

52 I.e. the *Apocalypse of Peter*.

53 Is. 34:4. The Hellene quotes a version of Is. 34:4 that includes the phrase "and every power of heaven will dissolve," which is found in *Codex Vaticanus* and Eusebius of Caesarea's *Commentary on Isaiah* II 7, where he notes that it was asterisked in Origen's *Hexapla*. At 4.16.3 below, Macarius's quotation is that of the received text of the LXX. Goulet ([2003], 411) suggests that the Hellene is here quoting this verse of Isaiah as it was transmitted in the *Apocalypse of Peter* (the text he has been drawing on throughout this passage), while Macarius quotes the received text of Is. 34:4, either because (if he is drawing on a pagan source) he does not recognize that the Hellene has quoted the verse from *Apocalypse of Peter*, or because he does not accept this apocryphal work..

54 Mt. 24:35.

55 Thus the Hellene presents the understanding that Christians give to Christ the role of the Platonic Demiurge; alternatively, this may be another insertion on the part of Macarius (see note 36 above).

56 Mt. 11:25; Lk. 10:21.

57 Jn. 3:27.

58 Dt. 26:15. Goulet would add the phrase σου ἐκ τοῦ οὐρανοῦ, which would make the quotation accord with the LXX, giving "Look down from your holy dwelling place, from heaven, and bless your people Israel" He argues that the Hellene must understand them

him who is master? And if the elements of the earth are destroyed, what will be the footstool of he who sits, when he himself says: "The heaven is my throne, and the earth the footstool for my feet"?[59]

8–9. 1. And as for the idea that the heaven and the earth will pass away, there you have it. But let us fumble about, as if in the dark, for another doctrine more fabulous than this, in the passage: "The Kingdom of heaven is like a mustard seed,"[60] and again, "The Kingdom of heaven is like leaven,"[61] and once more, "It is like a merchant who seeks fine pearls."[62] 2. These reveries are not appropriate for men, nor even for women lost in dreams. Whenever someone holds forth on matters that are great and divine he is obliged to use common things suited to humans for the sake of clarity, but not things so vulgar and unintelligible. 3. But these statements, besides being base and inappropriate for such great things, have in themselves no clear or intelligible meaning. 4. And, yet, it is quite proper that they be clear because they are not written for those who are wise or have understanding, but for children; if it is even necessary to ruminate on how Jesus says, "I thank you, Father, Lord of heaven and earth, that you have hidden these things from the wise and those with understanding and have revealed them to children,"[63] and in Deuteronomy it is written: "The hidden things are the Lord our God's and manifest things are ours."[64] 5. Therefore what is written for children and those without understanding must be most clear and not enigmatic, for if the mysteries are hidden from the wise, but are unreasonably poured out upon children and nurslings, it would be better to emulate their lack of reason and lack of learning. 6. And this is the great achievement of the wisdom of him who has come: to hide the rays of knowledge from the wise, but to reveal it to senseless infants!

10. 1. It is right to investigate another matter much more erudite than this (I speak ironically): "Those who are healthy do not need a physician, but those who are ill."[65] But Christ declaimed this to the crowds about his own

---

in order for the verse to be quoted in this context; this is correct, yet the words need not necessarily be added to the text.
59 Is. 66:1.
60 Mt. 13:31.
61 Mt. 13:33.
62 Mt. 13:45.
63 Mt. 11:25.
64 Deut. 29:28.
65 Lk. 5:31.

coming. 2. If, therefore, it is for those who are labouring under sins, as he says, that he put a stop to sins, did not our fathers labour, were our ancestors not made ill by sins?[66] If, in fact, those who are healthy have no need of a physician, and "he did not come to call the righteous but sinners to conversion,"[67] as Paul in fact says in this way, "Jesus Christ came into the world to save sinners, of whom I am the greatest";[68] if, indeed, this is so and he who has erred is called, and he who is sick is healed, and the unjust person is called, but the just person is not called, then he who is neither called nor has need of the Christians' healing would not err, but would be just. 3. For he who does not need healing turns away from the doctrine of the faithful [i.e. Christianity], and to the degree that he turns away, to that extent he will be just, healthy, and without error.

{Christian}

11. 1. *After such a refined and forceful speech, the entire audience that was present cowered, and the senses of the noble people were completely humbled. But we, seeing the rule of the New Covenant*[69] *dragged through the mud in this way, were stung in our mind and sick in our soul and all the senses of our body were agitated, so that we could almost have said, "Lord, save us, we are perishing!"*[70] *2. Encircled by such a surge of contrivances,*[71] *but encouraged from somewhere by an invisible ally, we stood fast against the threatening tempest, opposing to it the alliance of the Holy Spirit, and like an oarsman we began to rattle the oar of our tongue, and drove hard into the first wave.*[72] *3. This was the [question] concerning the form of the cosmos and how it passes away. In truth, just as the visible form of the*

---

66 Compare Augustine, *Letter* 102.8 (= Porphyry, *Against the Christians* fr. 81 [Harnack]) and Jerome, *Letter* 133.9 (= Porphyry, *Against the Christians* fr. 82 [Harnack]); see also 4.24.2.

67 Cf. Lk. 5:31–32.

68 1 Tim. 1:15.

69 Like Goulet, we consider the phrase κανὼν τῆς καινῆς διαθήκης to refer more generally to the "rule" of the gospel and promise of the *parousia*, just critiqued by the Hellene, rather than to the textual "canon" of the New Testament.

70 Mt. 8:25.

71 This translates τοσαύτῃ δὲ μηχανῆς ζάλῃ κεκυκλωμένοι, which Goulet translates as "*Cernés par un tel soulèvement d'engins de guerre.*" Macarius exploits the multivalence of μηχανή ("contrivance/siege engine"); this is also a good example of his penchant for characterizing the debate with the Hellene in martial terms.

72 Macarius is conjuring the image of oarsmen rattling their oars before setting out through the surf.

cosmos passes away, so too the pretence of the speaker passed away as the cloud of his sophistical wickedness was scattered and the cresting wave of his words broke.

4. Let us say, then, that the "form of this world" can be understood in various ways. For the "form of the world" can mean this transitory life full of groaning. You can also take the "form of the world" to mean the different ages of the body, which passes from infancy into boyhood, then into manhood, and then again into maturity, and finally into old age. 5. Indeed, "form" is nothing other than the appearance of something; for as the shadow that follows a man is a "form" and outline of a person, but quickly "passes away," dissolving when the light ends, departing and no longer affected by the ray of light, so too the appearance of things that exist corporeally here in this world, being a "form" and shadow of the world, does not have a stable and fixed state, but passes away in a brief period of time.

6. Consider also the "form" and semblance of the world to be those things which are falsely thought to be honours in human society: office, military command, authority, rule of a province, and, if you will, sovereignty itself. The "form" of all these things, or rather their splendour—for "form" can also mean "splendour"— is brought to an end by the balance of a brief amount of time.[73] 7. Someone who lived in the imperial palace yesterday, is assigned today to the most distant guard post. Someone else who presides over the tribunal of gubernatorial power is arrested and thrown into the prison of the condemned. Another who has fought a sea battle and shines with the splendid "form" of his success all of a sudden wanders, stripped naked, suffering miserably. Another, too, commanding an army and defeating barbarian ranks, so as to be enthroned second only to emperors, when some envious person's plot arises after the victory, instead of [obtaining] the splendid prosperity hoped for, is brought down into the dark pit of the dead. 8. Thus does the form of this world pass away, and "those who have must think as if they have not and those who rejoice must live as though afflicted."[74] 9. Someone else who sits on a stinking dunghill suddenly seems splendid and distinguished, having cast off the hateful form

---

73 "The balance of a brief amount of time" (βραχεῖα καιροῦ ῥοπὴ παρήγαγε); Macarius is using the metaphor of the "tipping" (ῥοπή) of a balance beam, thus, "when even a small amount of time can result in a great change of circumstances."

74 Cf. 1 Cor. 7:29–31. Like the Hellene, Macarius quotes the passage as referring to possession generally, while the received text has "have *wives* as though not having them."

of shame.⁷⁵ Another, worn down with nothing but an old sheepskin and a worn leather pouch,⁷⁶ pitifully roaming the whole countryside, becomes fortunate for some reason, and appears admirable to the ruling authorities, robbed by chance of the "form" of poverty. 10. Thus neither are sorrows lasting for people, nor do joys tarry and remain long; rather, every "form" always passes away. Cyrus deposed Croesus, stripped him of his power; Tomyris, winning victory over Cyrus, deposes him. Neither one nor the other kept the "form" of his Kingdom.⁷⁷

11. Consider the "form of the world" to be the beauty of cities, and you will learn how it has departed and [still] passes away even to this day. The city called Babylon was the royal metropolis of the Assyrians: Eight hundred and fifty stadia in circumference, fifty cubits in width and rising to two hundred and fifty in height,⁷⁸ it was an invincible and impregnable [city]. Subsequently, under the Persians it lost all the comeliness of its "form" and finally, having been laid waste, preserves no trace of its former good fortune.

12. At another time, the people of Macedonia appeared admirable, when the fear of the strength of their sovereignty hung over both land and sea. But now, subdued by the rod of Roman rule, they are taxed in the manner of subjects and have lost their former renown. It would be superfluous to mention how many toparchies⁷⁹ have drifted away like smoke or how many royal women have perished or how many illustrious men's fame has completely come to naught.

13. Thus, if someone wants to consider the whole universe by means of reason, he will find that the form of the world is carried away by time and is unable to persist. Consider life itself thoughtfully, and you will find that it rightly changes. Is not the child who was at first raised without injury today consumed by the years of his age, his mind worn away by anxiety little by little? Does not someone who in his youth has the full flower of strength and is manifestly worthy of being commander of the [praetorian] guards,⁸⁰

---

75   An allusion to Job upon the ash heap (cf. Job 2:8, 42:10).
76   The sheepskin garment and worn leather pouch are marks of an impoverished beggar.
77   Compare Herodotus, *History* I.79–86, 205–214.
78   Compare Herodotus, *History* I.178; Herodotus's description gives a circumference of four hundred and eighty stadia and a wall fifty cubits thick and two hundred high.
79   The toparchy was a sub-unit of territorial administration in the Hellenistic Near East; as an example, see the descriptions of the division of Palestine/Judaea into toparchies in Pliny, *Natural History* 5.70 and Josephus, *Jewish War* 3.54–55.
80   Δορυφόρων ἄρχοντος, δορυφόροι, or "spear-bearers," was the usual Greek term for the emperor's Praetorian Guard, see e.g. Plutarch, *Galba* 13.1. The fifth-century historian

having taken pride in his exploits and been full of life, today wastes away, lying in a bed?

14. Investigate time itself philosophically, if you wish, and you will find that it is not fixed stably, but like a stream passes quickly. Was it not spring, long ago, painted with the many-coloured beauty of flowers, splendid and magnificent with their sweet bouquet, which has a charming and delightful effect on souls? Did not the sight of every budding sprout bring unspeakable pleasure? Did not the pure streams of the springs pour swiftly into the clear-flowing torrents of rivers? Was not the sea most amenable to navigation for sailors? Did not the dry land, like a mother, urge on those who work the land to plough the soil? Were not shepherds happy and rejoicing as they walked, surrounded by the bleating of their lambs? Did not the many-toned melodies of songbirds resound in the air, blending in an indescribable and endless bliss? Does not all of creation, as if crowning itself with spring, deck itself out with eminent and splendid ornament? And, when summer was not yet at its peak, did not the pleasant "form" of spring pass away?

15. Flowers, having sparkled gracefully for a while, but then withered, all the grass parched by the burning heat, stalks of the crops wilted by the heat, have betrayed the decrepitude of their own nature. Springs and rivers fighting the fiery heat and unable to conquer it sink below their low marks. Songbirds, unlike the cicadas, chirp temperately.[81] From the midst of the aether, the seething flame roasts all the leaves of the plants; the transition to dry [weather] makes everything bare and plain. There is a drinking cup of flame placed before every land animal. Fountains take on a hardened crust and ape the nature of stone, unable to endure the burning heat. The whole "form" of the world of spring passes away and summer evinces the parched, fiery nature of things. 16. See that this "form," too, is not stable, but quickly flies from our midst like a dream. Summer appeared. The farmers' fields were seen to be close to harvest. Ripe fruits appeared on the trees and grapes darkened in the vinedressers' vineyards. One cut the crop with the scythe and, rejoicing, picked an ear from the stalk, deeming

---

Zosimus claims that Constantine disbanded both Maxentius's and Licinius's Praetorians (*New History* 2.17.2), and this has sometimes been taken to indicate the end of the Praetorian Guard. Eusebius (*Life of Constantine* 4.65.1), however, has the δορυφόροι at Constantine's deathbed. Macarius is likely using the term as a general designation for the emperor's personal security force, which, beginning under Constantine, was comprised of men selected from his new cavalry troops, the *Scholae Palatinae*; for a general introduction to the Roman military in the fourth century see Elton (2006).

81 Reading A against Goulet, who conjectures οὐ μετρίως where A reads μετρίως.

BOOK 4

the summer harvest the judge of his labours, while another revelled as he picked a red apple and took pleasure in the scent as he handled the fruit, as if rejoicing in a prelude to autumn. 17. Every crop on the threshing floor was splendid and the abundance of wheat and barley provided food for the farmers; and great was the toil of those who gathered in the harvest, and their bodies were marked by the broiling sun.[82] One gathered sheaves with the scythe, while another tossed the heaps with the winnowing fan; someone else removed the light chaff, while another cleaned the grain in sieves and another put it in a bag. Like bees in a honeycomb, they divided the harvest amongst themselves.

18. And what happens after this? Consider the matter with me. The harvest comes to an end and the "form" of summer has abruptly run its course. The time of autumn appeared at its height, the roundness of the grapes weighed down the grapevine, the tents of those who guard the vineyard rang with laughter, luxury succeeded the dry and toil-filled time of harvest, everyone cut the bunches of grapes from the vines. The fine charm of it all was a delight for the soul: when the vines high on the trellis, as if having senses, selected the fruit, while others below, plump as if pregnant, bent down presenting the offspring they had borne of their nature at the height of full ripeness, [offspring] which, as they were swaddled, the pickers worked to place in vats and made dry wine in the protection of wine jars. All was joyous, the produce delicious.

19. Then after this—to cut my oration short—winter rushed in, the season in which we are now practicing such subtlety of speech, in which we spin such threads of words, weaving a many-coloured fabric of questions, the season which freezes the air with relentless icy cold and binds the land with harsh winds. Shutting civilized nature indoors, barring all the heat that comes from the heavenly firmament, it made our earthly realm sullen and most hateful, and made us, who before rejoiced in the open air, into prisoners. Now, just yesterday, snowflakes dimmed the whole "form" [of the world], stealing away the joy of all the senses, with the result that what has been said about the passage, "The form of this world passes away," is clear.

20. Where, tell me, is spring, and then summer, or again, autumn? Indeed, this season, winter, will also cease and pass away, will it not?[83]

---

82 Literally: "sizzling fire signals touched their bodies."

83 Due to the loss of the beginning of the *Apocriticus*, this remark is one of the few extant details as to the setting of the fictional debate.

Where do cool breezes completely get the upper hand over the other winds? Where does the power of honours ever last? Where does calm ever get complete control over the sea? Where does the same inclination of the zodiac embrace the world? What among things that have come into being does not partake of alteration? And what created nature denies change? What among things that have been made is not used to being altered on a daily basis? 21. But you, for your part, you want the world not to pass away, as if it was the Unbegotten? But if this is what you want, give it the status of the Unbegun, raise the conception of it to that of the Eternal itself, do not give it youth, and it will not assume old age, it will refuse an end. For that which has no origin is, naturally, ageless. That which has no beginning, logically, is without end. That which is unbegotten, naturally, is unchangeable.

22. Now, if you think it is correct that the form of the world does not pass away, judge it to be unchangeable and eternal. But according to this doctrine, not only is the heaven not generated, nor only the earth, sea, rational or irrational animals, nor birds, but every [created thing] will be eternal and deny their essence as generated beings. 23. But no human being will accept a doctrine so full of thoughtlessness, not even among the Scythians and the barbarian peoples. Rather, he will say that there is what is generated, and what is ingenerate, and that the former passes away and the latter remains the same.[84]

24. Paul, then, knowing that the whole form of the world will pass away, rightly said: "Those who have, be and think as though having not."[85] For the possession that disappears from its possessor in a span of solstices, seasons, hours, and changes is not secure. "Nor [should] he who delights delight," for that in which he delights is easily changed. 25. Nor is there a day so long and without end that we rejoice as if it always has its splendour, but the sun rises and then sets, at one moment it seems calm and at another wintry, so that the form of the [day] comes and goes. 26. Nor is there a night so greatly unquenchable that, given the depth of its darkness, we will

---

84 Apart from ignoring the distinction (common among pro-Nicenes by the end of the fourth century) between ἀγέννητος ("ungenerated") and ἀγένητος ("uncreated," that is, not having a temporal or spatial point of origin), pro-Nicenes understood the former to refer only to the Father, while the latter applied to persons of the trinity. Macarius also takes no account of the standard Platonic exegesis of Plato's *Timaeus* (e.g. Porphyry, *Commentary on the Timaeus* Fr. 25–27 [Sodano]), which argues that the world is γένητος only insofar as its contents are mutable, not in the sense that it has a temporal origin in its entirety; in fact, Porphyry avers that no one would entertain the latter view.

85 Cf. 1 Cor. 7:29.

sleep for aeons, but rather, sometimes darkness lasts ten hours, sometimes twelve. The "form" [of night] is not stable and immutable.

12. 1. That is enough about the phrase "The form of the world passes away." Next let us see what the "cloud" is and who those are who, having been taken up on the cloud to a rendezvous in the air, will be with the Lord forever. Let us not interpret the apostolic meaning superficially, ruminating on the letter like irrational animals, but rather like rational animals, dining at the table of reason, let us search carefully after the Apostle's meaning, for here he philosophizes mystical principles for us. 2. He says that the corruption that accompanies human nature because of free thought and choice[86] is completely destroyed in the second coming of Christ, and as if snatched away from the great mire of things here, the pious are caught up out of mortal life.

3. For just as the nature of the waters, being something that is salty, bitter, and most heavy, lies lower down in the seas and in the lakes, but when caught up into clouds swiftly traverses the air, so too he [Christ] will draw up human nature, which is immersed in the bitterness of life and sunken in the sea of death, quickly and with angelic power, which he [Paul] names "clouds" allegorically because of the way it behaves. 4. For because the type of cloud is sometimes high and aloft, but at other times lies close to the ground and makes contact with the earth, and there are times when they descend down into the deepest valleys. In a similar way, the essence and speed of the angels, which serves the glory of the Creator, sometimes comes down to the earth serving God, and at other times it ascends above, having completed the course of its ministry. For this reason, he likens the angelic nature to clouds because of the similar way they act.

5. In this way, the angel, having taken Habbakuk up from the middle of Judaea like a cloud takes water up from a lake, carried him, and placed him above the pit in Babylonia.[87] Indeed, it is recorded that Jacob saw angels ascending and descending from heaven.[88] 6. Hence customarily, the

---

86 That humans incur corruption by their own choice is an early Christian commonplace: see e.g. Theophilus of Antioch, *To Autolycus* 25; Origen, *On First Principles* 1.8.1; Athanasius, *On the Incarnation* 7.

87 Cf. Dan. 14:33–39. Habbakuk, who is in Judaea, is ordered by God's angel to bring dinner to Daniel, who is imprisoned in a lions' den in Babylon. After Habbakuk protests that he has never been to Babylon and does not know where the lions' den is, the angel picks Habbakuk up by the hair and carries him to the den.

88 Cf. Gen. 28:12, where Jacob sees angels ascending and descending a ladder as part of a vision in which God promises land and progeny to Jacob's descendants.

divine and prophetic tablets plainly call the angels "clouds." For instance: "I will command the clouds not to rain on the vines";[89] for if the "vine" is, allegorically, nothing other than the People,[90] then angels, naturally, would be the clouds that furnish a shower of visions to the People. In another instance, "And behold one like a Son of Man coming with the clouds of heaven,"[91] that is, with the angels. 7. In order that we might know that Daniel refers allegorically to the angels with whom the Son of Man was coming, the Evangelist says: "When the Son of Man comes, and all the angels with him."[92] For he explains what the "clouds" in the Book of Daniel are, with which the Son of Man has come, stating [they are] "angels" in the passage: "When the Son of Man comes, and all the *angels* with him."[93] 8. And again, elsewhere it [i.e. Scripture] names the angelic order "cloud" in the passage: "A cloud and darkness encircle his throne and fire moves about before him."[94] For there too, in the second judgment of Christ's coming, it [i.e. the psalm] signifies the angelic order as a cloud that surrounds and guards the divine tribunal, and reveals, as "darkness," the invisible and inexplicable dispensation of the incarnation. It has spoken enigmatically of his vengeance in the form of flaming "fire" that flashes from the cloud, while by "throne" it tells you of the seat of forbearance[95] and points to the harsh judgment of the Law, but by "justice" it indicates the evangelic gift, in order that whatever it [i.e. the Law] subjects to judgment, this the gift of the Gospel justifies by grace. 9. And in another place: "He places clouds as his stepstool."[96] And a pillar of cloud went before the People during the day and led the People out.[97] 10. But in order that we might know that the statement the Apostle makes about clouds concerns angels, I will point out what is given in the Gospel, where it says: "When the Son of Man comes

---

89 Is. 5:6.
90 For the vine as the People of God see e.g. Ez. 15:2; Jn. 15; *Didache* 9.
91 Dn. 7:13.
92 Mt. 25:31.
93 Mt. 25:31.
94 Ps. 96:2 (LXX). The received text of this verse reads: "A cloud and darkness encircle [him, justice and corrective judgment surround] his throne and fire moves about before him"; Macarius omits the phrase within brackets. Goulet would restore the missing phrase ([2003], 264), but there is no need for this addition, for the verse serves Macarius's point as quoted.
95 Reading μακροθυμίας ("forbearance") against the μακρομυθίας of Goulet's text, which is a misprint, for Goulet's "*longanimité*" translates μακροθυμίας.
96 Ps. 103:3 (LXX).
97 Cf. Ex. 13:21–22, where God leads the Israelites out of Egypt, guiding them with a "pillar of cloud" during the day and a "pillar of fire" at night.

in his glory, he will send out his angels into the four corners of the world and they will assemble his elect from one end of the earth to the other."[98] You see that the just are gathered together and in some way taken up "on a cloud" to a rendezvous with the Lord.

11. That the Apostle was accustomed, for the most part, to speak metaphorically about the nature of things, I will at once make plain and clear for you. For wishing to speak about knowledge and ignorance, he likened knowledge to day and ignorance to night, saying "The night is almost gone, but the day draws near, so let us walk decently as in the day,"[99] and again: "But you are all sons of light and sons of the day."[100] And saying these things, he did not at all mean sensible light or sensible day, but light that is authentically intelligible and blessed, and a mystical day that radiates incorruptibility. 12. So here too then, with a universal end seizing the inhabited world and with humanity flowing away like water, there will be a need for a trumpet, thunder, and an intelligible cloud so that the world will be frightened by the trumpet,[101] Hades will be shaken and rocked by the thunder, and those who stream like water pouring from the vessel that is the earth will be brought together from one end of the earth to the other by the mystical cloud into Christ's presence, that is, before the fearful and just tribunal, where the King will place those taken up upon the cloud in ranks on the right and left.[102] For the trumpet call will not be made by a trumpet made of horn or a bronze pipe, but by an angelic voice, and it will raise up all those who have set aside corruption after having themselves become light and airy. For as Elijah was led away by horses into heaven[103]—angels they were in respect of the nature of the thing, but in the story they were fiery horses and they revealed the speed of the chariot of fire—so too here [they are led away] in a cloud which is in its actual nature angelic, but is termed a "cloud" for the purpose of treating the subject.

14. But since you said that each of the things that have come to be is happy in its particular place and is unable to accept a foreign abode, know that each of the entities having a principle of essence that is generated, is preserved by abiding in what is different, not in what is like itself, such as what is moist in what is dry, like water in a jug, what is hot in what is cold,

---

98 A composite quotation of Mt. 25:31, 24:31; Mk. 13:27; Rev. 7:1 (cf. Goulet [2003], 416).
99 Rom. 13:12a, 13a.
100 1 Thess. 5:5.
101 Cf. 1 Thess. 4:16.
102 Cf. Mt. 25:33.
103 2 Kings (= 4 Regn. LXX) 2:11–12.

like fire in air, and then vice versa, what is dry in what is moist, like the earth in the abyss, what is cold in what is hot, like hail in a thunderstorm. 15. For each welcomes permanence in another, while it is impossible that a body remain a distinct element within the same element. No one has found another fire in a fire or found in water another kind of water, but in water people find earth, while in earth they uncover veins of hidden water. What is dry, moreover, resides happily in what is moist and in what is dry what is moist customarily makes its home. Thus embers of fire are often found hidden in the cold, and in fire cold spots imperceptibly remain. So too what is heavy is friend and sharer with what is light, like the body with the soul, and what is light wants to rest in what is heavy. 16. For every nature of every entity has its distinct constitution not *vis à vis* itself but *vis à vis* another principle; for example, if justice did not exist, the principle of injustice would not subsist. Likewise, if the pious man were not apparent, no one would be able to discover the impious man, nor what is heavy apart from what is light, nor what is hot without what is cold. And if one wanted to traverse the universe by means of reason, he would find that each predication is made in relation to other beings.

17. Therefore, it is not strange if clouds take humans up from the earth, delivered from corruption and released from the mire of vice, for what clouds are in relation to water angels are in relation to humanity. If, then, clouds do not exert any effort to lift up water, angels transporting the nature of humans exert even less. 18. That the divine Word likens humans to water you can learn from the prophet who says, "Behold many nations like water," and: "Multitude of many nations, like a stormy sea, so will you be troubled; backs of many nations, like water you will rumble."[104] Now then, if "waters" are humans, there must be an intelligible "cloud," which, as [a cloud does in the case of] water, will make the earthly essence light.

19. And do not let Paul's statement trouble [you], when he says "We who are alive will be taken up,"[105] as if he seems to be mistaken because the resurrection [i.e. of the faithful] did not come in his lifetime. For he liked to include himself in his account of [human] essence and not to shun his kinship, for he thought, reasonably, that all were included in him, in so far as he was human, and he, loving truth, determined that he subsisted in all, and was speaking in anticipation of the time, or rather, he shortened the

---

104 Is. 17:13a and 17:12b, passages which liken human nations to troubled waters.
105 1 Thess. 4:17.

time [i.e. for parenetical effect]. This is what a friendly person does, or anyone who loves the kinship of a shared nature.

13. 1. Since enough has been said to you on this point, let me comment briefly on the saying about the gospel [cited] by you, which reads as follows: "And the Gospel of the Kingdom will be proclaimed throughout the whole world and then the end will come."[106] 2. It is possible, in fact, to take the word "end" in many ways: the word of peace is the end of war; the learning of knowledge is the end of ignorance; the flame of piety is understood to be the end of impiety; the tablets of liberty are seen as the end of tyranny; the accomplishment of virtue is the end of vice; the gleaming lustre of self-control is the end of intemperance; unpretentious morals and integrity are the end of knavery, villainy, and trickery; the unalloyed, sober, and steady mind is the end of folly, revelry, and frenzy.

3. If, indeed, when the Gospel had been proclaimed clearly, these [evils] ended and every corner of the world moved towards the celebration of piety, rejecting the ancient error of their way of life; if the heretofore intemperate human race today dwells in the citadel of self-control and loves the beauty of chastity like a pearl; if some who until now worshipped temples of idols now seem reputable, having become polished temples of the Holy Spirit;[107] if those who used to have an insatiable thirst for blood and forged swords against their own people, spending on slaughter and themselves expended in rancour now have the bond of indissoluble peace and unbroken friendship; if those who once had ignorance thick as the darkness of gloom today fire their minds with the learning of wisdom brighter than the sun; if an inhuman tyrant tormented the world and now indulges it with royal philanthropy; if vice besieged rational nature,[108] but virtue [now] stands guard, sheltering it; if villainy and deceit used to make reason helpless, but [now] the morals of free men light up the mind—how is it not clear, persuasive, and manifest from this exposition of circumstances that used to be evil and are now good that the world has come to know the end of a way of life that had become a tragedy?

4. But if you are looking for a universal end and a bodily one, and it pleases you to have an answer according to the literal sense, be patient for

---

106 Mt. 24:14.
107 Cf. 1 Cor. 6:19.
108 On humans as the eminently rational creation see e.g. Origen, *First Principles* 1.8.1; Constantine, *Oration to the Saints* 13; Athanasius, *On the Incarnation* 8; Gregory of Nyssa, *On the Making of Man* 10–11.

a moment and you will know what you seek—that the end does not tarry, but is at the gates and that the Gospel is still unknown to many people.[109] 5. Seven peoples of the Indies that live beyond the southeastern desert, who have not yet heard one word from the Evangelists, as well as the Ethiopians who are called "long-lived," in the southwest right at the mouth of Ocean, who legislate against committing any injustice and suffering any injustice, drink milk and eat meat, and live around one hundred and fifty years and never get sick or feeble until they die—these have not learned the word of the Gospel.[110] 6. What do I say to you of the Western Maures,[111] or the peoples across the Danube, the river of the North, which, fed without limit by thirty-five tributaries, flows in summer and in winter, is wide and impassible, which, navigable by thousands of barges, encloses the whole country of the Scythians, where twelve nomadic barbarian peoples more harsh than savage beasts reside (but Herodotus will tell you their names and teach you about their customs and laws)[112] to whom the word of the Gospel has not come, but who as yet have made do with evil ancestral traditions and maintain a horrible and dreadful way of life? But the divine Gospel must be proclaimed to all as a witness,[113] then corporeal life will have its end. 7. For when the evangelical word of incorruption makes every people obedient with its testimony about the pure life after death, then at that time the Word, while not responsible for the punishment of the Gentiles, which it predicted and prophesied, and which damage they brought upon themselves by means of self-chosen vice, will deem it right for the ruin of destruction to arrive. 8. Thus, the source of time prolongs the times because of human recalcitrance and saves the appointed time and makes the approach of the appointed time very slow. For wisely, since we do not know it, the Master of the ages, turning and spinning the axes of time, makes the slowness of

---

109 An allusion to Mt. 24:14, quoted above at 4.13.1.
110 Macarius draws on ethnographic commonplaces. On Indians compare especially Herodotus, *History* III.98–98, for Ethiopians at the mouth of Ocean compare *History* II.21 (though Herodotus rejects the notion that the source of the Nile is Ocean); on Ethiopian customs compare *History* III.23. On the "four corners of the world" as a patristic commonplace see e.g. Irenaeus, *Against Heresies* 3.11.8; cf. Mk. 13:27.
111 The Maures are not mentioned in Herodotus, suggesting that Macarius is "improvising" upon Herodotus from memory (cf. Goulet [2003], 417), or drawing on a source dependent on Herodotus.
112 On the Ister (Danube) and its tributaries see Herodotus *History* IV.48–50; for Herodotus's list of Scythian tribes, see *History* IV.16–21; for his ethnography of the Scythians see *History* IV.2–20.
113 Cf. Mt. 24:14.

times great and hides [from us] the determined amount [of time].[114] 9. For if the disciples of the philosophers, [living] in the mud of the body, have obtained such intelligence that they can make a triangle into a rectangle and a rectangle into a triangle while preserving the definition of the form of both, and not destroy the figure of the triangle when transforming this form into the rectangle, nor corrupt the nature of the rectangle when, in turn, transforming it into a triangle; rather, they mystically change each thing by some principle of wisdom, neither corrupting nor confounding the definition of either one,[115] it is no great thing if the Father of Wisdom, having determined that the end would be short in duration, will make this end short or long depending on what is useful for humans, neither making the entirety of time something less, nor altering the hour of the event. In this way he makes a day a thousand years,[116] but not many days—rather, it is still one day. 10. It is not that he carved the day up into a thousand years, but rather that he stretched out a span of a thousand years within one day, without disturbing the calculation of either thing. For he did not pull the day apart forcibly into a thousand years as if stretching it out, but kept it intact, perfect, and whole in its particulars; nor again did he efface the thousand years, chopping the intervals up to fit into a single day, but rather unifying the definition of the nature of them both.

11. Thus it will not help us to be impatient, if, having determined that the end is coming quickly, he delays it. For he does not disregard the appointed time of the end, and, in his incomprehensible understanding, prolonging what is brief and quick, he makes no mistake. For our sake he alters the succession of dates, diverts time, and cuts life short, if it is advantageous for living beings, or on the contrary extends it, if it is useful and good.

And now, confessing these things to be so, [let us] put to the test the question that follows, since you have a sufficient answer about "the end."

14. 1. We must still examine the case of Peter and Paul, and those of their way of thinking. How, when he [Christ] said to Peter, "Tend my sheep"[117]

---

114 Macarius ignores the shortening of time promised in Mk. 13:20.
115 Macarius seems to be describing geometric dissection; that is, the "cutting" of geometrical figures into pieces that can be arranged into new figures with the same area as the original. Euclid's proof of the Pythagorean Theorem was a well-known geometric dissection involving rectangles and triangles (Euclid, *Elements* I.47; see also Proclus, *Commentary on the First Book of Euclid's Elements* 426–429).
116 Cf. 2 Pet. 3:38, which cites Ps. 90:4 (89:4 LXX) to explain the delay of the end.
117 Jn. 21:15.

and to Paul, "Speak, do not be silent, because I am with you and no one will harm you,"[118] did he allow each of them to receive a different punishment? 2. For when he saw the former crucified and the latter decapitated, he patiently and very fittingly allowed it; but not before their struggles or the instructions and actions of their teaching, but [only] after the toil that they piously endured, teaching the earth, calming the much-troubled sea, raising islands from the depths of error in which they were sunken, filling things under heaven with pure light, purifying souls soiled with wickedness, rekindling with [their] admonitions minds that were wounded and nearly extinguished, shattering the darts of disobedience and breaking the swords of sins. Nobly defending the oppressed, [they were] the most powerful brothers-in-arms of those suffering injustice, the greatest seekers of the lost, and the support and help of the fallen. After revealing to the world many marvellous deeds, they received capital punishment by the Cross and decapitation.

3. But they met with such an end so that the praise of their glory would be greater, like the best and most unshakable soldiers who are more highly honoured by the king time when, fighting for the fatherland and people, they expose themselves to the point of death for love of their own [people]. Now presently, because of these leaders, the phalanx of demons, having been driven off, leaves the multitude of the faithful to live in peace, and since the tumult of the enemies who lead the people astray has been stopped, the progress of life is left free from fear, because the rampart of piety is firm and the fold of the faith is fortified.[119] 5. What are these noble men reported to have done next after such a spectacle? They plaited the evergreen garland of martyrdom; they made the unfading crown of confession. Having enlisted believers for Christ up and down the inhabited world, they understood that they had to show them what sort of struggles the crown of faith is woven from, in order to persuade them not merely to believe but even to suffer for the sake of piety.[120] 6. For believing an account is not at all difficult, but rousing the faith with toil is glorious, and an account that has been proclaimed is often untrue, but a deed that guarantees the nature of something effects a solemn verification of the account. For this reason they sealed their lives with a violent death, faithfully leaving those who witnessed it zealous and winning the prize of great success. For

---

118 Acts 18:9–10.
119 On the intimidation of demons by the martyrs see Origen, *Against Celsus* 8.44.
120 An allusion to Phil. 1:29.

what they endured in suffering willingly they left as a farewell gift to their disciples, they who had become the model of unconquerable courage. 7. But then in order that after many good contests they might be crowned in the final struggle, they went on; they were allowed to enter into the great and famous theatre of suffering, one by decapitation, the other on a cross, whereby they slashed the tail of the serpent.[121] For the one, when his head was cut off, baited the snake with blood, as if it were milk,[122] while the other slashed it vigorously with the Cross.

8. And before their teaching and preaching, Christ protected them from suffering, rescuing Peter and Paul from countless Jewish ambushes, but when the multitude of the Gentiles had come to know their preaching, when the seeds of the faith finally took root, when they had persuaded the mountainous regions and territory beyond the borders to cling to the citizenship of heaven,[123] then he sent them to the famous glory of martyrdom. 9. And he commanded this very appropriately, on account of the many rumours of the fickle that there were at that time, for there were many who were then whispering and hissing through their teeth in jealousy, saying: "The deeds of Peter and Paul can also be accomplished by magic and their portents could come from some kind of spell."[124] 10. Indeed, if their demise had appeared to be ordinary and like everyone else's, their case would be nothing great or very marvellous, but if their death was unusual and strange, and if it was unlike those who conquer punishment through magic, but rather was endured patiently even as they were undergoing painful tortures, when many who had previously been brought to the tribunal to receive their sentence suddenly became unseen and invisible and this stage trick was clearly seen to be magic.[125] 11. Hence it was not right for those who had become heralds of the heavenly Kingdom to do such a thing, but rather to really suffer and to show themselves stronger than tortures and by this to demonstrate that, though suffering, they were not overcome, having

---

121 For the tail (σπεῖρα) of the serpent see Rev. 12:4.
122 Cf. 2 Tim. 4:6.
123 On the "citizenship of heaven" as the Christian polity see Phil. 3:20.
124 Compare, for example, Simon Magus in the *Acts of Peter*; Arnobius, *Against the Nations* 1.52.
125 See especially Philostratus, *Life of Apollonius* 1–5, which recounts Apollonius of Tyana's trial before Domitian, where he is charged with sorcery and vanishes. In Philostratus's narrative, however, the sage disappears only after being acquitted. Compare also Eusebius (of Caesarea?), *Against Hierocles* 39.3: "... if in submitting to trial he is not a sorcerer, by escaping from it and from those around the emperor himself, I mean the guards posted around him, he is clearly revealed as a sorcerer."

as they did a reasoning power hard as adamant and unconquerable, and like fire they remained unmoved when struck by the sword.

12. It is for these reasons and because of stupid reasoning [i.e. on the part of the fickle mentioned above] that the saints have been allowed to suffer wrong in the world, since great is the blame given to such as these by crass people. For even when the just are protected [by God] when they are being punished, they are blamed by the unjust, who say, "If they had been allowed to die by painful sufferings, they would not have remained steadfast, but have speedily recanted." 13. And if, conversely, battling the tortures with great patience, they are victorious, they are likewise whispered about by the unscrupulous, who say, "If they were pious, when they were condemned they would not have been overlooked by all-seeing Providence." 14. Thus God, who very much cares for and loves his worthies, snatches some away from sufferings and permits others to suffer, in each case refuting the murmuring of these absurd detractors. 15. For look how Daniel and those with him conquered fire and mastered lions,[126] in order that the Babylonians would know that they were servants of that [God] who made fire and created wild beasts. For since the Babylonians divinized fire, but the boys confuted its caustic power, fittingly were those worshipping the Great God seen to be greater than the god of the Assyrians. 16. But conversely, in order that those worshipping God who had completely escaped the tortures prepared by the Babylonians would not seem unmanly and fearful of the sufferings, for this reason Christ prepared the worshippers of piety to bear the toil of pains nobly, in order that he demonstrate by this too that both those who suffer and those who do not suffer maintain the same opinion towards the Master. 17. Now look at Peter and Paul, who being steadfast against the fear of pains, have given proof of their love for the Saviour in the face of tortures, so that those who are certainly enemies of piety might not find occasion in this for slander and fatuity, saying that Christ had obtained his following by cajolery, but that if he had given them over to adversity they would have refused his company.

15. 1. So, as to the question of why he [Christ] allowed Peter and Paul to suffer, it is fair to say that these are the reasons, but let us elucidate that topic of yours which comes next, namely, what is said about the Antichrist, for he [Christ] says, "See that no one shall lead you astray, for many shall come in my name."[127] 2. If I provide you with the entries and words recorded in

---

126 Dan. 3:24, 6:17–24.
127 Mt. 24:4–5.

BOOK 4   229

chronographies, you will recognize beyond doubt the prescience of Christ, since many misusing the title "Saviour" have enticed many by the way they seemed, and led them in the end to their own destruction.[128] 3. For example, Mani in Persia, who made a show of using the name of Christ,[129] corrupted with error many satrapies and many lands of the East, and even corrupts them today, secretly invading the inhabited world with his destructive seeds.[130] 4. Another in Phrygia, Montanus, having in this way been called by the name "Lord," putting on a fictitious show of asceticism, showing that he was the dwelling place of a wicked demon, has led into error all of Mysia up to Asia; and so strong was the demon lurking and hidden in him that almost the [entire] inhabited world was drowned in the spell of error.[131] 5. What shall I tell you about Cerinthus and Simon, or Marcion, Bardaisan, Droserius, or Dositheus of Cilicia, or myriad others, the throng of which I hesitate to mention, as all these and their followers, having appropriated the name of Christianity, have wrought their unspeakable error in the world?[132] They have made countless prisoners [their] spoils. 6. For example,

---

128 Acts 5:36–37 mentions, for example, Theudas and Judas the Galilean, two first-century figures who led movements in Roman Palestine and whom early Christians considered to be among the "false messiahs" predicted in Mt. 24:4–5. As for the "chronographies" Macarius mentions, he may well have the *Chronicle* and associated *Chronological Tables* of Eusebius of Caesarea in mind, as Mani, Montanus, Marcion, and Bardaisan, all mentioned in what follows, are referenced in the *Chronological Tables*.

129 "Made a show of using the name of Christ" (τὸ ὄνομα τοῦ χριστοῦ ὑποκρινάμενος); here again the text displays its penchant for theatrical metaphors—ὑποκρίνω ("to play a part on the stage," hence, "make a show of," "pretend"), compare above 3.8.16 and 3:29.2 (the Christian), 3.30.2 (the Hellene), etc.

130 Manichaeism was often described as a foreign, "Persian" infiltration of the Roman Empire; compare the language of Diocletian's edict of 302 CE, which expresses the fear that "there is danger that ... they will endeavour, as is their usual practice, to infect the innocent, orderly, and tranquil Roman people, as well as the whole of our empire, with the damnable customs and perverse laws of the Persians as with the poison of a malignant serpent" (*Comparison of Mosaic and Roman Law* XV.3; the proscription of Manichaeans was reiterated by Valentinian I and Valens in 372 CE [*Codex Theodosianus* XVI.5.3]).

131 Montanus and his associates Prisca and Maximilla were second-century Christians who claimed to be prophets inspired by the Holy Spirit; their movement, dubbed "Montanism" and/or the "Phrygian" heresy by late ancient Christian heresiologists, propounded an imminent eschatology. For an early heresiological account of Montanism see Eusebius, *Ecclesiastical History* 5.16–19.

132 Cerinthus was an early second-century "gnostic" Christian. According to Irenaeus (*Against Heresies* 1.26.1–2), he taught that the universe was created by an ignorant Demiurge distinct from the primary God as well as an adoptionist Christology. Simon, or "Simon Magus" (i.e. Simon "the Sorcerer") is often considered the proto-typical heretic in early

those who believe in these antichrists or antigods no longer want to use the name "Christians," but from the name of their leaders they love to be called "Manichaeans," "Montanists," "Marcionites," "Droserianists," and "Dositheists." 7. You see the destructive legions of many antichrists fearfully spurred on against Christ and the Christians, and yet you say that none of those the Saviour predicted has come? You observe the ranks of armed antigods, and yet you reject the Saviour's foreknowledge? One must not reject, but agree with what he said!

16. 1. Enough about these points. Come, let us examine the subtle phrase in the *Apocalypse of Peter* that speaks about the heaven and the earth as though they are things being put on trial: "The earth will present all those judged to God on the Day of Judgment and it will itself be judged with the heaven that surrounds [it]."[133] 2. But that it is not because of a fault of heaven or any wrong of the earth that they are going to be judged is obvious, while the report of the divine words is not false, and this is evident and especially unambiguous. 3. For although we should reject the *Apocalypse of Peter*, we are compelled by the prophetic and evangelical voice to [consider] the *Apocalypse of Peter*, even against our will, for the prophet says,[134] "The

---

Christian heresiology (e.g. Eusebius, *Ecclesiastical History* 2.13.6), though little is known of his doctrines. He is first mentioned in Acts 8:9–24, where he offers Peter money in exchange for the power to bestow the Holy Spirit (hence the origin of the term "simony"). Marcion was a native of Pontus who became a well-respected Christian teacher in Rome in the mid-second century; he wrote the *Antitheses* (no longer extant), a work that compared accounts of God in the Old and New Testaments to argue that the God described in the former is a lesser, just God, while the God proclaimed by Jesus is the perfect, highest God. Bardaisan was a philosopher and polymath of Edessa in the latter half of the second century. He is described by some heresiologists as a Valentinian gnostic (e.g. Eusebius, *Ecclesiastical History* 4.30); of his many works only the *Book of the Laws of Countries*, which deploys ethnographical knowledge in an argument against fatalism, is extant. A "Droserius" appears in the heresiological *Dialogue of Adamantius* (early fourth century) as a proponent of Valentinian gnosticism. Dositheus was a Cilician heretic, he is known only from Macarius. See above 3.43.26, where Macarius describes him as an Encratite, that is, one who advocated strict sexual and alimentary continence.

133 Cf. the Ethiopic version of *Apocalypse of Peter* §4, which C. Detlef and G. Müller translate as "and all this shall the earth give back on the day of decision, since it shall also be judged with them, and the heaven with it." Macarius's quotation of the passage differs from the Hellene's (4.6.1 above) with its inclusion of κρινομένους ("those judged").

134 Macarius rejects the *Apocalypse of Peter* as such, but he acknowledges canonical utterances contained within it; in other words, Macarius appears to argue that the passages of *Apocalypse of Peter* quoted by the Hellene, Is. 34:4, and Mt. 24:35 are all, in essence, the same prophetic utterance. This may account for the difference between the Hellene's and

heaven will be unrolled like a book scroll and all the stars will fall, as leaves fall from a vine, as leaves fall from a fig tree,"[135] and the Gospel says: "The heaven and the earth will pass away, but my words will not at all pass away."[136]

4. Now, it is necessary to avoid a superficial interpretation of these statements. But even if we wish to expound the actual words, we will say it in a hidden way and secretly, making the doctrine persuasive with a figure. 5. What then? The natures of things must now be questioned, as well as their coming to be, [that is] whether [a specific thing] has come to be on account of something, or has come to be for its own sake. For everything made by the Wisdom of the Creator[137] in the creation has come to be either for its own sake, or for the sake of something [else], such as wells, springs, rivers, dry land, mountains, the sea, plants, trees, crops, air, aether, heaven, the sun, stars, the many-phased moon, aquatic creatures, winged creatures, land creatures, quadrupeds; each has not appeared only for the sake of its own existence so that creation obtains completeness through them, but for the sake of humans, in so far as they receive every assistance from them and reap a fitting service from them. 6. But humans are not created for the sake of any other thing, but they have existence for their own sake, so that they alone glorify the Wisdom of the Creator, the rational Wisdom that finely crafted them,[138] and give glory continuously, not as if giving praise and honour to the Creator as a gift—for He has eternal superiority before the creation of the cosmos and humans—but as if by giving glory they enjoy the gift of the one who is glorified and from him they are strengthened in respect of principle of their own essence. 7. For just as one gazing at the sun and praising the ray of light over and over again does not gratify the sun with any encomium—for even before his words it had the ornament of its own brilliance—but gazing at it takes pleasure from the light, makes himself honoured by virtue of where he directs his attention, so too a person honouring the Maker gives no gift to

---

Macarius's quotations of Is. 34:4; that is, Macarius may be quoting his text of Isaiah while the Hellene may be quoting the text as it appeared in the *Apocalypse of Peter*.

135 Is. 34:4.
136 Mt. 24:35.
137 Here Macarius writes, literally, "Wisdom of the Demiurge," using the standard Platonic term for the creator (δημιουργός), while a few lines below in 4.16.6 he uses the biblical terms ὁ κτίσας ("the Creator") and ὁ ποιήσας ("the Maker"); because Macarius uses the Platonic and biblical terms interchangeably we have followed him in the translation.
138 On creative Wisdom see e.g. Prov. 8:22–30 and Wis. 7.

the Creator, but associating himself with divinity, becomes divine. And just as someone who draws near to fire is warmed but does not himself give warmth to the fire, but rather he is warmed by the fire, so too does he who gives glory with genuine praises to [him who] aids him fills himself with glory and much favour. 8. Now since humans exist, as has been said, for no other reason than their own glory, they receive created things as servants for [their] service. The cosmos, then, was certainly created on account of humans, but humans did not come into being for the sake of the cosmos, but for their own sake and for their own honour.

9. Since, then, the cosmos was given for human habitation, after the manner of a great house, but man, upon receiving the creation as his abode, exceedingly neglected his own existence and did not protect the principle of [his] noble lineage, having taken a draught of thoughtlessness he betrayed the favour of Him who granted it, dishonouring and blaming the gift of the Almighty and unlawfully acting quite drunk towards the Divine. For this, seeing [man] behaving madly against, still not paying attention to, and giving offence to the beautiful things [of creation], so that man not ultimately dash even against divine things and fall and be completely destroyed, the Creator determined to send them through death as if into another country in order that, having been loosed from their external surroundings and having vanished when they did, man would come next into an incorruptible mode of life.

10. Hence, since these things have been determined to be mortally dangerous and the master has been expelled from his house, it is necessary that the house also suffer something unpleasant. For as one who guards a tent in a vineyard[139] remains[140] as long as it is right and fit, [that is] until the fruit of the vines has been harvested, but allows the tent to pass away so that it is destroyed and the leaves of the vine fall away and the admired magnificence of the vines passes, so too it is necessary that human nature and substance, residing as if within the tent of the cosmos, leave it once the fruit of piety has been harvested, departing thence, and the beauty of the heaven and earth be extinguished, since the rational essence of humans has left, at the proper hour of the time appointed beforehand.

11. To whom will the splendour of the cosmos be of service any longer? For whom will the streams of the rivers be useful? For whom will the seas

---

139 Cf. Is. 1:8. The "tent," or σκηνή, of one who watches over a vineyard would be a simple "hut" or "lean-to" built of branches.
140 Reading A against Goulet's emendation.

be navigable and the land arable? The crops and seeds of plants and fruits will be counted as nothing when humans are not present. For whom will the heaven kindle the august lamps of its luminous bodies? When the crown of created things has left their midst, will not all vanish? And it will be undone with them, suffering, in a way, with them and judged with them, desiring to be transformed with them and cleansed of all the marks of punishment. 12. For as all people, after being consumed in a universal end, will receive the principle of a second existence in incorruption, so too the whole cosmos, when utterly destroyed with them, will receive a greater beauty in a second [existence], having put off with them [i.e. humans] the garment of misery and having put on with them the robe of impassibility.

13. For if a silversmith who has broken and destroyed a silver vessel that was made long ago renews it by subjecting it to fire to make it stronger without undoing and destroying its whole character as a vessel, yet removing the imperfection from the vessel, he makes it beautiful and new again. Now, if someone who saw it in the first, ugly state <then saw it renewed>, would he not rightly say that the whole vessel has been destroyed, but that its definition as a vessel remains unaltered? Thus, since the whole cosmos is, because of the filth of disobedience that has come to be in it, so to speak, cast into the crucible of the consummation, it must receive a second, better definition of essence, so that one seeing the existence of the second creation in beauty will marvel greatly at the word of the Saviour, who says "The heaven and the earth will pass away, but my words (*logoi*)[141] will not pass away"[142]—that is, this phaenomenal world will pass away, but the Creator's *logos*, remaining in creation, will not pass away, but existing still, this same [*logos*] will renew the whole [universe].[143]

141 Macarius is reading λόγοι here as particular "reason principles" or "thoughts" within the *Logos*.
142 Mt. 24:35.
143 In this complex passage, Macarius invokes the Aristotelean phrase λόγος τῆς οὐσίας ("definition of essence/substance") (*Categories* 1a2) together with the Neoplatonic/early Christian conceptualization of λόγοι/reason principles in the mind of the Demiurge. Macarius's analogy appears confused, however. A material vessel, when purified in a crucible and re-formed can be termed a "vessel"; that is, the name and definition "vessel" applies both to the original, ugly vessel and the re-shaped, beautiful vessel; they share the same "definition of essence" and are synonymous (e.g. *Categories* 1a6–7). The universe, however, when refined in the consummation, takes on a different "definition of essence"; that is, the universe in its pre- and post-consummated conditions do not share the same account of their essence (the former is perishable, for instance, while the latter is imperishable). For

234 MACARIUS, *APOCRITICUS*

14. And if the structure of a house is destroyed by neglect, the design of the builder of the structure is not destroyed. He will rebuild the fallen splendour and will make the house worthy of a better service, with the result that the fall of the house will be considered to have happened for the better. In the same manner, indeed, according to this paradigm, the Creative *Logos* and Indefatigable Builder, having framed the cosmos, will rebuild as splendid what has suffered from much neglect and finally crumbled and is about to perish in vain. For it is necessary that the whole nature and subsistence of created beings, apart from incorporeal beings, receive a second, better creation.[144]

15. Look! The prophetic Word gave us a philosophical teaching by way of an image, saying: "As leaves fall from the vine and as leaves fall from a fig tree."[145] For as the falling of leaves is considered to be the consummation of the comeliness of both the vine and the fig tree, though of course the principle of [the leaves'] existence is not destroyed, but remains to effect [an even] better blossoming, so too heaven, having cast down the comeliness of its starry vaults at the consummation, will receive a second [comeliness], better than what it had before. 16. Consider for me, if you will, both the mystical enigma[146] and the explanation—of the many myriad trees that shed their leaves, it mentions only the vine and the fig tree, not the apple, nor the pear, nor even the willow, though it sheds a thicker shower of leaves, because only the fig tree and likewise the vine do not shed their leaves bit by bit, but all at once. 17. This is probably because each receives the greatest care from the farmers. Thus by these [plants] the passage signifies enigmatically that God, deeming heaven worthy of much solicitude, will not in the end neglect it when it suffers, but like a farmer he will fill it up with all solicitude and ornament. 18. Or perhaps somehow [the Word refers to these plants], because of the accusation associated with them—for at one time a disgraceful tunic was stitched together for Adam

---

Macarius, it is the permanence of the λόγοι or "reason principles" in the Demiurgical *Logos*, expressed in both the pre- and post-consummation universe, that ensures its continuity as the universe.

144 Following the reasoning from 4.16.13 above, Macarius seems to argue that the reason principles (λόγοι) in the Demiurgical *Logos* will be productive of a new nature (φύσις) and subsistence (ὑπόστασις) on the phaenominal plane.

145 Is. 34:4.

146 Τὸ μυστικὸν αἴνιγμα ("mystical riddle/enigma"); the vocabulary of biblical exegesis blends here with that of mystery cult—the enigmatic/symbolic saying reveals hidden, "mystical," truth/meaning to the initiated reader.

from the fig tree,[147] while at another time shameful nudity and reproach came to Noah because of the vine.[148] Since, therefore, passing away is imputed to the cosmos and heaven because of human failings, though it seems that these [human failings] have appeared because of the vine and fig tree, it fittingly said: "As leaves fall from the vine and as leaves fall from the fig tree."

19. But, indeed, this statement seems even more mystical: "The heaven will be rolled up like a book."[149] For when the astrologers no longer read the heaven like tablets, and there is no longer anyone able to philosophize from the writing tablets above, the lecture must be ended, for the students are no longer in school, and the book of the teacher's lessons [must] be rolled up and then reopened in a new and mystical way, when humanity, created according to the image of blessed essence, will be stripped of its affliction, or if I may say, its agedness, when the soul receives the pure crown of glory, when it obtains freedom from painful and harmful things.[150]

20. But since, it says, heaven is the throne of the Creator and the earth his footstool,[151] when these things disappear, where will he who is seated be, and where will his "words" be found? Understand this saying in a sense befitting God and do not confine the Incomprehensible to a throne or footstool! For it is not that we should learn that the Divine is seated, having the earth as a footstool under his feet, that the prophet has inscribed this text for our instruction, but in order that we imagine in our mind the Creator's greatness, without apportioning it into quantity and quality, but knowing it in the power of his unspeakable beauty. 21. For if neither the human eye nor mind has comprehended[152] the heaven, and has not accurately seen the limit of the earth, how much greater would be he who makes the heaven his chair and the earth his footstool? Now, it is certainly not the case that the one who is so seated must suffer when the chair is removed and the footstool likewise taken away, since even before the creation of the heaven and the earth the Divine had a mystical and immoveable throne, as the prophet says "Your

---

147 Cf. Gen. 3:21.
148 Cf. Gen. 9:20–27.
149 Is. 34:4a.
150 The preceding passage makes use of the imagery of late ancient education: "writing tablets" (δέλτοι) were the reusable wax tablets used by students to compose lessons and take notes on a master's lecture (διατριβή); the master is commenting upon, or reading from, a book-roll.
151 Is. 66:1.
152 Cf. 1 Cor. 2:9.

throne, God, [is] forever and ever,"[153] and again "Your throne, Lord, [is] from long ago, you are from eternity";[154] but somewhere another divinely-inspired utterance calls out, saying "You, Lord, have founded the earth and the heavens are the work of your hands; they will be destroyed, but you will remain,"[155] and again: "You are [always] the same and your years will [never] cease."[156] 22. And even if the heaven and the earth suffer something, they will obtain a stronger grace, but their architect, being more ancient and having as the principle of his essence that he is ingenerate, will not suffer anything with them when what is created is destroyed, since he alone has the honour of eternity.

23. Similarly, about the change of created things and natures—the prophet has given an utterance about their destruction, saying: "All will be made old like a garment, you will turn them like a wrap and they will be changed."[157] For as a cloak is knowledge of the fuller, "turning" it in the wash cleans it, and "changing" it makes it brilliant and conspicuous,[158] so too the All-wise and Creative Nature will wipe and cleanse the creation that has been aged for many ages by the dirt of wickedness and make it like a new and brilliant cloak.

24. So much for the interpretation of this utterance according to the literal sense, but I will relate for you another interpretation according to the allegorical sense, so that you may see that the teaching of the divinely-inspired sayings is something multifaceted and admitting of multiple perspectives. For you must understand the passing away of heaven and earth mystically, and must be instructed mystically about the principle of human existence. 25. For, receiving its subsistence from heaven and earth, humanity came to exist as both rational and irrational, taking soul from heaven and body from earth. And the rational exists in the soul, which is also the throne of the divine Word, if, at least, a person orders his way of life[159] in accordance with the principle of his own dignity. But the irrational

---

153 Ps. 44:7 LXX.
154 Ps. 92:2 LXX.
155 Ps. 101:26–27a LXX.
156 Ps. 101:27b LXX.
157 Ps. 101:27b–c LXX.
158 Cf. Mk. 9:3.
159 "Way of life" translates ὑπόθεσις, which can mean "purpose" or "proposal for action," and hence, as here, "way of life," though here it also connotes the "theme" or "subject" of a given piece of oratory. Thus, a rational person will act like a well-trained rhetor: because the soul is the seat of Divine Speech/*Logos*, a rational/*logikos* person will fittingly compose his life as a rhetor composes a fitting speech/*logos*.

exists in the body, which accordingly is the footstool of the Creative *Logos*, who late in time deemed it worthy to become embodied as human, using flesh as a footstool. John the Baptist relates the matter of this mystery as if a secret, "I am not fit to undo the strap of his sandal,"[160] and another of the saints, seeing this portent, says "Worship the footstool of his feet, because it is holy,"[161] for it is not the element of earth that he says to worship (for it is completely accursed),[162] but the salvific and only-begotten body which he wove together in some unutterable way with divinity. 26. Since, then, the human being is fitly [termed] "heaven and earth," and is appropriately [termed] "throne" and "footstool" of the Creator when the divine Word says "I will reside and walk among you,"[163] but it [i.e. human being] has been disturbed by many experiences of evil, and turns this way and that, agitated by affairs so that it is no longer able to be a residence or throne of the Maker. For this reason God has economically determined that all humanity will pass away in a universal consummation from this painful life, and that all the splendour here below will fall from glory after the manner of the stars, and that it will disappear together with them, so that they will receive a second mode of existence in a second life and the saying that states: "There will be a new heaven and a new earth"[164] will be fulfilled.

17. 1. These [matters have been dealt with] sufficiently, but next, regarding your objection concerning the parable, I will add some remarks about the mustard seed, leaven, and pearl, [to show] that he [i.e. Christ] very fittingly likens the Kingdom of heaven to these things. For great realities that have an invisible constitution are not explained by great themes, but rather by things that among humans are considered simple, small, and of no account. 2. If, then, you are willing to examine the diligence and that arduous labour and attention of those who do philosophy, you will discover precisely the theme of the present discourse. For when they seek to comprehend in thought the prodigious expanse of land that is full of mountains and hills and laden with peaks, they do not represent it by means of something exceedingly bulky and with a great body, but by means of a small point that completely lacks mass, which cannot be divided in depth or breadth.

---

160 Lk. 3:16.
161 Ps. 98.5 b–c LXX.
162 If Macarius means that the ground is accursed, in contrast to the custom of worshipping it, his authority is Gen. 3:17.
163 2 Cor. 6:16. Where the received text has "among them," Macarius reads "among you."
164 Is. 65:17.

And so they compare this great and massive earth, and in order to grasp it from a point they pursue their speculations, devoting the entire day to the matter and embracing a whole night's labour of study. For they represent it [i.e. the earth] as a small grain within a figurative conception of the heaven. There are also those who measure the heaven, which is incomprehensible to human nature, with a small sphere. 3. You should know this from the wisdom of Aratus of Cilicia who, investigating the nature of things visible and especially of heavenly things, inscribed in a small sphere the whole course of the upper regions, representing such great orbits of the heavenly bodies with such a sorry little device.[165] What need is there to mention to you those who dare compare the atomic nature, on account of its delicacy, to the All-wise and Unbegotten Essence?[166]

4. If, then, you do not deny the intelligence of the philosophers, for what reason do you censure likening the Kingdom of heaven to leaven? What is there about yeast worthy of slander, [yeast] which readies flour into something life giving for humans, and though something most small, harnesses the qualities of myriad measures for the making of bread? For strengthening and leavening the just-moistened billows of flour, it perfects a well-arranged and easy-to-digest combination, and brings to successful completion the principal sustenance of life. But without leaven, bread tastes bad and is slack, and is not fit to the taste or as nourishment. 5. If, then, the Kingdom of heaven has strengthened a way of life that had fallen into disorder, in a way "leavening" into appropriate order what was previously dispersed as slack, un-nourishing, loose, and censurable, what is strange in this matter? What is alien about the act of perfecting? What is distressing or out of the ordinary about this occurrence, if the Principle of hypercosmic realities, in sympathy with us, mixed himself with us, bringing our essence through this communion into alignment with the virtue proper, if I may say, to its allotted condition? This is similar to the leaven that a woman takes (the creation, clearly) and hides in three measures of dough,[167] [that

---

165 Aratus of Soloi in Cilicia (c.315–240 BCE) was well known in the Hellenistic and Roman worlds for his writings on astronomy. Macarius's reference to those who represent the earth as a small grain (κέγχρος) refers to Aratus and/or his commentators; compare Achilles Tatius's introduction to Aratus's *Phaenomena*, which imagines placing a grain (κέγχρος) in the middle of an inflated balloon or bladder (φῦσα) to conceptualize a stationary earth within the heavens (*Isagoga excerpta* 4.59–64).
166 Macarius assumes (correctly) that the Hellene, as a Platonist, would agree in condemning Epicurean atomism and "atheism."
167 Mt. 13:33.

is] in the past and present times and the future, for mixing and making the ages, to perfect the beginning, middle, and end, to complete the human body, spirit, soul, and seal with grace the height, depth, and breadth.[168]

6. And if it is likened to a mustard seed, it is not slighted, but glorified.[169] For the mustard seed, being small and exceedingly miniscule, is very pungent and hot, and draws out and cleanses head congestion. Sprinkled liberally on food at table it effects the health of the guests. It thins the thickness of hidden phlegm, while it also cuts the moisture of harmful fluids. When sown, it is as if it is invisible on account of its fineness, but when it sprouts, it resembles tree trunks in height.

7. So if, indeed, the passage likens the activity of the Kingdom of heaven to a mustard seed, [which] cleansing serpentine evils from the heart, drying [the heart] of the liquids of intemperance and all moisture of lack of discipline, calms a great fever and imperceptibly draws out the mass of the bile of sins and heals people, while as if mingled in the gathering of the crowd it makes the thoughts of souls steadfast, and contrives to make the whole rational being healthy, stinging with reproaches and cutting with teaching, heating and lighting the fire of rationality with compassion, lying down and rising up together with those who study divine things, being sown in the cosmos and revealing the hypercosmic fruit of virtue, thrown into the earth and leading the earthly up to sanctification—if indeed then its labour is so great and efficacious of good things, it is fittingly likened to the mustard seed, on account of the subtlety of its actions. For it is not [likened] to a bean or any other of the legumes, whose principle the Hellenes in their folly asserted to be divine,[170] but to the mustard seed, on account of purity, and likewise to the pearl on account of its great value.

8. As this first and peerless adornment in the cosmos[171] comes into existence in a watery environment (clearly, in the flesh), so the divinity of the one who has resided [among us] has come into being in the flesh, and filling the flesh with untroubled light, adorned the life of those who

---

168 Cf. Eph. 3:18. There are Platonic resonances here as well, cf. *Timaeus* 73a–c.
169 Mk. 4:31; Mt. 13:31; 1 Thess. 5:23.
170 Macarius has in mind Pythagorean reverence for the bean (e.g. Diogenes Laertius, *Lives of the Philosophers* 8.19, 24, 34; Porphyry, *Life of Pythagoras* 43–44; Iamblichus, *Life of Pythagoras* 24).
171 Literally "cosmos in the cosmos" (κόσμος ἐν κόσμῳ), a pun difficult to capture in English. The "world" or "cosmos" (κόσμος) is a beautifully ordered whole, while "cosmos" can also refer to any type of adornment, like a pearl. Macarius uses the same word play above at 2.31.4.

travail in virtue, making to shine with many virtuous actions whomever has procured this pearl sincerely through good works.

9. Thus the Salvific Word likened himself to the things just mentioned in a manner appropriate to the Divine and plausibly—not implausibly as you claim, not presenting mysteries as if to children or as if to the ignorant, but to men who are sound and perfect in mind, and are also children who have not tasted the depravity of the Devil.[172] But from those who are wise in evil and from those who have detestable thoughts in their perversity, he concealed the treasures of the heavenly doctrines and closed the doors of real understanding.

18. 1. These responses are sufficient, in my judgment. Hence, if it seems good, let us examine the question about the sinners who are called and the just who are not called, and the meaning of those who are healthy and those who are sick who need a physician.[173]

2. By this, Christ clearly indicates two orders: one, the healthy (the just, clearly), the other, the ill (which he also explicitly calls "sinful").[174] He has taught about two rational essences and natures: one that lacks and another that does not lack, indicating the angelic and human *hypostases* [respectively]. 3. And the substance of the angels, being just, is never called to repentance, for it is not accused of anything about which it should repent. It measures [its] correctness with an infallible ruler, as it is near the highest and entirely eudaimonic bliss, [and] as it is allotted the pure abode, as it studies[175] the pure and unmixed ray of light, as it has received the highest region of incorruption to inhabit. It is free of hubris, blame, and blemish, and uncontaminated by stain, guile, and evil, and drives away the affliction of sins, and does not need correction nor any conversion. 4. This incorporeal essence of the hypercosmic beings, therefore, which is indeed the guardian of indestructible rank, having a way of life that consists in blameless virtue, a life of innocence and unalloyed love, being in the presence of the Just with justice, is never reproached. Being within the enclosure of immortality, it is a life[176] without illness and old age; having a

---

172 The contrast between the "perfect man" (ἀνὴρ τέλειος) and "children" (νήπιοι) at Eph. 4:13–14 appears to have been combined with the celebration of childhood innocence at Mt. 18:3 and 1 Cor. 14:20.
173 Cf. Lk. 5:31.
174 Lk. 5:31.
175 Φιλοσοφοῦσα, literally, "philosophizes."
176 Αἰών ("life," or "aeon"), a title for hypercosmic, eternal beings in late ancient cosmologies.

pure and enduring dwelling place, it exists forever together with the King of the Ages.

5. Human nature, by contrast, is also rational and a participant and receiver of noetic light, having the capacity not to fall short of the angelic glory in any way, but, having chosen, with advice, the way of sloth, it fell from the better [state], becoming passionately attached to the matter of pedestrian things; plastering itself with the rubbish of these cares, and having sunken in a lake of deceit, the soul grew feeble and the mind disabled. 6. Thus, it took to its bed, burning with the fever of sins, being utterly consumed by the suffering that had befallen it, it did not have law, it did not know obedience, or order, or reason, or philosophical thought, or the practice or life of [the] ascetic rule. Afflicted, it has been cast into the sickbed of the body, a stranger and alien of the sacred regions, foreign and hostile to the heavenly teaching, not seeing the brightness of the court of the blessed, having spread before it a great veil, an ignoble abode,[177] beautyless quarters, it is cast out from the company of the pious assemblies and barred from divine providence. 7. As a result [the Divine] was almost afflicted as well by so great a change and transformation in the rational essence (as utterly good Providence knows compassion, even though it does not experience passion) and commiserated the fall that had come from negligence, so that God the Word, in order that rational nature might rise up, descended in sympathy, so as to call the unjust to justice, and to make those harmed by sin healthy by grace, with the result that the healer opportunely says to the one healed: "Behold, you are healed, sin no more."[178] 8. So he who toils not took on the weakness of those who toil, and what is undefiled received the tinge of that which suffers, and what is most high [took on] the property of what is humble, and what is blessed [took on] the lump that was accursed,[179] with the result that the immortal was braided together with the mortal, and

---

177 Cf. Heb. 10:20.
178 Jn. 5:14.
179 Τὸ φύραμα, translated here as "lump," denotes something mixed together, like dough; here it refers to the compound of soul and body in the human being (see 4.16.25 above, where the human being derives its *hypostasis* from soul and body). The word appears in Rom. 11:16 ("If the dough offered as first fruits is holy, so is the whole lump" [RSV]), as well as 1 Cor. 5:6 ("Do you not know that a little yeast leavens the whole lump?"), and was often read Christologically and soteriologically in terms of the Son's assumption of humanity; cf. e.g. Gregory of Nyssa: "... the Lord of the creature ... becomes Man while still remaining God, being both God and Man in the entirety of the two several natures, and thus humanity was indissolubly united to God, the Man that is in Christ conducting the work of mediation, to Whom, by the first fruits assumed for us, all the lump is potentially united" (*Against*

became a door[180] for what was shut out, and the Creator became an entrance for the creature, with the result that the incorruptible was mysteriously united with the corruptible and what is without sin reclined together on the sick bed with sinners, yet did not fall together with them, but raised them up together with him, so that the entire economy was effected by his immutable nature and principle, and he who was true to the Law came to be with those who were lawless, and that what is just gladly accepted the way of life of the unjust and took up the organ [i.e. of the body] of those who had been condemned, and using this medium and service, almost led back to their proper strength by means of his exceeding love of humanity those who had been thrown out and were almost stinking with the disease of disobedience in his own proper strength by means of his exceeding love of humanity. 9. For this is proper to the nature that is perfectly good: not to rejoice only in the just whom he possesses,[181] nor to take pleasure simply in those who are healthy, nor to participate brilliantly only with hypercosmic realities, but also to lead the unjust to the enjoyment of just things, and to lead the afflicted by the hand to the health of the strong, and to lead those harassed in the world of wickedness to the good order of hypercosmic realities, and to make all into one herd,[182] kept safe by the great herdsman, [a herd that] resides on the earth, above the earth, and is well ordered.

10. Now, it is possible to see that starting right from the beginning he called to sinful human nature, saying to Adam: "Adam, where are you?"[183] and saying to Cain "Have you sinned; be quiet,"[184] he taught Enos to call upon the Divine, <***>[185] begetting [Methusaleh], calling him [i.e. Enoch] to repentance and making him pleasing to God by this repentance,[186] calling Noah and through him saving his kinfolk. And he called Abraham

---

Eunomius 2.12 [NPNF 122]). Here Macarius alludes to Rom. 11:16 and 1 Cor. 5:6 to liken the effect of the incarnation to the leavening power of yeast in dough.

180 Cf. Jn. 10:9.

181 Cf. Lk. 15:7.

182 Macarius's term here is ἀγέλη ("herd"), but is a clear allusion to Jn. 10:16 ("I must herd these [sheep] and they will listen to my voice, and they will become one flock [ποίμνη], a single flock.").

183 Gen. 3:9.

184 Gen. 4:7.

185 We agree with Goulet in positing a *lacuna* here; "he taught Enos to call upon the Divine" seems to refer to Gen. 4:26, while the clauses that follow in the manuscript ("begetting him, calling him to repentance and making him pleasing to God by this repentance") likely allude to Gen. 5:22, a passage that concerns Enoch.

186 Cf. Gen. 5:22.

himself through faith, but once he erred he [God] made him a tablemate and hearth mate with the angels.[187] He called to all sinners in general who were beaten by the stripes[188] of disobedience. Even if you mention the patriarchs and those of Moses's day and the prophets themselves—all were called and through the call all showed themselves to be just by not dismissing the caller's call nor disdaining the gift of munificence.

11. But it is necessarily the case that the angels who are with him, being just and enjoying the good fortune of the realm of justice, are not called; for who would call inside those who are inside, as if they are outside? Clearly it is necessary to lead with goodness those who have been cast far off from the heavenly halls and to call with love of humanity to those who are afflicted, not to those who are healthy, to prescribe homeopathic remedies, and to administer what is able to soothe the ailment of those who are fevered and suffering terribly, and to sit beside those who are aggrieved by treachery or illness.

12. But if humanity had preserved the law of the first injunction and observed the precept of the command,[189] the Creator would not have become physician; nor would the Maker have entered into the shabbiness of that which he called, if human nature had been inside the heavenly latticed gates and had a life without illness and incorruptible. 13. But since, as I was saying, it [humanity] neglected the injunction that was given and disregarded the lordly order, the maladies of sins adhered to it and a swarm of injustices harassed the soul. Once rationality had been abandoned, fear immediately set in, and [humanity] was in need of an advocate and compassionate healer.[190] Immediately the host called back him who had committed injustice, saying, "Where are you?" and saying to another: "What have you done?"[191] Calling another he separated him from men.[192] To another he says, "Go out from your land and from your

---

187 Gen. 18:1ff.
188 Cf. Is. 53:5; Lk. 12:47.
189 Macarius may allude to God's command in Gen. 2:16–17 against eating of the tree of knowledge, as suggested by the elaboration of the divine economy that follows. Irenaeus (*Against Heresies* 3.48.3 and 5.16.2) appears to hold that the Word would have become incarnate even had Adam and Eve not sinned, in order to reveal the perfect image of the Father. In the time of Macarius, however, theologians were more likely to follow Athanasius (e.g. *On the Incarnation*) in viewing the incarnation as a remedy for transgressions which, though foreseen, were not inevitable.
190 Cf. Ps. 111:10 on the propaedeutic use of fear.
191 Gen. 3:9, 4:10.
192 Perhaps a reference to Cain in Gen. 4:14–15.

kinfolk," and to another: "The time of every person passes before me; now therefore, do what I tell you."[193]

14. He spoke to one, but thundered to all, calling all to repentance and correction, when he said to another "Loose your sandal of old habits, for I have come down to deliver the afflicted,"[194] and to another "'I am the commander-in-chief of the divine powers, now I have drawn near'[195] and do not be shaken by the cares of bodily waves"; to another "Whom shall I send, and who will go to the people?";[196] to another: "Receive my words in your mouth."[197] 15. He deified another, calling him "son of man,"[198] and plainly talked about another as "son of [my] desires."[199] He called and invited all after [their] transgressions, at one time, as physician, treating those who were wasted away, at another time, as just, admonishing the unjust no longer to live unjustly; at one time, as the divine *Logos*, making rational beings gods,[200] then, as Christ, making them christs; as incorruptible, making them incorruptible, then, being immortal, guiding mortals into immortality. He called every race of men into the happy well-being of blessednesss, and calls them up to the present day.

16. For do not think that he called them only during the time when he had become human, but that he neglected to call them before the incarnation and after his blessed assumption of the flesh, but that he calls all those who transgress and summons them indefinitely, or rather, in the aorist, saying "I came not to call the just, but sinners,"[201] that is, "I came also to Adam, and I came also to the sons of Noah; I came to the patriarchs and to all the human tribes alike." 17. For if he was saying, "I am not present," or "I have not come now to call," then he would rightly be thought only to have called some at that time, when he was incarnate. But here he says "I came not,"[202] from the outset showing that the time of

---

193 Gen. 12:1, 6:13–14.
194 Ex. 3:5, 8.
195 Jos. 5:14.
196 Is. 6:8.
197 Jer. 1:9.
198 Cf. Ez. 2:1.
199 Goulet notes that this phrase recalls Dan. 9:23, which in the LXX reads ὅτι ἐλεεινὸς εἶ ("because you have received [my] mercy") but in Theodotion reads ὅτι ἀνὴρ ἐπιθυμιῶν σὺ εἶ ("because you are a man of [my] desires") (Goulet [2003], 421).
200 On the saints as gods see Jn. 10:34–35, quoting Ps. 82:6.
201 Mk. 2:17.
202 Macarius reads the aorist of Mk. 2:17 (οὐκ ἦλθον καλέσαι) as pointing to the perfective aspect of the verb, that is, that the action of "calling" is a single, undivided event, whereas if

BOOK 4

his *parousia* is limitless, and that he makes his call from the beginning up to the consummation.

18. But if many of those who are called have put off coming to the call, it is not the fault of the one who is calling, since neither is the sun, which summons all people [to see] with its own brightness, the cause of blindness for those lying asleep in their drunkenness. Rather, they are the cause of darkness for themselves with their voluntary choice of vice. Likewise, Christ calls all to the ray of the Father's love of humanity, but if some, being drunk on the demon's evil, choose darkness over the blessed light, this choice of life must not be ascribed to Christ but to human nature and choice, which has the power to incline to the better and the worse alike, whichever way it wills and wishes.

19. Since the present grand theme has been addressed sufficiently, we must be silent. But if another passage of the divine teachings presents an *aporia* for you, as if it scratches at you, bring this out into our midst, holding nothing back, for in this too there will be more than casual exercise.

19. 1. *He, as if moved by some high-flown diatribe, offered us at length a Homeric quotation, saying with a great mocking chuckle*:

Homer with good reason enjoined the Hellenes to calm their manly courage, when he recounted Hector's rash proposal, speaking in verse to the Hellenes:

"Keep still Argives," he says, "hold your fire young Achaeans,
for Hector of the flashing helmet wants a word with you."²⁰³

And now we all sit in a similar silence, for the interpreter of Christian doctrines has promised and confirmed that he will explain the principal obscurities of the Scriptures!

2. But tell us then, my good friend, as we attend to what you are explaining, why the Apostle says: "But such were some [of you]!"—here he clearly means wretches—"but you have been washed, you have been made holy, you have been justified in the name of the Lord Jesus Christ and in the Spirit of God"?²⁰⁴ 3. For we marvel and our soul is truly puzzled at this: that a person who has just once been washed of such stains and pollutions will appear pure; if, having been mixed up in such stupid defilement in his

---

Christ had meant to say that he came at a specific historical moment he would have used the present or perfect tenses.

203 Homer, *Iliad* 3.82–83. The words are Agamemnon's, who urges the Greek to hold fire as Hector steps out of the battle line to arrange single combat between Paris and Menelaus.
204 1 Cor. 6:11.

life—fornication, adultery, drunkenness, theft, sodomy, poisonings, and myriad foul and dirty things—and having only been baptized and having called upon the name of Christ, he is easily freed and all the guilt sloughs off like the old skin off a serpent.[205]

4. Who would not dare, then, to do wicked things both mentionable and unmentionable, and attempt things that have never been put in words and actions that have never been done, knowing that he will receive absolution from such accursed deeds by having merely believed and being baptized and by hoping to obtain forbearance after doing them from the one who is coming to judge both the living and the dead?[206] 5. These [statements of Paul] encourage him who hears them to sin. They teach [him] to do what is lawless on each and every occasion. They are intended to banish the teaching of the Law and [encourage the idea] that what is just prevails in no way in its own right against what is unjust. They introduce an unlawful way of life into the world and teach that impiety is not to be feared at all, when a person can put away a heap of myriad injustices once he has merely been baptized.

20–21a. 1. So that is the refined artifice of that statement. Yet let us expressly examine the question of the monarchy of the One God and the polyarchy of the gods that are worshipped, since you do not even understand how to explain the doctrine of monarchy. 2. For "monarchy" does not mean *existing* alone, but *ruling* alone. But he rules, evidently, over [beings] of the same kind and like him, as the Emperor Hadrian was monarch not because he was alone, or because he ruled cattle and sheep, which shepherds and cowherds rule, but because he reigned over humans of the same species and having the same nature [as he]. Likewise, God would not properly be called "monarch" unless he ruled over gods—for this is fitting for divine greatness and great heavenly dignity.

3. For if you say that angels stand beside God, being impassible, immortal, and incorruptible in nature, which we term "gods" on account of their nearness to the Godhead, what does this dispute about the name amount to, beside the conclusion that the difference is only one of nomenclature? 4. For she who is called "Athena" by the Greeks, the Romans call "Minerva," but the Egyptians, Syrians, and Thracians name her differently. Certainly nothing is changed or detracted from the appellation of "god" by the

---

[205] On the cheapness of the grace offered Christians cf. Origen, *Against Celsus* 3.49, Julian, *Caesars* 336b.
[206] Cf. 2 Tim. 4:1.

BOOK 4   247

difference in name.²⁰⁷ 5. Now, whether one names them "gods" or "angels," the difference is no great thing, since their divine nature is testified to²⁰⁸ when Matthew writes thusly: "And Jesus replying said, 'You err, not knowing the Scriptures or the power of God, for in the resurrection they will neither marry or be given in marriage, but they will be as angels in heaven.'"²⁰⁹

21b. 1. Therefore, as it is agreed that the angels participate in divine nature,²¹⁰ those who give the appropriate reverence to the gods do not think that the god is *in* the wood or the stone or the bronze from which the mere image is fashioned, nor if a piece of the statue is broken off do they judge the divine power to be diminished. 2. For the wooden statues and the temples were established by the ancients as a memorial, so that those passing by and coming in would come to think about God, or taking leisure and purifying themselves from all else, that they would make use of prayers and supplications, each one asking of them whatever he needed. 3. For if one makes an image of a friend, he does not at all think the friend himself is *in* it, or that the limbs of the friend's body are enclosed within the limbs of the painting, but he [wants] to honour his friend through the image. But the sacrifices offered to the gods do not so much give honour to them as much as they are evidence of the motive of those sacrificing and of the fact that they must not approach them ungratefully. 4. But, fittingly,

---

207 In his response to this section (4.26.1 q.v.), Macarius argues that the Hellene's argument is based upon a misunderstanding of the Aristotelean concept of homonymy (*Categories* 1a1–2). In fact, the Hellene is arguing that (Christian) angels and (Hellenic) gods, like the ethnically specific names for a particular deity, are polynyms, a concept left undiscussed in the *Categories* but inferred by later commentators, for example Porphyry, who writes that "... polynyms are things that have several different names, but one and the same account [i.e. of essence] ... Polynyms seem to be the opposite of homonyms" (Porphyry, *Commentary on Aristotle's Categories* 69.1 [trans. Strange]).

208 Again, the Hellene means that "god" and "angel" are polynyms because they refer to beings sharing a common definition of essence, here "divine nature."

209 Mt. 22:29–30.

210 "Participate in divine nature" translates θείας φύσεως ... μετέχειν. Goulet ([2003], 311) notes an interesting marginal gloss on this phrase: οὐκ ἐστὶν ἀληθὲς τοῦτο ("this is not true"). The sense of the genitive absolute is somewhat ambiguous in this clause, as is the relation between angels' participation in divine nature and the beliefs about divine beings being contained in statues expressed in the subsequent clause. The sense seems to be "Therefore, just as we agree [with you, i.e. Christians] that angels participate in divine nature, so too those who give the appropriate reverence to the gods do not think that the god is *in* the wood or the stone ..." The translation, however, attempts to retain the ambiguity of the genitive absolute. See also Goulet ([2003], 425).

the shape of the statues is anthropomorphic, since humans are considered to be the finest of living beings and the image of God.[211] And it is possible to confirm this dogma from another passage, which maintains that God has fingers with which he writes; it says: "And he gave Moses the two tablets of stone written by the finger of God."[212] 5. But even the Christians, imitating the construction of temples, build great houses, within which they gather to pray, even though nothing hinders them doing this in [their own] homes, since clearly the Lord can hear them everywhere.[213]

22. 1. But if one of the Hellenes is so empty in his opinions as to think the gods reside within the statues, how much purer is the thought of one who believes that the Divine entered into the womb of Mary the Virgin and became an embryo and once born, was swaddled, covered with the blood of afterbirth and bile and with things still much more incongruous than these?

23. 1. I would also like to show, from the Law, the oft-seen name of the gods, in the passage that calls out and with great awe admonishes: "You shall not speak ill of the gods and you shall not speak badly of the one ruling your people."[214] For here it does not mean [any] others than those thought by us to be gods, as we know from the passage "Do not follow after *gods*,"[215] and again: "If you follow after and worship other *gods*."[216] 2. That it means not men, but gods, and those considered such by us, not only Moses but also Joshua his successor says to the people: "And now fear him and worship him alone and forsake the gods which your fathers worshipped."[217] And Paul says, not about men but about incorporeal beings: "If those who are called gods are many and there are many lords, both on earth and in heaven, for us rather there is one God and Father from whom is everything."[218] 3. Thus you are in every way mistaken in thinking that God

---

211 This discussion of statues and sacrifices encapsulates common apologetical arguments; compare for example Celsus in Origen, *Against Celsus* 7.62; Sallustius, *Concerning the Gods and the Universe* 16; Julian, *Letter* 89B).
212 Ex. 31:18.
213 The Hellene may be slyly invoking the logic of Jn. 4:24 and Lk. 17:21.
214 Ex. 22:27.
215 Cf. Jer. 7:6, 9.
216 Deut. 13:3.
217 Josh. 24:14.
218 Cf. 1 Cor. 8:5–6; the Hellene's quotation expands on the received text: "For even if there are so-called gods." In his response, Macarius quotes the passage as "For even if there are gods." Goulet ([2003], 428) notes that these do not reflect any known variants of 1 Cor. 8:5–6. The Hellene's assertion that Moses references and honours the Hellenic gods can

is irritated if another is called "god" and has his appellation, when rulers do not begrudge their subjects homonymy,[219] nor masters their slaves. It is indeed not admissible to think God more mean spirited than men![220]

24. 1. Enough about the existence of the gods and that it is necessary that they be honoured. But it remains necessary to explain the resurrection of the dead. For why will God do this? And the succession of creatures up to now, by which he decided the species are preserved and not interrupted, will he abruptly undo what he legislated and regulated from the beginning? But what once seemed good to God and has been preserved in this way forever ought to be the same forever, not be condemned by the one who created it, nor should it be destroyed, as if brought into being by a human and established as mortal by a mortal. 2. Hence it is irrational if, after the whole [cosmos] is destroyed, the resurrection follows; if he will resurrect one having died, if you will, three days before the resurrection and along with him Priam and Nestor, who died thousands of years before, and others before them, since the creation of humanity.[221] 3. But if one wants to investigate this fully, he will find the matter of the resurrection a heap of ridiculousness. For many have often been lost at sea and their bodies consumed by fish; many others, have been devoured by wild beasts and birds. How, then, will their bodies rise, and what sort of bodies?

4. Come, let us investigate what I said closely. For instance: someone is shipwrecked, then mullets eat his body, then some fishermen eat the [fish] that ate him, and they, in turn, are devoured by dogs; crows and vultures completely consume the dogs when they die. Now, how will the body of the sailor be reassembled, digested as it is by so many animals? And indeed, another [person] is destroyed by fire and another brought to an end by

---

be compared with Julian, *Against the Galilaeans* apud Cyril of Alexandria, *Against Julian* 238c–d; 290b.

219 Here the Hellene uses the term "homonymy," and Macarius seems to grasp that this is meant in a technical, that is grammatical or Aristotelean, sense in his reply at 4.29 below. The Hellene's comparison is that, just as a ruler does not begrudge his subjects' sharing the same appellation "human," God does not bristle at other beings having the homonymous appellation "god."

220 A tacit contrast may be intended here between the jealous god of Exodus 20:5 and Plato's maxim that the divine cannot harbour jealousy (*Timaeus* 29d).

221 Compare Augustine, *Letter* 102.8 (= Porphyry, *Against the Christians*. fr.81 [Harnack] and Jerome, *Letter* 133.9 (= Porphyry, *Against the Christians* fr.82 [Harnack]). Goulet ([2003], 429) also notes a parallel with Ambrose, *De bonis mortis* X.46; see also discussion in Courcelle (1964), 160.

vermin—how and in what manner will they turn back into the distinct subsistent individuals they were originally?[222]

5. But you will say to me that this is possible for God, which is not true. For he is not capable of everything. For instance, he is not able to cause Homer not to have been a poet, or Ilium not to have been conquered. Nor, of course, two when doubled being four, can he make it add up to one hundred, even if it seems pleasing to him. 6. But neither is God ever able to become evil, even if he wants, nor, being by nature good, would he be able to sin.[223] Now if he is such that it is impossible for him to sin or to be evil, this is not ascribed to God as a deficiency. Those who have from nature a disposition and fitness for something, and are then prevented from doing it, are clearly prevented by deficiency. But God has as his nature to be good and is not prevented from being evil, but at the same time that he is not prevented, he is unable to become evil.[224]

24b. 7. But consider how irrational this is if, on the one hand, the Creator overlooks the heaven, a beauty more marvellous than one has ever conceived, when it is dissolved and the stars are fallen, and the earth destroyed utterly, while on the other hand, he will raise the putrified and corrupted bodies of humans, one group [of bodies] that were excellent, but others that were unattractive, disproportioned, and unpleasant to the eyes before they died. 8. But even if he is able easily to resurrect [them all] with a proper composition, it is impossible for the earth to hold [all those] who have died since the creation of the cosmos, if they were to rise.[225]

---

222 ὥς οἷόν τε εἰς τὴν ἐξ ἀρχῆς ἐπανελθεῖν ὑπόστασιν. The problem of the resurrection of human bodies metabolized by animals was perennial in discussions about the resurrection. J. Pépin (1964) argues that Porphyry developed a version of this argument. Goulet ([2003], 276–278) cites parallels in Pseudo-Justin, *Questions and Responses to the Orthodox* 15 (= Porphyry, *Against the Christians* fr. 93 [Harnack]) and Augustine, *City of God* XXII.12, 20. A closer verbal parallel is Cyril of Jerusalem, *Catechetical Lectures* 18.2.

223 On the necessary goodness of the divine see *Timaeus* 29d.

224 On the union of necessity and freedom in the first principle see Plotinus, *Enneads* 3.8.4. Here and above at 4.2.4 the Hellene's argument that an omnipotent God need not contradict logic, his own essential goodness, or the natural order is associated explicitly with Porphyry by Didymus the Blind (*Commentary on Job* 280.22–28): "Some, among whom are Porphyry and those like him, sophistically assert that, if all things are possible for God, then he is able to lie, and if all things are possible for the believer, then he is able to make a bed or make a man."

225 The Hellene's objections to the resurrection here strongly resemble those rebutted in the treatises *On the Resurrection* ascribed to Athenagoras (esp. chapter 4) and Justin, *1 Apology* (esp. chapters 2 and 4).

25. 1. *Having let fly such a clever harangue,*[226] *the Hellene seemed to confuse us with questions and to have cast us into the throes of helplessness. But we, earnestly supplicating that which secretly reveals deep things from the shadows and which teaches men the clearest knowledge,*[227] *replied to each of the statements in the right way, saying to the picked man:*[228]

Your propositions are great and exceedingly obscure, but receive a response cleverer than they, as Christ supplies the exposition for you through us. Listen as we speak about the first topic first, the second in a second discourse, then the third together with the fourth and fifth, then the sixth with the seventh question.[229]

2. First, then, we must speak about the utterance of the Apostle, which says: "And such were some of you, but you have been washed, but you have been made holy, but you have been justified in the name of our Lord Jesus Christ and in the Spirit of our God."[230] Here, then, will be the proemium of our theme.

3. The creature, after committing offence is accustomed to receive the free gift of mercy from the Uncreated Nature,[231] to be saved by grace, and to be released from the judgment of sins, since one who becomes a worker of evil and is punished by the legal reckoning of the judge is saved only by the philanthropy of the king,[232] having merely entreated [him] and supplicated him a single time. 4. For when the law has rigorously convicted a person in order to preserve justice, the king, being lord of the law, has

---

226 Possibly an allusion to Socrates's characterization of Thrasymachus's self-satisfaction with his speech in Plato, *Republic* 344d.

227 Goulet identifies a possible allusion to Dan. 2:22: "He reveals deep and hidden things, knowing what lies in shadow."

228 "To the picked man" = τῷ λογάδι. This is another of Macarius's heroicizing gestures. In classical Greek literature "picked men" are the most skilled warriors chosen for the most difficult battles. In later usage, the term can also refer to "choice phrases" (e.g. Photius, *Bibliotheca* 491B), and so could be translated here as an instrumental dative "saying with a choice statement," but given Macarius's desire to portray the debate as heroic single combat "picked man" is more likely.

229 On the import of this comment for the overall structure of the *Apocriticus*, see the Introduction.

230 1 Cor. 6:11.

231 This notion is both Christian (e.g. Athanasius, *On the Incarnation* 8) and Platonic (e.g. *Symposium* 191b).

232 "The king" translates ὁ βασιλεύς. Where Macarius seems to refer generally to a ruler, the word has been translated "king," while when he appears to refer to contemporary examples of rule it has been translated "emperor." On Macarius's ambivalent attitude to emperors and empire see the Introduction.

shown him mercy, not warping justice by this act, but proving his power as master from his sympathy and correcting injustice not by chastisement but by saving the unworthy. 5. Now many who have received a sentence of death from the law have, by appealing to the emperor, had it overturned, which demonstrates that the philanthropy of the emperor is stronger than [evil] deeds. For in this is the promise of lordly power preserved— in generously remitting the slave's debt and in gratuitously restoring the convict's dignity. 6. But any action whatsoever is judged exactly as is due; there is no help from the judge, and it is evaluated on its own merits. If, therefore, the Font of Grace were to extend nothing of grace to humans, but were to judge everything by the measure of the Law, it would no longer be grace, but the inquisitor of habits and actions.

7. And why for us who have accomplished nothing worthy of light did the Creator supply light as a gift? Why for created beings did he prepare an abode, beings not at all aware of the reason for the abode? 8. For if all that God gives is a gift and grace, and though he receives nothing from creatures he makes creatures wealthy, it is reasonable also that he would free sinners of their fault, as a father has pity on sons who behave senselessly. But it would not be just that the natures of creatures obtain lustre by their own virtue, since then the beauty of goodness would be hidden and the generosity of the Creator be invisible. 9. For if the universe had not been granted life by illumination from what is superior and the nonexistent did not receive existence from the existent, having this as a gift given from grace, not as something given in exchange, each of the visible things would be invisible and would not have its shining comeliness. But now, since it has this gift from the Almighty, it glows with beauty and reveals this favour.

10. But if it is pleasing to you, let us now examine the matter of this subject from the beginning, and let us lay bare the doctrine concerning those who sin and do not sin—that the Law does not have the power to save those who have committed faults, while he who gives the law, in so far as he is master of the Law and Lord, can free [them] of [their] fault.[233] 11. For this even the laws of truth have proclaimed and the nature of things teaches in a truth-loving way: that the Law does not rise up to a master's glory and absolve the unjust of their sins on its own authority and extend a master's grace to those worthy, nor does he who rules the Law and is Lord descend to legislative pettiness and form a legal opinion based on subtle

---

233 Cf. Gal. 3 and Rom. 7.

assessments of sins, feigning poverty by pretending to count pennies, and conceal the gift of his authority while he puts on a pretence of fastidious precision, and like the Law judge those convicted and administer justice to each according to his works. 12. But it is fitting to all and divinely professed to others, that the Lord, as lord, forgive sin, but that the Law, as law, exact revenge for faults, in order that the grace of authority be manifest and the right action of what serves authority be evident, and so that the rank of each not be outraged by the handing down of a single judgment from the confusion [of their proper roles]. But the one, as servant, will be seen to toil, while the other, as lord, will be seen to have a wealth of freedom.

13. One can, then, understand this from a true similitude and a fine example. For yesterday and the day before, not long ago at all, some who were entangled in illicit deeds and were to be chastised with an appropriate punishment, but bowed to the imperial train, petitioning that his reign be perpetual, were released from any supposition of guilt and put behind them the judicial decision. 14. But others, free of every spot and blemish, who did not partake even of common crime and theft, nor had feigned to honour royalty, like the unpurified and ungrateful, immediately received the awful chastisement of destruction, enjoying no advantage from living without reproach nor gaining any profit from being clean of any accusation. But on the contrary, being full of conspicuous good works—in their estimation—they have been destroyed as if by their own provocation. 15. But those who put on a careful show, who are makers and doers of myriad evils and full of illicit pursuits, who believed that desperate people are readily saved by the emperor, and come [to him] with a pitiable expression and pathetic attitude, have been saved, punished for none of the faults they committed. 16. For each of these types of people, his own opinion helped to cause his life or death. Because the emperor succoured those who were mindful of their salvation, while to the others he gave punishments worthy of [their] pretension.

17. If, then, faith is stronger than injustices, while the faithlessness of the blameless is rightly punished, why should the Apostle be blamed when he says "But such were some of you"—liable to and subjects of legal sentences, you endured the inexorable trial of retribution—"but you have been washed, but you have been sanctified, but you have been justified in the name of our Lord Jesus Christ and in the Spirit of our God."[234] 18. For if you wish to know the force of these statements accurately, the explanation

234 1 Cor. 6:11.

will be clear to you. For he does not simply say "you have been washed" or "sanctified" or "justified," but he says "in the name of the Lord." For as the forms of the letters have power and are manifest to all when they are written by the emperor's hand, sufficient to free the accused and sufficient to raise an army full of phalanxes and to give full liberty of speech to all subjects, but when written by any other particular hand they have the same style of handwriting, but not the same effect, so too the water, when marked by the sign of the name of Christ, is potent and powerfully fortifying, and serves for all as a purification sufficient to wash the stain of evil, quick to cleanse the imperfections of wickedness. 19. For the name of the Saviour Jesus, when made over the water, mystically makes it no longer common water, but set apart and unspeakably able to wash not only the exterior of the visible body, but also what is itself hidden in the conscience, and to arm the reasoning powers, like a camp, and to fill with life the one washed in it—with the result that he no longer fears the threat of the Law, which hung over the guilty from the beginning, who takes refuge in the framer of the Law himself, and receives from him the armour of grace that is able to stab at the battle line of the passions.

20. See, therefore, the sequence and consistent arrangement! See how the teaching of the apostles blazes! He does not first say "You have been sanctified" but "You have been washed" first. For first one is washed, then made clean; that is, made holy. For just as a nitron dipped in water washes away dirt, so does the name of Christ, when combined with the waters, cleanses of [his] faults the one who goes down into them and makes [him] shine with the blaze of grace. Then after sanctification it makes him just, every unjust action having been stripped away.

21. But these things happen, he says, to the saved in on other way than "in the name of the Lord and of the Spirit of God." In an inspired way and entirely fittingly he taught that the grace is furnished from the Trinity to believers, saying "in the name of the Lord and Spirit," and not simply "of the Spirit," but of God's Spirit, naming the one Godhead of the three, not saying "in the *names*" but "in the *name*." 22. For the one name of "God" applies to the Son and to the Father and to the Holy Spirit, and God is one in three subsistent entities and is so named,[235] and the believer accepts neither Father without the Son, nor does the Son lead anyone to the Father apart from the Spirit. For behold how he spoke mystically: "But you have

---

[235] Cf. Athanasius, *On the Incarnation and Against the Arians* 10 (PG 26:1000); Basil, *Letter* 214.4.

been washed, but you have been sanctified, but you have been justified." For him whom Christ washed, this one the Spirit made holy, while him whom the Spirit made holy, this one the Father justified, and not because Christ, washing, is not able to make holy, or the Spirit, making holy, does not have the strength to justify, or the Father, justifying, is in some way too weak to wash or make holy whom he wishes. For the Father, the Son, and the Holy Spirit are similarly competent to wash, make holy, and justify everything, but because it is fitting that the Son, as Son, make sons, and the Holy Spirit make holy, as Spirit, and the Father, as Father, to justify what has been made holy, in order that the name of three subsistent entities be known in one essence.[236] 23. For the Apostle, having been taught this idea in the Gospel, where it says, "Going out, you shall teach all the nations, baptizing them in the name of the Father, and of the Son, and of the Holy Spirit,"[237] upon the occasion of baptism inherited the name of the Trinity, saying: "But you have been washed, but you have been made holy, but you have been justified in the name of our Lord Jesus Christ and in the Spirit of our God."[238]

24. But if some, as you say, have taken the gift as an encouragement for sin, and retailing grace, through it market the passions of vice, buying the hubris of shameful deeds, that is no fault of the gift giver. For by calling, he does not encourage the one called to behave licentiously, since the host who invites friends to a drinking party never instructs them to drink themselves into a stupor, but on the contrary to be sober and to keep pure from excess with all sincerity. Likewise, he who out of generosity calls people to the heavenly table and the spiritual cup does not enjoin them to fill up on vices, but to prepare to receive this advantage with a calm demeanour and not to make their freedom and the promise of noble birth an excuse for slavery. 25. But if it happens that some disregard the host and gorge themselves on an irrational way of life, he who gives the gift does not renege on his promise, but he who receives [the gift] and acts badly in his excess harms himself, not he who gave the gift. For his intention is to set one table of

---

236 Compare and contrast Gregory of Nyssa, *To Ablabius* (GNO III.3, 47.21–27): "About the Divine Nature we have not learned that the Father does anything on his own which the Son does not take part in, or again, that the Son effects anything particular to himself apart from the Spirit, but every effect that extends from God to creation, and is named according to our various perceptions of it, begins from the Father and proceeds through the Son, and is perfected in the Holy Spirit."
237 Mt. 28:19.
238 1 Cor. 6:11.

joy for all and to lead the guests to one condition. 26. But if some, led like cattle by their own calculating, come to act with hubris, they suffer excessive heartburn, unable to digest the communion of beauty. For many, indeed, as you say, having misrepresented the matter by this reasoning, have gone astray from the aforementioned grace, even unto old age caking the muck of vice upon themselves. And having been zealous for the pursuit of loathsome deeds, and having taken mind to expel the heap of vices in one fell swoop in baptism, they separated themselves from the accursed life for a moment, but carrying no sign upon the forehead that would encourage pity,[239] perishing by an excessive hardening of the intellect, and by testing the gift and setting aside the good, have brought harm upon themselves.

26. 1. I suppose this has answered your questions about the Apostolic teaching, but next I will thoroughly address your sophism about monarchy and examine the doctrine of the gods and the One God.

If it was, for the most part, by way of an image that you were eager that we accept the doctrine of the monarchy of God and of the gods ruled by him, it must reasonably be asked if the nature of things is accustomed to being preserved in homonymy.[240] For we have found that it is not the thing that has acquired its true nature from the name, but the name from the thing, as [one predicates] of fire that it is hot, as well as of what is near fire, for both are hot. But both do not have the essence of heat, the one is hot by nature, while the other is so by position, and the one has heat in itself, while the other derives heat from another—and so the word [i.e. "heat"] does not at all indicate for us a single nature from homonymy.[241]

2. Thus the Apostle, in order that he might teach the authentic Godhead and offer correction, by distinguishing the essence from homonymous [beings], declared to the disciples that one is God by nature and is properly termed "lord,"[242] while the others are gods by relation and "lords" merely

---

239 Cf. Rev. 7:3ff.

240 "When things have only a name in common and the definition of essence which corresponds to the name is different, they are called homonyms" (Aristotle, *Categories* 1a1).

241 When Macarius argues that "what is near fire" is hot "by position" he uses the phrase τῇ θέσει and may have in mind Aristotle's placing of θέσις within the category "relative" (πρός τι) (Aristotle, *Cat.* 6a37; 6b12). His argument is that, just as the word "hot" is predicated essentially of fire, but only relatively in the case of what is accidentally hot, the word "god" is predicated of God essentially but only relatively in the case of other beings. Here he seems to misunderstand the Hellene's point, which was that gods and angels are polynymous, named differently but sharing the same definition of essence (see 4.20–21a.3–5 above).

242 Contrast with Gregory of Nyssa, To Ablabius 42.,13–43.1.

in name, saying: "For even if there are gods, as indeed there are, and many lords, ours is the One God, from whom is everything, and One Lord, Jesus, through whom is everything."[243] 3. See how he says "For even if there are gods" in place of "gods who are such only in name, but not gods in the proper sense," "but ours is the One God," that is, the god who is God essentially. The definition of essence testifies to the Godhead, the appellation of the name does not confirm what is so designated, but rather the nature of the thing validates the truth [of the name].[244]

4. He rules the gods, then, and is lord over them and has power over them not being one of them from homonymy, but being alone unoriginated and being lord over things begotten. For they have received being from him, but he has not derived seniority of honour from them. And he was the Creator of their being, while they have not taken their origin of subsistence from themselves. And he knows how to preserve those whom he rules, but they bring no benefit to him by being ruled. 5. But he is not envious that many are called "gods" and "lords," if by being in proximity and close relation to him they are in contact with the principle of the Godhead. But if they slacken and become in any way distant, they experience the same thing as those who turn away from the ray of light and live in the shadow of darkness in the gloom.

6. That is something un-tyrannical, then, and just—ruling beings that are unlike, on account of the sublimity of his essence. For one who is lord to beings of a different kind by virtue of his superiority in nature does not govern them despotically with tyrannical force, but directs them benignly by the firmness of love. 7. But Hadrian, or some other world ruler, being a human being and reigning over humans like himself, did so by the law of domination and tyranny; not ruling over beings of a like nature by the precept of consistency,[245] he rather enslaved fellow kin by constraint and violence. 8. But he committed great injustices, beating down portions of essence, not the essence, and wronging the species, not subduing the genus; for a human, in so far as he is human, is unable to be lord over a human being, but only in so far as he rules or takes on tyrannical power, thereby

---

243 1 Cor. 8:5–6.
244 If this sentence is read in terms of Aristotle's *Categories*, then Macarius is arguing that "god" and "godhead," when predicated of God, designate primary substance (*Categories* 2a11). Again, contrast Gregory of Nyssa's *To Ablabius*, which rejects the idea that predications can be made about the nature of God's essence.
245 I.e. with the ontological and natural order. Macarius uses the same phrase at 3.25.5 (ὁ τῆς ἀκολουθίας θέσμος) to refer to the consistency of nature and the biblical narrative.

subduing the same race and enslaving it. In so far, then, as he plays tyrant over nature by force, he does not have authority by nature, but shows by savagery that he is more powerful than those like him.

9. But God, ruling alone and holding monarchy in its true sense, rules originated beings, being unoriginated; has power over creatures, being uncreated and without beginning. He does not govern beings like him, but unlike him, caring for them. 10. For as the sun illuminates whom it does, making them shine by participating in light, while it is not at all ever illuminated by them, so too God sanctifies those who draw near to him by the principle of rational thought, divinizing[246] them and [giving] them the most blessed gift from himself, while he, of course, does not receive the ornament of virtue from them. If indeed, then, the sun, which when it illuminates someone with its light causes him to be called "bright" just as it is, provides nothing to those illuminated by way of the principle of diminution of its own essence, while it does not prevent those things brightened by it from being called "bright," being bright by essence, it causes those things that are brightened to be called "bright" by relation. 11. In the same way, consequently, God as monarch and being eternal in nature does not prevent the angels being called "gods," divinizing them by the position of their rank, neither dividing his own proper essence among them nor giving to them a portion of his specific nature. 12. Hence, he who venerates him who is God by nature is blessed, while he who venerates what is god by relation is greatly disappointed, deriving an insecure benefit from his worship. 13. For he who draws near fire for the sake of warmth is warmed by it and lit by its light, while he who aims for warmth from a piece of copper or iron drawn out of the fire fails in his aim, for after a short while the piece that has belied its nature returns slowly to its own proper natural state, having neither helped the one who has it in any way to be warm nor providing him with a bright light. So too, he who wishes to obtain the beatitude of the highest virtue is not disappointed when he asks this from him who is God according to nature, but he who asks it of an angel or some being of incorporeal and transcendent rank, which is a god by relation and not by nature, is greatly harmed, because he wishes to receive that which the possessor himself is deprived of when he gives it.

---

246 Divinization is promised to the saints in much early Christian literature (see e.g. Athanasius, *On the Incarnation* 54.3); it has biblical warrant in Jn. 10:34–35 (quoting Ps. 82:6) and 2 Pet. 1:4.

BOOK 4   259

14. But God, giving everything to all, possesses all, refuses poverty. As the sun furnishing its rays to those who see them simultaneously serves them and is not deprived of its light, as a teacher giving learning to students simultaneously makes the students wise and possesses wisdom, so power went out from Christ and simultaneously drove illnesses from those it struck,[247] and remaining fully in Christ, it was not separated [from him]. 15. This should be a convincing reply for your question about God and gods and the monarchy possessed by the one true God[248] who rules.

27. 1. It remains that we speak in a measured way about the subject of the angels and their incorruptibility, and how in the Kingdom of heaven "they neither marry nor are given in marriage, but are like the angels in heaven."[249]

2. Christ, wanting to show the beatitude of those who are in the heavenly country and to declare unhappy those who reside in the corruption of the earth and who have received their existence from the filthy birth of beings of the flesh, who are begotten and beget and fall faster than leaves,[250] says: "Those deemed worthy to enter into the indestructible palace of life receive the way of life that the angels have, being released from corporeal mixture and union and finally no longer experience death or birth, separated from corporeal interweaving and bonds." [He says this] in order that any of those who think rightly, having heard of the rational essence in heaven, which rejoices in the principle of immortality, might compose his life in imitation of them [i.e. the angels], and be zealous in his deeds for their glory, abstaining from marriage and shirking the symbols of corruption, and finally that, passing through the gates of death, he might come into the hall of the blessed (that is, of the angels) being relieved of his burden. 3. Not, indeed, after having fashioned images in the figure [of angels], as you yourself say, speaking to a shadow and rejoice in a mere appearance, making himself acquainted with inanimate material things as if they were animate, being entertained by the dead apparitions of letters, presenting his intercession to a mute creation, thinking that the Divine lurks in stone and wood, deluded that the uncontainable order is contained by copper

---

247 Cf. Lk. 6:19; Mk. 5:30.
248 The expression "the one true God" is applied to the Father at Jn. 17:3 and either to the Father or to the Son at 1 Jn. 5:20; these passages inform the formula of the Creed signed at the Council of Nicaea: "true God from true God."
249 Cf. Mt. 22:30.
250 For the comparison of humans to leaves see Is. 64:6, as well as Homer, *Iliad* 6.146.

and iron, irrationally surmising that the ungraspable is grasped in a dead image. 4. For even if, for the most part, angels have appeared in the form of men, they did not [in themselves] look like this, but were invisible. But if someone either paints or casts in bronze [an image of the Divine] according to this [human] likeness, he does not make it according to what it truly is, nor would he enclose its nature. And even if he perfects it to the letter, he wears himself out, totally exhausted, wanting to give a tactile form to that which cannot be touched. 5. For even if the divine Word somewhere recounts a "finger of God" and that tablets were marked by it, and [mentions] feet, a head, a tongue, or an ear, it did not utter this to divide the Lord into parts, but rather, it sympathetically taught the invisible essence to pass into a visible form, mystically fashioning a visible sign that corresponds to the weakness of the world, in order that man, seeing things in divine visions that accorded with his own conventions, would not fear as he received the oracles of things to come, but be strengthened by a vision that was akin to his way of seeing, in order that from visions commensurate [with his nature] he might approach the ineffable mysteries.

6. Hence, with good reason, in every mystical discourse, for the sake of the [divine] economy, the Divine acts according to the natures of those he aids, degraded not even if he be revealed as a plant, since it is not possible for created beings to see the ingenerate plainly, nor for corporeal beings to approach the incorporeal, nor for compounded beings to grasp what is uncompounded; for someone who in his sleep sees a lion or column or a river does not see a true river or column or lion, but by a trick of the eye sees a dream which is insubstantial when judged by the scrutiny of knowledge. 7. Thus, someone hearing of God's feet, hands, fingers, tongue, or ear, having been instructed about them and understanding something appropriate to the Divine, would not judge them to be corporeal feet or hands, but an image of things that reside in the imagination. 8. Thus angels appeared to Abraham, disclosing a human form to his vision, but were not human by nature, preserving the principle of incorporeal beings. And the actions they performed were human and not a false imitation of human nature. They who did them were in truth angels, and they did not temper their own nature by this act, but adapted their appearance for a vision proper to Abraham. While taking food and drink they did not consume them like Abraham, but consumed what they were offered like fire. They did not become full from it like those who are hungry, nor did they excrete the remainder, as is customary,

as dung.²⁵¹ 9. They did each thing in a manner fit for each thing; for appearing to humans they maintained the particular way of humans, so that they would not cause a great offence against the just man [i.e. Abraham] by refusing to eat, and thus show that their own nature was inhospitable to him. But again, so that they not seem to be completely changed into human nature, they preserved precisely the limits of status, although they took grain like men from Abraham. Eating it, they consumed it as angels, experiencing no sweet taste in their mouths by corporeal sense of taste, but consuming the food by incorporeal contact. 10. And since these things manifestly occurred in truth, Abraham does not make the epiphany of those he saw into a figure, nor does he carve a statue resembling [them] or paint on a board, thinking that he could see in these those he had entertained, but in the hidden treasury of the soul he kept the memory of them and had all his cares calmed.

(28) 11. But if it seems better to you that the Divine consent to live in a statue, and not to have become incarnate in Mary because of the inferiority of the passions, hear the more complete mystery of this doctrine: that the perfectly all-sufficing and Creator *Logos*, being sufficient in power, great, alien to passions, has not feared what among us [seems] to be a cause of shame. 12. For in this he is impassible, in that being born with that which experiences passions he is not ashamed; in this he is undefiled, in that he does not take on the inferiority of evil. The Word, therefore, became incarnate, not descending into a sick or inferior flesh, but elevating the things of the flesh up to his own incorruption.²⁵² 13. For as the sun descending into moisture does not take on moisture and is not found to be muddy, but drying the moisture from the mud it hardens it completely into scales, without its rays becoming turbid, so too God the Word, being the intelligible sun,²⁵³ descending into flesh, does not take up any sickness from the flesh nor is he caught up in the passions, overcome, and falling into the infirmity of vice. But on the contrary, he leads it up from the slippery places, and uprooting it from what holds it, sets it in a Divine state of blessedness, heating that which was badly wasting away

---

251 On Abraham's angelic visitors neither eating nor drinking see Tob. 12:19.

252 On this Christological doctrine cf. Athanasius, *On the Incarnation* 54; Gregory of Nyssa, Christological *Letter to Theophilus*.

253 Christians since at least the time of the *Letter of Barnabas* (5.10) had been wont to apply to God such texts as *Republic* 509c and Xenophon, *Memorabilia* 4.13. According to Pliny the Younger (*Letter* 96), Christians faced the sun when praying to Christ; cf. Tertullian, *Apology* 16.9.

and strengthening that which had been abandoned in sins, in order that it become invincible and unchangeable and conquer the assaults of inferior things, so the flesh would keep its essence and refuse the slandering of its essence and preserve its definition and repudiate the confusion of this definition.

14. For this reason, he [i.e. Christ] fulfils the perfection of the [divine] economy not in something else, but in the flesh, and not in [some kind of] undefined flesh, but in flesh human and virginal, in order that he show that, taking [material] in the beginning—the virginal earth[254]—he had made the flesh, a dwelling place of mind, thoughts, and soul, and now from one who was a virgin and a young woman he arranges a temple for himself, not needing human hands or art.[255]

15. Now, what is more honourable: mud[256] or a virgin? A human being or mortar? I think that a human being is preferable over mortar and a virgin more honourable than clay. If, then, God is not ashamed to take clay from the earth, but rather forms and works the human being out of muddy matter, why should he resist assuming a human being taken from a human being? Or why would he question taking flesh from a virgin? Is it not without any hesitation or delay that he will assume the more honourable lump of earth and make it a uniquely-made, god-bearing statue,[257] residing within which he shakes the inhabited world with the thunder of [his] virtue and illuminates all with the lightning of the grace of [his] gift? 16. For if the one you [Hellenes][258] call Prometheus makes man,[259] being ashamed of nothing in any way, and Zeus made a woman whom Athena girded,[260] you applaud the myth and solemnify the matter, seeing no shame, not thinking there to be any passion, not scrutinizing the question of private parts.[261] For it is much more shameful (if there is any shame at all!) to make parts and to

---

254 Mary is also compared to virgin earth by Irenaeus, *Against Heresies* 3.21.1.
255 This doubling of "virgin" and "young woman" suggests that Macarius is aware that the Hebrew of Is. 7:14 means "young woman," rather than "virgin," as was often noted in polemics against Christian readings of Isaiah. Macarius's image of Christ's body as a temple conflates Jn. 2:19–21 with Mk. 14:58.
256 Cf. Gen. 2:1.
257 "Uniquely-made" translates the adverb μονογενῶς and is a word play on μονογενής ("Only-begotten"); compare Basil, *On the Holy Spirit* 5.12, commenting on 1 Cor. 11:12 ("... in order to show that the god-bearing flesh was formed from the human lump").
258 Second person plural, thus "you Hellenes," not merely the Hellenic interlocutor.
259 E.g. Pausanias, *Description of Greece* 10.4.4.
260 Hesiod, *Theogony* 570–574.
261 Κεκρυμμένων μορίων, literally "hidden portions," a euphemism for genitalia.

hide them with some clothing than to pass through them for the sake of the economy and profitable teaching.²⁶²

17. For he who makes a residence and then refuses to reside in it is his own accuser and pitiless judge, because when he was craftsman he considered there to be no cause for shame, but after its completion, he discredited the success of his own labours, judging the artful creation unworthy of habitation. So too, the Divine that made the human being is seen to act unjustly if in fact he is ashamed to accept a portion in its condition; if he refuses to accept his [i.e. the human being's] condition, he rejects the whole art of his effort; by refusing, he discredits all his own wisdom, because making a likeness of his own glory, he decided that it would be shameful to dwell within [it].

(29) 18. Hence we should be afraid to accept such an opinion about God. We should bristle at the thought of being overly curious about the mind of the Maker, and we confess that he assumed flesh, but do not believe that he resides in inanimate and mute statues. Nor should we call the elements of the cosmos "gods"—earth, water, fire, and air.²⁶³ And even though the stars "run" and have an unending course, we do not deify them.²⁶⁴ For as no one has crowned the horses that race, but rather their driver and charioteer,²⁶⁵ so too not to the stars but to God, who kindled them, do we reserve honour. 20. And even if a statue were to speak and seem to communicate, neither to these do we grant honour or glory. Nor if Moses says "Do not speak ill of the gods"²⁶⁶ do we think he speaks about these [gods] or mentions them, for [he refers] to the gods "to whom the Word of God came,"²⁶⁷ as if they are the warm things which the fire warmed. But the Word of God never spoke through stones or pieces of wood, nor furnished sensation to insensible things. Humans, in their empty thinking, melting gold and working silver, have requested oracles from them, as if from gods; crippled in mind and blind in their thinking, they are not dissuaded by the insensibility of stone statues from thinking they have a soul. They do not judge and rightly weigh the fact that that which is inanimate has no sensation of honour nor again of outrage, it does not repay the one who praises it with honour or the

---

262 On the incarnation as a medium for teaching see Athanasius, *On the Incarnation* 11.
263 For the commonplace that pagans worship the elements see e.g. Rom. 1:25; Gal. 4:9; Aristides, *Apology* 3; Eusebius, *Theophany* 1.2; Athanasius, *Against the Gentiles* 9.
264 The noun θεός, "god," is derived from the verb θεῖν, "to run," by Plato (*Cratylus* 396d).
265 For God as charioteer see Eusebius, *Gospel Preparation* 11.7.
266 Ex. 22:27.
267 Jn. 10:35.

one who abuses it with retributions. 21. Now Moses does not say not to disrespect inanimate gods. For how can what is insensible be disrespected? By what could it ever be grieved? But who is so dumb, idle, and stupid as to disrespect that which is unable, because of the torpor of matter, to perceive the outrage of disrespect? Since they are neither gods nor beings having sensation, they will not be reproached, or repay anything, as they are dead in nature and by definition without motion. 22. But if they have the names and titles of gods, they do not sully the Divine, any more than dogs do when honoured by human names. Many, out of recklessness, have given divine names to the profane. Wronging the Divine in no way by this, they have only revealed their folly. For if someone is called a god and is in no way divine he will outrage the title and impugn the name, being subject to a merciless and irremediable accusation. 23. Now, do not think that the All-Powerful God is distressed and vexed by this, if some thoughtless people also drag down the name "divine" to apply it even to serpents. For they punish themselves sufficiently, having applied the undefiled name of the primary and indestructible essence to worthless material.

24. These words are enough for you concerning your unconvincing pedantry about the gods.

30. 1. It remains that I ask that you apply your mind to the explanation I am about to give concerning the resurrection of the flesh. And do not interrupt me [with applause or groans], you or any of those seated here. For I already knew that some are not a little disgusted that we are going to speak about the resurrection.[268] Hence, since the topic is complex and requires a complex inquiry, the thinking of those present must be complex.

What then? With what likeness or what plausible argument might we relate the doctrine of the resurrection to you? For, along with persuasiveness what we say ought to use likenesses that are worthy of being believed and plainly evident. For it is not the stylistic veneer that reveals the nature of what is being examined, the truth of the subject knows how to solemnify the nature of the discourse, since appearances falsify what is being examined. 3. Often, a vessel or a piece of money dipped in plating that seems golden deceives the eye, keeping hidden the unworthiness of its material, and one who, so far as appearance goes, does not seem vile, contradicts this semblance by the vileness of his deeds. So too a discourse,

---

[268] The repugnance and absurdity of the doctrine of bodily resurrection, like the incarnation, was a commonplace in anti-Christian polemic; see for example Celsus, *True Logos* (in Origen, *Against Celsus* 6.72–75); Minucius Felix, *Octavius* 11.

when delivered solemnly, enchants the ear and imperceptibly harms the soul with wordiness, offering no firm account of virtue. Thus one must flee sophistical cleverness in every way and must consider unalloyed knowledge with beauty.

4. First, then, let us examine this in a worthy manner—whether what has been generated came to be from being or non-being. And if from being, it is not logical to ascribe generation to it, but if [generation] must be ascribed, the reason why is clear. But if it has been brought into existence from non-being, one accords subsistence to he who just before did not subsist. 5. For that which brings the nonexistent into being will restore to a great extent what has been generated and has been dissolved, and will deem it worthy of an improving addition or dispensation. For it is peculiar to the Unoriginated Nature to transform the existence of originated beings for the better and to lead beings labouring in temporal existence to renewal and oil those dulled by the rust of vice with grace and to make what is worn out worthy of a second creation and re-formation. 6. For the cosmos, when it takes this better form and dress, does not destroy the plan on which it was founded,[269] but on the contrary, reveals it, donning a beauty better than it had before. For to remain in a state of identity is fit for the Divine alone; for creation it is fit to accept change and alteration. Now the present life and state of affairs is like a pedagogue leading us to the festival of the immortality to come and prepares us to encounter the sublime splendour.[270] 7. Life now is like a womb with an infant, holding the entire subsistence of things in the lightless forgetfulness and obscurity of ignorance, and the universe must be expelled like a foetus from the amniotic sac that is the present age and receives a second course of life in the light of the pure abode. 8. But you want corruption to be unending and to reproduce sordidly and to die loathsomely and to procreate and to be born and to be eclipsed by forgetfulness; that evil wax wanton and misfortune increase; to be consumed by want and wasted by poverty; to suffer evil by day and to be lulled to sleep at night; to eat with pleasure

---

269 "The plan on which it was founded" translates ὑπόθεσις—"proposal," "plan," or, literally, "thing placed under," "basis." The term conveys the (divine) intentionality and purpose behind the cosmos, which Macarius claims is unaltered despite phaenominal change.

270 Macarius applies to life the image that Paul had applied to the Law (Gal. 3:24) and Clement of Alexandria to the *Logos* (*Pedagogue* 1.7). On creation as a foreshadowing of the final consummation see e.g. Irenaeus, *Against Heresies* 4.38.3; Origen, *On First Principles* 3.6.1; Gregory of Nyssa, *On the Making of Man* 16.17, 21.

266   MACARIUS, *APOCRITICUS*

and then be weighed down by painful fullness and to fall ill with hunger; that there be slavery and mastery in the same place; that the rich should stand and the poor be abased; that the old fall and the young rise up; that breasts swell and infants be suckled; that our thoughts be troubled and that we be sickened by suffering; to hate the country and be fond of the city; that we flee equity and pursue inequity; that the nature of things be tormented by great inconsistencies; that we be depressed in winter and scorched in summer; that we be brightened by the flowers of spring in their own season and be nourished by autumnal fruits; ploughing of the earth and tilling of clods; that the tips of trees and plants be pruned; to have change from season to season; that like receive judgment from like; that savagery lurk tyrannically among the nations; that thrones of vainglory be set up in the world; that the East rebel and the West be in turmoil; that the North be contentious and the South be quarrelsome; that the dry land and the sea alike be in a state of agitation;[271] that the weaker give orders and the stronger be commanded; that false accusation prevail and those falsely accused of things be ruined; that life be a tragedy and living be a comedy; and in general, that corruption, having bound the inhabited world with violent chains, should bring about its destruction in this wretched state and that an Ogygian plague[272] spread across the whole universe insatiably day by day.

9. And [you want] the hateful veil of these things never to pass away and the shameful mantle never to be removed;[273] that the soul never be released from inhuman shackles; that lament not be silenced and grief never be put to rest; that the evil that waxes not be quenched and that successive moral depravities not be cut off; that the might of world rulers not be put to death and the insolence of those who hold dynastic power not be cut down; that the struggle of those who groan not be relieved and the tears of those who wail not be comforted; that the virtues of ascetics not shine forth and the insolence of the arrogant not be quenched; that the works of the unjust not be chastised and the perfection of the just not be seen; that zeal for sorcery not be judged and the guilelessness of the sincere not be honoured; that rational nature not be glorified as far

---

271 The references to trouble and rebellion in the North, South, East, and West could refer to literal political unrest in various regions, or to natural or climatic "agitation."

272 The reference is to the mythical king Ogyges (cf. Pausanias, *Description of Greece* 9.5.1) and a primaeval flood said to have occurred during his reign (cf. Eusebius, *Gospel Preparation* 10.10.7).

273 For the heavens as a perishable garment see Is. 51:6; Heb. 1:12.

as possible and that irrationality not be cast away as it ought; that those who suffer piously not be crowned and those who live impiously not be brought to shame; that those enduring hardship for the sake of virtue not be elevated and those luxuriating in licentiousness not be humbled; that the fonts of the blood of fratricides not be purified and streams and rivers not lose their turbidity; that winter never cease and the torch-like heat not abate; that the air not appear as a pure vessel or the heaven expel the thickness of gloom; that the earth not be set free from pollution or the sea rest from being sailed;[274] that the cosmos not turn like a wheel and not preserve [its] essence and not change [its] form; that everything in every respect, with the exception of the hypercosmic realm, not receive renewal and not receive an unalloyed newness of life; that the sophistry of deceit not be impugned and the knowledge of sagacity not be kindled; that the superciliously dignified not fall and the tablet of solemnity not be read; that the knitted brow of false pretence not look sullen and the face of self-control not be made to appear luminous; that the temporary way of life not disappear and those who are now worn down not receive perpetual life; that rational thought not be set free from endless worry, reproach, and outrage, or that the pile of care not be crushed; that the cosmos not be stripped of disorder or cast off the ugliness within it. Instead, you want the sorrowful garment to exist forever and misfortunes to consume it everlastingly.

10. For the corruption and destruction that seem universally to be planted firmly in the cosmos are also the beginning for incorruption and the starting point for salvation. For subsequently, the ornament of life will turn out well, when rational nature will receive a second, indestructible principle of creation. 11. For it is for the sake of human beings that the universe is transformed, since it was also for them that it was deemed worthy of creation in the beginning.[275] For human beings came into existence for their own sake, not for the sake of another. But heaven and earth and the particulars in them were fashioned on account of humans and it is necessary that when they receive alteration and transformation that the universe be altered and be cleansed together with them. 12. For as an artisan who has first built a house, which in time is worn out and

---

274 Sailing the seas was often represented as an act of human folly or turpitude, see e.g. Aratus, *Phaenomena* 110–111; Lucretius, *On the Nature of Things* 2.1ff and 5.1004–1006; Ovid, *Metamorphoses* 1.94–95; cf. Ps. 107.23.

275 On creation being for the benefit of human beings see Theophilus, *To Autolycus* 18; Gregory of Nyssa, *On the Making of Man* 3.1.

is destroyed by collapse, rebuilds it once again and deems it worthy of stronger construction and greater charm, not being overly concerned about how the first, second, and third layers of stones were originally arranged in the building, but rebuilds by arranging the last [layer] first and the first last and the middle here and there, and in this does not fret at all about the form of the handiwork or about causing the composition of the art to be criticized, but dressing the house with fitting adornment and having beautified the form of the exterior, he receives effusive praise for his art. 13. In the same manner, indeed, God, who is the artisan of a rational "house" and who made humans in the beginning and who constructed an august residence of divine power,[276] [a residence] comprised of many races having the same nature, like stones, [a residence] built many aeons and ages ago and that has fallen into many passions of sins and has finally been destroyed and ruined altogether, will raise [it] up once again, and will lead nature by means of precise knowledge and lordly wisdom and will gather together what has been scattered, allowing none of what has crumbled to be destroyed; and even if he arranges the first in the last rank, and even if he leads the last up to the first glory, he will not fret about the matter, giving to each an account of the resurrection adapted to it.

14. Now, even if Priam, as you say, or Nestor has been dead for thousands of years, and even if someone else died three days before the resurrection, none of them will experience inordinate grief or boundless joy when they rise up, but each will obtain the wages due for his own works, not blaming or praising the doctrine of the resurrection, or its swiftness or slowness [in coming], but rather praising with hymns or finding fault with his own way of life. 15. For with God, the passage of a thousand years is counted as one brief day,[277] and a brief period of time, if it seems right to him, is a period of countless ages; so these are the words of those who debate trifles, when they say: "If he raises the one who died three days ago at the same time as the one [who died] a thousand years ago, he does a great injustice."

16. For, also, those who received life a thousand or two thousand years ago enjoyed a life of five hundred years or longer, and he who died three days before [the resurrection], living not all of thirty years[278] and these full of suffering, changed his life, so it is no great thing if for the sake of

---

276 For the body as a house or temple cf. 2 Cor. 5:1; 1 Cor. 6:19.
277 Cf. Ps. 95:5; 2 Pet. 3:8; Justin, *Dialogue with Trypho* 81.
278 Presumably an allusion to the age of Jesus at the outset of his public ministry (Lk. 3:23).

consolation he sees the resurrection as soon as he dies. For on a scale, I think, and with a measure and a yardstick the Divine weighed rightly the life of each person, and deemed it just that some live seven hundred years and that, once they died, they continue to rest many years, giving rest to the immense mass of their bodies,[279] while others live fifty years, in great hardships, and to give them the resurrection right after, in order that they be consoled of their difficulties quickly.

17. Thus you ought to reject a concept that is so impoverished and poor and not think that those who died long ago and rise up after a long delay are done an injustice, nor sing the praises of that childishness by saying: "How is it possible that someone shipwrecked and eaten by fish, then, when the fish have been eaten by men, and then, when the men are killed and eaten by dogs, and finally, when the dogs are eaten by buzzards, will live again and receive the resurrection, when he has been destroyed by so many animals."[280] 18. For these are not the words of sober and alert men, but of those who are asleep in drunkenness and draw pictures of their dreams, if they think the Maker of fire is not capable of accomplishing something like what fire does, when he effects the resurrection.

For when silver or gold lie in the earth, and lead, and tin, or bronze and iron are, so to speak hidden, it is fire that burns the earth and smelts the material, drawing out only the bronze, only the lead, or again the tin and the iron, allowing none of the substance to be destroyed, except perhaps for something earthy in it that can be destroyed. 19. If, then, the power of fire is so potent and has such an effective energy that it draws out pure matter from matter and preserves unspoiled the essence of each, even if the gold falls into myriad streams, even if it is distributed in numberless bits and disseminated in mud, clay, mounds of dirt, dunghills, fire, when applied to all, causes the reality of what is concealed to come out intact, what then shall we say about the one who caused the nature of fire to subsist? 20. Does he not equally have the strength to alter humans, though they be laid up in myriad materials, a rational treasure more precious than gold, and make whole those who have died, whether those in the earth, in the sea, in rivers, or in lakes, or those eaten by beasts or birds, or those pulverized into fine, invisible dust, or will he be found less powerful than fire and will he appear more impotent that the syllogisms which you speak?

---

279 Macarius seems to identify the patriarchs with the giants of Gen. 6:4; the previous verse (Gen. 6:3) records the abridgement of human life to one hundred and twenty years, perhaps leading to Macarius's conflation here.

280 Compare Gregory of Nyssa, *On the Making of Man* 26.1.

21. For your insane idea about God not being able to do everything, thinking that it will wax persuasive based on crafty reasoning, like a pillar without a foundation, will not stand. 22. Whence, then, might we explain to you God's capacity to do everything? From the [nature of] the Divine essence itself, or from what is appropriate to it? Or testing the logic of the first and the second? First, if you wish, from the Undefiled Nature itself we shall reply to the sense of what you have asked, [namely] that: 23. if God is able to make what has been originated cease to exist, then it is necessary that the originated becomes unoriginated, but if we posit this, the principle of two unoriginateds follows; or rather, there would be nothing that is originated, but the entire universe would be unoriginated. But a great absurdity spills over from this notion. For thus what is unoriginated would also be originated, as the unoriginated passes into the definition of the originated, once again the principle of the originated will not subsist. For who would be the maker of the originated, if the unoriginated did not exist? 24. And this question is similar to the former: whether God is able, being unoriginated, to make himself originated. But, since some say it is inconceivable that the unoriginated become originated, he is unable to do this. <***>[281]

25. But, as the just [God] will render justice, effecting retribution for those who have been mistreated. For if he did not do this, his power would seem, correctly, to be thoroughly silly: making everything and insulting it with the law of creation, while spitting upon things and neither honouring things that eagerly pursue virtue in life, nor judging things that honour vice in their living, but rather allowing what is beautiful and its opposite to be plunged alike into oblivion, neither crowning virtue as virtue nor exposing vice as vice; not accepting the ascetic discipline of those who toil and not castigating the insolence of intemperance; not bringing joy to the poor man who suffers evil nor making an example of the rich man who lives in luxury;[282] not judging the effeminacy of the coquettish nor glorifying the austere way of life, but rather, put simply, to be silent, as if the vacillations of human nature did not exist, and not place under examination its vice or virtue. 26. This doctrine does not accord with divine providence; this scheme is no brother to the Unalloyed Nature. Far distant from this unsullied oversight—completely alien, strange, foreign

---

281 Goulet conjectures a lacuna and suggests that a passage preserved in Latin by the sixteenth-century writer Francisco Torres (see Fragment 2, below) might belong here.
282 Possibly an allusion to the parable of the rich man and Lazarus (Lk. 16:19–31).

BOOK 4   271

to it—is this neglect of his creatures, a doctrine that utterly destroys the creation, rejoicing over humans that have been left to pass into obscurity.

27. Thus all things will be resurrected and a second existence will be granted to them, but he will judge the world for its wrongdoings, save those who have believed in him consistently, and chastise those who have neither wanted to accept him nor honoured the mystery of [his] manifestation.

28. For the foals marked by the emperor's sign and seal are deemed worthy of the emperor's court and stable, even if they are of no bodily worth and lack vigour and are hesitant in the race. Even if they are poorly proportioned, they are honoured and remarkable on account of the mark. But whatever [foals] do not have the seal, even if they are agile, even if quick, even if they can't be caught [in the race], and even if their sires are fast, even if remarkable, they are driven out of the imperial courts—and this is no made up story or the account of some wordsmith, but the account of observed facts and a true report. In the same manner, therefore, whoever has been stamped with the salvific sign, whoever bears the All-Ruling name marked on the tablet of his soul,[283] whoever has judged confession in God more powerful than his own sins, these escape the danger of the coming judgment; these sail unscathed past the so-called Charybdis by keeping the eye of faith fixed unwaveringly on the common torch of salvation and magnanimous redemption of him who sojourned.

29. For as he who dons a strong, large breastplate fitted with mail is invulnerable in battle and unassailable in the midst of dangers, so too he who dons the confession of the Almighty does not fear the threat of universal judgment.[284] 30. For just as fire does not enflame that which is called "incorruptible" or burn a sword, but illuminates and heats them, so neither fire nor judgment will ever touch things dipped in what is named"incorruptible", but will flee from what ebars that name.

31. For as the sun illuminates the one whose eye has the ability to see when it is opened, but leaves the eye in shadow when it is closed, not wronging or grieving the faculty of vision, it is the one who possesses the faculty of vision who harms himself. He suffers no injustice from the solar ray, but brings darkness upon himself through the same organs which enabled him to see in collaboration with light, making a judgment of light when he sees the sun and a judgment of shadow when he does not see the

---

283 On the necessity of "sealing" see Jn. 6:27; Rom. 4:11; 2 Cor. 1:22; Eph. 4:30; Rev. 9:4; cf. Heb. 1:3.
284 Cf. Eph. 6:10ff.

sun, appointing himself the arbiter and judge of these matters. 32. So too, someone who believes in God and remains in contact with that which is intelligible and divine light is found to be a companion of the God in whom he believes, fleeing from the darkness of ignorance and unlearning and being nourished by the lustre of heavenly dogmas, aiming to attain salvation for himself on account of seeing the Divine, and having a strong and mighty protection in his belief in the salvific cure. 33. But he who has had his eyes gouged out by willing unbelief and has turned away from the common light of day swims in darkness like a creature of the deep, having imperfectly succeeded in virtue; even if he evinces self-control apart from the light, he does not enjoy praise; even if he has fellowship with his neighbours he does not receive honours; even if he acts with justice and does not use the light as the determinant of his action, his actions are culpable and he does not escape accusation. 34. Even if his soul has been instructed by natural justice and he hates robbery and rejects theft, does not adulterate the custom concerning others' wives, does not trample on or commit outrage against his neighbour, fights on behalf of his fatherland, suffers on behalf of his kin, and plumes himself with the manifold beauty of his works, he is unpurified and does all for nought, since he does not accept the infallible authority as the determinant of his actions. 35. For just as without light the beauty of the beautiful receives no praise, and without measure the principle of measured things cannot be fulfilled, so too good action and every virtuous deed and disposition which does not accept as inspector the sleepless eye that sees everywhere, is like a pearl buried away in the clay, the beauty of which does not see the light but has been hidden in rubbish.

For who, tell me, will crown the self-control of he who is self-controlled? Who will honour with pay the soldier after his valour? Who will judge which wrestler is worthy of prizes? Is the race run against itself not reprehensible?[285] Are the successes of the combatant not for nothing without the general? Is the struggle of the self-controlled person not pitiable unless there is someone to crown him? Is the tribute of subjects not useless without the emperor? 37. So too, every act of justice that is not done in the name of and for the glory of the Creator is denuded of the perfection of good [works]. But on the contrary he who believes there is an overseer and judge who has power over his deeds and actions, even if he be under a curse, even if he be a minister of unseemly customs, even if he be a zealot for abominable practices, and if he places the examination

---

285 Macarius has in mind such texts as 1 Cor. 9:24; Heb. 12:1; 2 Tim. 4:8.

of his own deeds under the eye of the Creator, like one afflicted who bares the passions of his body to a philanthropic physician, is freed from every malady and disturbance, and casts away the myriad bruises of his faults;[286] for the Saviour has the power to sa<ve ...>

---

286 Cf. Is. 53:4–5.

FRAGMENTS

Fragment 1, from Book 4

(Nicephorus, *Epikrisis* 12.37–51
[Greek text in Featherstone (2002)])

For they,[1] by putting forward this Macarius as a witness and advocate of their own error and, by all appearances, receiving and embracing his words, have by all means entirely skewered themselves upon other wicked things. For they would rather collect whatever contradicts the sacred doctrines of the Church—perhaps because they are ruled and disposed about such things by an old habit—they were glad to embrace them enthusiastically, and to accept with delight not only the doctrines of the atheist Manichaeans and hateful Arians, but also the thought and crippled doctrines of the impious and apoplectic Origen, and undertook to teach the same things as that wretched man:[2]

> That the chastisement threatened and prepared by God for impious people in the time to come will have an end.

And this will be found easily by anyone who tracks it down at the end of the fourth book [of the *Apocriticus*], from which they have excerpted the present passages. At the moment, we shall not mention that among some he [i.e. Macarius] is suspected of holding the doctrines of the Jewish-minded Nestorius.

---

1 The iconoclasts who compiled the *florilegium* that included quotations from the *Apocriticus* and against whom Nicephorus is writing.
2 The demonstrative pronoun is ambiguous; "that" wretched man could refer either to Origen in the immediately preceding clause or to Macarius, whom Nicephorus associates here and in the following quotation with Origen and the Origenist doctrine of *apokatastasis*, that is, the ultimate return of all things to God (and thus an end to punishment in Hell).

Fragment 2, from Book 4[3]

A. (Turrianus [1552], 27)

Hear what the blessed Magnetes, who wrote before the time of Constantine the Great, said in this passage in his fourth book in response to a certain Theosthenes[4] who impugned the New Testament, which I shall translate into Latin:

> There is nothing that the divine nature is unable to do; it could cause sun and cloud to be the same, and likewise cause what has happened not to have happened and what has been done not to have been done. But how and when it is possible neither to explain nor understand. So consequently, he says, although God can do everything, he nevertheless does not do whatever is possible, but whatever he wills. But he wills what is consistent, and what is consistent is what is appropriate, and is in truth *what follows logically*,[5] that is, what is fit and coherent.

So says this author.

B. (Turrianus [1581], 14a)

Although God can do everything, he nevertheless does not act *according to capacity*,[6] as Magnetes, a most ancient and ecclesiastical author states in his apologetic books against Theosthenes the pagan. That is, he does not do whatever he can, but whatever he wills. But he wills, he says, what is consistent, what is consistent is what is appropriate, and again what is appropriate is what is coherent.

C. (Turrianus [1583], 5)

God, then, just as the divine Scriptures state, wills anything whatsoever that he creates on heaven and earth. Nevertheless, he wills what is consistent; in truth what is consistent is what is proper. Just so writes Magnetes, an ancient and ecclesiastical author, against the pagan Theosthenes.

---

3 Goulet is probably correct in suggesting that this fragment, quoted and summarized by Turrianus in several works, probably belongs at the *lacuna* at 4.30.24.

4 Turrianus mistakes the text's dedicatee as the name of the Hellene, and does so consistently, as the subsequent fragments show.

5 The italics represent Turrianus's quotation in Greek of the phrase ἅπερ ἀκόλουθον, the philosophical and ethical sense of which he translates correctly in the next clause.

6 The italics represent Turrianus's quotation in Greek of the phrase καθὸ δύναται.

Fragment 3, from Book 4[7]

(Turrianus [1578], 95)

Cyril then adds: "if, therefore, handkerchiefs and girdles, which are outside the body, heal when touched by the sick, how much more will he [be able] to raise the body of a deceased prophet!"

Next, Magnetes, a most weighty author about twelve hundred years ago, in his fourth book against Theosthenes, a pagan who assailed the gospels, [writes]:

> The bones, he says, of the prophets are not bones of the dead,[8] because God is the god only of the living.[9] About this it is written: "The Lord preserves all their bones."[10] It is clear, therefore, that the bones of the saints are not dead, but rather are full of virtue. If, then, "fringes,"[11] because of he who wears them, give the virtue of health to a believer and effect a cure through touch alone:
>
>> *"How can we not say that the saints, who are more worthy than inanimate fringes, have the power to cause believers who have an unfailing resolve to participate in better things, [believers] whom Christ put on like a cloak when they were living in the body, and honouring them after death, has made them like a purple robe of royal dignity".*[12]

His meaning is, how can we say that the saints, who are more honourable than inanimate fringes, are unable to vouchsafe better things to those who believe without wavering? Those with whom, when they lived in the body, Christ clothed himself as with a cloak and who, after their death, he made like a purple robe of royal dignity. A little bit before the same author states:

> The heresy of the Manichaeans and that of Marcion make out the bodies of martyrs to be *abominable*,[13] that is, that they are abominable and horrible, and do not differ from the tombs of criminals. But Scripture says that 'in the eyes of the Lord the death of his saints is precious.'[14] But if it is precious, writes this

---

7 The passage quoted probably responds to the Hellene's critique at 4.24b.
8 Compare Sirach 49:10.
9 Compare Mt. 22:32.
10 Ps. 33:21 (LXX).
11 See e.g. Mt. 9:20, 14:36, where individuals are healed by touching the "fringe" of Jesus's garments.
12 Turrianus quotes the italicised text in Greek.
13 Turrianus quotes the Greek word βδελυκτά.
14 Ps. 115:6 (LXX).

author, and honourable with God, how can we hear from these impostors that they are not so among men?

Fragment 4, from Books 2 and 5

(Turrianus [1572], 144ff.)

[Against a criticism that Anacletus (bishop of Rome, late first century) argued the primacy of the Roman See based on a false etymology of the name "Cephas" from κεφαλῆς ("head"), Turrianus explains that the etymology, while philologically incorrect, was designed to appeal to the presuppositions of a largely Grecophone audience. To support his case he looks to the *Apocriticus*.]

Yet we can adduce here the example of the Evangelists, who sometimes took up a word based not on the exact truth of the thing but on common habit and opinion. The author is Magnetes, a most ancient ecclesiastical writer who, in the second and fifth books he wrote against Theosthenes, who objected to discrepancies among the Evangelists and other falsifications in the Gospel, says that:[15]

> While one Evangelist said, "putting a sponge around a reed," another, because of its[16] likeness to a stick, said, "putting [a sponge] around a 'hyssop,'" since a "reed" was what had to be named. Then, while one Evangelist said, "wine," "vinegar" is in fact what was given at the Cross (that same vinegar which they drew from the vessel they set there when they arrived at Calvary and the Cross). This, he says, was because the Evangelists observed the law of history and wrote nothing more than the very things that were said amidst that tumult and furor. Therefore, they clearly judged it right that their history would be free of all suspicion, "*if the text of the history was found not to be especially elaborate but unfabricated*"[17], that is, if the text of the history was found not to be nicely written, but simple.[18]

---

15 Turrianus presents what follows in Latin. The passage is a parallel to the extant Greek text in the Athens manuscript (2.28.4–6), but does not match it exactly. This makes sense, given that Turrianus states that he is about to adduce evidence from Books 2 and 5; the passage here may thus be a conglomeration or summary of the passage in Book 2 and a similar treatment of variant readings in the gospels from the lost Book 5.

16 I.e. the "hyssop": see 2.28.6 for the passage Turrianus is aiming to summarize.

17 The italicised text is quoted in Greek by Turrianus.

18 On Macarius's notions about ancient historiographic practice see 2.28.4–6.

278   MACARIUS, *APOCRITICUS*

Fragment 5, from Book 5

(Turrianus [1557], 36b–38a)

Nor was I in fact the first to discover these passages, but fourteen hundred years ago, Magnetes, a most weighty author, said, at the very end of the fifth of the apologetic books he wrote to Theosthenes against those who calumniate the Gospels, about the faith of Abraham:[19]

> For because he had faith, he was pleasing to God through good works, and thereby was deemed worthy of the Almighty's friendship. By doing them he made his faith shine greater than the sun and, with faith, lived his life well. Therefore, being befriended by God he was honoured. For knowing that faith is the foundation of virtuous action, he established it as a deep foundation, building up the mass of mercies upon it. For building one upon the other, by laying brick upon brick, he erected a high tower upon them both, not using faith unattested by works, nor again letting works stand bare apart from faith. Knowing that faith is a seed that produces much, he attended to everything conducive to the seed: soil, plough ox, his ploughman's purse, yoke, plough, and whatever the knowledge characteristic of farmers teaches. For as a seed is not sown without these things, and without seeds the principle of the things just mentioned accomplishes nothing, so too faith, which is in a way a mystical seed, is sterile and abides alone, unless it sprouts through good works, and likewise the gathering of good deeds will be an idle affair and completely without result unless it has faith entwined together with it. Therefore in order to show that it was by faith that Abraham radiated the grace of good works, divine Scripture says that "Abraham had faith in God and it was reckoned unto him as righteousness."[20] You see how faith caused the perfection of virtue that he already possessed to be reckoned as righteousness, as seed causes the land to bear fruit. For as a lamp causes the quality of the oil placed within it to shine, so faith, placed within Abraham just as in a lamp has caused the virtue of his works to radiate. Abraham, since he was schooled in a way of life based on equality, naturally embraced his neighbours and was of service to them and honest with them, loving lack of corruption in giving and receiving, giving endless relief to those in need, and abstaining absolutely from wicked pursuits. But even in showing oneself to have these fine and honourable characteristics, no one was reckoned "unto righteousness," no one was by nature virtuous, since no one was such as this except God alone, but neither did anyone have faith. Abraham, however, had faith in God, and these and similar fine virtuous actions were reckoned to Abraham "unto righteousness."

---

19 In the quotation that follows, Turrianus first provides the Greek in full and follows it with a more or less faithful Latin translation; here we have only translated the Greek.
20 Compare Gen. 15:6; Rom. 4:3.

BIBLIOGRAPHY

Abbreviations

ANF = A. Roberts, J. Donalson, A.C. Coxe, A Menzies, eds. (1885–1897) *Ante-Nicene fathers: the writings of the fathers down to A.D. 325* (Buffalo and New York, N.Y.)
CCSG = Corpus Christianorum Series Graeca (1977–) (Turnhout)
CCSL = Corpus Christianorum Series Latina (1953–) (Turnhout)
GCS = Die griechischen christlichen Schriftsteller der ersten drei Jahrhundert (1897–) (Leipzig and Berlin)
LCL = Loeb Classical Library (1911–) (Cambridge, Mass. and London)
LXX = Septuagint
NPNF = P. Schaff and H. Wace, eds. (1890–1900) *A Select library of Nicene and post-Nicene fathers of the Christian church* (New York)
PG = J.P. Migne et al., eds (1857–1866) *Patrologia Graeca* (Paris)
PGL = G.W.H. Lampe, ed. (1969) *A Patristic Greek Lexicon* (Oxford)
PL = J.P. Migne et al., eds (1844–1880) *Patrologia Latina* (Paris)
SC = Source Chrétiennes (1942–) (Paris)

Primary Literature

Note on bibliography of primary literature: The titles given in this bibliography are those used in the text and notes. We have given titles in English, except in cases where no English title is in common use or the common title is a transliteration of the Greek (e.g. *Progymnasmata*). For each work, we provide a reference to a well-known translation, an original language edition, or both.

Note on translations: When an English translation is listed in this bibliography, it is also the translation quoted in the notes. Where no English translation is listed in this bibliography, any English translation in the notes is ours.

Biblical literature: see *The New Oxford Annotated Bible with the Apocrypha: New Revised Standard Version*, 4th edition (Oxford, 2010).
Apocryphal Early Christian Literature: see J. Elliot (1993) *The Apocryphal New Testament* (Oxford).

Achilles Tatius, *Isagoga excerpta* = E. Maass, ed. (1898) *Commentariorum in Aratum reliquiae* (Berlin)
Acta Alexandrinorum = H. Musurillo, ed. and trans. (1954) *Acts of the Pagan Martyrs* (Oxford)
Acts of Archelaus = M.J. Vermes and K. Kaatz, trans. (Eng.) (2001) (Turnhout)
(Ps.) Adamantius, *Dialogue of Adamantius* = W.H. van de Sande Bakhuyzen, ed. (1901) *Der Dialog des Adamantius*. GCS 4 (Leipzig)
Aelius Theon, *Progymnasmata* = George A. Kennedy, trans. (Eng.) (2003) in *Progymnasmata: Greek Textbooks of Prose Composition and Rhetoric*. Writings from the Greco-Roman World 10 (Atlanta)
Ammianus Marcellinus, *Histories* = J.C. Rolfe, ed. and trans. (1936–1939) (Eng.) LCL 300, 315, 331 (Cambridge, Mass.)
Amphilochius of Iconium = C. Datema, ed. (1978) *Amphilochii Iconiensis opera*. CCSG 3 (Turnhout)
Anonymous, *Commentary on Dionysius of Thrace's Art of Grammar* = A Hilgard, ed. (1901) *Commentaria in Dionysii Thracis artem grammaticam, Scholia Londonensia*, in idem, ed. (1901) *Grammatici Graeci* vol. 1.3 (Leipzig)
(Ps.) Anthimus, *To Theodore* 8 = G. Mercati, ed. (1991) *Studi e testi* 5 (Rome)
Aphthonius, *Progymnasmata* = George A. Kennedy, trans. (Eng.) (2003) in *Progymnasmata: Greek Textbooks of Prose Composition and Rhetoric*. Writings from the Greco-Roman World 10 (Atlanta)
Apocalypse of Peter = [Ethiopic] J. Grébaut, ed. and trans. (Fr.) (1910) "Littérature éthiopienne pseudo-Clémentine." *Revue de l'Orient Chrétien*, n.s. 15: 198–214, 307–323; C. Detlef and G. Müller, trans. (Ger.) and R.M. Wilson, trans. (Eng.) (1991–1992) *New Testament Apocrypha* (Louisville, Kentucky)
Apocryphon of John = J. Robinson, ed. (2000) *The Coptic gnostic library: A complete edition of the Nag Hammadi codices, vol. 2* (Leiden)
Apollodorus, *Library* = J.G. Frazer, trans. (Eng.) (1921) *Apollodorus. The Library*, 2 vols. LCL 121–122 (Cambridge, Mass.)
Aratus, *Phaenomena* = J. Martin, ed. (1956) *Arati phaenomena* (Florence)
Aristides, *Apology to the Greeks* = B. Pouderon, M.-J. Pierre, et al., ed. and trans. (Fr.) (2003) *Aristide: Apologie*. SC 470 (Paris)
Aristophanes, *Frogs* = J. Henderson, trans. (Eng.) (2002) *Aristophanes. Volume IV*. LCL 180 (Cambridge, Mass.)
Aristotle, *Categories* = J.L. Ackrill, trans. (Eng.) (1992 [1963]) *The Complete Works of Aristotle*: 3–24 (Princeton)
———. *Physics* = R.P. Hardie and R.K. Gaye, trans. (Eng.) (1992 [1963]) *The Complete Works of Aristotle*: 315–446 (Princeton)

—. *Metaphysics* = W.D. Ross, trans. (Eng.) (1992 [1963]) *The Complete Works of Aristotle:* 1552–1728 (Princeton)
Arnobius, *Against the Nations* = G.E. McCracken, trans. (Eng.) (1978) *Arnobius of Sicca: The Case against the Pagans*. Ancient Christian Writers 7–8 (Mahwah, New Jersey)
Artemidorus, *Oneirocriticon* = White, R.J., trans. (Eng.) (1975) *The Interpretation of Dreams* (Park Ridge, New Jersey)
Athanasius *Against the Gentiles* = R.W. Thomson, ed. and trans. (Eng.) (1971) *Contra Gentes and De Incarnatione*. Oxford Early Christian Texts (Oxford)
—. *Apology against the Arians* = H.G. Opitz, ed. (1940) *Athanasius Werke Band 2.1* (Berlin); A. Robertson, trans. (Eng.) NPNF II.4: 100–147
—. *Life of Antony* = R. Gregg, trans. (Eng.) (1979) *Athanasius: Life of Antony and the Letter to Marcellinus*. Classics of Western Spirituality (Mahwah, New Jersey)
—. *On the Incarnation* = R.W. Thomson, ed. and trans. (Eng.) (1971) *Contra Gentes and De Incarnatione*. Oxford Early Christian Texts (Oxford)
—. *On the Synods of Ariminum and Seleucia* = H.-G. Opitz, ed. (1940) *Athanasius Werke. Band II: Die Apologien. Lieferungen 6–7* (Berlin); A. Robertson, trans. (Eng.) NPNF II.4: 451–480
—. *Orations against the Arians* = M. Tetz, et al., eds. (1998) *Athanasius Werke, B. 1: Die dogmatischen schriften, fasc. 2* (Berlin)
Athenagoras, *Embassy* = M. Marcovich, ed. (1990) *Legatio pro Christianis: Athenagoras*. Patristische Texte und Studien. (Berlin)
—. *Plea for the Christians*. B.P. Pratten, trans. (Eng.) ANF I: 129–148
Augustine of Hippo, *City of God* = B. Dombart and A Kalb, eds. (1955) *Augustinus. Opera*. Corpus Christianorum Series Latina 47–48 (Turnholt)
—. *Debate with Fortunatus* = R. Teske, trans. (Eng.) (2006) *The Manichaean Debate*. The Works of Augustine: A Translation for the 21st Century I/19 (Hyde Park, NY)
—. *Retractions* = B. Ramsey, trans. (Eng.) (2010) *Revisions*. The Works of Augustine: A Translation for the 21st Century I/2 (Hyde Park, NY)
Basil of Caesarea, *Letters* = Roy J. Deferrari, ed. and trans. (Eng.) (1926–1934) *Basil: Letters*, 4 vols (London and Cambridge, Mass.)
—. *On the Holy Spirit* = B. Jackson, trans. (Eng.) NPNF II.8: 1–50
Blasphemies of Diodore, Theodore, and the Impious Nestorius = J. Behr, ed. and trans. (Eng.) (2011) *The Case against Diodore and Theodore* (Oxford)
Chromatius, *Tractate on Matthew* = J. Lemarié and R. Étaix, eds. (1977) *Spicilegium ad Chromatii Aquileiensis opera*. CCSL 9a suppl. (Turnhout)
Cicero, *On the Republic* = C.W. Keyes, trans. (Eng.) (1928) *Cicero. On the Republic. On the Laws*. LCL 213 (Cambridge, Mass.)
Clement of Rome, *1* and *2 Clement* = B. Ehrman, ed. and trans. (Eng.) (2003) *The Apostolic Fathers, Vol. I*. LCL 24 (Cambridge, Mass.)

Clement of Alexandria, *Excerpts from Theodotus* = F. Sagnard, ed. and trans. (Fr.) (1948) *Clément d'Alexandrie: Extraits de Théodote*. SC 23 (Paris)

—. *Exhortation to the Greeks* = O. Stählin and U. Treu, eds. (1972) *Clemens Alexandrinus B. 1: Protrepticus und Paedagogus*, 2. Aufl. GCS 12 (Berlin); W. Wilson, trans. (Eng.) ANF 2: 171–206

—. *Pedagogue* = O. Stählin and U. Treu, eds. (1972) *Clemens Alexandrinus B. 1: Protrepticus und Paedagogus*, 2. Aufl. GCS 12 (Berlin); W. Wilson, trans. (Eng.) ANF 2: 209–296

—. *Stromateis* = O. Stählin, L. Früchtel, and U. Treu, eds. (1985) *Clemens Alexandrinus B. 2., Stromata I–VI*. GCS 52 (Berlin)

—. *Who is the Rich Man Who Shall Be Saved?* = L. Früchtel, O. Stählin, and U. Treu, eds. (1970) *Clemens Alexandrinus, B. 3*, 2. Aufl. GCS 17 (Berlin); W. Wilson, trans. (Eng.) ANF 2: 591–604

(Ps.) Clementine Recognitions and Homilies = B. Rehm et al., eds. (1953–1992) *Die Pseudoklementinen. B. I–III*. GCS 42, 51 (Leipzig and Berlin)

Codex Justinianus = P. Krüger, ed. (1877) *Corpus iuris civilis. V.2: Codex Iustinianus* (Berlin)

Codex Theodosianus = C. Pharr, trans. (Eng.) (1952) *The Theodosian Code and the Sirmondian Constitutions: a translation with commentary, glossary, and bibliography* (Princeton)

Comparison of Mosaic and Roman Law = M. Hyamson, ed. and trans. (Eng.) (1913) *Mosaicarum et Romanarum legum collatio* (London and New York); translation of XV.3 revised by S. Lieu, in I. Gardner and S. Lieu, *Manichaean Texts from the Roman Empire* [Cambridge: Cambridge University Press, 2004], 117–118

Constantine, *Oration to the Saints* = M.J. Edwards, trans. (Eng.) (2003) *Constantine and Christendom: The Oration to the Saints, The Greek and Latin Accounts of the Discovery of the True Cross, The Edict of Constantine to Pope Sylvester*. Translated Texts for Historians (Liverpool)

Cyril of Alexandria, *Commentary on Matthew* = J. Reuss, ed. (1957) *MatthäusKommentare aus der griechischen Kirche*. Patristische Texte und Studien 61 (Berlin)

Cyril of Jerusalem, *Catechetical Lectures* = E.H. Gifford, trans. (Eng.) NPNF II.7: 1–157

Damascius, *On First Principles* = C.É. Ruelle, ed. (1889, 1899) *Damascii successoris dubitationes et solutions*, 2 vols (Paris)

Didymus the Blind, *Commentary on Ecclesiastes* = *Pap. Tura. Eccles.* 281.16–22 in G. Binder (1958) "Eine Polemik des Porphyrios gegen die allegorische Auslegung des Alten Testaments durch die Christen," *Zeitschrift für Papyrologie und Epigraphik* 3: 81–95

—. *Commentary on Job* = A. Henrichs, ed. (1968–1985) *Didymos der Blinde. Kommentar zu Hiob*. Papyrologische Texte und Abhandlungen 1–3, 33 (Bonn)

Diogenes Laertius, *Lives of Eminent Philosophers* = R.D. Hicks, trans. (Eng.) (1925) *Diogenes Laertius: Lives of Eminent Philosophers*, 2 vols. LCL 184, 185 (Cambridge, Mass.)

(Ps.) Dionysius the Areopagite = C. Luibheid, trans. (Eng.) (1987) *Pseudo-Dionysius: The complete works*. The Classics of Western Spirituality (New York)

Dionysius of Halicarnassus, *On Literary Composition* = L. Radermacher and H. Usener (1929) *Dionysii Halicarnasei quae extant*, Vol. 6: 3–143 (Leipzig)

Doctrina Addai = M. Illert, ed. and trans. (Ger.) (2007) *Doctrina Addai; De imagine Edessena/Die Abgarlegende; Das Christusbild von Edessa*. Fontes Christiani 45 (Turnhout)

Epiphanius of Salamis, *Panarion* = F. Williams, trans. (Eng.) (2012) *The Panarion of Epiphanius of Salamis*, 2 vols, 2nd ed. Nag Hammadi and Manichaean Studies 79 (Leiden)

Eusebius (of Caesarea [?]), *Against Hierocles* = C.P. Jones, trans. (Eng.) (2006) as "Eusebius's Reply to Hierocles" in *Philostratus, Apollonius of Tyana*, vol. 3. Loeb Classical Library 458 (New York)

Eusebius of Caesarea, *Chronicle* and *Chronological Tables* = R. Helm, ed. (1956) *Eusebius Werke. B.7: Die Chronik*. GCS 47 (Berlin)

—. *Ecclesiastical History* = E. Schwartz, T. Mommsen, F. Winkelmann, eds. (1999) *Eusebius Werke. B.2: Die Kirchengeschichte. Teil 1–3*. GCS N.F. 6. (Berlin)

—. *Ecclesiastical Theology* = E. Klostermann, G.C. Hansen, eds. (1991) *Eusebius Werke B.4. Contra Marcellum. De ecclesiastica theologia*. GCS 14, 3. Aufl. (Berlin)

—. *Gospel Demonstration* = I.A. Heikel, ed. (1913) *Eusebius Werke, B. 6: Die Demonstratio evangelica*. GCS 23 (Leipzig)

—. *Gospel Preparation* = K. Mras and É. des Places, eds. (2012) *Eusebius Werke, B. 8.1–2: Die Praeparatio evangelica. Teil 1–2*. GCS 43/1–2. Berlin; E.H. Gifford, ed. and trans. (Eng.) (1903) *Praeparatio Evangelica* 5 vols (Oxford)

—. *Commentary on Isaiah* = J. Zeigler, ed. (1975) *Eusebius Werke, B. 9: Der Jesajakommentar*. GCS (Berlin)

—. *Commentary on the Psalms* = PG 23

—. *Theophany* = S. Lee, ed. (1842) *Eusebius of Caesarea, on the Theophania* (London); idem, trans. (Eng.) (1843) *Eusebius of Caesarea on the Theophania* (Cambridge)

Eusebius of Emesa, *Homilies* = É.M. Buytaert (1953, 1957) *Eusébe d'Emèse: Discours conserves en latin, texts en partie inédits*, 2 vols (Louvain)

—. *On Faith* = É.M. Buytaert (1953, 1957) *Eusébe d'Emèse: Discours conserves en latin, texts en partie inédits*, 2 vols (Louvain)

Eustathius of Antioch, *Against the Ariomaniacs* = J.H. Declerk, ed. (2002) *Eustathii Antiocheni, Patris Nicaeni, Opera Quae Supersunt Omnia*. CCSG 51 (Turnhout)

Evagrius of Pontus, *Antirheticus* = D. Brakke, trans. (Eng.) (2009) *Talking Back: A Monastic Handbook for Combatting Demons.* Cistercian Studies 229 (Collegeville, Minn.)

—. *Eulogius* = R.E. Sinkewicz, trans. (Eng.) (2003) *Evagrius of Pontus: the Greek ascetic corpus*: 29–59. Oxford Early Christian Studies (Oxford)

Galen = works collected in C.G. Kühn, ed. (1821–1833 [repr.1964]) *Opera Omnia. Medicorum Graecorum opera quae exstant* (Hildesheim)

[Gelasius], *Ecclesiastical History* = G.C. Hansen, ed. (2002) *Anonyme Kirchengeschichte (Gelasius Cyzicenus, CPG 6034).* GCS N.F. 9 (Berlin)

Gospel of Truth = J. Robinson, ed. (2000) *The Coptic gnostic library: a complete edition of the Nag Hammadi codices, vol. 1* (Leiden)

Gregory Nazianzen, *Letters* = P. Gallay, ed. and trans. (Fr.) (1964, 1967) *Saint Grégoire de Nazianze. Lettres*, 2 vols. Collection Budé (Paris)

—. *Oration 33* = PG 36: 213–237

—. *Third Theological Oration* = F. Williams and L. Wickham, trans. (Eng.) (2002) *On God and Christ: St. Gregory of Nazianzus, The Five Theological Orations and Two Letters to Cledonius.* Popular Patristics Series (Crestwood, NY)

Gregory of Nyssa, *Against Eunomius* = W. Moore and H.A. Wilson, trans. (Eng.) NPNF II.5: 35–314

—. *Commentary on the Song of Songs* = H. Langerbeck, ed. (1960) *Gregorii Nysseni opera, vol 6.* (Leiden)

—. *Homilies on the Song of Songs* = R.A. Norris, Jr., trans. (Eng.) (2013) *Gregory of Nyssa: Homilies on the Song of Songs.* Writings from the Greco-Roman World 13 (Atlanta)

—. *Letters* = A.M. Silvas, trans. (Eng.) (2006) *Gregory of Nyssa: The Letters.* Supplements to Vigiliae Christianae 83 (Leiden)

—. *Life of Moses* = A. Malherbe, E. Ferguson, and J. Meyendorff, trans. (Eng.) (1978) *Gregory of Nyssa: The Life of Moses.* The Classics of Western Spirituality (New York)

—. *On the Making of Man* = PG 44: 124–256; W. Moore and H.A. Wilson, trans. (Eng.) NPNF II.5: 386–426.

—. *To Ablabius* = F. Mueller, ed. (1958) *Gregorii Nysseni opera*, vol. 3.1 (Leiden)

—. *To Theophilus* = F. Mueller, ed. (1958) *Gregorii Nysseni opera*, vol. 3.1 (Leiden)

Gregory Thaumaturgus, *Panegyric for Origen* = H. Crouzel, ed. and trans. (Fr.) (1969) *Grégoire le Thaumaturge: Remerciement à Origène.* SC 148 (Paris); M. Slusser, trans. (Eng.) (1998) *Gregory Thaumaturgus: Life and Works.* The Fathers of the Church 98 (Washington, D.C.)

(Ps.) Herodian, *On Solecism and Barbarism* = A. Nauck, ed. (1867 [repr. 1965]) *Lexicon Vindobonense*: 294–312 (St Petersburg [Hildesheim])

Herodotus, *Histories* = C. Hude (1927) *Herodoti Historiae* (Oxford)

(Ps.) Hermogenes, *Progymnasmata* = George A. Kennedy, trans. (Eng.) (2003) *Progymnasmata: Greek Textbooks of Prose Composition and Rhetoric.* Writings from the Greco-Roman World 10 (Atlanta)

Hesiod, *Theogony* = G. Most, trans. (Eng.) (2006) *Hesiod*, 2 vols. LCL 57, 503 (Cambridge, Mass.)
Hierocles of Alexandria, *Commentary on the Golden Verses of Pythagoras* = F.G. Köhler, ed. (1974) *Hieroclis in aureum Pythagoreorum carmen commentarius* (Stuttgart)
Hilary of Poitiers, *On Matthew* = J. Doignon, ed. and trans. (Fr.) (1978–1979) *Hilaire de Poitiers: Sur Matthieu*, 2 vols. SC 254, 258 (Paris)
History of the Monks in Egypt = E. Schulz-Flügel, ed. (1990) *Historia Monachorum*. Patristische Texte und Studien 34 (Berlin)
Homer, *Iliad* = D.B. Munro and T.W. Allen, eds (1920) *Homeri Opera. T. 1–2*. Oxford Classical Texts (Oxford)
—. *Odyssey* = T.W. Allen, ed. (1922) *Homeri Opera. T. 3–4*. Oxford Classical Texts (Oxford)
Hyginus, *Fabulae* = H.I. Rose, ed. (1963) *Fabulae, recensuit, prolegomenis commentario appendice instruxit* (Lyons)
Iamblichus, *De Anima* = J.F. Finamore and J. Dillon, eds and trans. (Eng.) (2002) *Iamblichus: De Anima*. Philosophia Antiqua 92 (Leiden)
—. *Life of Pythagoras* = U. Klein, ed. (1937) *Iamblichi de vita Pythagorica liber* (Leipzig)
Ignatius of Antioch, *Letters* = B. Ehrman, trans. (Eng.) (2004) *Apostolic Fathers, Vol. 1*. LCL 24 (Cambridge, Mass.)
Incomplete Commentary on Matthew (Opus Imperfectum in Mattheum) = PG 56: 611–946
Irenaeus, *Against Heresies* = A. Rousseau, et al., eds and trans. (Fr.) (1965–1982) *Iréné de Lyon: Contre les hérésies*. SC 100, 152, 153, 210, 211, 263, 264, 293, 294 (Paris)
Jerome, *Against Helvidius* = W.H. Fremantle, G. Lewis, and W.G. Martley, trans. (Eng.) NPNF II.6: 334–346
—. *Against the Pelagians* = C. Moreschini, ed. (1990) *Dialogus adversus Pelagianos*. CCSL 80 (Turnhout)
—. *Commentary on Galatians* = PL 26; A. Cain, trans. (Eng.) (2010) *St. Jerome: Commentary on Galatians*. The Fathers of the Church 121 (Washington, D.C.)
—. *Commentary on Matthew* = T. Scheck, trans. (Eng.) (2008) *St. Jerome: Commentary on Matthew*. The Fathers of the Church 117 (Washington, D.C.)
—. *Tractates on the Psalms* = G. Morin, et al., eds. (1958) *Tractatus sive homiliae in Psalmos. In Marci evangelium. Alia varia argumentum*. CCSL 78 (Turnhout)
—. *Questions on Genesis* = P. de Lagarde, et al., eds. (1959) *Hebraicae quaestiones in libro Geneseos. Liber interpretationis hebraicorum nominum. Commentarioli in psalmos. Commentarius in Ecclesiasten*. CCSL 72 (Turnhout)
John Chrysostom, *Homilies on 1 Corinthians* = PG 61: 9–382
—. *Homilies on Ephesians* = PG 62: 9–176
—. *Homilies on John* = PG 59: 23–482
—. *Homilies on Matthew* = PG 57:13–472; 58: 471–794

—. *Instruction and Refutation Directed against Those Men Cohabiting with Virgins* = Elizabeth A. Clark, trans. (Eng.) (1982) *Jerome, Chrysostom, and friends: essays and translations* (Lewiston, NY)

—. *On the Necessity of Guarding Virginity* = Elizabeth A. Clark, trans. (Eng.) (1982) *Jerome, Chrysostom, and friends: essays and translations* (Lewiston, NY)

Josephus, *Jewish War* = H. Thackeray, R. Marcus, A.H. Wikgren, trans. (Eng.) (1997 1998 [rev. ed.]) *Josephus: Jewish War.* LCL 203, 210, 242, 281 (Cambridge, Mass.)

Julian, *Against the Galilaeans* = Emanuella Masaracchia, ed. and trans. (Ital.) (1990) *Giuliano Imperatore, Contra Galilaeos: Introduzione, testo critico e traduzione.* Testi e commenti 9 (Rome)

—. *Caesars* = C. Lacombrade, ed. and trans. (Fr.) (1964) *L'empereur Julien.* Œuvres *complètes*, vol. 2.2 (Paris)

—. *Letters* = J. Bidez, ed. and trans. (Fr.) (1960) *L'empereur Julien.* Œuvres *complètes*, vol. 1.2 (Paris)

Justin, *First Apology* and *Second Apology* = M. Marcovich, ed. (1994) *Iustini Martyris Apologiae pro Christianis.* Patristische Texte und Studien 38 (Berlin)

—. *Dialogue with Trypho* = M. Marcovich, ed. (1997) *Dialogus cum Tryphone. Iustini Martyris.* Patristische Texte und Studien 47 (Berlin); T.B. Falls and T.P. Halton, trans. (Eng.) (2003) *Dialogue with Trypho. Justin Martyr.* Fathers of the Church 3, rev. ed. (Washington, D.C.)

(Ps.) Justin, *On the Resurrection* = M. Heimgartner, ed. (2001) *Pseudojustin— uber die Auferstehung.* Patristische Texte und Studien 54 (Berlin)

—. *Questions and Responses to the Orthodox* = J.C.T. Otto, ed. (1881, repr. 1969) *Corpus apologetarum Christianorum saeculi secundi*, vol. 5, 3rd ed., 2–246 (Jena)

Lactantius, *Divine Institutes* = Anthony Bowen and Peter Garnsey, trans. (Eng.) (2004) *Lactantius. Divine Institutes.* Translated Texts for Historians (Liverpool)

Letter of Aristeas = A. Pelletier, ed. and trans. (Fr.) (1962) *Lettre d'Aristée à Philocrate.* SC 89 (Paris)

Libanius, *Progymnasmata* = Craig A. Gibson, trans. (Eng.) (2008) *Libanius's Progymnasmata: Model Exercises in Greek Prose Composition and Rhetoric.* Writings from the Greco-Roman World 27 (Atlanta)

Life of Syncletica = E. Castelli, trans. (Eng.) (1990) in V. Wimbush, ed., *Ascetic Behavior in Greco-Roman Antiquity*: 265–311 (Minneapolis)

Livy, *History* = B.O. Foster, F.G. Moore, A.C. Schelsinger, et al., trans. (Eng.) (1919–1959) *Livy. History of Rome*, 14 vols. LCL 114, 133, 172, 191, 233, 295, 301, 313, 332, 355, 367, 381, 396, 404 (Cambridge, Mass.)

Lucian, *How To Write History* = K. Kilburn, trans. (Eng.) (1956) *Lucian. Volume VI.* LCL 430 (Cambridge, Mass.)

—. *Passing of Peregrinus* = A.M. Harmon, trans. (Eng.) (1936) *Lucian, Volume V.* LCL 302 (Cambridge, Mass.)

Lucretius, *On the Nature of Things* = W.H.D. Rouse and M.F. Smith, trans. (Eng.) (1924 [rev. ed. 1992]) *Lucretius: De rerum natura*. LCL 181 (Cambridge, Mass.)
Methodius of Olympus, *On the Resurrection* = G.N. Bonwetsch, ed. (1917) *Methodius Olympius: Werke.* GCS 27 (Berlin)
—. *Symposium* = G.N. Bonwetsch, ed. (1917) *Methodius Olympius: Werke.* GCS 27 (Berlin)
Nemesius of Emesa, *On the Nature of Man* = G. Verbeke and J. Moncho, eds. (1975) *De Natura Hominis* (Leipzig); P van der Eijk and R.W. Sharples, trans. (Eng.) (2008) *Nemesius: On the Nature of Man.* Translated Texts for Historians (Liverpool).
Nicephorus, *Critique [Epikrisis]* = Michael Featherstone, ed. and trans. (Eng.) (2002) "Opening scenes of the Second Iconoclasm: Nicephorus's *Critique* of the citations from Macarius Magnes." *Revue des Études Byzantines* 60: 65–111.
Origen, *Against Celsus* = M. Marcovich, ed. (2003) *Contra Celsum Libri VIII.* Supplements to Vigiliae Christianae 54. (Leiden); H. Chadwick, trans. (Eng.) (1953) *Origen: Contra Celsum* (Cambridge)
—. *Commentary on John* = E. Preuschen, ed. (1903) *Origenes Werke Band 4: Der Johanneskommentar.* GCS 10. (Berlin); R.E. Heine, trans. (Eng.) (1989, 1993) *Origen: Commentary on the Gospel according to John*, 2 vols (Washington, D.C.)
—. *Commentary on Matthew* = E. Klostermann, et al., eds. (1935, 1941, 1968) *Origenes Werke X und XII. Commentarius in Matthaeum.* GCS 40, 41.1–2 (Berlin)
—. *Commentary on Romans* = E. Klostermann, E. Benz, and U. Treu, eds. (1976) *Origenes Werke, Band XI. Commentarius in Mattheum II.* 2. Aufl. GCS 38
—. *Dialogue with Heraclides* = J. Scherer, ed. and trans. (Fr.) (1960) *Entretien d'Origène avec Héraclide* (Paris)
—. *Fragments on Job* = J.B. Pitra, ed. (1884) *Analecta sacra spicilegio Solesmensi parata*, vol. 2: 361–391 (Paris)
—. *Homilies on Genesis* = P. Habermehl, ed. and trans. (Ger.) (2011) *Origenes Werke mit deutscher Übersetzung. Band 1/2* (Berlin)
—. *Homilies on Jeremiah* = E. Klostermann and P. Nautin, eds. (1983) *Origenes Werke. Band 3. Homiliae in Ieremiam, Fragmenta in Lamentationes.* 2.Aufl. (Berlin)
—. *Homilies on Leviticus* = G.W. Barkley, trans. (Eng.) (1990) *Origen: Homilies on Leviticus 1–16.* The Fathers of the Church 83 (Washington, D.C.)
—. *On First Principles* = P. Koetschau, ed. (1913) *Origenes Werke. Band 5: De Principiis.* GCS 22 (Berlin)
—. *On Prayer* = P. Koetschai, ed. (1899) *Origenes Werke. Band 2: Contra Celsum V–VIII, De oratione.* GCS 3 (Berlin)
Ovid, *Metamorphoses* = F.J. Miller and G.P. Goold, trans. (Eng.) (1977, 1984) *Ovid: Metamorphoses.* LCL 42, 43 (Cambridge, Mass.)

Pausanias, *Description of Greece* = W.H.S. Jones, trans. (Eng.) (1917–1935) *Pausanias: Description of Greece.* LCL 93, 188, 272, 297–298 (Cambridge, Mass.)
Pelagius, *Commentary on Romans* = de Bruyn, Theodore S., ed. and trans. (Eng.) (1993) *Pelagius: Commentary on Romans* (Oxford)
Philo of Alexandria = Philo's works are collected and translated in F.H. Colson, et al., trans. (Eng.) (1929–1962) *Philo.* LCL 226, 227, 247, 261, 275, 289, 320, 341, 363, 379, 380 (Cambridge, Mass.)
Philostratus, *Life of Apollonius of Tyana* = C.P. Jones, trans. (Eng.) *Philostratus: Life of Apollonius of Tyana.* LCL 16, 17 (Cambridge, Mass.)
Pionius, *Martyrdom of Polycarp* = B. Ehrman, ed. and trans. (Eng.) (2003) *The Apostolic Fathers, Vol. I.* LCL 24 (Cambridge, Mass.)
Plato = J. Burnet, E.A. Duke, W.F. Hicken, W.S.M. Nicoll, eds. (1922, 1995) *Platonis Opera,* 5 vols. Oxford Classical Texts (Oxford)
Pliny the Elder, *Natural History* = H. Rackham, et al., trans. (Eng.) (1938–1963) *Pliny: Natural History.* LCL 330, 352–353, 370–371, 392–394, 418–419 (Cambridge, Mass.)
Pliny the Younger, *Letters* = B. Radice, trans. (Eng.) (1969) *Pliny: Letters and Panegyricus.* LCL 55, 59 (Cambridge, Mass.)
Plotinus, *Enneads* = P. Henry and H.-R. Schwyzer, eds. (1964–1982) *Plotini Opera.* (Oxford)
Plutarch, collected *Moralia* in F.C. Babbitt, et al. trans. (Eng.) (1927–2004) *Plutarch: Moralia,* 16 vols. LCL 197, et al. (Cambridge, Mass.)
Porphyry, *Against the Christians* = Adolf von Harnack, ed. (1916) *Porphyrius, Gegen die Christen 15 Bücher. Zeugnisse, Fragmente und Referate.* Abhandlungen der königlich preussischen Akademie der Wissenschaften Jahrgang 1916, Philosophisch-historische Klasse 1 (Berlin)
—. *Commentary on the Timaeus* = A.R. Sodano, ed. (1964) *Porphyrii in Platonis Timaeum commentariorum fragmenta* (Milan)
—. *Isagoge* = Jonathan Barnes, trans. (Eng.) (2003) *Porphyry: Introduction.* Clarendon Later Ancient Philosophers. (Oxford)
—. *Letter to Anebo* = A.R. Sodano, ed. and trans. (Ital.) (1958) *Porfirio. Lettera ad Anebo* (Naples)
—. *Life of Plotinus* = P. Henry and H.-R. Schwyzer, eds. (1964–1982) *Plotini Opera.* (Oxford); M.J. Edwards, trans. (Eng.) (2000) *Neoplatonic saints: The lives of Plotinus and Proclus by their students.* Translated Texts for Historians (Liverpool)
—. *Life of Pythagoras* = A. Nauck, ed. (1886) *Porphyrii Opuscula* (Leipzig)
—. *On Abstinence* = A. Nauck, ed. (1886) *Porphyrii Opuscula* (Leipzig); G. Clark, trans. (Eng.) (2000) *Porphyry: On Abstinence from Killing Animals.* Ancient Commentators on Aristotle (Ithaca)
—. *On the Cave of the Nymphs in the Odyssey* = A. Nauck, ed. (1886) *Porphyrii Opuscula* (Leipzig)

—. *On Statues (Peri Agalmaton)* = Andrew Smith, ed. (1993) *Porphyrii fragmenta*. Bibliotheca Teubneriana (Stuttgart and Leipzig)

—. *Commentary on Aristotle's Categories* = Steven K. Strange, trans. (Eng.) (1992) *Porphyry. On Aristotle's Categories*. Ancient Commentators on Aristotle (Ithaca)

—. *Sentences* = L. Brisson, ed. (2005) *Porphyre: Sentences*. Histoire des doctrines de l'antiquité classique 33 (Paris); J. Dillon, trans. (Eng.) (2005), in Brisson (2005)

Proclus, *Commentary on the First Book of Euclid's Elements* = G.R. Morrow, trans. (Eng.) (1970) *A commentary on the first book of Euclid's Elements* (Princeton)

—. *Commentary on the Timaeus* = H. Tarrant, et al., trans. (Eng.) (2007–2013) *Proclus: Commentary on Plato's Timaeus* (Cambridge)

Sallustius, *Concerning the Gods and the Universe* = A.D. Nock, ed. and trans. (Eng.) (1926) *Sallustius: Concerning the Gods and the Universe* (Cambridge)

Second Treatise of the Great Seth = J. Robinson, ed. (2000) *The Coptic Gnostic Library: A complete edition of the Nag Hammadi codices, vol. 4* (Leiden)

Socrates, *Ecclesiastical History* = G.C. Hansen, ed. (1995) *Kirchengeschichte*. GCS N.F. 1; A.C. Zenos, trans. (Eng.) NPNF II.2

Sozomen, *Ecclesiastical History* = J. Bidez and G.C. Hansen, eds. (1995) *Kirchengeschichte*. GCS N.F. 4; C.D. Hartranft, trans. (Eng.) NPNF II.2

Strabo, *Geography* = H.L. Jones, trans. (Eng.) (1917–1932) *Strabo: Geography*, 8 vols LCL 49, 50, 182, 196, 211, 223, 241, 267 (Cambridge, Mass.)

Suda = A. Adler, ed. (1928–1938) *Suidae Lexicon*, 5 vols (Leipzig)

Tatian, *Address to the Greeks* = M. Marcovich (1995) *Tatiani Oratio ad Graecos*. Patristische Texte und Studien 43 (Berlin)

Tertullian = see the collected works of Tertullian in ANF 3

Theodore of Mopsuestia, *Against Julian* = A. Guida, ed. and trans. (Ital.) (1994) *Teodoro di Mopsuestia, Replica a Giuliano Imperatore. Adversus criminations in Christianos Iuliani Imperatoris*. Biblioteca Patristica 24 (Florence)

Theophilus of Antioch, *To Autolycus* = R.M. Grant, ed. and trans. (Eng.) (1970) *Theophilus of Antioch: Ad Autolycum*. Oxford Early Christian Texts (Oxford)

Turrianus (Torres), Francisco, (1552) *Antapologeticus pro libro suo de residential pastorum* (Florence)

—. (1557) *Dogmaticus de iustificatione ad Germanos adversus Luteranos* (Rome)

—. (1572) *Adversus Magdeburg. Centuriatores* (Florence)

—. (1578) *Apostolici Constitutiones* (Antwerp)

—. (1581) *Epistola de definition propria peccati originalis* (Ingolstadt)

—. (1583) *Epistola scripta ad quondam in Germania theologum, contra Ubiquistas Arianistas* (Ingolstadt)

Unfinished Commentary on Matthew (Opus Imperfectum in Mattheum) = PG 56: 611- 946

Vegetius, *Epitome of Military Science* = N.P. Milner, trans. (Eng.) (1993 [rev. 1996]) *Vegetius: Epitome of Military Science* (Liverpool)

Xenophon, *Memorabilia* = E.C. Marchant, trans. (Eng.) (1968) *Xenophon: Memorabilia and Oeconomicus*. LCL 168 (Cambridge, Mass.)
Zostrianos = J. Robinson, ed. (2000) *The Coptic Gnostic Library: A complete edition of the Nag Hammadi codices*, vol. 4 (Leiden)

Secondary Literature

Adkin, Neil. (1992) "The Date of St. John Chrysostom's Treatises on 'Subintroductae'" *Revue Bénédictine* 102: 255–266
Amato, Eugenio and Jacques Schamp, eds. (2005) *Ethopoiia: La representation de caractères entre fiction scolaire et réalité vivante à l'époque impériale et tardive*. Cardo 3. (Salerno)
Ayres, Lewis. (2004) *Nicaea and its Legacy* (Oxford)
Barnes, Jonathan. (2003) *Porphyry. Introduction* (Oxford)
Barnes, Timothy D. (1973) "Porphyry *Against the Christians*: Date and the attribution of fragments." *Journal of Theological Studies* 24: 424–442
—. (1994) "Scholarship or Propaganda? Porphyry *Against the Christians* and its historical setting." *Bulletin of the Institute of Classical Studies* 39: 53–65
Behr, John. (2004) *The Nicene Faith*, 2 vols (New York)
—. (2011) *The Case against Diodore and Theodore* (Oxford)
Beatrice, Pierre Franco. (1992) "Towards a new edition of Porphyry's fragments against the Christians," in M.-O. Goulet-Cazé, G. Madec, and D. O'Brien, eds, ΣΟΦΙΗΣ ΜΑΙΗΤΟΡΕΣ, *Chercheurs de Sagesse, Mélanges Jean Pépin* (Paris), 347–355
—. (1996) "Traces du texte occidental chez le païen de Macaire de Magnésie," in D.C. Parker and C.B. Amphoux, eds, *Codex Bezae. Studies from the Lunel Colloquium 1994*. New Testament Tools and Studies 22 (Leiden), 317–326.
Blondel, Charles, ed. (1876) ΜΑΚΑΡΙΟΥ ΜΑΓΝΗΤΟΣ, Ἀποκριτικὸς ἢ Μονογενής. *Macarii Magnetis quae supersunt ex inedito codice edidit C. Blondel* (Paris)
Bochet, Isabelle. (2011) "Les *quaestiones* attribuées à Porphyre dans la *Lettre 102* d'Augustin," in S. Morlet, ed., *Le traité de Porphyre contre les Chrétiens* (Paris), 371–394
Borzì, Salvatore. (2003) "Sull'autenticità del *Contra Hieroclem* di Eusebio di Cesarea." *Augustinianum* 43: 397–416
Bouffartigue, Jean. (2011) "Porphyre et Julien contre les chrétiens: intentions, motifs et méthodes de leurs écrits," in S. Morlet, ed., *Le traité de Porphyre contre les Chrétiens* (Paris), 407–426
Bowersock, Glenn, W. (1990) *Hellenism in Late Antiquity* (Ann Arbor)
Brubaker, Leslie and John Haldon. (2011) *Byzantium in the iconoclast era, c. 680–850* (Cambridge)

Burgon, R.W. (1871) *The Last Twelve Verses of the Gospel according to Mark* (London)

Bussières, Marie-Pierre, ed. (2013) *La littérature des questions et réponses dans l'Antiquité profane et chrétienne : de l'enseignement à l'exégèse : actes du séminaire sur le genre des questions et réponses tenu à Ottawa les 27 et 28 septembre 2009* (Turnhout)

Caird, G.B. (1954) *Principalities and Powers* (Oxford)

Clark, Elizabeth A. (1977) "John Chrysostom and the *Subintroductae*" *Church History* 46: 171–185

—. (1999) *Reading Renunciation: Asceticism and Scripture in Early Christianity* (Princeton)

Cook, John Granger. (2000) *The Interpretation of the New Testament in Greco-Roman Paganism.* Studien und Texte zu Antike und Christentum 3 (Tübingen)

Courcelle, Pierre. (1964) "Anti-Christian arguments and Christian Platonism from Arnobius to St. Ambrose," in A. Momigliano, ed., *The Conflict between Paganism and Christianity in the Fourth Century*: 151–192 (Oxford)

Crafer, Thomas W. (1906–1907) "Macarius Magnesius, a neglected Apologist." *Journal of Theological Studies* 8: 401–423; 546–571

—. (1914) "The Work of Porphyry against the Christians and its reconstruction." *Journal of Theological Studies* 15: 360–395; 481–512

—. (1919) *The Apocriticus of Macarius Magnes.* Translations of Christian Literature, Series I, Greek Texts (London)

Croke, Brian. (1983) "Porphyry's Anti-Christian Chronology." *Journal of Theological Studies* 34: 168–185

Davis, Stephen J. (2001) *The Cult of Saint Thecla: A Tradition of Women's Piety in Late Antiquity* (Oxford)

DelCogliano, Mark. (2010) *Basil of Caesarea's Anti-Eunomian Theory of Names: Christian Theology and Late-Antique Philosophy in the Fourth Century Trinitarian Controversy* (Leiden)

Digeser, Elizabeth DePalma. (2002) "Porphyry, Julian, or Hierocles? The Anonymous Hellene in Makarios Magnes' *Apokritikos*." *Journal of Theological Studies* 53: 466–502

Duchesne, L. (1877) *De Macario Magnete et scriptis eius* (Paris)

Dumortier, Jean. (1949) "La date des deux traités de saint Jean Chrysostome aux moines et aux vierges" *Mélanges de science religieuse* 6: 248–251

Edwards, Mark J. (2009) *Catholicity and Heresy in the Early Church* (Surrey)

—. (2012) "Alexander of Alexandria and the *Homoousion*," *Vigiliae Christianae* 66: 1–21

Frassinetti, Paolo. (1949) "Sull'autore delle Questioni pagane conservate nell' Apocritico di Macario di Magnesia." *Nuovo Didaskaleion* 3: 41–56

Goulet, Richard. (2011) "Porphyre et Macarios de Magnésie sur la toute-puissance de Dieu," in S. Morlet, ed., *Le traité de Porphyre contre les Chrétiens* (Paris), 205–230

Grant, Robert M. (1973) "Porphyry among the Early Christians," in W. den Boer et al., eds, *Romanitas et Christianitas. Mélanges J.H. Waszink* (Amsterdam), 181–188

Grillmeier, A. (1975) *Christ in Christian Tradition* (Edinburgh)

Hägg, Thomas. (1992) "Hierocles the Lover of Truth and Eusebius the Sophist." *Symbolae Osloenses* 67: 138–150

Harnack, Adolf von. (1911) *Kritik des Neuen Testaments von einem griechischen Philosophen des 3. Jahrhunderts. Die im Apocriticus des Macarius Magnes enthaltene Streitsschrift*. Texte und Untersuchungen 37.4 (Leipzig)

Harvey, Susan Ashbrook. (2006) *Scenting Salvation: Ancient Christianity and the Olfactory Imagination.* (Berkeley)

Hausschildt, H. (1907) *De Porphyrio philosopho Macarii Magnetis apologetae Christiani Apokritikon auctore* (Bonn)

Hoffmann, R.J. (1994) *Porphyry's Against the Christians. The Literary Remains* (Amherst, NY)

Johnson, Aaron. (2012) "Hellenism and its Discontents" in S. Johnson, ed., *Oxford Handbook of Late Antiquity* (Oxford): 437–466

—. (2013) "The Author of the *Against Hierocles*: A Response to Borzì and Jones." *Journal of Theological Studies* 64: 574–594

Jouanna, J. (1999) *Hippocrates*, M.B. DeBevoise, trans. (Baltimore and London)

Kecskeméti, Judith. (1994) "Personnages tragiques et personages comiques dans les homélies dramatisées des prédicateurs grecs," *Euphrosyne* 22: 45–61

Kelley, J.N.D. (1995) *Goldenmouth: The Story of John Chrysostom, Ascetic, Preacher, Bishop* (Ithaca, NY)

Krueger, Derek. (2006) *Writing and Holiness: The Practice of Authorship in the Early Christian East.* Divinations: Rereading Late Ancient Religions (Philadelphia)

Lane Fox, Robin. (1987) *Pagans and Christians* (Harmondsworth)

Lévêque, Pierre. (1969) *Aurea catena Homeri: une étude sur l'allégorie grecque* (Paris)

Leyerle, Blake. (2001) *Theatrical shows and ascetic Lives: John Chrysostom's attack on spiritual marriage* (Berkeley)

Lim, Richard. (1995) *Public Disputation, Power, and Social Order in Late Antiquity.* Transformation of the Classical Heritage 23 (Berkeley)

Livingstone, Elizabeth A. (1997) "Macarius Magnes." *Oxford Dictionary of the Christian Church* 3rd ed. (Oxford), 1015

Ludlow, M. (2000) *Universal Salvation* (Oxford)

Magny, Ariane. (2010) "Porphyry in Fragments: Jerome, Harnack, and the Problem of Reconstruction." *Journal of Early Christian Studies* 18: 515–555

—. (2011) "Méthodologie et collecte des fragments de Porphyre sur le Nouveau Testament chez Jérôme," in S. Morlet, ed., *Le traité de Porphyre contre les Chrétiens* (Paris), 59–74

Marrou, Henri. (1956) *A History of Education in Antiquity*, G. Lamb, trans. (New York)
May, G. and K. Greschat, eds. (2002) *Marcion und seine kirchengeschichtiche Wirkung* (Berlin)
Mercati, Giovanni. (1941) "Per l'Apocritico di Macario Magnete. Una tavola dei capi dei libri I, II, e III," in *Nuove note di letteratura biblica e cristiana antica*. Studi e Testi 95 (Rome), 49–71
Meredith, Anthony. (1980) "Porphyry and Julian against the Christians." *Aufstieg und Niedergang der Römischen Welt* II.23.2: 1119–1149
Minns, Denis and Paul Parvis, eds. (2009) *Justin, Philosopher and Martyr: Apologies* (Oxford)
Morlet, Sébastien, ed. (2011) *Le traité de Porphyre contre les Chrétiens: un siècle de recherches, nouvelles questions*. Collection des Études Augustiniennes, Série Antiquité 190 (Paris)
Muehlberger, Ellen. (2008) "Ambivalence about the Angelic Life: The Promise and Perils of an Early Christian Discourse of Asceticism." *Journal of Early Christian Studies* 16: 447–478
Munnich, Olivier. (2011) "Recherche de la source porphyrienne dans les objections 'païens' du *Monogénès*: l'enjeu des citations scriptuaires," in S. Morlet, ed., *Le traité de Porphyre contre les Chrétiens* (Paris), 75–104
O'Neill, J.C. (2003) *Paul's Letter to the Romans* (Harmondsworth)
Palm, J. (1959–1960) "Textkritische zum Apokritikos des Makarios Magnes." Regiae Societatis humaniorum Litterarum Ludensis. Humanistiska Vetenskapssamfundet I, fasc. 4 (Lund)
Papadogiannakis, Yannis. (2012) "Eratopokriseis." In R. Bagnall, et al., eds, *The Encyclopedia of Ancient History*. (Hoboken, New Jersey)
Pépin, Jean. (1964) *Théologie cosmique et théologie chrétienne*. Bibliothèque de Philosophie contemporaine—Histoire de la philosophie et philosophie générale (Paris)
Quiroga, Alberto. (2007) "From *Sophistopolis* to *Episcopolis*. The Case for a Third Sophistic." *Journal for Late Antique Religion and Culture* 1:31–42.
Rives, James B. (1995) "Human Sacrifice among Pagans and Christians." *Journal of Roman Studies* 85: 65–85
Räisänen, Heikki. (2003) *Paul and the Law* (Tübingen)
Robertson, Jon. (2007) *Christ as Mediator* (Oxford)
Sanday, W. and A. Headlam. (1907) *A Critical and Exegetical Commentary on Romans* (Edinburgh)
Schaulkhauser, Georg. (1907) *Zu den Schriften des Makarios von Magnesia*. Texte und Untersuchungen 31.3 (Leipzig)
Schott, Jeremy M. (2005) "Porphyry on Christians and Others: 'Barbarian Wisdom,' Identity Politics, and Anti-Christian Polemics on the Eve of the Great Persecution." *Journal of Early Christian Studies* 13:277–314

—. (2009) "Philosophies of Language, Theories of Translation, and Imperial Intellectual Production: The Cases of Porphyry, Iamblichus, and Eusebius." *Church History* 78: 855–861
Sellers, Robert V. (1940) *Two Ancient Christologies* (London)
Sherwin-White, A.N. (1973) *The Roman Citizenship* (Oxford)
Van Hoof, Lieve. (2010) "Greek Rhetoric and the Later Roman Empire: The Bubble of the 'Third Sophistic.'" *Antiquité Tardive* 18:211–224.
Volgers, Annelie and Claudio Zamagni, eds. (2004) *Erotapokriseis: Early Christian Question-and-Answer Literature in Context. Proceedings of the Utrecht Colloquium, 13–14 October 2003* (Leuven)
Volp, Ulrich. (2011) "… for the fashion of this world passeth away": The Apokritikos by Macarius Magnes—An Origenist's Defence of Christian Eschatology?" H. Pietras and A. Dziadowiec, eds, *Origeniana Decima: Origen as Writer. Actes du Colloquium Origenianum Decimum, Krakow, 31 août–4 septembre 2009. Bibliotheca Ephemeridum Theologicarum Lovaniensium* (Leuven)
—. (2013) *Makarios Magnes,* Apokritikos: *Kritische Ausgabe mit deutscher Übersetzung. Texte und Untersuchungen zur Geschichte der altchristlichen Literatur* 169 (Berlin)
Waelkens, Robert. (1974) *L'Économie, thème apologétique et principe herméneutique dans l'*Apocriticos *de Macarios Magnès. Recueil de travaux d'histoire et de philologie de l'Université de Louvain 7e série, fasc. 4* (Louvain)
Wagenmann, J.A. (1878) "Compte rendu de Blondel et Duchesne." *Jahrbücher für Deutsche Theologie* 23: 138–142
Young, Frances M. (1971) "A Reconsideration of Alexandrian Christology," *Journal of Ecclesiastical History* 22: 103–114
—. (1997) *Biblical Exegesis and the Formation of Christendom* (Cambridge)
Zachhuber, Johannes. (1999) *Human Nature in Gregory of Nyssa: Theological Background and Philosophical Significance.* Supplements to Vigiliae Christianae 46 (Leiden)
Zamagni, Claudio. (2011) "Porphyre est-il la cible principale des 'questions' chrétiennes des IVe et Ve siècles?," in S. Morlet, ed., *Le traité de Porphyre contre les Chrétiens* (Paris), 357–370

INDEX OF BIBLICAL PASSAGES

Genesis
   2:8 (141)
   2:16–7 (243)
   3:9 (242, 243)
   4:7 (242)
   5:22 (242)
   6:13–4 (244)
   12:1 (244)
   15:6 (278)
   18:1f. (242–3)
Exodus
   3:5, 8 (244)
   13:21–2 (220)
   22:27 (204, 248, 263–4)
   31:18 (204, 248, 260–1)
Leviticus
   11:29–32 (187)
   12:2–8 (187)
   14:34–57 (187)
   15:19–33 (187)
Numbers
   19:14–22 (187)
Deuteronomy
   7:13 (220)
   13:3 (248)
   14:22–19 (187)
   18:4 (187)
   25:4 (176)
   26:1–15 (187, 211)
   28:66 (117)
   29:28 (212)

Joshua
   5:14 (244)
   24:14 (248)
1 Kings
   19:11–12 (139)
2 Kings
   2:11–12 (221)
Job
   1:1–3 (130)
   2:7–9 (131)
   9:8 (135, 137)
   15:25–26 (101)
   40:25 (123)
Psalms
   8:709 (177)
   19:7 (124)
   21:7 (122)
   33:21 (276)
   44:7–8 (124, 235–6)
   68:22 (117)
   90:12 (149)
   92:1–2 (161, 236)
   96:2 (220)
   98:5 (237)
   101:26–7 (236)
   103:3 (220)
   113:4 (139)
   115:5 (276)
   117:27 (124)

Isaiah
  1:8 (232)
  2:3–4 (124)
  5:6 (220)
  6:8 (244)
  14:29 (193)
  17:12–13 (222)
  34:4 (203, 211–2, 231f.)
  53:2–7 (115)
  65:17 (237)
  66:1 (212)

Jeremiah
  1:9 (244)
  7:6, 9 (248)
  11:19 (116)
  23:29–30 (140)

Ezekiel
  2:1 (244)

Daniel
  3:24 (228)
  6:17–24 (228)
  9:23 (244)
  14:33–9 (219–20)

Habakkuk
  3:4 (117)

Tobias
  12:19 (260–1)

Matthew
  4:6 (104, 148f., 162f.)
  4:9 (163)
  4:19 (61)
  8:1–4 (73)
  8:25 (213)
  8:28–34 (103, 108f.)
  9:1–8 (73)
  9:24 (64)
  10:28 (119)
  10:34 (71)
  10:37–8 (64–8)
  11:25 (204)
  12:48–50 (71–5)
  13:31–3, 45–6 (204, 212, 238f)
  14:20 (134)
  14:21 (62)
  14:25 (103, 112f.)
  14:31 (138f.)
  16:13–17 (164)
  16:18–9 (149–50)
  16:22–4 (68, 104, 164f.)
  17:14–19 (65, 78–9, 161–2)
  17:20–1 (104, 148, 160f.)
  18:22 (104, 150)
  19:13 (132)
  19:17 (128)
  19:21 (111, 128f.)
  19:24 (103, 110f.)
  21:19 (62)
  22:29–30 (204, 247, 259f.)
  24:4–5 (203, 210, 228f.)
  24:11 (210)
  24:14 (203, 209–10, 223f.)
  24:35 (211, 231f.)
  25:31 (220)
  26:15 (145)
  26:39 (103, 106f., 119f.)
  26:26–8 (155f.)
  26:41 (107)
  26:53 (127)
  26:64 (84)
  27:46 (65, 82f.)
  28:1–10 (84f.)
  28:19–20 (114, 140f., 255)

Mark
  1:17 (61)
  2:17 (244)
  5:9 (126f.)
  5:23–43 (63)
  6:43 (134)
  6:48 (103, 112f.)
  8:33 (104)
  10:18 (64, 75–8, 106)
  10:23 (132)
  14:35 (107)
  15:36 (82f.)
  16:15 (62)
  16:18 (104)

INDEX OF BIBLICAL PASSAGES

Luke
- 2:1 (126)
- 3:16 (237)
- 4:2 (61)
- 4:9 (104)
- 4:13 (121)
- 4:25 (64)
- 5:14 (241)
- 5:31 (204, 212–3, 240f.)
- 6:45 (75–77)
- 7:11–17 (72)
- 8:30 (126f.)
- 10:9 (241–2)
- 10:21 (211)
- 12:4 (106)
- 14:26–7 (64–8)
- 17:6 (104)
- 17:11–19 (73)
- 18:18 (128)
- 18:19 (64, 75–8)
- 18:25 (132)
- 19:17 (134)
- 22:46 (107)
- 23:4 (141)
- 23:46 (65, 82f.)

John
- 1:27 (145)
- 2:1–11 (73)
- 3:27 (211)
- 5:31 (65, 80–1)
- 5:46 (101, 107, 123f.)
- 6:13 (134)
- 6:53 (146f., 152f.)
- 6:55 (156)
- 6:63 (104)
- 8:12–13 (80–81)
- 8:43–4 (65, 86f.)
- 9:1–34 (73)
- 10:35 (263)
- 11:1–44 (72)
- 12:4–5 (145)
- 12:8 (103, 113f., 140f.)
- 12:31–2 (65, 94f.)
- 14:6 (80)
- 14:10 (99)
- 18:31 (62)
- 19:29–30 (82f.)
- 19:33 (65, 90f.)
- 21:15 (151, 209, 225f.)

Acts
- 5:1–11 (104, 150–1, 168f.)
- 12:5–19 (104, 151, 171f.)
- 16:2–3 (104, 174f.)
- 18:9–10 (209, 226)
- 22:3 (175, 183f-4)
- 22:25–7 (104)

Romans
- 5:20 (104, 178, 189f.)
- 6:3–4 (158)
- 7:12–14 (178, 188)
- 9:1 (176)
- 9:18 (196)
- 13:12–3 (139, 221)

1 Corinthians
- 6:3 (209)
- 6:11 (204, 245f., 251f.)
- 6:19 (268)
- 7:25 (179, 196f.)
- 7:29–31 (203, 205f., 214f.)
- 8:4 (178, 194–5)
- 8:5–6 (204, 248–9, 257f.)
- 8:8–10 (178, 194)
- 9:5 (152)
- 9:7 (104, 176f., 184f.)
- 9:9–10 (176–7, 188f.)
- 9:19–23 (174–5, 181f.)
- 9:32 (164)
- 10:20 (105, 178f)
- 15:56 (178)

2 Corinthians
- 5:1 (268)
- 6:16 (237)
- 11:13 (152)
- 11:29 (181)

Galatians
  2:12 (151, 172f.)
  2:18 (175)
  3:10 (177)
  5:2–3 (104, 177f, 185f.)
  6:14 (96)
Philippians
  3:2 (174)
1 Thessalonians
  4:15–17 (203, 207–9, 222–3)
  5:5 (221)
  5:8 (66)

1 Timothy
  2:4 (196)
  4:1–3 (104, 179, 200, 246)
Hebrews
  4:12 (69–71)
2 Peter
  3:38 (225, 268)
Apocalypse of Peter
  §4 (203, 210–1, 230f.)

INDEX OF PROPER NAMES

Abraham 44, 139, 156, 242, 260–1, 278
Adam 10, 15–6, 19, 87, 91, 121, 138n184, 234, 244–4
Anacletus (bishop of Rome 79–92 CE) 277
Ananias and Sapphira 4, 11–2, 37, 104, 150n244, 168–71
Antioch 7, 11–2, 14, 32, 46–8, 52, 69–70, 173n354
Apollonius of Tyana 7, 14, 31–2, 36, 90n163, 106, 111n53, 117–8, 210, 227n125
Apuleius of Madaurus 36, 111n53
Aristotle 2, 27–8, 38, 50, 75n82, 76n87, 77n90, 86n148, 88n152, 153n258, 181n403, 206n29, 208n35, 209n42, 247n207, 256n240–1, 247244
Arius/Arian 5, 6n9, 7, 43, 77n89, 121n102, 274
Assyrians 215, 228
Athena/Minerva 246, 262
Augustine of Hippo 1, 7, 40, 55, 173n354, 196n468, 201n494, 208n35

Babylon/Babylonians 58, 151n249, 215, 219, 228
Bardaisan 6, 48, 229
Berenikē (Queen of Edessa) 42, 45–6, 63
Beliar 66, 131, 163

Bithynia 1, 31
Blondel, Charles 41, 43–4, 51, 91n167, 143n207, 178n390

Cain 242–3
Canaanites 140
Celsus 1, 5, 7, 28–30, 33, 39n131, 84n136–137, 85n143, 89n160, 92n171, 101n215, 106n28, 107n33, 111n51, 147n227, 176n366, 177n374, 248n211
Cerinthus 6, 48, 229
Cephas (alternate name for Peter) 277
Charybdis 271
Cilicia 6, 48, 175, 201, 229–30, 238
Constantine 18, 117n87, 136n167, 216n80, 223n108, 275
Cyprian of Carthage 160

Daniel 219n87, 220, 228
Danube 224
Diocletian 2, 30–1, 53, 126n125, 229n130
Dositheus 6–7, 48, 201, 229–30
Droserius 6, 48, 229–30

Edessa/Edessenens 42, 45–6, 63, 230n132
Egypt 36, 111n53, 139, 220n97, 246
Enos/Enoch 242
Ethiopians 147, 224
Eunomius 50, 81n114

Eusebius of Caesarea 1, 7, 18, 23n92, 31, 34–5, 46, 63n17, 80n109, 96n194, 106n27, 116n81
Ezra/Esdras 16, 33, 107, 123

Fabian (bishop of Rome, 236–250 CE) 160

Galatia/Galatians 7–8, 37, 48, 177, 183, 188, 201
general 9, 58, 175n362, 180–3, 185, 272
  generalship 153
  Christ as general 121
Goulet, Richard 21–2, 24n93, 28n97, 29, 32, 33n112, 35, 39, 41–5, 47–8

Habbakuk 117
Hadrian 53, 246, 257
Hagar 66n27
Harnack, Adolf von 21–2, 35, 41–2, 51
Hellenic/Hellenes/Greeks 61, 87, 88, 89n161, 109n42, 114, 152n252, 189n440, 192, 204, 245, 247n207, 248, 262
  the Hellene, identity of 21–40
Herod the Great 126
Herod Antipas 11, 33, 83, 151, 171–2
Herodotus 89–90, 105n26, 147n224, 215n78, 224
Hierocles, Sossianus 1, 30–32, 35, 51, 106n27, 210n49
Homer 57, 88n152, 116n81, 245, 250, 259n250
Horeb 139

Irenaeus of Lyon 160
Isauria/Isaurians 7, 48, 201

Jerome of Stridon 35–8, 111n53, 113n62, 114n69, 148n233, 150n244, 152n255, 173n354, 176n366, 213n66, 249n221
Jeremiah 116, 140, 155

Jerusalem 66n27, 67n27
Jesus 75, 81–3, 90, 103, 105–6, 112–3, 117–8, 134–5, 138, 144–5, 148–51, 161–3, 165–6, 179, 188, 211–3, 245, 247, 251, 253–5, 257
John the Baptist 164, 211, 237
John (Evangelist) 6, 75, 82–3, 90–1, 145
Joshua 248
Judaea 110, 126, 219
Julian (Roman Emperor, 361–363 CE) 2, 28, 32–5, 40, 51, 54, 82n120, 83n131, 100n206, 107n33, 107n36, 109n42, 110n45, 110n48, 111n54, 112n54, 114n69, 144n211, 148n234, 152n255, 175n363, 176n366, 209n41, 249n218

Lycaonia 7, 48, 201
Luke (Evangelist) 82, 147

Macedonia/Macedonians 58, 215
Mani/Manicheans 201, 229–30, 274, 276
Marcion 6, 10, 48, 94n181, 229–30, 276
Mark (Evangelist) 82, 108, 112, 124, 126, 147
Mary (mother of Jesus) 74n71
Mary Magdalene 84, 140, 204, 248, 261
Mathew (evangelist) 79, 82, 84, 108, 124, 147, 209, 247
Montanus 6, 229
Moses 16, 32–4, 103, 107, 117, 123–5, 172–3, 177, 243, 248, 263–4

Nicephorus (Patriarch of Constantinople, 806–815 CE) 42–6, 62, 274
Noah 235, 242, 244

Origen of Alexandria 15n521, 18, 71n52, 98n201, 101n213, 140n189, 147n226, 155n269, 173n354, 211n53, 274

Palestine/Palestinian 126, 140, 160
Paul 3, 8, 97, 104, 111n53, 148n230, 151–2, 158, 173–202, 203, 205–210, 214–223, 225–8, 246–8
Persia/Persians 6, 186n424, 215, 229
Peter 3, 75, 104, 136–8, 149–52, 164–173, 203, 209, 225, 227–8
Phrygia 6, 229
Pilate, Pontius 62, 65, 83, 91–3, 106, 114, 116, 119, 126
Pisidia 7, 48, 201
Plato 30, 111n51
Polycarp of Smyrna 159
Porphyry 2, 9–10, 27, 35–40, 42, 51, 85n143, 86n147, 86n148, 111n53, 113n62, 114n69, 147n226, 147n227, 148n233, 150n244, 152n255, 173n354, 175n366, 176n367, 176n370, 206n28, 208n35, 213n66, 247n207, 249n221, 250n222, 250n224
Philosophy from Oracles 193
Prometheus 262

Red Sea 36, 111n53
Rome/Romans 5, 8–9, 88, 92–93, 104, 126, 160, 175–7, 182–4, 209, 215, 246, 277
  as "Queen City" 171

Sarah 66n27
Satan/the Devil 11–15, 17, 97n197, 104, 149–50, 164–5, 193n449
  as Accuser (διαβόλος) 4, 24, 61, 65, 86–7, 98–101
  as Tempter 121
Scythians 218, 224, 246
Sea of Galilee 25, 36, 110n46, 112–13, 133
Senate, Roman 83
Simon Magus 5, 227n124, 229n132
Sinai 139, 161
Syria/Syrians 6, 45–8, 52, 69–70, 201n496

Timothy (disciple of Paul) 8–9, 104, 174
Thecla 68–9
Theocleia 68
Theosthenes (dedicatee of *Apocritus*) 55, 105, 204, 275, 276, 277, 278
Tiberius (Roman emperor, 14–37 CE) 46, 63, 92, 126
Troy/Ilium 250
Turrianus (Francisco Torres, 16th century Jesuit scholar) 4, 45, 195n462, 275–8

Volp, Ulrich 18n73, 41–3, 55n195, 196n470

Zeus 262

SUBJECT INDEX

Acts of Pilate 46, 63n17, 144n212
Apocalypse of Peter 4, 22–3, 203n7, 210–1, 230–1
angel/angelology 4, 17, 19, 24, 27–8, 67, 96, 101, 127, 154, 164, 167–8, 171, 199, 204, 207, 209, 219–22, 240–1, 243, 259–61
   Gabriel 140
   as polynymous/homonymous with "gods" 246–7, 256–7
apostles 3, 8, 36–8, 70, 133, 136–40, 152, 161, 164, 169, 173, 188, 192, 254
Apotactics 48, 201
Antichrist 24, 99, 101, 188, 228, 230
ascetic(s)/asceticism 6, 46–7, 128n138, 197, 199n486, 201, 229, 241, 266, 270

baptism 19, 91, 158–60, 200, 255–6
barbarian(s) 88, 90, 109, 125, 147, 180–1, 214, 218, 224
breast/breast milk 153–4

Christology 12–17
circumcision 15, 37–8, 71, 151, 173–5, 181–3, 186–7
creator/creation 6, 13, 18–19, 30, 72, 77–9, 89, 94–5, 107–8, 134–8, 156, 167, 177, 201, 205–13, 216, 231–37, 242, 249–50, 266–8, 272–3
   see also Demiurge

cross/crucifixion 16, 68, 88, 92, 97, 117, 121–3, 141–3, 159, 165, 171, 210, 226–7, 277

Demiurge 26–7, 85n143, 94, 205n25, 211n55, 231n137
demons/*daimones*/demonology 10, 16–17, 35, 68, 84, 103, 105, 108–10, 124–8, 161, 178, 192–5, 226
Doctrina Addai 46, 63n17

Emperor 52–4, 84, 92, 97–8, 106, 117, 126, 180–1, 184, 200, 214, 246, 251–4, 271–2
Encratites 6, 9, 48, 201
Eremites 6, 48, 201
Eucharist 4, 13, 155–7
Evangelist(s) 36, 81–4, 87, 90, 134, 220, 224, 277

Gentiles 151, 159, 172–3, 187, 224, 227
gods/goddesses 166–7, 195, 204, 244, 246–9, 256–9, 263–4

icon(s) 42–3, 45–6, 62–3, 274n1
idol(s)/statues 9–10, 46, 63n17, 139, 178, 192–5, 223, 247–8, 261–3
îhîdāyê 70n50

Jews/Judaism 8, 72, 80, 83, 86, 88, 91–3, 98–101, 110, 116, 118, 120–24, 126, 141, 151, 159, 171–9, 181–4, 227, 274

SUBJECT INDEX

Judgment 23, 84, 94–7, 136, 151, 168–70, 203, 210, 220, 230, 251, 271

Kingdom (of God, of Heaven) 13, 67–8, 101, 103, 110–11, 126, 128–9, 130, 131–2, 149–50, 166, 209, 212, 215, 223, 227, 237–9, 259

Law of Moses 125, 173, 176

magic 36, 111n53, 175, 227
monarchy 256–9

Nicaea, Council of 2n2, 15, 143n204
New Testament 22, 154, 173, 203, 275
see also Old Testament

Ogygian Plague 266
Old Testament 154
see also New Testament

Passion 4, 14, 82–3, 91–2, 106, 115–23, 141–2, 145, 165
physician 19, 63, 119, 129, 170, 180–2, 204, 212–13, 240, 243–4, 273
Platonists/Platonism 1, 5, 26, 28n97, 39, 85n143, 193n450, 206n30, 206n33, 208n35, 211n55, 233n143, 238n166
poor/poverty 36, 91, 103, 110–11, 113–14, 128–32, 140, 145, 190, 266, 269–70
prophet(s) 115, 123, 137, 139–40, 155, 161, 164, 186, 192, 211, 222, 230, 235–6, 243, 276

resurrection 4, 83, 92–4, 140, 145, 204, 210, 222, 247–9, 264, 268–9
Rule of Truth 36, 111, 154, 166

sacrifice(s) 9, 116, 178, 187, 192–5, 247
serpent(s) 15, 66, 78, 91, 99–101, 118, 122, 142, 158, 193, 195, 227, 239, 246, 264
sin 9, 10–14, 17, 52, 67, 91, 95, 97, 110, 122, 144, 150–2, 158, 160, 164, 170, 189–91, 213, 226, 239–43
sophist(s)/sophistic/sophistry 54, 56, 59, 99–100, 118, 141–2, 152, 165, 200, 207, 214, 256, 265–7
Son of Man 13, 84, 220, 244
Synod of the Oak (403 CE) 49, 54
suneisaktoi/subintroductae 47, 70n50

Temple, Jerusalem 107, 148–9, 162–3
temple(s) 110, 126, 169, 194, 223, 247–8, 262, 268
Theotokos 74n71
Thyestean Feasts 146
theatre 54, 105, 108, 150, 171, 174, 227
  acrobats 174
  costumes/masks 175
tyrants/tyranny 15, 54, 68, 121–2, 158, 223, 258

virgins/virginity 197–200, 202, 248, 262

wealthy/wealth 25, 47, 110–1, 128–33, 159, 168–9, 185, 252
women 29, 36, 47, 52, 62, 86, 94, 111, 141, 212, 215

INDEX OF THEOLOGICAL, PHILOSOPHICAL, AND RHETORICAL TERMINOLOGY

amplification (*amplificatio/auxesis*) 56–7
anacoluthon (ἀνακόλουθον) 90
anagogy 138
antistrophe (ἀντιστροφή) 196n466
aporia 55, 245

catachresis (κατάχρησις) 26, 133–4
chreia (χρεία) 58

epanaphora (ἐπαναφορά) 196n466
essence (*ousia*) 2, 27, 49, 74, 86n148, 96–7, 124–5, 134–6, 157, 163–4, 166, 189, 200, 218–9, 222, 232, 235–6, 238, 240–1, 255–9
definition of essence (λόγος τῆς οὐσίας) 56, 88n152, 221, 231, 233
ethopoiia (ἠθοποιία) 57, 65n17

form (σχῆμα) 26, 203, 205–8, 213–9, 225

godhead (θεότης) 5–6, 14, 16, 27, 75, 122, 125, 145, 167, 246, 254, 256–7

homonymy 27–8, 56, 77, 247, 249, 256–7

ingenerate (ἀγένητος/ἀγέννητος) 218, 236, 260

nature (φύσις) 2, 16–17, 26–8, 53, 73, 76–81, 87, 96–8, 100, 120, 125, 133–5, 144, 147, 153, 157, 163, 166–7, 178, 187, 189, 191–3, 206–8, 210, 216–9, 221–3, 225–6, 231–43, 245–7, 250–2, 256–8, 260–1, 265–70, 275

Only-begotten/unique (*monogenēs*/μονογενής) 15, 44, 70n50, 72–4, 76n84, 103, 117, 120–3, 137, 143–4, 156, 165–7, 185

parrhēsia (παρρησία) 106n29, 132n152
polynymy 247
position (θέσις) 27–8, 76n87, 256, 258
progymnasmata 57

question and answer literature (ζητήματα καί λύσεις) 3, 55, 105n25, 113n63

reductio ad absurdum 24, 26
retorsion 34

solecism 90
synkrisis (σύνκρισις) 31–2

Word (*logos*/λόγος) 12–17, 19–20, 74, 77, 87, 101n212, 107, 115n78, 116, 122–4, 133, 135, 140–5, 157, 167n324, 183–5, 208, 222–4, 233–7, 240–1, 244, 260, 261, 263, 265